HEADY DAZE
THE MISSION YEARS 1985-1990

D1354958

Also by the Author:

Salad Daze

HEADY DAZE
THE MISSION YEARS 1985-1990
WAYNE HUSSEY

OMNIBUS PRESS

Copyright © 2023 Omnibus Press
(A division of the Wise Music Group
14–15 Berners Street, London, W1T 3LJ)

Cover designed by Fabrice Couillerot
Cover image © Paul Skellett
Colourised by James Mountford
Picture research by the author

ISBN 978-1-913172-16-9
Special edition 978-1-913172-17-6

Every effort has been made to trace the copyright holders of the photographs
in this book but one or two were unreachable. We would be grateful
if the photographers concerned would contact us.

A catalogue record for this book is available from the British Library.

Printed in the Czech Republic

www.omnibuspress.com

Heady Daze is dedicated to the memory of Steve Watson (1959-2019). Known to some as Sex-Pistol, others Winker, and others just as Stevie. Beloved and sadly missed by all.

Also departed and remembered fondly: Chris/Chrys Bocast, Steve Spring, Dave Kentish, Hambi Haralambous, Janice Long, Maartin Allcock, Ken Adams and Dick Rabel.

Contents

Preface And Disclaimer

Being in a reasonably successful band in the second half of the 1980s was a mucky, messy and oft-times morally dubious business… but *so* much fun. And hysterically funny for those of us that liked a good laugh. In contrast to the popularly held perception of The Mission as being moue-faced, maudlin, black-clad and taking-ourselves-far-too-seriously, we *loved* a good laugh. There's a lot of mucky, messy, morally dubious laughs in this book. I can't vouch for their absolute veracity, though. The memory is fragile, malleable, nebulous and unreliable – coloured by our excesses, desires, disappointments, beliefs, hearsay and emotions.

So, this book may well be a pack of lies. Or the unmitigated truth. It really depends on what you, dear reader, prefer to believe. I *have* dutifully researched, as well as trawled the memory banks of myself and others, but have written without being slavish to fact. These are *my* memories and I can't demand absolute accuracy of them, so neither should you. My story is certainly based on very true events but even the most honest of men are prone to exaggeration in the pursuit of self-mythology, wouldn't you agree?

My apologies for putting words into the mouths of others. Conversations are recorded here but I must confess that liberties may well have been taken in their recall. Who can remember verbatim a conversation that took place merely an hour ago let alone 35 years? It's the *gist* of the conversation that's important rather than the actual words. It's the *gist* that is remembered.

As with my previous book, *Salad Daze**, I set out with the intention of covering a lot more of my life than I ended up doing in this second volume, *Heady Daze* (consequently, a third volume will likely follow in the near future). The writing process itself is a journey into the unknown. We remember what we can't forget, though each memory often triggers an avalanche of other long-forgotten memories. Once the avalanche starts it's impossible to control where it goes. Mostly, the remembering has been enjoyable and brought with it new and hitherto unrealised appreciation for the life I have lived. Occasionally, though, the memories have been more difficult and uncomfortable to confront, but they are just as integral to my story. That being said, regret is not an emotion I often feel, although my mistakes have been many. The road I've travelled has led me to where I am today and where I am today is a good place to be.

Wayne Hussey
São Paulo, April 2022

---

* *Salad Daze* is, for the reader who doesn't know, my first book, published by Omnibus Press in 2019. Still currently available at all reputable and non-reputable outlets I believe.

How To Find The Playlists
On Youtube And Spotify

For each chapter in this book I have constructed a playlist that pertains to the content of that particular chapter, or were 'hits' in the time period I am writing about. Designed to enrich the reading experience, we have set up playlists for you with Spotify and YouTube (see instructions below). Where I was unable to find a particular song that's listed in the book I have substituted it with another that has some relevance, however tenuous.

I must add that a few of these choices are purely for context, but most are because I love the songs. My heart continues to beat fiercely, insanely, to the same incessant rhythm of love for music that propelled me to pick up a guitar in the first place. And in music there is redemption. Believe you me. It's because of music that this book exists. It's only right that there should be a soundtrack to its reading. You don't even need to read the book to enjoy the playlists!

For Spotify:
Open and log in to the Spotify app, type 'husseysaladdaze' into the search engine. Upon results go to the husseysaladdaze Profile. On 'Overview' click on 'All' and choose the folder husseyheadydaze and you will then have access to the playlists for the prologue and all 20 chapters. Choose the corresponding number for the chapter you are currently reading.

For YouTube:

Type 'Wayne Hussey' into the search engine, and then click on the 'Wayne Hussey – Official' icon. Once on the official channel page, highlight playlists, and, again, choose the corresponding chapter for the one you are currently reading.

A Précis...

PLAYLIST:
1. Jo's So Mean – The Flowerpot Men
2. Good Thing – The Woodentops   3. Ace Of Spades – Motörhead
4. Rock And Roll – Led Zeppelin   5. New Year's Day – U2
6. Fascination Street – The Cure
7. Search And Destroy – Iggy & The Stooges
8. Break On Through (To The Other Side) – The Doors
9. This Charming Man – The Smiths   10. Rip It Up – Orange Juice

Based on real events.

Cast:

Craig Adams – Early twenties, lank, manky dark hair, snub-nosed, skinny but evidently prone to chubbiness if he stayed off the white diet powders for any length of time. Wears tight skinny-legged black jeans with black winkle-picker scuffed-up boots, usually with a short-sleeved black T-shirt emblazoned with a band name and logo, Motörhead or The Stooges being the most frequent. Nicknamed Lurch.

Wayne Hussey – A mid-twenties rock'n'roller who likes to wear sunglasses at all hours. Long dyed-black hair, usually backcombed in the style of Siouxsie Sioux or Robert Smith, sizeable conk (that's *conk*), thin-lipped, and as skinny and brittle as a dead leaf with a pallor akin to the frozen wastes of Siberia.

5

Scene – The front room at 27 Ashville Grove, Headingley, Leeds LS6, late October-ish 1985. A typical end-terrace house – from the street the front door opens into the front room, which is furnished with a beaten-up sofa facing the fireplace, a matching armchair to the left, and a TV set and video recorder on the right in the corner by the bay window, which overlooks the tiny front garden and the street. There's a small table in the bay, on which sits a telephone.

The phone rings. Wayne picks up the receiver.

WAYNE (impatiently)
Yep?

Cut to Craig standing in a red telephone box. It's grey and raining outside, a typical West Yorkshire late Autumn day.

CRAIG
Huss, Addo here. D'ya wanna go t'Fav for a pint, like?
I got summat I wanna talk about.

.WAYNE
Yeah, sure. I'll meet you at the bus stop in half an hour, gotta do me hair first. You got any of that Aquanet Extra Super Hold left?

Forty minutes later, hair suitably coiffed, Craig and Wayne are sat on the top-deck back seat of a double decker number 19 bus heading into town, each dragging on a Silk Cut.

CRAIG
So, is Stevie getting the whizz delivered before the weekend? I fancy Friday night out down the Warehouse and then onto t'Phono.

A Précis...

WAYNE

Dunno. He was up in his room when I left. Don't think he's very happy. He went into town to buy the new Flowerpot Men single and, 'cos he was a bit pissed, in his befuddlement he ended up buying The Woodentops instead. Got home, staggered up to his room, put it on, realised his mistake and threw the record out of the window along with his stereo, speakers n' all. Came crashing down into the street, smashed to smithereens. Right funny, it was.

CRAIG (laughingly)
What, from the top floor? Did it hit any of the students from across the street?

In response Wayne shakes his head in the negative. Remembering he's on the phone, he answers.

WAYNE
Nah.

CRAIG
Shame. Aw, I love Stevie, he's a right Sex Pistol.

WAYNE
So, whassup?

CRAIG
Ah, I wanna leave the band. I can't stand that pompous twat anymore.

WAYNE
Yeah, I know what you mean.

CRAIG
Fancy leaving with me and starting a new, proper band?

WAYNE

Yeah, bloody right. Who's gonna be the singer though?

CRAIG

*Ah, you can be the singer; you're better looking than me and
'appen to have, and be, a bigger knob.*

WAYNE, (evidently missing the jibe, carries on):
*And singing bass players look crap, dunnay? Look at Sting
and that bloke out of Level bloody 42.*

CRAIG

Aye, 'nuff said.

WAYNE

*But I'm gonna have to write words for the songs.
I ain't ever really done that before.*

CRAIG

*Ah, just string any ol' bollocks together, it's only stupid journos and other
singers that take any notice of the words anyway.*

WAYNE

*Puh, that sounds easy enough, that's what I'll do then.
Right, what about a band name?*

CRAIG

*Oh, don't worry about that. We'll just use summat for the time
being that'll annoy the shit out of 'im. Something better'll
come up later one day when we're whizzing.*

A Précis…

WAYNE

And what about getting other people in the band? You know I don't like many people, most of 'em are dicks. Prefer dogs, meself. But I don't wanna play with a drum machine anymore, they can't chop 'em out.

Wayne laughs throatily.

CRAIG, (ignoring the crap joke, doesn't join in but replies):
I know this bloke, Mick, plays with The Lorries. He's mental and he likes his whizz. We could nick 'im.

WAYNE

Sounds brilliant. Can he play?

CRAIG

Dunno but he hits 'em hard.

WAYNE

Well, that's good enough for us then. What about another guitarist? I know I'm pretty good meself, like, but I'm gonna find it hard to sing and play them tricky guitar parts at the same time.

CRAIG

We could put an ad in the back of Melody Maker *and down at Jumbo.*

WAYNE

Yea: guitarist wanted for new soon-to-be famous band. Must be from The North. Experience and technical ability not essential but must be slinky. No Manchester United supporters need apply.

CRAIG

Hang on, you're not from The North, you're from Bristol!

WAYNE

Yeah, but I lived in Liverpool for six years before
I moved to Leeds – that makes me an adopted northerner.

Craig, in Roger Moore stylee, raises his left eyebrow.

CRAIG

Really? Ee, Wayne, there's neither mickling nor muckling with thee, lad.
So, what kind of band shall we be then?

WAYNE

I reckon a cross between The Doors, Led Zeppelin, U2 and The Cure.

CRAIG

Yeah, and with a bit of Iggy and Motörhead thrown in we'll be laughing.

WAYNE

Too bloody right. A bit rock, a bit goth, but with tunes.

CRAIG

And we can dress up in me mam's old blouses and get some of those
cheap skinny black jeans down the market.

WAYNE

Yeah, I like that and, you know, as singer, I could wear a bit of lippy as
well, that'd be tarty. Goes with me surname.

10

CRAIG

Yeah, and t'other blokes in the band have to be good looking too,
we can't have any ugly buggers. Image is reet important, I reckons.
Look at Durran Durran, they don't have any real mingers in their ranks,
do they? Well, their guitarist was a bit rough but they got shot of him.
And, thinking about it, I 'spose that Rick Rhodes bloke ain't really
the rugged, handsome sort either, is he? I'll shut up.

WAYNE

And we could go on tour all the time, none of this staying at home lark,
none of this taking months in the studio spending days on a piddlin'
snare sound or a bit of feedback. Get in there, bang 'em down,
and get out on tour, see the world. That's where the real action is.
Whizz, booze, sex and no sleep.

CRAIG

Brilliant.

WAYNE

Yeah, and we'll have a ton of records in the charts, we'll get on
Top Of The Pops *and get played on Radio 1, and I'll get me*
ugly mug on the cover of Smash Hits *and* Melody Maker.

CRAIG

Aye, but we won't talk to the NME, right?

WAYNE

Damn right. Hate those bastards. They're always going on about those
poncey jingly-jangly guitar groups like Orange Squash and
The Smiths. Bloody rubbish if you ask me.

CRAIG

Yeah, and The Woodentops.

WAYNE

Yeah, all this anti-rockist stuff is crap, innit? We'll be the ones to put a bit of sex, drugs, and rock'n'roll back into the mix, eh? Just say no? Puh. Just say yeah, I reckon.

CRAIG

Our stop's coming up, come on, Huss, ring the bell.

Ten minutes later: Sat in the corner of The Fav – The Faversham, a favoured student pub in Leeds, near the university. Craig with a pint of Stella in one hand and a newly lit ciggie in the other; Wayne with a pint of Strongbow and black and a newly lit ciggie in his grubby mitts. Craig takes a drag and exhales.

CRAIG

And we'll win all the readers' polls in the music mags, we'll play arenas and stadiums and headline Reading Festival a couple of times.

WAYNE

And we can split up on tour a few times as well, that always makes for a good news story. Let's take the press and the whole soddin' music business for a bit of a ride, I reckon.

CRAIG

Yeah, and I'll take too many drugs and have a nervous breakdown and leave the band.

WAYNE

In America.

CRAIG

Can't wait.

WAYNE

And in 25 years' time, uh, when will that be?

CRAIG

Hang on…

Craig counts on his fingers.

CRAIG

…ten, twenty, twenty-five… that'll be 2010, 2011, summat like that.

WAYNE

Here, you're good at maths, you can do the band's accounts. Anyway, yeah, in 2011 we'll get back together to celebrate our 25th anniversary and play sold-out shows all around the world.

CRAIG

Aye, if we're still alive.

WAYNE

And the record company will wanna release a greatest hits album.

CRAIG

Bloody 'ell! Greatest hits? You're pushing it a bit there, aren't you, Huss?

WAYNE

Well, you gotta dream big, Addo, me laddo. Reach for the stars and we might just pull ourselves up out of the gutter. 'Ere, that's a

13

good lyric, that. I'll have ta remember that. Anyway, what's up with ya?
We're gonna be the best band in the world. Maybe not the
biggest but defo the best.

CRAIG
'Ey up, Huss, that girl you shagged in the bogs at the Warehouse last
weekend has just walked in.

WAYNE
Oh, bloody 'ell. I'm off 'ome. See you later, mate.

CRAIG
Yeah, sure.

Addo takes another long draw on his Silkie and laughs to himself as Huss scurries out of the door of The Fav.

The entire history of The Mission is distilled to its core essence in the previous fictional conversation between Craig and I, based on sleeve notes written by me for the compilation album *Serpents Kiss – The Very Best Of*, released by Universal in 2014; one of those cheap releases you may have found, if you were lucky, in the racks at Tesco or Sainsbury's for a fiver. I've adapted and enhanced it, and used it again here because I think it's revealing of the way we used to think, and still think to a large degree, about ourselves and the band. But I'm guessing as you've paid for yer Sunday roast you'll want more than just beef* and spuds. How about a few Yorkshire puddings?

Well, here goes…

---

* If you're veggie, like me, or vegan, then substitute beef for a Quorn roast roll.

CHAPTER 1

Take My Hand
And Lead Me

PLAYLIST:
1. The Power Of Love – Jennifer Rush   2. Cloudbusting – Kate Bush
3. Bring On The Dancing Horses – Echo & The Bunnymen
4. Cities In Dust – Siouxsie & The Banshees   5. Rain – The Cult
6. The Whole Of The Moon – The Waterboys
7. Serpents Kiss – The Mission   8. Wake (RSV) – The Mission
9. Naked And Savage – The Mission
10. Running Up That Hill – Kate Bush
11. A Night Like This – The Cure
12. Like A Hurricane – Neil Young   13. She Sells Sanctuary – The Cult

It was late October 1985. Earlier in the year, *Eastenders* had begun its long-standing tenure on BBC One. The size of a large crusty farmhouse loaf, the first mobile phone in the UK made its maiden call. Dire Straits' *Brothers In Arms* became the first CD release to sell a million. Roger Moore, who had played James Bond since 1973, had bowed out in his final appearance as '007' in *A View To A Kill*. Written by Frank Clarke and directed by Chris Bernard, two ace-faces around town when I lived in Liverpool, rom-com *Letter To Brezhnev*, which starred Clarke's sister Margi, was the alternative hit film of the year. Margaret Atwood published the eerily prescient dystopian novel *Handmaid's Tale*. At number one in the UK singles chart, and destined to be the biggest selling single of the year, was Jennifer Rush with her nauseating 'The Power Of Love', while the Top 10 was littered with the likes of John Parr, Jan Hammer and Level bloody 42. Odious. But take a sneaky-peaky a bit further down the chart and at number 20 was the soul-soaring 'Cloudbusting' by Kate Bush, Echo & The Bunnymen were at 21 with the regal 'Bring On The Dancing Horses', Siouxsie & The Banshees were at 23 with the majestic 'Cities In Dust', my ol' mates The Cult were at 25 with the breast-beating 'Rain', and further on down at number 56 were The Waterboys, just starting to make their way up the chart with the glorious 'The Whole Of The Moon'. Sift through all the fool's gold and, despite some distracting barnets, there were a few genuine and precious 24-carat nuggets.

Elsewhere, Everton were crowned English champions as well as winning the European Cup Winners' Cup Final on 15 May, but were denied a unique treble when they lost 1–0 to everyone's arch-enemy, Manchester United, in the FA Cup Final at Wembley. But football was ill. Shorts were getting shorter, hair was being permed, moustaches being grown, and the average top footballer was taking home a mind-boggling £25,000 basic per annum – 2.5 times more than the average working man. Those that had a job. There were more than three million unemployed in the UK, and it had been that way since the late Seventies. More disturbingly, hooliganism was rife and killing the beautiful game. On 29 May, all English football clubs were banned from European competition for five years after 39 people, mostly Italians, were crushed to death in a violent confrontation between Liverpool FC and Juventus fans before the European Cup Final match kicked off at Heysel Stadium, Brussels. It would be the darkest stain in the history of Liverpool FC, my team since 1965. The game was played despite the incident, and Liverpool went on to lose 1–0 to Juventus in what was a largely inconsequential match under the circumstances. It came only a couple of weeks after 56 people had lost their lives in a fire at Bradford City's Valley Parade, and a 14-year-old boy had been killed when Leeds fans rioted at Birmingham City the previous month. The terraces were merely a reflection of British society at the time. Dark days.

Not-so-Great Britain was helmed by the harridan Margaret Thatcher, who had her feet firmly under the desk at 10 Downing Street. As charming and compassionate as Covid-19 – and just as devastating – having now been in office for six years, she was systematically bringing the country to its knees. The divide between North and South, the haves and have-nots, the toffs and the plebs, the bosses and the workers, was getting ever wider. It was a miserable time. The country was suffering. And to compound it all, our band, The Sisters Of Mercy, split up.

Craig Adams and I had become fast friends, copesmates[1], partners in debauchery and indecorous behaviour in the two years that I was guitarist with The Sisters Of Mercy. We left at the same time. Well, about three hours apart to be exact. Craig left first. Our relationship with the despotic Andrew Eldritch was proving to be intolerable and after Craig had slung his hook along with his bass guitar to the floor and stormed out of rehearsal, he and I had adjourned to our local – The Faversham in Leeds – and decided we were going to leave TSOM and form our own band.

The first decision Craig and I had to make for our fledgling band was what kind of line-up we wanted. The drum machine was all well and good while we were with TSOM, and it did set us apart from the 'riff-raft' of guitar bands, but by this time both of us had become bored with the immutable Dr Avalanche. We fancied playing with a real, live, flesh and blood, belching, farting, joke-cracking, drug-taking, long-haired, Clash and Led Zeppelin-loving, huge-hearted drummer. But who? There was really only ever one choice.

Craig had started playing in a Leeds covers band, the impeccably monikered Elvis Presley's From Hell, for shits and giggles and free beer. As well as our dear Mr Adams on bass, the band featured Grape, who had previously been in The Expelaires with Craig, on vocals; John from the Batfish Boys on guitar; and, on drums, a certain Mick Brown who, at the time, was plying his trade with Leeds legends in waiting Red Lorry Yellow Lorry.

Craig and I had managed to persuade TSOM's A&R manager, Max Hole (nicknamed 'Arse', I presume, because of an allegiance to Arsenal Football Club) at WEA Records, to whom we were still contracted, to pay for us to record some demos. With studio time duly booked in late October at the Slaughterhouse Studios in Greater Driffield, where I'd previously produced fellow Leeds band Salvation, we approached Mick to see if he would come and help us out by playing drums. And by driving. Mick loved being behind the wheel, having been a long-distance lorry driver before he exchanged gear sticks for drumsticks, and returning to said profession after he'd later hung up his bandana and drumming shorts.[2] So, with little persuasion needed, we enlisted Mick to drive the hire-van to shift our gear from Leeds to the Slaughterhouse and to sit behind his kit and bash away at our new tunes.

Colin Richardson[3] was the house engineer at the time, and he and I had hit it off as a 'production team' during the Salvation sessions earlier in the year so it was an easy, and comfortable, working relationship from the off.

We had the use of a large, empty warehouse just across the street from the studio in which to record the drums. We set up Mick's kit, mic'd it up and lay tie-lines across the road from one building to the other and fed my guitar and Craig's bass, which were both set up in the studio, through his headphones, and we recorded the basic tracks in this way. In different buildings. Nowadays it's commonplace to record with collaborators having never even been on the same *continent*, let alone in the same room, but back then this was something new to us. We quickly laid down four tracks: 'Serpents Kiss', 'Wake (RSV)', 'Naked And Savage' and 'Burning Bridges' (sic)[4]. By the second or third day Craig's and Mick's services were no longer required so, loading up the van with drums and bass gear, they made their way back to Leeds, leaving me in the studio with Colin for an extra day or so to finish the guitars and record the vocals. Once again, as with my school band Humph, followed later by ...And The Dance after we'd jettisoned Hambi,[5] I became singer by default. Craig and I did talk about getting someone else in to sing, but we didn't know of anyone and, more importantly, we didn't like anyone enough to consider asking. I wasn't sure about singing and was certainly far from confident I could carry it off, but being better looking than Craig (ahem) and with a little past experience of stringing nonsensical words together to form a song, I decided I'd give it a whirl.

With the recordings finished but not yet properly mixed, Craig and I sent a cassette of rough mixes off to Mr Hole at WEA. A few days later I received a call asking Craig and I to come into the office for a meeting with him and Rob Dickins, the label's head honcho. Travelling down to London on the train, Craig and I, both very excited, speculated why we'd been invited – certainly, if we were going to be rejected Max could've just informed us over the phone. The prospect of WEA saying they loved our demos, and wanting to extend our contract and give us a bumper advance to form a new band and record an album, was uppermost in our expectations. How bloody deluded we were. When we arrived in Soho, we were shown into Max's office at WEA on Brewer St and asked if we wanted a beer and if there were any new albums we wanted.

'Nah, we don't want any Twisted bloody Sister or Strawberry soddin' Fruitcake or Switchblade or whatever they're called, but we'll have the beer. And then can we get on with this, please?' was my reply.

Rob Dickins joined us shortly thereafter and the conversation went something like this:

Dickins: 'We've had a listen to your tape. And while we like the songs we don't think you can really sing, Wayne.'

Hole: 'In fact, we've drawn up a short list of other singers we think you could work really well with.'

Addo: 'Go on.'

Dickins: 'Sal Solo from Classix Nouveaux.'

Huss: 'He's rubbish.'

Hole: 'Gavin Friday from the Virgin Prunes.'

Huss: 'Rubbish.'

Dickins: 'Peter Murphy.'

Huss: 'Oh, gawd, he's the worst of the lot.'

Dickins: 'Andi Sex Gang.'

Hole: 'Nik Fiend.'

Addo: 'All bloody rubbish.'

And on and on it went... It was so excruciatingly apparent that the unfortunately named Dickins–Hole comedy duo didn't *get* what Craig and I wanted to do, preferring to simply see us both as potential guns for hire for some other tosspot nincompoop front man. Well, I could be my own tosspot nincompoop front man, I was sure, with a bit of practice.

'Okay, we obviously don't see eye to eye on this, so are you gonna release us from our contract?' I enquired.

'No, we're gonna keep you contracted until the option comes up,' Dickins replied.

Craig, with his ire being gradually irked: 'Well, when's that then?'

Hole, smirkily: 'In about 12 months' time.'

'And so what are we supposed to do in the meantime, then? You know, to live and to survive?' I reasonably questioned.

'That's not our problem. What we'd suggest is you find yourselves a new singer, go out and play some gigs and build up an audience. Write some new and more commercial songs and then come back to us in six months or so,' was 'Arse' Hole's considered advice.

'Okay, thanks for all your help and encouragement. Will you pay for us to finish and mix our demos?' I, again, reasonably requested.

20

Dickins replied: 'Okay, lads, I have to go to another meeting now,' insinuating that it was with someone *far* more important than us, 'and no, we're not going to give you any more money for any more demos; you'll have to find the money yourselves if you want to finish them. And have a think about what we've suggested here today.'

'Cheers. Can we take a few beers for our journey back to Leeds, please?' asked Craig in a moment of inspired pragmatism.

'Sure.'

We both grabbed a six-pack each and left the offices of WEA for the last time, never to return.

The truth is the opinion of the two besuited record company execs did cut deep, and wound, and reinforced my own doubts as to whether I was cut out to be a front man. While I may have come across as the cockiest cock of the north, I was beset with a whole host of insecurities that I kept at bay as best I could by soaking 'em in alcohol or dusting 'em down with a little of the ol' sniff-sniff. I could sing, I knew that, but was my voice unique enough? Did I possess that elusive star quality, charisma or whatever you wanna call it, to elevate myself and our band above the flotsam of a million other bands? I wasn't sure, and WEA's rejection fed right into my own uncertainties. To compound matters even further, one evening around this time I dropped a tab of acid and listened to Kate Bush's recently released stunning *Hounds Of Love* over and over on headphones, and that threw my self-confidence into a complete tailspin. I surely wasn't good enough to compete or compare with the brilliance of Kate's vocal work, who was I bloody kidding? And if I couldn't be as good as Kate then what was the point? For days I vacillated, hemmed and hawed, but with Craig's encouragement I was gradually reconciling myself to the idea that, yes, fuck 'em, I could do it and we'd show the bastards. And then maybe another day or two later, I was once again listening to music at home and played The Cure's *Head On*

The Door, which had been released earlier that summer. You know what? **I *can* do this**. This *isn't* beyond my capabilities. I was finally persuaded and resolved to being the best singer-front man I could be, comparisons to Kate Bush notwithstanding. I'd played behind Pauline Murray, Pete Burns and Andrew Eldritch, even Knopov[6] and Hambi, and watched and learned and picked up skills and tricks from all of them. I was ready at long last, with my comrade in arms, Craig, in the trenches alongside me, to lead a band into a serious, concerted assault on the music business.

Our immediate pressing concerns were: first, to raise cash to pay for the mixing of the tracks we'd recorded at the Slaughterhouse; second, to persuade Mick Brown to leave the established Red Lorry Yellow Lorry and to join us in our new and untried venture; and third, to find a second guitar player.

To solve the first conundrum we met with Craig's dad, Ken Adams, in The Fav. Over pints and fags we laid out our masterplan, as brief as it was, and asked him to loan us a couple of hundred quid, to which he thankfully and quickly agreed. 'You wanna 'nother couple of pints, lads, to celebrate?' he said, his generosity spilling over into revelry. 'Aye, that'd be great, Ken. Ta.' Much toasting and jubilation ensued.

It took much cajoling and the plying of Mick with copious amounts of drugs and drink – and it stands as great testament to Mick's loyalty to the Lorries that it was indeed amounts copious – before he eventually succumbed and deigned to join our burgeoning gang. Sandy, Mick's girlfriend, was to become an essential member of our team over the next dozen or so months and was convinced far earlier than Mick that he should leave the Lorries to join us. The fact that we persuaded her to deny Mick his conjugal rights until he said yes to our proposition may have been a deciding factor, too. Job number two – done.

Next: a guitarist. Being a guitar player myself of a certain élan, finding another player up to my exacting standards was always going to be a difficult task. One person that came recommended to us was Simon Hinkler, who had previously played with then relatively unknown Sheffield bands Artery and Pulp.[7] With Sheffield being only 30 miles down the M1, we considered him certainly worth a shot. Arrangements were made and he appeared on my doorstep one Friday afternoon. He arrived dressed in a coat that wasn't quite afghan, but enough for Craig, Mick and me to quickly glance at each other and roll an eye or two. And to compound our initial impression the first words out of his mouth were, 'Alright lads, shall I skin up?' *Oh, God*, I thought, and almost demanded he leave straight away. Now, you know damn well it's not because I was averse to the ingestion of the occasional drug or two myself but, for me, smoking spliffs is something you do at the *end* of the working day when you have nothing else to do. It's certainly not a get-up-and-get-at-'em drug, is it? Mick, Craig and I were all heavy amphetamine users at this time, and the last thing we wanted for the band was a stoner. So we declined his offer, but Simon went ahead anyway and got himself righteously stoned, too stoned to even understand the chords and riffs of the songs I was trying to teach him. He was so out of it that I couldn't even tell if he could play guitar.

Simon ended up staying at mine for the weekend and while I grew to like him, I could see that his dope smoking would end up being a huge hindrance if he were to join the band. Even indulging in the occasional white line with me, he just seemed to be perennially stoned, with the guitar parts of the songs seemingly well beyond his capabilities. This conclusion he resigned himself to before he'd even left my house on Sunday afternoon. As he was leaving he said, 'I'm sorry, Wayne, I really don't think I'm up to scratch. I think you should cast your net wider and look for someone else.' It was a shame as he was a decent lad, good company and *very* pretty.

So the wearisome process of auditioning guitarists that we'd hoped to avoid if Simon had worked out was now our best option. We sent out the word and placed an ad in the Musicians Wanted section in

Melody Maker for a guitarist. Without expressly stating who we were, we were inundated.

There were a few guitarists in Leeds we knew that were up for the job, but they were all either too ugly, or played with no discernible style, or in some cases both. Some applicants came from further afield, but we could ascertain from their phone calls that they were either: (a) a psychopathic nutter, (b) a heavy metal fan, (c) a Manchester United supporter, or (d) an *NME*/Smiths devotee[8], all of which were duly winnowed as chaff from the wheat and excluded from any invitation to attend the auditions.

After setting up at Parkside rehearsal rooms in Leeds, we spent four or five days auditioning guitarists. Of course, we missed a few oddballs via our crude system of screening and we were forced to endure torturous, if not sometimes amusing, episodes auditioning ill-suited candidates. Among them was one chap who entered the room in a long overcoat, which he refused to remove despite the stifling heat, who produced from a black plastic bin bag a guitar with the price tag still dangling from the headstock. We rattled quickly through a couple of tunes with him playing along, very ineptly it has to be said, at the end of which, without saying a word, he deposited his guitar back into the bin bag and exited the room, despite our offer of a cup of tea and a fag. After his departure we all agreed that he must've nicked the guitar from a shop en route and was in a hurry to get going again before anyone caught up with him. To add credence to our theory the soddin' kleptomaniac also walked off with one of our guitar straps and a guitar cable.

Among the more well-known names that arrived to audition were Steve Skinner, who'd been playing with Edwyn Collins, and Vince White, latterly of The Clash MkII, who was furiously chewing either gum or the inside of his own cheeks. I attempted to show him the chords to one of the songs and he was all 'Nah, let's just jam, man'. Once a hippie…

My old school pal, Brian Powell, also travelled up from Brighton to have a go. One after another they came and went, dozens of the buggers[9], none of them quite right.

Towards the end of the auditions I received a phone call from Simon, explaining that he'd had second thoughts; he felt he'd let himself down badly during his previous visit with us, and could he, please, have another go? Yeah sure, why not – what did we have to lose apart from more time? I don't know whether it was because we'd already spent time with Simon or because our patience had worn thin with the seemingly interminable audition process, but when he returned to Leeds he was sans afghan, wasn't stoned, didn't skin up – just plugged in his guitar and blew every other auditionee to kingdom come. An overwhelming frisson erupted in the room and the four of us grinned at each other as we played together knowing that, now, our band was complete.

We started rehearsing five days a week, eight hours a day, honing the songs I was writing, a task made easier because of the demos I'd recorded, which we used as reference and a starting point. It took Simon, who we quickly and affectionately nicknamed 'Slink', a little while to come to terms with the notion of playing someone else's guitar lines when he'd previously been in bands where the members had worked out their own individual parts in a rehearsal room. I'd take in porta-studio demos with already written guitar, bass and drum parts and say 'this is the song, this is how it goes, and this is what you need to learn to play.' I wasn't *so* dictatorial as to not allow input from the others, and the truth is that Simon, when given space to come up with his own guitar parts, would produce some lovely stuff to complement what I was playing. But he did, as I once did with Eldritch, bristle a little with resentment at being told what to play, and this would prove to be a source of growing dissension on his part, I felt, throughout the initial period of our working together. But I was nothing if not motivated and demanding and, putting this minor friction aside, we knuckled down and rattled through the new material and soon had a full set of songs – including a rollicking version of Neil Young's 'Like A Hurricane' – rehearsed and ready to go. But go where?

Then serendipity came to stay. Or rather, my mate, The Cult's Billy Duffy. Towards the end of the year Billy called and said he was in Manchester visiting his folks and asked if it was alright to pop over to Leeds and say hello. Of course it bloody was. Anyway, he came to stay at mine that night and we sat in with a few beers and spent a very pleasant evening catching up. The next morning Billy came with me to rehearsals and sat there and listened while we stormed through our set, at the end of which he suggested we come on tour with The Cult. They had earlier that year enjoyed their biggest hit to date with the classic and evergreen 'She Sells Sanctuary' and had more recently released their era-defining album *Love*. In January 1986 they were embarking on a European tour and we were invited to join as their support band. To help ease our dire financial situation Billy magnanimously offered for us to travel on their sleeper coach with them and for our five-man crew to travel with theirs on their bus. The only problem was we had no money and, as of yet, no band name. Two fairly substantial obstacles.

Endnotes

1   A partner or colleague, associate, accomplice in plots and schemes. 'Misshapen time, copesmate of ugly night' – *The Rape Of Lucrece*, William Shakespeare (1594).

2   In fact, Mick, in his post-Mission days, would end up driving trucks for Oasis and our arch-nemesis The Sisters Of Mercy, among others.

3   After his stint at the Slaughterhouse, Colin Richardson went on to become one of the top producers in the heavy metal field, and all its murky sub-genres, producing over 100 albums including hits for Slipknot and Sepultura. And he was such a nice, quiet lad when I knew him.

4   The title as listed on the tape box, but which had become 'Bridges Burning' by the time it was re-recorded and released on The Mission's debut album, *God's Own Medicine*.

5   Humph, Hambi & The Dance and …And The Dance being three of my previous bands. See *Salad Daze*, my previous book.

6   David Knopov, lead singer in the Ded Byrds/Walkie Talkies, a band I was in for 18 months or so when I first lived in Liverpool. Again, please see *Salad Daze*.

7   Pulp, fronted by the engaging Jarvis Cocker, went on to huge success in the mid-Nineties after years of scrabbling around on the fringes. Simon's girlfriend when he first joined the band, and for several years after, was Jarvis' sister, Saskia. I remember Jarvis coming to a Mission show or two in the early days when we played in Sheffield, sitting in the corner of the dressing room being very quiet and quite timid. Quite unlike the Jarvis we all came to publicly know and love.

8   Actually, in fairness, I have a lot of time for Johnny Marr's guitar playing, and Andy Rourke was/is a very good bass player too, although conversely and to be frank, I found a lot of The Smiths songs to be musically quite pedestrian. I know I'm brooking the trend somewhat by expressing this opinion and no doubt it will incite wrath and indignation on the part of the fanatical zealots that believe The Smiths to be the messiahs of indie music, but really, some of it was a bit twee, wasn't it? Just like The Mission were a bit rock, right? The Smiths songs I do like I love, but most of 'em I can live without.

9   Q: How many guitarists does it take to change a light bulb?
A: One, and the rest of 'em to stand around to watch and boast 'Ahh, I could do that.'

CHAPTER 2

Foreign Tongue
In Familiar Places

PLAYLIST:
1. The Death Of Peter X – Artery
2. Like A Hurricane – The Mission (from the album *Salad Daze*)
3. Blood Brother – The Mission
4. Where Was? – Guthrie Handley w/Wayne Hussey
5. Giving Ground – The Sisterhood
6. This Corrosion – The Sisters Of Mercy
7. Serpents Kiss – The Mission   8. Wake (RSV) – The Mission
9. Naked And Savage – The Mission

VIDEO PLAYLIST:
1. Serpents Kiss – The Mission

I was onstage at the Electric Ballroom. Tonight was the night we were going to unveil our new band name and logo. We'd had a backdrop made specifically for the occasion. The place was full and we were playing well to a particularly receptive audience. My initial puke-inducing nerves had by this time dissipated and I was well settled into the performance, as were my fellow band mates. We'd reached the planned point in the set where we'd reveal our backdrop. With great pomp and ceremony, I announced, 'You thought you were coming to see The Sisterhood tonight? Well, tough, 'cos we ain't called that anymore.' And as I started to play the opening guitar riff to the next song and as the band crashed in, so the backdrop was supposed to fall and unfurl. I looked out at the audience, expecting to see faces filled with wonder and awe, but all I could see was confusion and, in some cases, blatant laughter. *What the hell is going on*, I thought. I quickly glanced behind me to see a couple of roadies scurrying around behind Mick's drum kit. I looked up at the backdrop to see that the right-hand side had got snagged on the lighting rig, unveiling THE MISS. It took a good minute or two for the roadies to eventually yank it to the floor to reveal the ION. Oh, bloody hell, that hadn't gone to plan...

With a pressing need to raise funds so that we could afford to do The Cult tour, we started to ask around about management. Up to that point I'd been dealing with the business aspect of the band the best I could. I certainly harboured no desire to go the route of Eldritch and manage the band for which I was the singer, guitarist and principle songwriter. I'd seen first-hand the damage it had wreaked on Andrew's creativity, health – both physical and mental – and personal relationships. Simon suggested a friend of his, Tony Perrin from Sheffield, who had managed Artery, Simon's previous band. Artery were fairly popular in their home town, but even at this stage, before we'd played a gig or released a record, we were already in a different league to what Tony had been used to. Whether he was up to the task was a genuine concern of mine. Nonetheless, I invited Tony to travel to Leeds to meet with us. Craig, Mick and I all immediately liked him and were impressed with his philosophy and idealism. He thought in a very similar way to us. We agreed that we wanted to infiltrate the mainstream and subvert from within, shake it up a bit as it had all gone a bit staid and conservative under the mid-Eighties Thatcher regime and the Tory policy of 'me, me, me'. There was no merit in being staunchly independent or alternative if we weren't competing with the big boys. We informed Tony that we needed an immediate influx of cash to pay for us to tour with The Cult, a golden opportunity too good to miss. While The Cult's generosity had helped, we still needed £5,000 for hotels, crew wages, and bits and bobs. We gave Tony until the following Sunday to raise the cash and if he did so, the job was his. He got it. Tony approached Dave Hall, a Leeds-based operator who ran one of the north-west's premier fly-posting gangs.[1] Fly-posting was big business and woe betide anyone that strayed outside their strictly enforced areas of demarcation. Huge turf wars could flare up and be contested with weapons of butchery such as knives, bicycle chains, metal pipes and knuckledusters. Dave wanted to branch out into the legitimate business of band merchandise and recognised the huge potential of getting into bed with us. He offered us a £10,000 advance − then unheard of for a brand-new, untested band − £5,000 of which was immediately payable. Dave and Tony met in the middle of the night at Woolley Edge motorway services on the M1, between Leeds and Sheffield, and Dave handed over the cash in a plastic bag containing fivers and tenners amounting to five grand. We had both our manager and the money to do the tour.

While putting together cassettes of demos and the Slaughterhouse recordings, I had, for convenience sake, been labelling the tapes as The Sisters, more as reference rather than with any real intent of permanently using the sobriquet. When Craig and I had left the 'Dritch, both parties had come to the understanding that neither would use the name The Sisters Of Mercy. We never had any intention to do so, despite some later claims to the contrary by Andrew and certain factions of the music press. Relations between myself and Andrew had remained reasonably amicable and cordial up to this point. But, I believe as much to do with his presumption that we wouldn't, couldn't and 'how dare we' get anything together, let alone in such a short space of time since the dissolution of TSOM, our relationship inevitably began to sour. I don't know if you're like me but if someone tells me I can't do something then I want all the more to do it. If someone tries to stop me doing what I set out to do then I will persist all the more, and use every device available to me to achieve my aims. This was clearly a case in point. The more Eldritch objected to our rapid development – and don't forget he had the corporate weight of WEA on his side at this point – the more determined I became that we'd ride this particular horse all the way to the finishing line. With The Cult tour fast approaching we needed a name for our band and as Andrew, in cahoots with Dickins-Hole, was proving obstructive, we decided to antagonise the bugger by going out as The Sisterhood, the name by which a group of fans had called themselves while following TSOM. I knew perfectly well that it was an inflammatory and provocative act and would, once and for all, demolish any bridges between me and Andrew and certain sections of the TSOM audience that would doubtlessly side with him. In hindsight, it was perhaps not the smartest move, but I was hitting out in retaliation the best way I could see how. It was also coldly calculated that maybe this situation would serve us well in the music press: after all, what new band doesn't crave publicity? And let's be clear here, the decision on our part to name the band The Sisterhood was also an attempt to provoke WEA into releasing us from our contract. Maybe we could use it as a bargaining tool with which to negotiate our way out of our fast-becoming untenable position. Craig and I were angry at the shackles we felt Eldritch and WEA were attempting to tether us with. While the name The Sisterhood would suit our purposes in the short term, we all knew it was temporary until we could come up with something better. We had a plan of action long before we eventually changed our name. So, pretty early on we decided to ride the press storm and use it to our advantage, and for a few months our barney raged very publicly across the pages of the UK music press. Andrew enjoyed this caper too, and I think it's fair to say that both parties benefited from the mischief. Back and forth, insult followed insult, my most memorable perhaps being 'Eldritch is as enigmatic as a boiled egg', while Andrew claimed I was so stupid that I wouldn't realise 'Giving Ground' was about me. Sometimes garrulous to a fault, I quickly learned how, with a well-aimed barb in interviews and press statements, to conjure a 'pull quote' that would make an attention grabbing headline. It was a baptism of fire in dealing with the jackals of the music press, but I'd had good teachers – in Pete Burns and Von (Eldritch) himself – in how to deal with the scurrilous breed. Then the lawyers got involved. They couldn't sue us, couldn't force us to cease and desist. We knew we had not done anything illegal by using the name The Sisterhood. Morally it was maybe another matter, but we didn't bother ourselves with such trivial and ethical considerations. We *did* enjoy the battle, and when it was spent we left it there. Andrew, on the other hand, continued with his grievances both publicly and with letters from his lawyers months after we had become The Mission. The only thing it had cost us was some legal bills and maybe the moral high ground. It was never gonna reach court, and the rumours of big financial losses and paying off Eldritch to the tune of £25,000 were mendacious and wishful thinking on the part of some of his more extremist supporters.

We embarked on the European tour with The Cult as The Sisterhood, sometimes being billed, against our instruction I hasten to add, as ex-Sisters Of Mercy.[2] This was to prove particularly galling at our first ever gig, a supposed low-key event at the then trendy London club Alice In Wonderland, on Monday 20 January, 1986. Billed as The Sisterhood, some wag with an eye to door profits started the whisper that it was, in fact, a secret gig by the reformed Sisters Of Mercy. Of course the place was packed and, with nerves getting the better of us, particularly me, we were abysmal, weeks of rehearsal flying completely out the window at the first scent of an audience. It didn't help that those in attendance came expecting 'Alice' and 'Marian', with some visibly and verbally disgruntled that instead they were getting the then unknown 'Wasteland' and 'Serpents Kiss'. Still, as dreadful as we were we convened back at the Columbia Hotel in Lancaster Gate après show and celebrated as if we were The Rolling Stones having just played Wembley Stadium.

We can't have been all bad, though, as, fortuitously, having seen us play and recognising that we had *something*, Martin Horne from top London agency ITB[3] approached us. Up to that point we had been working with Andy Woolliscroft at Station, who had been the Sisters' agent, and it was felt by all concerned that maybe it was a conflict of interest, much like it'd be if we'd been using the same lawyer. So, we gladly took Martin up on his offer to become our new agent, severing yet another tie with our past. In fact, Martin became an integral member of our extended family for more than 20 years.

The day after our Alice In Wonderland debacle I had arranged for us to record a Radio 1 session for my old Liverpool pal, DJ Janice Long[4] – our first radio play anywhere in the world. Janice became an important supporter of the band in the early days and played us at a time when no one else would and we were being roundly ignored by that exalted champion of new bands, John Peel.[5] Peelie loathed us from day one and never entertained the possibility of us appearing on his show. I preferred to see that as vindication that we were indeed headed in the right direction.[6]

Two days later and we were on The Cult's tour bus heading for the Netherlands. This, lest we forget, all within the space of three short months since Craig and I had departed TSOM. That's quite an achievement and testament to our drive, resolve and good fortune. Eldritch despised the fact that we'd managed all this without him.

It was the first time any of us had ever been on the sleeper coaches that are so widely deployed by 'proper' touring bands, but it didn't take us long to feel at home, and we were soon cracking beers and chopping lines and playing Zeppelin and Hendrix tapes at raucous volume in the back lounge. It was certainly a big step up from The Flying Turd.[7]

Our first show was in front of a sold out audience of 2,000 in Utrecht, and we stormed it. The audience, not knowing who we were, were slow to warm to us, but by the end of our 40-minute set we had most of 'em on our side, dancing and cheering in a way that we'd never previously managed in the Netherlands with TSOM. Our previous experience of Dutch audiences was of stoned, sedate hippies that tended to gawk at us through clouds of pungent marijuana smoke rather than get animated or involved.

Most nights we'd sit up in the hotel bar after the show until close to dawn, drinking with our buddies The Cult, and then we'd spend our days sleeping it off in our bunks on the bus as we travelled to the next town to do it all again. The camaraderie between the two bands during this time was very special, and a memory I still cherish. We learnt a lot from Billy, Ian, Jamie and Les, and we aspired to reach the position the band held at that time. Kindred spirits we were and, as the song goes, blood brothers.

From the Netherlands the tour rolled through Belgium, France and Germany. Needless to say our amphetamine use was out of control, although none of the members of The Cult touched the stuff, preferring their booze, with front man Ian, long before their conversion to teetotalism, guzzling the best part of a bottle of brandy a night. I would regularly go four or five days and nights without sleep during this time, which did my state of mind nor my vocal cords no good, Mick very often keeping me company on my voyages into derangement. I took to greeting people with a snog, tongues 'n' all – male or female, friend or stranger, it made no difference to me. Of course some, quite rightly so, took exception to my invasive form of salutation. One night a young lad, a fan who had simply asked for an autograph, revealed his objection to me sticking my tongue down his throat by biting said oral appendage and drawing blood. Ian stepped in and gave him a good slapping to compound the situation. 'Don't bite me mate's tongue, it's rude,' Ian chided.

Billy, when he'd see me coming, would say, 'Don't you bloody well try and snog me, 'Ussey.' It was, coincidentally, the first thing Liam Gallagher would say to me when we were first introduced a good few years later, my reputation obviously preceding me. What is it with these Mancs, eh – don't they like a bit of foreign tongue? Anyway, having to sing the next night with a swollen tongue taught me a valuable lesson – don't put your gustatory organ, or anything else for that matter, where it's not invited.

The Cult, being the headliners, were obviously the main pull for the tour, with Ian and Billy off regularly doing interviews. As a band, we even got to do a couple ourselves, with one TV interview in Paris being particularly memorable for Mick's hilarious reply to the question, 'How long have you been together?'

'What, me personally?'

Mick became the heart and soul of the band. Ask any of us, including our crew, who our favourite member was and we'd all say Mick. He was the one that would act as peacekeeper when things got fraught, he'd be pragmatic and earthbound when things looked like spinning out of control, and he became best friend and Father Confessor to us all. He'd endlessly encourage us to express, and *be*, ourselves. And if I was hoovering up lines of speed he'd join me, he'd smoke spliffs with Simon and down pints with Craig – all at the same time – and still be the most coherent out of the lot of us. Mick did his very best to make sure that everything remained copacetic within, and around, the band. Mick is Taurus, an Earth sign. Craig is Pisces and Water, Simon is Fire and Scorpio, while I am the Gemini twins and Air. The four elements – a perfect balance. And it was.

Mick also became very adept at smuggling drugs across borders. The morning after we'd played in Hamburg, The Cult took an early flight into Berlin to appear on a TV show, leaving us alone to travel on their big tour bus. Loath to dump the speed and dope we had on our persons before hitting the corridor[8] through East Germany, Mick hatched a plan to hide them on the bus. He tightly wrapped up our illicit supplies in silver foil paper and dropped them into a carton of milk he was drinking from. When we were inevitably stopped at the border and asked to exit the bus so the guards could bring on the sniffer dogs, Mick just left the carton on the floor in the back lounge. A few minutes later the guards and dogs exited the bus and let us go, the drugs undetected. Several miles down the road and Mick fished out the goodies from his milk saying, 'we'd best have a line, then, to celebrate'. Which reminds me of another episode a couple of years later, on the return from our first jaunt to South America. Arriving into Heathrow from São Paulo, Mick and I grabbed our bags and walked together through customs. I, of course, get pulled over and into a small side room while Mick waves to me as he cheerfully walks straight through. I get seriously done over, the whole strip search thing, rifling through all my luggage etc., but they find nothing. They may have thought I looked stupid but I certainly wasn't stupid enough to ever wittingly carry drugs across borders. I was released and continued through to the arrivals area, where the rest of the band and the crew were stood waiting for me with big grins on their faces. 'Ah, I knew if I walked through customs with you that I wouldn't get pulled over,' boasts Mick, 'just like groupies, they always go for the singer first', he said with a chortle. Ha bloody ha. We get into the waiting minibus to ferry us to the Columbia Hotel in London and en route Mick searches his pockets for a cigarette lighter. 'What the fuck is this?', and he pulls out a small white paper wrap. 'Shit, it's coke. I forgot I had that. That could've gotten nasty. Best chop 'em out to celebrate our safe homecoming, then.' He wasn't

36

called Lucky Mick[9] for nothing. As I had inadvertently saved his bacon, he graciously passed me the first line.

With The Cult tour over, the first thing we did when we arrived back in London was sack Simon. We'd noticed that he really wasn't entering into the spirit of *all for one and one for all.* When The Cult flew and we were on the bus alone, on arrival at the hotel we'd help carry their bags, as well as ours, into the lobby. Simon only ever picked up his own. Sometimes when we had a quick changeover between bands we'd help our crew load the backline off the stage and onto the truck. Simon was never to be seen. It's not a big deal, really, and a simple word to the wise would've probably sufficed, but with our senses and emotions ravaged by the excesses of three weeks on tour these incidents became exaggerated and we felt there was no other recourse but to get rid of him. After a few days back in Blighty, and with some semblance of sober thinking being restored, we asked him to rejoin. I think, though, this episode scarred Simon, as sensitive as he is, and fostered feelings of insecurity in him for the remainder of his original four-year tenure with the band. His insecurities also later led to a power struggle within the band between him and I that he was never going to win and that would ultimately lead to his 'permanent' departure in 1990.[10]

A few weeks off and I returned to the Slaughterhouse to mix the 'Serpents Kiss' recording. Having already expended the funds endowed to us by Ken Adams I'd struck a deal with the owner of the studio, Russell, for some more free studio time. On his own Prism label roster there was an artist, Guthrie Handley, who was recording a single. I'd spend a couple of days playing guitar on a track or two and in return I could mix our four tracks for free. Good deal. Later in the year, when Guthrie's single 'Where Was?' was released, I was slightly taken aback by Russell's blatant opportunism, a stroke straight out of *my* book. My star was in the ascendancy at the time and Russell had plastered my name – in slightly smaller type than

Guthrie's – across the front cover, and I'd been given a 50 per cent writing credit on the song, which I can unreservedly say I didn't deserve. It was solely Guthrie's song. Flattered and thankful nonetheless, it's a pleasant enough ditty that reached numbers 14 and 63, respectively, in the UK's independent and national charts.

In the first week of March 1986, we had three UK shows booked as The Sisterhood, at which we were going to unveil our new name. The dispute had gone on long enough with Eldritch, and as he had released a single entitled 'Giving Ground' under the same name, The Sisterhood, to stake his claim to the name, we were legally forced to change ours. No matter: we were ready, with the perfect new moniker already decided. Suitably fuelled, Mick and I had stayed up in Ashville Grove one night and, with our cats Kevin and Max running up and down the hessian-papered wall, we drew up a list of potential band names, most of which – Love Patrol and Sons Of Cain being just two examples – were drug-induced silliness. A serious contender, until morning at least, was The Crystal Religion, obviously a reference to our amphetamine habits. We'd also scribbled down The Mission, suggested by my Mission stereo speakers and the fact that I was chronicling all our ideas in a Mormon missionary journal my parents had bought me one Christmas when they still harboured vain hopes that I would, indeed, one day serve a Mormon mission. In the cold, harsh light of day, and once we had consulted with the other two, Craig and Simon, the consensus was that The Crystal Religion was rubbish and The Mission was the one.

By the way, 'Giving Ground', to these ears, is a turgid affair with little, lyrics aside, to redeem it. It's obviously aimed at yours truly, and if we're talking about songs penned by the 'Dritch that have a dig, then it's hellaciously pallid in comparison to the later and, I'm loath to admit it, outrageously brilliant 'This Corrosion'. While 'Giving Ground' is Andrew's song and he produced it and released it on Merciful Release – because he, like us, was still contracted to the blood-sucking WEA – he had to employ one of his minions to vocal it for him. He should've left it at that. He'd won the battle: we'd acceded and changed our name. But he went on to record an entire album of this dreariness, entitled *Gift*, an enterprise designed, as well as to prevent us from using the name, to extricate himself from his publishing deal. Andrew, as had so often been the case, was inspired to create by spite and intended perniciousness; he has always been at his best when he's had someone or something to inveigh against. I, along with Craig, forced his hand into making what was perhaps the nadir of his entire recorded output, an accomplishment I took great pleasure in detailing in my scathing one star review of the album in *Sounds*[11], issue dated July 26, 1986. Listening to the album now my opinion hasn't changed; it still sounds musically vapid to me, but it does act as an indicator to where Andrew would journey with his next album, TSOM's *Floodland*.

Our first show that week, and second ever UK show, was at the Electric Ballroom in Camden, on Thursday, February 27. Two or three songs in and a backdrop was to unfurl to reveal our new logo[12] and name. Akin to a scene from *Spinal Tap*, the unveiling didn't have quite the impact we'd hoped for. Some might even say it was a portent of things to come, but we were to prove all doubters and naysayers wrong over the next few years. That night, Ian Astbury and Billy Duffy joined us onstage for an extended encore. It was rumoured that Andrew was in attendance, but he didn't make his presence known to us and would no doubt have slinked away when Astbury started chanting 'Eldritch is bald' over and over.

Saturday, March 1, and we were scheduled to perform at Leeds University but the show was cancelled due to an injunction served on us by Andrew's lawyers. This made it all the more extraordinary when, the very next night, he turned up again in the audience as we played at Birmingham Powerhouse, apparently commenting to a mutual friend how good he thought the songs were; ironically the very songs of mine he had rejected in Hamburg the previous year.

This show was also reviewed by the *NME* – our first review in that particular rag – and, shockingly, it was a favourable one. Always previously at odds with the self-appointed arbiter of taste while with TSOM, it was a huge surprise to actually read within their pages something positive about us. But our credibility wasn't to last; the mamamouchi[13] *NME* turned on us as quickly as it'd take to fry an egg on the surface of the Sun. Yet another vindication of us making the right moves.

Sounds also ran a feature on us just after the Cult tour, sending out Neil 'Spud' Perry[14] to interview us in Paris, our first meeting. Neil was to become a good friend to us, as much as a journalist can be I guess, and a firm supporter, one of the very few, of the band among the hack fraternity.

On April 27 we flew down to Valencia in Spain to play two shows at E-Discoteca Mansies, one at midnight and the second at 5 a.m. The day before I had bitten into a rock-hard Mars Bar and, thinking it very crunchy, had swallowed half of one of my molars that had broken off with the first chomp. With no time to visit the dentist before we left I was in acute pain. The promoter, Robert Mills, a charming but roguish native of Catalonia who boasted a huge handlebar moustache and long, dark hair swept back into a ponytail like a Seventies German porn star, procured for medicinal purposes a small lump of dope that I ate to temper my agony. By the time we hit the stage at midnight I was stoned out of my gourd, the first and only time I have performed while in that state. I was about as useless as the P in 'psychosis'. How people can get stoned before a show and then go on to play I have no idea. Of course, I was pretty able to do so under the influence of booze, speed, coke and, later, even ecstasy, but holy cats, dope was another thing entirely.

After we finished our set the club emptied and with tiredness encroaching, despite the abundance of Spanish beer and wine, we managed to score some speed to liven us up for the second set, which was due to start at 5 a.m. By 4.50 a.m. there was no bugger in the club. But when we walked out onto the stage 10 minutes later the place was rammed. The gig was a sweaty early morning stormer, all the more remarkable for the fact that all the songs were new to the audience, what with us not having yet released even a single. Which signified a huge leap of faith by Robert Mills to bring us down there in the first place. It was a brave move on his part, and while not a fortune, it was still a fairly sizeable investment he had to make to do so. But it paid off for Robert, as he is still our favoured promoter in Spain some 30-odd years later. He could be quite a character and always had multiple deals going on, but he has forever been honourable to both myself and the band. I consider him to be a friend, one of the very few who work in the business. And the fact that he supports Liverpool alongside Barcelona is a huge plus in his favour.

We were impatient to get things moving and still being in deadlock with WEA we decided on a course of action that was perilously close to being illegal and could well have scuppered our plans and left us entangled in litigation until the end of time. We decided to go ahead and release the Slaughterhouse recordings as a 7- and a 12-inch vinyl single. The Leamington Spa-based Chapter 22 label, later home to Pop Will Eat Itself and Ned's Atomic Dustbin, and helmed by then manager of Balaam & The Angel, Craig Jennings, was the only label that would even entertain the idea of taking on the corporate might of WEA. Craig (Adams) and I, still contracted to WEA and with them owning the masters as they had partly paid for the recordings, had to sign a document ensuring that if WEA did come after us we would be personally liable for any legal ramifications, absolving Jennings and Chapter 22 from any financial recourse. What did Craig and I have to lose? We had nothing anyway. For us it was worth the risk.

Released on Friday 9 May, the single, entitled simply *The Mission – I*, featured 'Serpents Kiss' as the A-side and 'Wake (RSV)' on the 7-inch B, while 'Naked And Savage' completed the line-up on the 12-inch. It flew straight into the UK Independent Charts at number one, a feat hitherto unachieved by a debut single from a brand-new band. It stayed there for a couple of weeks before being knocked off the top perch by 'Bigmouth Strikes Again'. The Smiths opus quickly plummeted, though, with 'Serpents Kiss' returning to the summit for a further couple of weeks and then staying around in the Top 10 for the remainder of the year. At the year end *The Mission – I* was certified as the biggest selling independent single of 1986 and Craig Jennings and Chapter 22 were awarded a statuette by trade bible *Music Week* to commemorate the achievement.

Musically, 'Serpents Kiss' is a joyous and effervescent piece, set up by the spine-tingling opening guitar riff. The song itself is full of those shimmering guitar hooks and melodies I was becoming so adept at coming up with: twelve and six-string electric and acoustic layered guitars, all topped off with a trick I'd learnt to make the guitar sound sizzle. I'd slow the multi-track tape down to half-speed and then record the guitar part at the new, slower tempo. On playback, with the tape machine being put back to its normal speed, the newly recorded guitar part would play back with an octave higher radiance. It's a ploy I would return to regularly until the advent of bloody Pro Tools[15] and music being recorded to computer rather than tape. Sadly, despite all the technological advances and the huge plethora of plug-ins, it's impossible to recreate that effect in quite the same way without tape.

For the guitar solo I was struggling to come up with anything that wasn't predictable and obvious in normal E-A-D-G-B-E tuning. So, I tuned my guitar, a Starcaster, to an open chord. I have no memory of what notes the strings were tuned to, as it was a spontaneous act and not a conventionally known tuning. Each open string was in tune with the song, which for the musos among us is in the key of

C# minor. Then I asked Colin, the engineer, to roll the tape. I have no idea how but I got it in the first take – with that sudden rush of adrenaline and blind grasping at notes, not quite sure what exactly would be elicited from the guitar in that strange tuning. It worked, it sounded fresh and exciting, unplanned, unsculpted, untethered, the icing on an already very tasty cake.

The B-side to 'Serpents Kiss', 'Wake (RSV)', was my pithy response to Eldritch's 'Giving Ground'. It's a well-aimed lyric, which also ended up giving us the title of our debut album, *God's Own Medicine*, which would come later that year: 'For you, sunshine, it's a taste of your own medicine, God's own medicine for you.' The (RSV) addendum in the title is an abbreviation of RSVP, or *répondez s'il vous plaît*, which is usually found on invitations to social events that require a reply. I really didn't feel like I owed Eldritch a 'please', hence I dropped the 'P'.

The extra track on the 12-inch was 'Naked And Savage', and to this day I don't know what the song is about. That's maybe why I still enjoy singing it so much. As with most of my early Mission songs, the meaning is oblique, the lyrics scribed while speeding.

A few days after the single's release I was sat at home watching the *Old Grey Whistle Test* when they announced they would feature the UK Independent Chart the following week. I already knew we were going to enter the chart at number one, so I was straight on the phone to Tony Perrin, telling him that we needed to make a video for 'Serpents Kiss' and get it to the *OGWT* office before the end of the following weekend – a tall order, as this was already late Tuesday evening. We contacted Kevin from Leeds-based band The Mekons, and as music video production was an area he was looking to expand into he was only too eager to produce the video for us. Tony raised the money we needed (£2,000) and within less than 48 hours we were filming in Meanwood Park in Leeds. With no story-board as such, not having time to develop one, our idea was to film us messing about in the park. We assembled a few props, including a gas mask I kept in my bedroom for, um, emergencies; Thermidor, our plastic lobster mascot that travelled with us for years; a toy police helmet; various acoustic instruments; a few beach footballs and umbrellas; various silly hats; a trident and a pair of devil horns for Craig; and a pink Cadillac we borrowed from Dave Hall. It wasn't a particularly sunny day but, fortuitously, it didn't rain. With the cameras set to high colour saturation the film ended up looking very bright and vivid; an Eighties psychedelic vision as opposed to the en vogue retrogressive cliché of trying to look like you were filming in the Sixties. We clowned, we frolicked, we buffooned, we pranced, we ran and we jumped. We had so much fun shooting that video – more so than any video before or since. I wore black lipstick and at one point I bowed down and kissed the camera lens. Craig was stood trouser-less in a lake, with the devil horns on his head attempting to spear Thermidor with his trident. Simon mimed the guitar solo on a mandolin, while I kicked footballs at him. Mick used a log as his drum. Craig jumped off the edge of the world. It was improvised silliness that flew in the face of what was expected from us – the complete antithesis of goth. It was filmed and edited by novices with very little resources and all these circumstances fed into its sense of innocent exuberance. It was to be the best video we ever made, in my opinion, certainly the most played on British TV.

With a few late nights and early mornings we managed to finish it in time for *OGWT* to screen its TV debut the following Tuesday. It gave many their first sight of The Mission, and it shocked those who believed us to be the serious, humourless, po-faced goths they'd been led to believe we were. We're still to this day contending that errant and lazy assumption.

Serendipity once again helped our cause when the fledgling *Chart Show*[16], broadcast weekly on Friday evenings on Channel 4, entered into a dispute with the major record labels concerning payment for the use of their music videos. Not realising the value of primetime TV exposure, the silly, greedy corporations forbade the show from broadcasting their videos until the dispute was settled. The situation was a godsend to us. Being independent and not answerable to anyone but ourselves we gave Channel 4 carte blanche to show our video as often and as many times as they liked, without ever having to pay a penny. As a result, and because of our constant position in the Top 10, they broadcast the 'Serpents Kiss' video virtually every week while their spat with the avaricious record companies lingered on over the summer months. And each showing ensured the record remained in the chart. There was really nothing else like us around at the time, with the exception perhaps of The Cult and, while they were in the process of transforming themselves into AC/DC, they certainly weren't as much fun as we were.

Largely, and predictably, derided by critics, 'Serpents Kiss' is a re-telling of a night I spent with a pair of German sisters in their home. I had recently read *Moonchild* by the occultist Aleister Crowley, in which a serpent's kiss was described as an erotic greeting whereby a man would bite into a woman's bottom lip, drawing blood. The sisters and I dropped acid and it all became a slightly unnerving but sensual trip as I soon realised that they were both, in fact, maenads[17], when they started performing frenzied rituals and incantations over black candles. Of course, ever the adventurer, I went along for the ride and was instructed to perform the serpent's kiss, and more, on both the girls. I was more than happy to oblige. Unsurprisingly, the song that grew out of this experience led to the salacious rumour that I was a practising Satanist, a situation compounded when, not long after, we released the song 'Severina' with its further reference to Crowley and his *Love Is The Law, Love Under Will* maxim. Let me clarify right now that I was never a Satanist or a practitioner of magick. My curiosity was merely piqued by my near obsession with Jimmy Page and his immersion in the dark arts. I did on occasion, however, play the willing supplicant in the pursuit of kinky ritual sex. Well, who wouldn't?

All through the success of 'Serpents Kiss' we didn't hear a peep from WEA, except to ask to be put on the guest list for the London show of our upcoming Expedition 1 tour. We declined, saying if they wanted to come they'd have to buy tickets. As we did with all record labels. WEA didn't turn up. But almost every other major record label in London sent representatives who did.

Endnotes

1   Fly-posting in Britain was illegal but highly lucrative. Despite the illegality of the practice, record companies were all too willing to underwrite the perpetration of violence and sometimes vandalism to promote their bands' new releases on inner city sites – maybe a derelict building or a wall on a piece of wasteland – which were fiercely guarded by the crews that considered them to be their own sacrosanct fiefdom.

2   In the early days, unscrupulous (I know, it's a bit like a Dalmatian dog calling a leopard spotty) promoters would boldly emblazon the legend 'ex-Sisters Of Mercy' across all publicity. As we became better versed in contractual issues, we insisted on a clause being written in to our contracts to the effect that no mention of The Sisters Of Mercy was allowed on any posters or promotional material for any show, anywhere.

3   International Talent Booking agency was founded by agents Barry Dickins and Rod MacSween and located at 113–117 Wardour Street, literally right across the street from the old Marquee club.

4   Sadly, Janice passed away on Christmas Day 2021 while I was writing this book. She had been a supporter of both me and The Mission throughout. My first ever radio interview was with Janice in the late Seventies, when I lived in Liverpool and she worked at Radio Merseyside. The last time I

spoke with her was late 2020, an interview we did for her show on Radio Wales. She reminded me of the time we, along with Christine, her assistant at Radio Merseyside, had been out for the night in Liverpool. I'd got so blottoed that they'd had to take me home. I woke up the next morning with a bucket next to my bed, a glass of water at the ready, and naked with a ribbon tied around my dick. Out for the count, Janice and Christine had undressed me and put me to bed, enjoying a little giggle at my expense.

5   We recorded four songs for Janice at that session: 'Sacrilege', 'Severina', 'And The Dance Goes On' and 'Like A Hurricane'. A compilation of our Radio 1 sessions was released in 1994 as *Salad Daze*. We never did record a session for John Peel.

6   I don't wish to speak ill of the deceased – or, indeed, a fellow LFC supporter, and particularly someone as rightfully venerated as John Peel – but among all the good bands he did champion and to whom he gave their first breaks, Peel did also play an awful lot of rubbish. It was a running joke among us that you could record your hoover and get your dog to howl over the top of it, send it to Peelie, and he'd play it on his show before he'd play a Mission record.

7   As described in more detail in *Salad Daze*, The Flying Turd was a red and white Dodge minibus, owned and driven by Dave Kentish, which was used to convey TSOM from town to town while on tour. Excerpt from *Salad Daze*: 'the interior was tastefully carpeted from floor to ceiling in a lovely shade of shit brown, hence the appellation, The Flying Turd.'

8   In 1986, Germany was still divided into the Communist East and the Federal Republic of the West. Access to West Germany was quite simple and straight-forward, as much as any European border was at the time, while East Germany was generally a no-go zone for Westerners. Berlin was a city divided, again by East and West. The only way to get to West Berlin was either by flying in or travelling by road using one of three 'corridors', one from the north, another from the west, and the last one from the south of the Federal Republic. These 'corridors' were heavily policed by military, and while there were one or two officially sanctioned areas to stop – you could hardly call them motorway service stations – no traffic was allowed to leave the main road or stop at any unauthorised point. The route from West Germany all the way through to West Berlin was lined with shows of military might: tanks, fighter planes, marching soldiers and army bases. On entering and leaving East Germany,

47

without fail, the border guards would stop us and insist on searching our buses and trucks, sometimes causing delays of many hours.

9   'Mental' was another of our much-favoured nicknames for Mick, as was the ubiquitous 'Brownie'.

10 Until our 25th anniversary reformation in 2011.

11 *Sounds* was a UK weekly music paper, published from October 10, 1970, to April 6, 1991, which tended to focus on more progressive and rock-orientated music than its two rivals, *NME* and *Melody Maker*. There was also *Record Mirror*, which was more geared to chart music. My beauteous countenance graced the covers of all of them several times over. I was even on the front covers of *Smash Hits* and *Number One* bi-weekly mags, geared purely to a teenage pop audience, sharing my *Smash Hits* cover with a smaller photograph of that hateful she-devil, Margaret Thatcher.

12 We had a band logo long before we had a name. Acknowledging the value of the Merciful Release/TSOM logo that my previous band had employed to great effect, I came across what we were to adopt as the Mission logo one Sunday morning while browsing through a newspaper supplement: a photograph of French rescue workers pulling buried people out of the rubble of a collapsed building, with one of them wearing a cap with what looked like a Celtic knot embroidered on the top. I could sit here now and claim the logo held some deep meaning for me but it didn't – it was simply, to my mind at least, something that would look good on T-shirts and as a stage backdrop. One continuous unbroken line affectionately christened 'four fishes' by Mick, alluding to the fact that it does look like four contiguous overlapping fishes. It is deceptively simple in design but an absolute bugger to draw by anyone not ferociously skilled with a pencil and a compass. It has served us well and become synonymous with the band, with initiates worldwide only needing to see the logo to know it pertains to us, whether it be on a poster, an advert, the back of a leather jacket or a tattoo.

13 Someone who believes themselves to be more important than they really are.

14 Neil was ingeniously bestowed the nickname of 'Spud The Cork' by Mick, no one quite remembering why. Neil also co-wrote, with Martin Roach, the first Mission biography, *Names Are For Tombstones, Baby*, published in the mid-Nineties.

15 Digidesign released Sound Tools in the late Eighties, essentially a stereo digital-audio computer-based software editor, which evolved throughout the Nineties into the industry standard multi-track recorder Pro Tools. The introduction of Pro Tools into pretty much every studio in the land tolled the death knell of studios, sounding, to these ears at least, uniquely idiosyncratic. Everything became generic, complete with that horrible high-end fizz which was inherent in digital recording when it first became prevalent. The technology has now improved considerably and offers a lot of advantages over tape, but nothing could get the ticker of the producer going quite like seeing piles of tape littering the studio floor as the engineer is bent over the machine editing with a razor blade and a tape-editing block.

16 A precursor to MTV in Europe, *The Chart Show* was arguably Britain's best ever music show, eschewing jabbering VJs and presenters and tiresome interviews in favour of playing back-to-back music videos of the latest releases and chart hits including, fortuitously for us and bands of our ilk, the then thriving Independent and Alternative Charts.

17 In classical mythology, a Bacchante, a female participant in the orgiastic rites of Dionysus.

CHAPTER 3

God's Own Medicine

PLAYLIST:
1. The Dam Busters March – The Associated British Studio Orchestra
2. Garden Of Delight (Extended) – The Mission
3. Like A Hurricane – The Mission
4. The Crystal Ocean (Extended) – The Mission
5. Over The Hills And Far Away – The Mission
6. Dancing Barefoot – The Mission   7. Telegram Sam – T.Rex
8. I Am The Walrus – The Beatles   9. Panic – The Smiths
10. FFA – The Leather Nun
11. Spirit In The Sky – Dr & The Medics
12. Something In The Air – Thunderclap Newman
13. Quiet Life – Japan   14. Island In A Stream – The Mission

We'd been in the Slaughterhouse all week recording the follow-up when *The Mission – I* was released on Friday 9 May. I insisted we take a break from proceedings on the Saturday to watch Liverpool beat Everton 3–1 in the FA Cup Final at Wembley, to clinch their first domestic league and cup double. Things were going brilliantly for me.

The Mission – II was planned as a double A-side, with 'Garden Of Delight' on one side and our version of Neil Young's 'Like A Hurricane' on t'other of the 7-inch. The 12-inch included two new songs I'd recently written, 'The Crystal Ocean' and 'Over The Hills And Far Away', both destined to become evergreen live favourites. Again written while in the throes of amphetamine delirium, lyrically all three of my songs were essentially about sex and drugs, my predominant interests in life at the time, second (and third) only to music. It was unfortunate for me that as a lyricist, I was largely compared with the erudite Eldritch. I couldn't compete. I wasn't blessed with Andrew's intelligence, education, vocabulary, wit or emotional detachment, qualities none of which I could contrive. Make no bones about it, Andrew was an exceptional writer of words and particularly a master of the arts of enjambement and layered meaning. He'd also had five or six years' practice at it before I started to take lyric writing seriously. Mind you, it would sometimes take Von months to piece together a song, while my approach has always been more visceral, more immediate, sometimes dashing off songs in a matter of minutes. Get it done, get it down, and move on to the next thing, my belief being that a song is at its most potent when it is first written.

Over the course of the first few years of writing for The Mission I developed my own song language that had very little to do with everyday life. I realised from the very beginning that my lyrics weren't to everyone's, or should I say hardly anyone's, taste but that didn't concern me. They weren't the language of the common people – I always found that to be too prosaic a concept. And they were certainly apolitical: I'd leave that particular cross for the Citizen Smiths of this world to climb upon. Not for me the mundane, the terrestrial. I'm not everyman. Never have been, never wanted to be. My view has always been that song lyrics are more about how words *sound* rather than their meaning. They don't have to *mean* anything; it's music and just as the instrumentation has to sound right, so too do the words, being just another component of *the song*. Granted, for some, they're the most important component, but for most, not so much. I love Marc Bolan's lyrics, in 'Telegram Sam' or 'Jeepster' for example, but what do they mean? Who cares, they *sound* great. Written under the influence of LSD to primarily confound listeners who'd spent hours analysing Beatles lyrics, affording some serious scholarly interpretations, perhaps my favourite song lyric of all time is John Lennon's 'I Am The Walrus.' Goo-goo-g'joob. It's surrealist nonsense that paints such vivid pictures. Now, before you get all het up, don't think for a second I'm comparing myself to Bolan or Lennon. I am merely making the point that songs can mean whatever you want them to mean, or nothing at all. As for me, lyric writing has never come easily or naturally, so I framed my songs in the oneiric, the celestial, the otherworldly, the mystical, the esoteric and arcane; more concerned with the heart, the soul, the sensual and the carnal rather than matters of the mind. Yeah, I used clichés but twisted them. My songs, with a few exceptions, were always more voluptuary, about escape, transcendence and surrender to the senses, rather than social or political humdrum. If they meant anything at all. In the end, it all comes down to whether or not a song speaks to you, the listener, and that could be vocally, lyrically, instrumentally or any combination of the three. Some of the most powerful pieces of music that touch me deeply to my very inner core are instrumental classical pieces. As a certain bass player once said to me, 'Ah, you don't need to worry; it's only journalists and other singers that bother listening to the lyrics.' Not sure I'd wholly concur but I understood the sentiment.

Expedition 1 was a sold-out 12 shows in 12 days mad-dash through the UK, starting on Saturday 24 May, 1986, at Glasgow Queen Margaret Union and finishing in Stoke-on-Trent at Shelly's on June 4, a Wednesday. Along the way we played in our home-base city of Leeds on my 28th birthday, where the after-show party was adjourned to our favourite Leeds nightspot, the Warehouse. I duly got myself banned from the establishment that night by being caught in flagrante in the ladies toilets. To be fair, the whistle had been blown on me by an ex who was then working behind the bar at the club. She had seen me sashay off with a ravishing young beauty and, with the ugly green-eyed monster whispering in her ear, had gone running tittling and tattling to Blanche, the door lady who kept a firm hand over the goings-on. My pleas for leniency – it was my birthday after all and I was merely collecting a promised birthday surprise – fell on deaf ears and unceremoniously ejected I was, and instructed never to again darken their doorway. Unsurprisingly, I was allowed back in later in the year after we'd hit the Top 30, although my evil twin, Craig, did have to broker a peace deal for me with Blanche, promising that he'd keep me out of mischief. Craig as my moral compass, now there's a thought…

Our London show was at the Kentish Town & Country Club on Thursday 29. It was a big one for us, the biggest yet of our own. It was a sell-out, and with the majority of the London-based press and record companies in attendance, we doused our pre-show nerves with a vat-full of Blue Nun. As our intro music, 'The Dam Busters March'[1,] built to peak anticipation, we stood in the wings, awaiting the moment of our grand entrance. The atmosphere was electric. We marched onstage amid a cloud of dry ice to a big cheer. I started the opening guitar riff of 'Wasteland', at the end of which Mick joined in with a big crash on the kick drum and cymbal while Craig hit a big open chord on his bass. Clang. He broke his bottom E string and, as he hadn't a spare bass at the time, the show had to be stopped before it had even started, to allow for him (Jez, our guitar tech, hadn't yet mastered the art of changing strings) to replace the broken string chop-chop. To use a football analogy, it was like conceding an own goal in the first minute from which we never fully recovered. I'd call it a spirited draw in the end rather than the resounding victory we were hoping for. Still, it didn't stop the feeding frenzy among the record labels vying for our signatures on the dotted line, our little mishap not seeming to deter them one iota. Tediously, of course, the claws of the merciless press cabal were bared, and we were predictably savaged. Undaunted and resolute we marched on through that heady summer of 1986 playing our own shows, and festivals, both home and in Europe, building up an audience that was at once fanatical and legion.

By the time we released *The Mission – II* on July 14, we'd already settled on signing with Phonogram[2], and even though we had put pen to paper in the lobby of the Hamburg Metropol Hotel while on tour in late June, we demanded to honour our agreement with Chapter 22 by releasing the single through them. As with 'Serpents Kiss', it went slamming into the UK Independent Chart at number one, where it stayed for a couple of weeks before being toppled once again by the bloody Smiths, this time with their Metal Guru pastiche 'Panic'. While 'Panic' quickly came and went, 'Garden Of Delight' remained at number two for a month or more, while 'Serpents Kiss' climbed back up to number three. The single even crept into the national chart at number 45, where it hung around the lower echelons of the Top 50 for four weeks. We were getting ever closer to that elusive Top 40.

We were in London on Friday 11 July, and The Leather Nun were playing at the Hammersmith Clarendon, a long since demolished venue that was situated on the Hammersmith roundabout, right across the street from the Apollo.[3] The Nunnies, as they were affectionately known in our camp, are a Swedish band, which at the time were a fave of mine and Craig's. Their feel-good hit of that summer was the dance-floor smash 'FFA', their charming ode to the joys of fist fucking. We wangled ourselves onto the guest list and, determined to make a long night of it, made our way early to the Clarendon. Not long after we arrived I was accosted by a raven-haired seductress by the name of Rachel, a dancer she claimed to be. While snuggling up together in a darkened corner of the venue she was telling me about a friend of hers, the singer in the next band due onstage, third or fourth on the bill. The name of her friend was Julianne Regan and her band were called All About Eve. We watched and listened and I was blown away. Not particularly by the band or the songs but by Julianne's voice. It was the voice of an angel – heavenly, mellifluous and as fresh as spring water. She was a siren calling to me across that crowded, noisy venue.

'Hey, Rach, if you can introduce me to Julianne after they've finished their set then I'll go home with you tonight, if you want,' was my attempt at inducement.

'Well, I'll introduce you to Julianne but you've gotta work a bit bloody harder than that to go home with me. You can start by buying me a pint of cider and black, please,' Rachel replied. Concord duly struck, I won the introduction.

I complimented Julianne on her voice and asked if she'd be up for doing a bit of warbling on the album The Mission were soon to start recording. She said she'd love to, and after we exchanged phone numbers, she drifted back to her group of waiting friends and I returned my attentions to Rachel. Two things came out of that evening. I did end up going home with Rachel (I came six times that night so I knew it was love), and we were a couple for the next six months or so. And from that initial brief encounter, Julianne and I formed a life-long friendship and working relationship.

A week later, on Friday 18, we found ourselves in Milano to play the Suono Festival at the massive 80,000-capacity San Siro stadium, home to both AC and Inter football clubs. The Damned were head-lining while second on the bill were the truly comedic Dr & The Medics who had just scored a number one single in the UK with their note-for-note cover of Norman Greenbaum's 'Spirit In The Sky'.

It was a wet, miserable day, not at all like the hot Italian summer's day we, and the promoters, were hoping for. Only about a thousand people turned up. The stage was set up in the middle of the football pitch facing just one side of the terracing but, even so, a thousand-strong audience scattered about that huge space looked pathetically scant. And to compound the absurdity we were half the width of a football pitch away from them, the biggest distance an audience has ever been away from the stage in my experience. The walk from the dressing rooms at one end of the stadium to the side of the stage was exercise we were rarely used to. We had to time 'Dam Busters' to perfection or we'd be stranded in midfield as the crescendo reached its zenith, thereby missing our cue to enter the stage at the moment of maximum impact.

We played during daylight hours and it was a difficult show, despite our very best efforts. Towards the end of our set I was looking at the trek back to the dressing room and thinking to myself, *Mmm, I could do without that, I'm knackered.* So I threw myself around the stage in gay abandon for a couple of minutes and then feigned collapse. The band finished the last song and started making their way back to the dressing room, the distant cheers from the paltry audience being lost on the wind and in the rain. I was picked up by Stevie Sex-Pistol and a couple of stagehands and carried offstage, across the pitch and into our dressing room. Once there I was gently laid out on the tiled floor, concern etched on the faces of both band and crew. I jumped up and exclaimed, 'Tada! Ta, lads. Thanks for the lift. Anyone gotta ciggie?' I had to duck to evade the flying plastic bottle Stevie had hurled at my head. 'Wanker,' he declared, with some justification.

Later that night back at the hotel – the same hotel The Damned and The Medics were staying at – a big drinkie-poo ensued in the bar. After a couple of rounds I disappeared to my room with company, but not before Craig had started complaining that the Doctor had been unnecessarily rude to him.

Now, after almost 40 years of working together on and off, I like to think I know my beloved Evil Twin. The thing is, Craig is a very funny man, a brilliant raconteur and genuinely eccentric, but he's definitely not without his demons. Known among our crew as 'The Dark One', one drink too many and the constant stygian clouds that swirl around his brow become plainly visible. I have learnt to make myself scarce when his skies blacken, preferring to let other people deal with him when the tornado hits, which it invariably does. And as I did on this particular occasion. A perceived slight, a misheard word, or someone just looking at him 'wrong' would set him off. Woe betide anyone he had a grievance against. And there was absolutely no reasoning with him. Try, and you'd more than likely receive a punch in the gob for your efforts. I've seen him pull knives on fans, threaten journalists with a baseball bat, tell a Greek promoter that he had a gun in his hotel room safe and would go and collect it and shoot him in the legs if he didn't pay our fee before we went onstage. We were paid in full, but we haven't been back to Greece since. The tales are manifold, too many to recount here and now. As it was, the Doctor, who at the time did rather seem to think a lot of himself, if truth be known, had probably just said something slightly offhand to our Mr Adams. But the devil perched on Craig's shoulder was screaming in his ear that it was a deeply impugning affront, and retribution demanded to be wrought. The Doctor, probably sensing that Craig was getting a bit lairy, had slunk off to bed with his missus, one of the backing singers with The Medics. Craig gave them some time to clean their teeth, don their pyjamas and make themselves comfortable. And then, in an act of ingenious cunning, he walked to reception and claimed he'd lost his room key, giving what he thought was the Doctor's room number as his own. The night clerk duly issued Craig with a new key. Uh-oh. Making his way down the corridor, he then quietly let himself into the darkened room and leapt up onto the bed, only to be confronted by the visage of the Medic's tour manager, luckily not the Doctor himself, tucked up under the sheets with the *other* Medic's backing singer. Not to be deterred from his mission (excuse the pun), Craig was stood over the terrified couple, brandishing a broken bottle in his hand and screeching, 'Where is he? I'm gonna fucking kill him if he ever says anything like that to me again.' There was screaming and shouting, and a passing couple of roadies came to the tour manager's rescue and pulled Craig off the bed and out of the room before he could inflict any real damage. Somehow, this little skirmish made the gossip columns in the UK press. It didn't come from us, honest guv. And we weren't to hear the last of this contretemps either, as both bands were due to appear on the same day at the Reading Festival just a month later.

Somewhere among our increasingly busy summer schedule we were booked into Jam Studios, in the Finsbury Park area of London, for a few days to record with Tim Palmer. I had worked with Tim when I was with Dead Or Alive, as he had been the house engineer at Utopia Studios. When he had been suggested to us by Charlie Eyre[4] at Phonogram to co-produce our first album, I had readily approved of the idea. I didn't want a big-name producer, someone who'd come in and try to mould us to their way of thinking. We already knew how we wanted the band to sound and had produced the *Mission I & II* ourselves. All we really needed was someone to come in to help me realise the soundscapes in my head; and to oversee the whole project, as producing an album is a whole different barrel of monkeys to producing just a single. Tim was young – younger than me – but, with an already impressive résumé, a man in a hurry who didn't like to waste time. His whole ethos was to work fast and work hard and get the job done. Much like ours. We recorded three songs with Tim initially, just to prove to the Doubting Thomas's at the record label that he was the right man for the job. There was never any doubt in my mind. We recorded what was to be our next, third, single, the waltzing 'Stay With Me', along with potential B-sides 'Blood Brother'[5] and 'Let Sleeping Dogs Die'. Everybody was ecstatic with the results and Tim was signed on to do the album.

After a full week of pre-production rehearsals with Tim in London, we quickly nipped across the channel for two shows at the beginning of August: one in Amsterdam at a sold-out Melkweg, and the other we were third on the bill to The Ramones and PIL at the Seaside Festival in Veurne, Belgium. With just two independent single releases thus far, we were already being billed higher than bands that had been around for years and had released albums. Things were certainly moving very fast for us. It was like being in the eye of the hurricane. All around us was chaos but at the centre of it all we were calm and knew exactly what we wanted to do and how and when to do it.

On our return to Blighty we were booked into Ridge Farm Studios, a glorious residential farmhouse in the locale of Rusper, a village on the border between Surrey and Sussex. The studio itself was located in a mid-17th century mediaeval barn while accommodation and catering was provided in the main farmhouse, a 15-yard stroll from the studio. There was also a self-contained producer's cottage a little further away from the house and studio that afforded greater privacy. The buildings were set in 12 acres of gardens, orchards, meadows and woodland. It was idyllic.

We'd all arrived the evening before the scheduled first day of recording to claim our rooms, to set up the backline in the studio, and to settle in and relax. Tim had gone to bed at a reasonable hour, leaving us with his exhortation to follow suit so that we could get an early start the next day. At nine the following morning Tim descended the stairs and entered the band recreation room, where I was sat on the couch strumming a guitar and watching TV with the sound turned down. Tim, pleased as punch, said, 'Ah, great, you're up. We'll wake the others in a little while and get started early, shall we?'

'Nah, I wouldn't do that, they only went to bed an hour or so ago,' was my reply.

'Wow, okay. How do you know that – did you get up early?'

'Nah, I ain't been to bed yet myself; I've been up all night. I'll need a couple of hours kip before we start.'

Tim, visibly crestfallen, looked around the room and among the empty Liebfraumilch bottles and over-flowing ashtrays he spotted white powder residue on an album cover and put two and two together. Figuring he wasn't gonna be able to beat us, he decided the only way he could get the album done was if he joined us, so the next time lines were offered around Tim partook and kept up with us for the duration, working mostly 18-hour days in the studio. I have to say it's one of my favourite times recording. We were riding that hugely exciting first flush of success, our arrogance still tempered by an innocence, our self-belief fuelled by our newfound omnipotence, and an album's worth of great songs which we'd been constantly refining by playing them live for seven months. We felt we could do anything and everything. The world was at our feet.

Because Rachel, the dancer, was planning on visiting every now and then while we were at Ridge Farm, Tim and the rest of the band kindly insisted I take the producer's cottage. The seclusion would also help me write the lyrics I was still honing while we were recording, they suggested. It wasn't until a few months later, after Rachel and I had split up, that the band confessed they'd given me the cottage because they couldn't stand her being around. Unbeknown to me, she would glide into the band's recreation area while they were playing pool or watching TV and put on a cassette of a working mix of one of our songs and say to the others, 'Look, I've choreographed a dance for this song. Maybe I can do this in the video?' And then she'd dance for them – she'd had no training – in her freeform style while they'd be trying to stifle guffaws, saying, 'Yeah, that's great that, Rach. Have you shown Wayne yet?' To which she'd reply, 'No, I wanted to get you guys on my side first. Maybe you could learn a few of the steps and dance with me behind Wayne while he sings?' Cue guffaws released aloud. Despite Rachel having introduced us, Julianne later told me that among her friends and band mates she was affectionately known as 'Crazy Rachel'. Well, thanks for letting me bloody know, eh? Poor Rachel. But I liked her. She was funny and easy company, and we did have a good laugh together most of the time. She was perfect for me during this period as I was so busy and she made no demands on my time. She also turned a blind eye to my philandering, such was the nature of our relationship.

Not long after we had gotten together Rachel had whispered in my ear one evening, while in the throes of *l'amour*, 'You know I'm dying. Please love me to death.'

'What?' was my startled reply, completely disrupting my stroke.

'Yeah.' Pause. 'I only have six months to live,' she blithely informed me.

'Why didn't you tell me?'

'I'm telling you now, ya stupid sod.'

'Oh, Rach, I'm so sorry. Come here.' I pulled her to me and rested her head on my chest, stroking her hair. I didn't know what to say or how to react or whether to offer comfort or encouragement. We lay like that for a full five minutes or more in silence, with my heart heavy and fighting back the tears. And then she blurted out among gales of laughter, 'I'm only joking. Have you not heard of *la petite mort*? Hahaha.' She got me there.

That was 'Crazy Rachel' for you. But she did provide me with the final song title I needed for the album – 'Love Me To Death'.

While at Ridge Farm we'd hear this euphonious guitar playing emanating from one of the bedrooms on the ground floor from the other end of the house, in the owner and staff quarters. Intrigued enough to follow the sound one afternoon, Mick found the source and stuck his head through an open window. 'Here, that's reet good guitar playing, that. You should come and have a play with us one evening,' our affable drummer suggested.

'I'd love to,' replied the startled, long-haired guitarist.

61

'My name's Mick, what's yours?'

'Ah, you can call me Speedy. Speedy Keen.'

'And you can call me Mental.'

Mick returned to the studio and boasted, 'I've just met that bloke who plays guitar all day. He's an alright geezer. His name is Speedy King or summat.'

Ren, the house engineer corrected him. 'You mean Speedy Keen. You do know who he is, right?'

'No,' we all chorused.

It transpired that Speedy was in fact John David Percy Keen, songwriter, vocalist and multi-instrumentalist in the band Thunderclap Newman, who had enjoyed a huge number one summer hit in 1969 with the classic 'Something In The Air'. Not just that, Speedy had produced the *Motörhead* album and *L.A.M.F.* by Johnny Thunders & The Heartbreakers. We had rock deity among us and we didn't even know.

Ridge Farm was owned and established by Frank Andrews, a lovely old stoner who used to come and hang out in the control room of an evening, smoking his spliff while we were all manic on whizz. Frank had seen it all before many times over, having toured as lighting designer with such luminaries as Queen and The Rolling Stones, but he'd retired from the road in the mid-Seventies to set up the studio. Speedy Keen was an old friend of his who was, by 1986, a little down on his luck, so Frank had offered him the use of one of the bedrooms in the farmhouse. Speedy, who, as a young man had earned his nickname from indulging in the same leisurely pursuits we did, was by this time a more relaxed, gentle soul, more at home strumming an acoustic than shovelling piles of white powder up his nose.[6]

We were due to play the Reading Festival on Friday 22 August, again third on the bill to headliners Killing Joke, and Craig's friends Dr & The Medics. But as we hadn't played since the beginning of the month we figured we needed to do a warm-up show. And, to tell the truth, it was probably as much to do with cabin fever and our desire to get out and let off some steam, having been stuck in the studio for a couple of weeks.

Nearby was the Sussex market town of Horsham, which boasted a grotty little venue called Champagnes. We arranged a gig there on the Tuesday before our Reading appearance and, pre-internet days, we let the local radio station know we were playing a day or so before. Word quickly spread and the place was jammed, the crowd spilling out onto the street. It was sweaty mayhem and, obviously, post show we rounded up a host of likely looking candidates to invite back to the studio to continue the after-show knees-up. Over the next few years, playing Champagnes became pretty much an annual event for us as, inexplicably, we always found ourselves down in that neck of the woods come the summer, either rehearsing or recording. But on that first occasion, Speedy Keen had climbed up onstage and played a couple of songs with us. We all enjoyed it so much that we insisted he come to the Reading Festival with us to do it all again. Speedy needed little persuading.

During the weeks preceding Reading the music papers ratcheted up the conflict between us and the Medics, and more specifically between the Doctor and Craig. To circumvent anything really kicking off we came up with the sound idea of inviting some of our Hell's Angels friends from Nottingham Rock City to be our security for the day and to give us a motorbike escort to the festival site. I've never felt safer. The Angels were as good as gold, their presence calming rather than intimidating – or rather, calming *through* intimidation. No one was gonna pick a fight with us that day. Altamont it wasn't, thankfully.

It was at Reading Festival that I first realised we were actually already quite popular. While waiting to start our set I poked my head through the curtains drawn across the front of the stage and a huge cheer went up. I was really taken aback by that response, not expecting it at all. However, I remember not enjoying our performance, despite the crowd being on our side. We hadn't been able to do a soundcheck, so there were the usual problems with the sound onstage, and some of the monitors weren't working so we couldn't hear each other. The usual festival cack. I remember, towards the end of the set during our by now regular show closer, 'Shelter From The Storm', standing on the lip of the stage and looking down into the pit below me – that no man's land area between the stage and the audience. It was, apparently, a 15-foot drop. In an attempt to get closer to the audience and create some communion sadly lacking thus far in the show, I remember making the conscious decision to jump. I landed on my feet, albeit with a stumble, not hurting myself, too bloody pissed and amped up to feel any pain. Once I'd felt up the audience a little and they me, I was hoisted back up onto the stage by a couple of burly Angels. The legend became, and was perpetuated in almost all the reviews, that I had *fallen* off the stage. Not so. My leap may have looked a bit ungainly but I can assure you it was a jump and not a fall. Back in our trailer post show I vowed to Tony Perrin and anyone else who'd listen that I wouldn't play Reading Festival again until we were asked to headline. Guess what? We were back the following year to headline and again two years after that.

While recording one evening in Ridge Farm, we decided to hire a Fairlight CMI for a day or two. This was an 8-bit digital sampler made voguish in the UK by the pioneering work of Peter Gabriel and Kate Bush among others, and, at the time, costing more to buy than a Yorkshire terrace of two-ups, two-downs. We found a few usable samples, one of which was the ethereal sound you can hear at the end of 'Wasteland' on the album, leading into 'Bridges Burning'. A couple of others we used as well – thought we'd get our money's worth, as it wasn't cheap to rent. None of us, though, Tim included, were overly impressed with the Fairlight and the consensus was that it was just a fad and wouldn't catch on. Of course, the sampler came to revolutionise the music industry, so what did we know?

The Ridge Farm studio was housed in an old barn with big, old wooden doors opening up directly into the ground floor recording area. The control room was at the back of the building, up a flight of stairs overlooking the studio floor, a very similar set-up to the more celebrated Studio Two at Abbey Road, where The Beatles had recorded the bulk of their output. There was a big bay window in the control room overlooking the studio area, so as to be able to maintain some visual contact. Quite often, while recording my vocals downstairs on the studio floor with the lights turned low to enhance the mood, I'd look up to the control room window and see that buffoon of a drummer of ours, Mental Mick, either gurning, mooning, looning or with his hand on his crotch trying to disrupt my concentration. 'Ah, keep trying, mate, it takes more than your cock to put me off,' was my challenge for him to be ever more outrageous.

One night I was about to record a vocal and Tim's voice came through the intercom to my headphones. 'Hey, Mr Huss – just talk for a minute so we can get a level.' I started saying anything that came into my head, maybe part of the lyrics for the song I was about to sing, and then out it popped with no forethought: 'I still believe in God but God no longer believes in me'. I paused, and then said, 'TP, are you ready to record? Let's just get that down on tape as I'd like to use that at the start of the album.' The red light went on in the studio and I repeated the phrase two or three times to tape.

'Yeah, that's a good idea, Mr Huss, and Mick likes it,' came back Tim's voice in my ear, and as I looked up to the control room I could see Mick giving me the thumbs up with one hand while swinging his dick around in the other. He was very supportive and encouraging, was our Mick.

I'd kept in touch with Julianne from All About Eve, and one evening we invited her down to Ridge Farm to add some backing vocals to a couple of the songs. Needless to say we had to keep Mick away from the control room window while she was at the microphone.

Julianne sang on 'Severina', 'Dance On Glass' and 'Love Me To Death'. And we were all astonished by how brilliant she was. The purity of her voice and her harmony work was astounding. And the blend of our two voices together was and still is alchemical. For me, she has one of the best ever British voices; there are far lesser talents that are constantly being lauded while Julianne has been largely ignored and forgotten. I think it's criminal how she has gone unheralded by the UK music media. Shame on them.

While she was with us, Julianne had given me a cassette of All About Eve demos. I loved it and kept playing it to people who I thought could maybe help her and the band. First, our manager Tony Perrin, who liked it so much himself that he took on their management. Next was Charlie Eyre, who had signed us to Phonogram and would sign AAE as well. And then to our publisher, Dennis Collopy, at RCA Music. He would also sign AAE. As would Martin Horne at ITB, becoming their agent. In the long run, maybe some of those moves for AAE weren't necessarily the right ones, as they were perceived for a while as being in our slipstream, which initially helped them along but ultimately did them a huge injustice. In the end they were to distance themselves from us, and quite rightly so, and they found their own audience and enjoyed success on their own terms.

After three eventful weeks it was time for us to say goodbye to Speedy and Frank and the rest of the staff at Ridge Farm, and adjourn to the Primrose Hill area of London and Utopia Studios, to mix the album. We went from the sumptuous space and separate bedrooms we enjoyed in the English countryside to sharing a minuscule two bedroom flat that backed onto Utopia; the studio, not the mythical place. Still, we had a job to do and do it we did. There were a few additional overdubs to be recorded as we mixed, as well as my lead vocal for 'Severina'. For some reason I just hadn't been able to nail that one. We tried all kinds of scenarios to induce a decent vocal take: singing sober, drunk, speeding, straight, first thing in the morning and last thing at night, different microphones, naked with all the lights out, all the lights on, in the corridor, in the bathroom, but nothing seemed to work. In the end, and with a pressing deadline to meet to make our release date, Tim ordered me to leave him alone for an hour or so while he compiled a vocal from the various takes. Listening to it today I hear absolutely nothing wrong with the vocal, and now wonder why it was such a bugbear to me at the time and proved so difficult to sing. I've come to find there is usually one track on each album that gives me the same problem. I think I've worked out it's a psychological reluctance to let an album go when nearing completion.

I realised a long-held ambition while recording *God's Own Medicine*. I'd had the idea that we could rearrange 'Garden Of Delight' for a string quartet. I'd liked the string arrangements that Adam Peters had done for Echo & The Bunnymen's *Ocean Rain* album. Adam was also a member of one of Stevie Sex-Pistol's favourite bands, The Flowerpot Men. Tim managed to track Adam down, and invited him to the studio to hear my ideas for the arrangement. Adam was up for it and went away for a few days to work on the score.

We were booked into Angel Studios in Islington one afternoon to record with the quartet – two violins, a viola, and a cello. Adam was conducting, and it was all going swimmingly, if not a tad slowly, until Mick turned up. Now, traditional classical musicians are very union orientated and there are strict rules on playing only for a certain length of time before having an enforced break. For musicians that work in other fields it can seem a very disruptive policy. Work for half an hour then take a 10-minute break, even if you're in the middle of a take; clock-watchers, some might say. Mick, having been up all night on the ol' snortle, began to get increasingly frustrated at these constant interruptions. Yet another take had broken down halfway through the song and the leader of the quartet had declared, 'Let's have a break. Who wants a smoke?' That was it for Mick. 'I've fookin'

67

had enough of these knob'eads.' And he stormed out of the control room and into the studio while Tim and I looked on aghast at what was about to occur. Over the studio monitors we heard Mick shouting in his broad Yorkshire accent, 'Right, youse lot of fookin' skivers. That's a fookin' 'nuff. Just ger on wit' job, will ya. We're bleedin' paying yer t'work, not smoke tabs. Just do what that bloke there in the control room is telling yer to do, alright, and no more pissing around. Gerrit fookin' done.' And then he stomped back into the control room with a big fat Cheshire Cat grin on his face. 'There, that told 'em. You'll be havin' nought more problems with them buggers, TP.' Tim leant into the mixing console, pressed the talkback button, and said, 'Right, folks. Are we ready to have another go?' We didn't hear a peep out of the quartet for the rest of the afternoon and they played the song beautifully.

One of the songs we'd recorded with Tim before the album sessions, 'Let Sleeping Dogs Die', was considered too good for a single B-side, so we decided to save it for the album. Which meant that we needed a new song as the extra track for the 12-inch version of our next single, 'Stay With Me'. I came up with the idea of recording an acoustic version of our end-of-show anthem 'Shelter From The Storm'. I'd written 'Shelter' as a four-chord fast rocker that we could string out when the mood took us. It was the one kind of song we were lacking in our early sets. The problem was, though, we needed an audience in front of us to be able to perform it. Hence the idea of a quiet, acoustic version. I'd come up with the basic backing track using my Ovation 12-string acoustic and a mandolin, and then got Simon to overdub tracks of feedback and EBow[7] all through the song to give it an edge of uneasiness. Mick added some heavily reverb'd floor tom hits on the chorus and, fanny's your aunt, there you have it. When I came to vocal it, I tried it once or twice and decided it wasn't working as it was, so decided to write new lyrics for it. With the aid of a couple of bottles of Blue Nun and a little 'special catering',

I stayed up one night and completed a new lyric, 'Island In A Stream'. It came to my attention much later that both titles had been used before, 'Shelter From The Storm' was a Bob Dylan song and 'Islands In A Stream' was a Dolly Parton/Kenny Rogers duet. I wasn't really aware of either song at the time but their titles must've lodged somewhere in my subconscious and when, in my addled state, I was scrabbling around for titles I had alighted upon something that felt vaguely familiar to me. I've never claimed to be original.

The artwork for our first run of singles and *God's Own Medicine* was highly stylised, and yet another stick that the bile-slathering music press beat us with. All our front covers were illustrations created by Sandy Ball, Mick's girlfriend at the time. Ornate and florid, and alluding to goddesses, not of this world but a strange, ancient, arcane world of another time, the covers became as synonymous with The Mission as my black bolero hat and Ray-Bans. And when lined up next to each other, the 12-inch covers made a striking collection. Again, we were out of step with what was in vogue, but it was yet another indication of our determination to follow our own course. Causing even more irritation to the circling press vultures was the fact that I'd numbered the singles I, II, III, IV and V rather than title them with the lead song. Another obvious nod to Led Zeppelin, which seemed to raise the hackles of our detractors.

The recording of *God's Own Medicine* was completed from start to finish in just under five weeks – compared to some of our later albums, no time at all. And not that *GOM* suffers for it, either. For many, *GOM* is still arguably the best Mission album. It certainly holds that position in my affections. It has energy, it has consistently good tunes, it captures a band in a moment of unstoppable momentum, of glorious traction, arrogant and secure in the belief that there was no better band in the world at the time. It's fresh and still sounds it to me, and we hadn't yet fallen prey to the musical excesses and extravagances of which we were later sometimes guilty. It also heralded a period of commercial success for us, which in itself was exciting to live through for the first time. 1986 was a thrilling, exhilarating time to be in The Mission, and I think that comes across in the spirit and energy of *GOM*. Sure, some might argue that it now sounds of its time, but anything of real value needs to have a context, and when heard alongside anything else that was going on in 1986, *GOM* still more than stands up. Modesty never being one of my more exercised traits this, for me, was the album of the year.

Endnotes

1   1955's *The Dam Busters* recreates the true story of Operation Chastise when, in 1943, the RAF's 617 Squadron attacked three German dams with 'bouncing bombs'. Originally suggested by Mick Brown, we've used the opening theme off and on since our formation as our intro music. Composed by Eric Coates, 'The Dam Busters March' was originally performed for the film by The Associated British Studio Orchestra. It's a stirring, rousing, albeit slightly comical piece, which inspires patriotism if not downright jingoism. We always enjoyed a wry smile to ourselves when in Germany the audience sings along, not realising the origin of the theme. I imagine *The Dam Busters* isn't a popular film in Deutschland.

2   To ensure our release from WEA so that we were free to sign the new deal with Phonogram, we had to agree to a 2 per cent over-ride, payable to WEA. In essence this means they collected 2 per cent of income from sales of our first album, which would've amounted to a pretty penny all told, as *God's Own Medicine* sold over 500,000 copies.

3   At the time it was known as the Hammersmith Odeon, and is still called that by those old enough to remember Bowie killed off Ziggy Stardust there in 1973. It's had several names since and is, as I write, currently trading under the name Eventim Apollo.

4   Charlie Eyre, a typical public school toff and son of knighted Sir Graham, was our A&R manager at Phonogram. Despite his very obvious prejudices and a spritzed-all-over-with-an-aerosol-called-privilege sense of entitlement (and being a season ticket holder at Chelsea), Charlie was passionate in his belief in the band. He would fight our corner zealously in the regular internecine department disputes within Phonogram. Despite us eventually selling millions of records for them, it seems there were some within the company who held essentially the same opinion of us as did the music press.

5   'Blood Brother' is a song I primarily penned for Ian Astbury of The Cult when we finished the European tour. The Cult had recorded a session for BBC Radio 1 and in one track Ian had sung 'hat's off to Hussey, he's a good man'. It seemed only natural to return the compliment. A sweet little side story to this song is that there's a lyric in the last verse that reads 'Father, you're a good man, an honest man, a saint among men, and Mother, I wish I could tell you I love you'. While we were close, we'd never been a particularly demonstrative family, and I had never told my mum that I loved her. Until I put it in the song. The next time we played in Bristol and my parents came backstage after the show my mum caught me on my own for a few seconds as she was leaving and simply said 'I love you too'. I knew immediately it was her response to that line in 'Blood Brother'. Since then, neither of us have had any problem telling each other that we love them.

6   Sadly, Speedy departed this mortal coil in March 2002, succumbing to heart failure.

7   The EBow is a hand-held battery-powered electronic device that when held over a single guitar string causes the string to vibrate and sustain. It's supposed to emulate the sound of using a violin bow on the strings but, in my experience, sounds nothing like the cacophony I produce when I've used an actual bow on my guitar. I began using an EBow in 1981, when I was with Dead Or Alive, after seeing the guitarist in the band Japan use one in the video for their song 'Quiet Life'. I love Japan, one of those bands whose music has aged remarkably well. Their front man, David Sylvian, was quite possibly the prettiest pop star ever. Achingly beautiful. Very misunderstood in their day by the press (no surprise there, eh?) but very influential, nonetheless.

CHAPTER 4

Here Comes Success

PLAYLIST:
1. Success – Iggy Pop
2. *God's Own Medicine* (album): Wasteland, Bridges Burning, Garden Of Delight (Hereafter), Stay With Me, Let Sleeping Dogs Die, Sacrilege, Dance On Glass, And The Dance Goes On, Severina, Love Me To Death – The Mission

VIDEO PLAYLIST:
1. Sex Dwarf – Soft Cell   2. Close To Me – The Cure
3. Stay With Me – The Mission
4. Tomorrow Never Knows – The Mission (*Old Grey Whistle Test*)
5. Severina – The Mission (*OGWT*)

'Stay With Me', or *The Mission – III*, was released on Monday, October 13, 1986. It was our first release on Phonogram. No longer qualifying for the Independent Chart, however, it did make the UK Top 40 singles chart the following weekend at, wait for it, number 40! And boy, did we celebrate. Or at least tried to. A group of us, including the band, Jez, Grape and Stevie Sex-Pistol, convened at 27 Ashville Grove and we journeyed into Leeds to revel in our newfound fame and glory. Being a Sunday evening, not a lot of clubs were open, but nonetheless we found one city centre establishment that was plying its trade. We turned up to the door and the thick-set, shaven-headed doorman gave us the once over and, turning to his equally stocky mates and winking, brayed, 'Sorry, lads, or is it ladies? You ain't coming in here dressed like that.'

'But we're in the Top 40! Don't you know who we are?' I remonstrated.

'Don't give a toss if you're number one, you ain't coming in here dressed like a bunch of old grannies. It's not grab-a-granny night, you know. We have a strict dress code. No dresses on men.' He and his cronies snorted like a sounder of swine. I think they were laughing but I wouldn't swear to it.

'But this is a skirt I'm wearing, not a dress. Didn't your mother teach you anything?' was my Wildean riposte.

'Hey, big-conk, leave me mam out of this. No need to get personal. Now, fuck off,' was the Neanderthal's considered response.

And there our attempt to celebrate our first entry into the UK Top 40 ended, rather ignominiously. I thought my life would be changed in an instant by hitting the Top 40. I thought we'd be fêted and fawned over wherever we went. But no one, in Leeds at least, gave one jot that we were rubbing shoulders with the likes of Nick Berry and Huey Lewis & The News as one of the Top 40-selling songs in the whole of the UK that week. With our tails firmly between our legs, we took the bus home. Catching the off licence just before it closed, I stocked up on some cans of cider and went home to watch a film on late-night TV. I went to bed early. Alone. So this was what being a pop star felt like. What a huge, crushing disappointment.

We'd shot a video for 'Stay With Me' with the same Leeds-based crew that had filmed 'Serpents Kiss' with us. Why not? That had been such a huge success. However, this time the stakes were considerably higher, as exemplified by a budget of £25,000 compared with the paltry £2,000 'Serpents Kiss' had cost. In our naiveté, we thought we could pretty much do the same as before: work with no script as such, satirical ad-libs, horsing around to playback with various silly props. But this time we were way out of our depth, and the end result proved to be folly and unusable. A bigger budget and everyone gets serious. Sometimes, and certainly in this case, money inhibits and corrupts the imagination. We scrapped it, and Phonogram weren't best pleased. We met with a few other London-based video directors, closer at hand to the record company this time so they could keep an eye on proceedings.

We had a bizarre meeting with Tim Pope, the much-celebrated director who had made several memorable videos with Soft Cell and The Cure, among others. We met at the Phonogram offices on New Bond Street and, weirdly, Tim brought a lackey to talk for him. Tim himself didn't say a word. Mind you, neither did we, as we'd not been to bed and were in a serious state of disarray. I don't know what Tim's excuse was. Charlie Eyre and Tony Perrin spoke for us, while Tim had this other bloke acting as his mouthpiece. We sat mute on one couch, opposite him on another, and just stared at each other throughout the proceedings while the others did all the nattering. Not surprisingly it was deemed that The Mission and Tim Pope were not a match made in heaven, and consequently we ended up working with Tony Van Den Ende instead, who had previously directed Killing Joke and Samantha Fox! How disparate can you get?

After being informed that we didn't want to make a *goth* video, Van Den Ende, completely ignoring our brief, came in with a story-board based on two early 1920s classic German expressionist films, *The Cabinet Of Dr Caligari* and *Nosferatu*. But with a twist. Both Phonogram and the band initially baulked at the synopsis, but one of Van Den Ende's main attributes was his power of persuasion, and we ended up giving him the green light and a big bucket of cash. Replete with us sitting around in coffins in graveyards, plastic bats flying around suspended on clearly evident bits of twine, yours truly swinging on a huge pendulum and dancing with a torso-less mannequin, and with every over-the-top goth cliché that we could muster, the 'Stay With Me' video was supposed to be comical, very tongue-in-cheek – a *Carry On Goth*, if you want. Our hope was that it would be seen as such, but unfortunately most couldn't see past the bats and the coffins and the joke fell flat. It does make for hilarious viewing but perhaps not in the way we'd intended, merely compounding the fainéant assumption for many that we were, after all, a goth band.

The upside of being in the Top 40 was that we did start to hear our record on daytime radio every now and then. The panacea of being on Radio 1's A-list was still beyond us, mind, but we were played occasionally purely by virtue of the fact we were in the charts. And on Thursday evening later that same week I was rooted to *Top Of The Pops* to catch us being mentioned in the chart run-down. They even briefly flashed up a photograph of us! What elation! Lasted all of two seconds. The following weekend our single jumped up to number 30, sales clearly bolstered by the 5,000 copies of the limited-edition numbered record sleeves[1] we'd tediously spent a long afternoon signing in the Columbia Hotel. And *still* we weren't A-listed on Radio 1 and *still* we weren't invited to appear on *TOTP*, although they did show 30 seconds of our video that week, with the promise that if we climbed further up the chart the following weekend we'd get to go on. The midweek chart position[2] came in on the Friday and 'Stay With Me' was predicted to climb still further. Come Sunday evening when the chart was announced we'd failed to hold our position and the single had slithered down to number 38. Ah well. There'd be other singles and there was no time to sit around and mope.

Any disappointment was tempered by the fact that by this time our World Crusade tour (part 1) had commenced with a warm-up show at our home from home, Nottingham Rock City, on Saturday, October 25. It was essentially a sold-out month-long run through the British Isles to coincide with the release of *God's Own Medicine*.

Out there every night in front of an ever expanding fanatical, adoring throng was where we preferred to be. While it felt good to be in the charts, and to hear our record on the radio, and to see my ugly mug staring out from a front cover, it was onstage where I really felt alive. Away from the sniping, back-biting, sneering music business. Among *our* people. The kids, and they were mostly kids at this point, who came to our shows didn't give a hoot about midweek chart positions, or bad reviews, or seeing us on *Top Of The Pops*. A Mission show has always been, and still is, about communion. The shared experience. We demand from our audience exactly the same that they demand from us: involvement. If one of us reneges on the deal then the show, for me, is a failure. We could be blindingly brilliant some nights, fuelled by copious amounts of the usual as well as *love* from the audience. Other nights, fuelled by the same copious amounts, we could be abject, purely because that sense of communion, *love*, wasn't present. Whether we performed well or atrociously we were, and are, only ever as good as our audience. We are not a unique band in that sense; a host of other bands enjoy a similar symbiotic relationship with their following. And a following is what it became; a large group of young people hitchhiking, jumping trains and buses, getting from city to city by whatever means possible. The core of our following were The Eskimos[3], who took their place in the middle of the mosh pit every night and built human pyramids, four or five people high at times. They still do it today, but it rarely gets any higher than two, what with the extra weight most of us carry and the brittle bones that come with age. The Eskimos became so notorious that they even graced the cover of *Melody Maker*, one issue featuring their exploits on the road as they followed us around. From the very beginning we employed a strategy I'd cribbed from T.Rex. We purposely kept our ticket prices for shows as low as we could to make it affordable for younger followers, with little or no income of their own, to buy tickets. When we could we'd nightly fill our guest list with this horde of devotees and quite often bung 'em a crate of beer from our rider. These policies of looking after the following ensured full, if not sold out, venues of rabid fanatics, who became staunch long-term followers of the band, some of whom still follow us around to this day, albeit now staying in swankier hotels and travelling in more comfort than we do. The relationship between The Mission and our audience is one that most outsiders failed, and still fail, to understand.

As a young teenager in the early Seventies I had joined the fan clubs of T.Rex, Slade and The Sweet. I was ecstatic on the occasions an envelope would drop through our letterbox addressed personally to me, it being a newsletter, or a Christmas card, or a list of upcoming tour dates from one of my favourite bands. It made me feel closer to them, part of the gang, and I was utterly convinced that each band member knew me by name. Pre-internet, it was the only way we could, we assumed, have direct communication with our heroes. Whenever I wrote a letter to Marc or Noddy I'd naively believe it would reach them and they'd read it. It didn't occur to me that they'd have somebody reading and vetting the letters for them. It didn't occur to me that there'd be hundreds and thousands of other besotted teenagers writing similar lovesick missives to the objects of the same fantasies as mine. A year or two later, when my listening tastes had, shall we posit, matured, I'd grown out of the youthful proclivity of joining fan clubs. Bands like Pink Floyd and Led Zeppelin didn't seem to brook fandom of the hysterical teenage kind. But I always remembered how thrilling it was to the younger me to be a fan club member of a beloved band.

With that in mind, very early on we set up the Mission World Information Service (or MWIS) – a posh name for our fan club – in the attic room at Mick and Sandy's house. Initially a free service (for the price of an SAE[4]), its ranks grew rapidly until membership soon exceeded several thousand and it became a full-time job for two people to run the MWIS office, at which time we began to charge a nominal annual membership fee. For a fan's subscription they would receive a membership card, a badge, a signed photograph of the band, a signed Christmas card delivered in December, six bi-monthly newsletters, advance and exclusive ticket info for tours with discounts for members, exclusive merchandise offers, and at least one free fan club show per year. A veritable bargain at £1.50. Despite the subscription fees we still had to subsidise MWIS to the tune of a few thousand pounds a year to cover running costs, but we didn't mind because we considered it a vital way of being able to communicate directly with *our people*, and we were paid back in kind through ticket, merch and record sales. We'd receive bagfuls of mail each week from all points of the globe. Sandy, Mick's girlfriend and our artist in residence, and Gilly, my landlady, would sift through and sort into separate boxes for each member of the band. My box was always far fuller than anyone else's, a dubious perk of being the singer. Every time we were back at home in Leeds we'd all pop around to the office and sign a slew of postcards and photographs, ready for new memberships. One time when we were away for a fair while, they ran out of signed items, so Grape was enlisted to sign a few in our absence, faking our autographs. Next time I was home I received a letter from 'Leslie in Edinburgh'. She'd written, 'Thank you, Wayne, for all the lovely goodies. And particularly for the signed photo. One thing, though; have you forgotten how to spell your name? You've signed it Wanye.' Oops, busted. Bloody 'ell, Grape, the least you coulda done was spell my name right – I bet you did it on bloody purpose, didn't you? I wrote back and pleaded weary disorientation after a long tour and I daresay I was forgiven. It did make me wonder, though, just how authentic were the autographs I had received from my fave bands as a wide-eyed teenager.

I spent more time at MWIS than the other three. In the early days of the band I was always 'ON', even on days we were supposed to have off. I was so driven, so ambitious, every waking moment was spent working on and for the band. If I wasn't working on new songs or discussing artwork with Sandy or making plans with Tony Perrin, I'd spend my evenings at MWIS, sifting through the mail I'd received, answering some choice letters, and even going as far as often picking letters at random and using the office phone to call fans at home. Unsurprisingly, most people couldn't or wouldn't believe it was actually me calling them. Slowdive chanteuse Rachel Goswell will be mortified to learn that she's being outed here as an early member of MWIS. She has embarrassedly and laughingly confessed that she was indeed the recipient (victim?) of one of my fan club phone calls. I imagine the call would've gone something like this, as most of the calls I made to MWIS members did:

I ring the number. A female voice answers. 'Hello?'

'Hello, is that Rachel?'

'No, it's her mum.'

'Oh, okay. Can I speak with Rachel, please?'

'Who shall I say is calling?'

'Tell her it's Wayne Hussey.'

'Sorry, Wayne who?'

'*Wayne Hussey.*'

'Mmm, yeah, right. I'll tell her but she won't believe me.'

A few seconds go by. I hear footsteps approach the phone.

A voice, suspicious and cautious: 'Hello, this is Rachel here.'

'Hi, this is Wayne.'

'Wayne who?'

'That's exactly what your mum asked. Hussey.'

'Dave, is that you? Ah, it's you, isn't it, Rob?'

'No, it's Wayne Hussey, I swear.'

'Oh, come on. That's a pretty good imitation, I must admit, but who is this? Anyway, why would Wayne Hussey be calling me?'

'Well… I'm at the Mission office and going through some mail I've received and came across your letter and thought I'd give you a call.'

Stutteringly, 'Why? I mean, prove it.'

'Okay… in your letter you wrote 'Dear Wayne, I am a huge fan of The Mission and you are my favourite member. I have pictures of you on my bedroom wall. I used to like The Sisters Of Mercy but now I like The Mission better. I play guitar too and one day I'd like to be in a band and…'

'Stop, stop, that's enough. Oh my God, it is you! I can't believe you're calling me. None of my friends at school tomorrow will believe me.'

Most of the fans I called needed only a little convincing that it was really me on the other end of the line – wishful thinking kicking in, maybe – and once my identity was established and they had got over the shock, most would natter away like we were long-lost siblings. Just a few were completely incredulous and dumbstruck, as I no doubt would've been if Marc Bolan or Brian Connolly had ever given me a ring.

Certainly in the early days of our success I did attempt to maintain a connection with our audience. I was approachable and, dare I say it, readily available. There was no attempt on my part to contrive an aura of mystique by keeping a distance; a vexing trend which seemed to be prevalent again after the short-lived success of punk, a decade previous, in stripping away the barriers between the stage and the audience. With me, what you saw was what you got. Of course as the band got more popular and started to play bigger venues it became harder to sustain accessibility, try as I might. I remember playing the Philipshalle in Düsseldorf to a sold-out audience of 7,500. During the course of the evening I'd learned there were several coach-loads of fans who had travelled over from the UK. After the show, when everyone was back on their buses getting ready for the overnight trip back to Blighty, I insisted on visiting each bus to say hello and thank you for coming before they set off. There were gasps and looks of astonishment as I boarded the coaches, and much hugging and kissing ensued before I was allowed to alight. That gave them something to talk about on their long journey home. This was fairly typical of the kind of thing I was wont to do. Being inebriated helped. But these incidents sadly became more difficult to orchestrate, and gradually distance from our audience became a natural consequence of success. We still hosted fan club phone days, though, and played fan club-only shows, and fan club competition winners were invited to the studio while we were recording. It was still well worth the £1.50 to be a member of MWIS.

God's Own Medicine[5] was finally released on Monday, November 10, to wildly differing reviews. It certainly divided the media; either they were for us or (mostly) against us. Some were ecstatic, most vitriolic. There was very little indifference or middle ground, and everybody seemed to have an opinion. *GOM* entered the UK album chart at number 14, during the tour. By the time we hit Nottingham Rock City again later in the month it had been certified Silver, and within a couple of months, Gold.

I was never under any illusion that we were an innovative or seminal band. We were the sum of our influences as, if truth be known, most bands are. We all take from the past. It's what we add to the mix that makes us unique and individual. A constant criticism levelled at me, and The Mission as a whole, even before we released our first single, was we were unspeakably retrogressive, an anachronism. Our decision to cover 'Like A Hurricane', for example, was greeted with universal disdain; it wasn't such an uncool thing to do just a few years later when Neil Young had been revisited by credibility, but at the time there were hoots of derision emanating from all sides. In reality, our sound, a swirling concoction of shimmering guitars and impassioned vocals with a beady eye on the commercial pop charts, had little precedent. Every record we made sounded like The Mission, as distinctive in our own way as, say, T.Rex or Joy Division were in theirs. We were, and are, unique, and while the media largely couldn't

– or wouldn't – recognise it, the fact we soon amassed a huge and very loyal following confirmed that we didn't need endorsement from the likes of the *NME* and John Peel. With *Hammer Of The Gods*[6] as our tour bible, we believed in the 'big rock dream', and carried on its dissolute, hedonistic traditions at a time when the flavour of the month was the shambling, jaunty, jingle-jangle of the C86 brigade. Yuck. Most of it being far more retro than we ever were. This amid a moral climate of 'Just Say No', an ill-informed campaign propagated by the tabloid media that attempted to put the fear of God and the Devil both into a youth populace that indulged in drug-taking and casual sex. And all the while their journalists were snorting lines of coke and shagging each other in the toilets of Fleet Street. Despicable hypocrites.

It really was an awful time culturally, and we came along and added a splash of colour and outrage to an otherwise fairly conservative landscape. By 1986 it was almost like punk had never happened and the climate had reverted back to 1975, the worst period musically when I was growing up. I decided very early on that I, and we as a band, would *play the game*. Not playing the game would've been a cop-out. We bought the ticket and we were gonna take the ride to the end of the line. Our relationship with the media was – that word again – symbiotic. They loved to write about us, and me in particular. I was an open book: a colourful, loud-mouthed, opinionated, irreverent, amoral, arrogant, garrulous, ever ready with a quip, shameless, brazen, belligerent, drunken, puking, shagging, drug-taking, openly ambitious pop star. Oh, and honest at a time when honesty was not seen as valuable currency, repeatedly being asked by my record company to keep my trap shut. Sod that. I polarised the British media and the youth (those who cared) in a way that perhaps hadn't been seen since, I don't know, maybe Freddie Mercury.[7] On a smaller scale, of course. If The Mission had got to be as big as Queen, Fleet Street would have had a field day with me as much as they did with Liam Gallagher less than a decade later. I've always liked my pop stars to be larger than life, to not give a toss. Every proper rock star has to go through a period of disproportionate self-indulgence and immorality that is inconceivable to the average person on the street. That is the privilege of the rock star, to behave abhorrently. No one else can get away with it. We all enjoy, to varying degrees, living vicariously through someone in the public eye who lives their life with no discernible shame, regret or embarrassment, doing the things we'd love to do ourselves. I think Liam was the last great British pop star. It would be so tedious for rock stars to just turn up, perform and then go quietly home afterwards. I mean, come on, Ed Sheeran? Gimmeabreak.

I was a divisive character and undoubtedly more reviled than I was revered, but that didn't bother me. Anyone interested in pop/rock/alternative music in the UK between 1986 and 1991 could not have avoided me. You couldn't go two weeks without picking up one of the music papers and finding a photo, an interview, a review, a piece of gossip, or an irate letter about me on the letters page. We were fair game. If we were asked to dress up in Santa outfits for the cover of the Christmas issue we'd do it and have fun doing so. What, you want us to strip down to our underwear and then be covered to our heads by two tons of cold, wet sand in a freezing photo studio? Ah, nae bother. Don England football shirts and we'll put you and Craig on the cover of the *Melody Maker* 1990 World Cup issue. Yeah, why not? For that one they sent photographer Tom Sheehan all the way from London to Atlanta, Georgia, to photograph us in a hotel room on an afternoon off during a US tour. What a waste of money, probably ours. There wasn't anything we wouldn't consider, apart from maybe jumping from a moving plane without a parachute, a suggestion I'm sure was made at least once by the ever-charming *NME*. We made good pop stars. We were frivolous and fun, and good looking. What I mean by that is while none of us were what you'd call classically handsome – although Simon was a pretty boy

– we knew how to make the most of what God had given us. We dressed up, played the part, and we looked good. We were skinny, we had hair, lots of it, and we had our own teeth. I wore shades at night, even to the cinema, and how cool is that? La Dolce Vita. I took to drawing a beauty spot on my face, à la Madonna, that would be in a different place for the next photo shoot or TV appearance. By the time we performed on the *Old Grey Whistle Test* in early spring 1987 my beauty spot had strangely developed into a love heart. I wore dresses, skirts and armfuls of cheap bangles. I dressed like a cross between Boy George and Clint Eastwood, yet not as pretty as George or as handsome as Clint – more like a gothic Widow Twankey, if truth be known. And we had fun. And everyone could see we were having fun. And it irritated a lot of people no end to see us having so much fun. How dare we revel in the pantomime and show up the whole charade for what it really was? Everything about being in a successful band, with the exception of actually making the music, is ludicrous and preposterous. We knew that. We lived it and pointed out the absurdity of it all. The very fact that there were factions of the media that believed us to take ourselves seriously merely shows how easy it was to fool them. For a few years there I was ubiquitous in the UK music press, with most of it being just nasty, personal invective from moue-pussed journos with an agenda. I was such an easy target. As well as the hacks themselves, other bands and singers were always having a pop at me. But I didn't care. I figured as long as they were writing and talking about us then we were doing something right. I loved that we could get up people's noses so easily. We were never the darlings of the press illuminati like, say, Suede were in the early Nineties, but we did, thankfully, have our champions scattered among them like sleeper spies. Amid all the vitriol there'd be an occasional five-star album review or interview that didn't harp on about Eldritch or our drug intake, preferring to focus on the music we made instead. Not that I ever had any problem with talking openly about our drug use. It was never a closely guarded secret, was it? No topic was ever out of bounds with me.

While there is no such thing as an overnight success (it generally comes in degrees), it did seem to happen very quickly for The Mission. And while it is something you want, work towards and prepare for – for years, in some cases – and you know it's coming, can see and feel it coming, it still hits like the proverbial runaway freight train when it arrives, and catches you off guard with how intense and life altering it can be. No one can handle success that comes suddenly; you'd have to be some kind of sociopath if you didn't succumb to the first taste of it. It fucks you up. With success comes a fair degree of self-delusion, too. Solipsism is a prevalent trait among the newly famous, I find. And I was no different. Of course I had my head turned, so would you. I'd be walking to the Co-op thinking everyone was staring at me because I'd been on the cover of that week's *Melody Maker* or on *Top Of The Pops* the night before. It only began to dawn on me a few years later that they were more than likely staring because I was dressed in a full-length purple crushed-velvet coat replete with a mini-skirt over black leggings, and a big black hat and ribbons in my long, dyed-black hair, sporting Ray-Bans on a cold, grey, dismal winter's day. I'd like to think I was a sight for sore eyes but I may well have been the cause of those sore eyes. I wasn't *really* famous, not in the true sense of the word – not like Prince, or Madonna, or Dirty Den. In reality, the music papers only had a limited and specific reach, and while most of my friends and peers would pore over their every word, the general population didn't care a hoot for which new band they were championing that week as the best band ever. Television could make you famous, and at that time the holy grail for all bands (except The Clash, it seems) was to appear on *Top Of The Pops*. We were to do that a fair few times over the years, as well as appear on pretty much every other music-based show that was then broadcasting in both the UK and the rest of Europe. But I still didn't *feel* famous. Does anyone ever? And anyway, how do you really measure it?

Our exploding popularity in the UK was confirmed when at the end of 1986, readers' polls were announced in the music papers. We swept the board in *Sounds*, winning best band, best new band, best album, best single, best live act (shared jointly with Queen!), and I was voted second best male vocalist after Peter Gabriel and ahead of Jon Bon Jovi in third. We enjoyed very similar results in *Melody Maker*. That I also featured in the dickhead of the year and worst dressed categories came as no real shock, either. Bear in mind that we had achieved all of this in less than 12 months of the band getting together, another factor that made the music press suspicious of us. That we didn't feature at all in the *NME* polls – not even in most hated – was inexplicable, a mystery that was cleared up for me a few years later. I long suspected that the *NME* had implemented an editorial policy to demean us at every possible chance, and that votes for us in any category in their readers' poll were instantly binned. This was confirmed to me in '93 or '94 by an *NME* journo (we'll call him El Tel), who was a sometime acquaintance of ours, when he came backstage after we'd just played a London show. He'd been sent by the *NME* with the brief to write a review that was intended, with us a little down at heel at the time, to hammer the final nails into our coffin. El Tel would further confess that, in all good conscience (a hack with a conscience? There's a shock…) he couldn't – that he thought the show was very good. So I suggested he write a good review and see if they'd print that. He said he would. Did they print it? Of course they bloody well didn't. We weren't alone in their scorn, though; many bands suffering the same fate as us, if not quite as virulently. Every album, single, live show was reviewed with the intent of causing us damage both personally and professionally. A weaker man would've crumbled in the face of some of the reviews we received in the *NME*, being so decidedly venomous and viciously personal.

86

But I developed a thick skin – had to, or I'd have gone under. I learnt after a while not to bother reading the bunkum masquerading as journalism. As I said at the time, I didn't read most of my cuttings, I just weighed 'em. (Can't remember who originally said that – was it Mae West?) Interviews were conducted by journalists who would keep pace with every line and drink I ingested and imbibed. They'd be nice as pie to my face and then turn around and condemn me with their written words for my debauched ways. On the release of our second album, *Children*, in early 1988, I refused to speak with the *NME*, despite the record company's best beseeching and the mag's promise *to be fair this time*. Still, I refused. I didn't trust them one whit. And how right I was not to. We had arrived in Dublin for our show, scheduled the following day. I had a humdinger of a cold and so went straight to bed. I woke up the next morning feeling much the same the way. A doctor was called. He visited me in my room, took one look and declared he was gonna give me two shots – one a B12 and the other some magical cold cure. He had me pull down my pants and lean over the bed, an invitation I normally couldn't refuse. Ordinarily I might be excited at this juncture, but with a large hypodermic in his hand excitement was not the emotion I was feeling.

'Roight then, Mr Hussey, this first prick might hurt a bit, okay?' he advised, as he administered the injection.

'Was that it? Puh, I felt nothing,' was my insouciant reaction.

'Okay, good. Here's comes the second one, then,' my kindly doctor warned.

'Ow!' I howled, 'that bloody well hurts. A lot. You said the first one would hurt, not the second!'

'Ah, that's Irish psychology for you, Mr Hussey. Now be a good boy and pull up your pants and get back into bed. These little shots will get you through the show tonight, alright!' the quack said, as he counted the pile of fivers that Stevie Sex-Pistol was handing over on my behalf. Once the doc had vacated the room, Stevie said, 'Listen, there's this kid that's been waiting in the lobby all yesterday and all this morning hoping to talk to you. He's asking if you could do a short interview for the little local fanzine he writes for. He's come a long way and says he only needs 10 minutes. What d'ya reckon?'

'Oh, go on then. I can do 20 minutes before we go to soundcheck, okay?' I declared.

Despite feeling like death warmed up, I made my way to the lobby half an hour before we were due to leave the hotel. Stevie introduced me to *the kid*, and we found a quiet corner of the hotel bar where we sat and conducted the interview. Nothing out of the ordinary, nothing to be suspicious of. A week later the *NME* was published with a tagline on the cover advertising a 'Hussey Exclusive'. Yep, *the kid* worked for the *NME* and, of course, it was a blatant hatchet job. He didn't even use my name in the feature, preferring W★★★★ H★★★★★ instead. And I'd even bought the bugger a drink.[8] These are the levels that some British journalists and papers would stoop to. I found another journalist, who I considered to be 'one of our people' and who I'd invited into the sanctum of my London flat, rooting through my medicine cabinet in the bathroom. When I asked if he needed something he replied, 'Oh, no. Just looking to see what prescriptions you might be taking.' 'Why don't you just ask me, ya nosy git,' was my rebuff. Needless to say I didn't invite him to my home again.

The *NME* weren't alone in their venom. I did catch it from all sides. Essentially, though, the music press generally, and the *NME* in particular, were impotent in stemming the rise of The Mission. I believe that this is the issue that irritated them the most. In fact, I'd go as far as to say it's probable that all they achieved with their derogatory features and reviews and column inches dedicated to how awful we were was to create an 'us and them' scenario, making our relationship with our audience even stronger than it already was. What the press failed to realise was that by constantly spouting such puerile bile about me in particular, they actually helped to create a mythology and perpetuate the dichotomous role that I was always destined to fulfil, of being the pop star that was either loved or despised. And as a consequence, they became irrelevant to us and our followers. Still, throw enough shit at the wall and some will stick. While in the short term we were untouchable and unstoppable, their constant inculcation did have adverse long-term effects. By the time our star was on the fizzle in the Nineties it became impossible to alter the general public perception of me and the band and, try as we might, still some 30 years later we are damned as an aberration best forgotten when it comes to writing the history of rock music in the second half of the Eighties. An analogy I can draw is that of the actor who is typecast after playing a specific role very successfully early on in their career, and from then on that is how they are eternally regarded. They spend the rest of their life harbouring the ambition, and the talent, to play other, more sophisticated and diverse roles but feel trapped by the expectation of the media (that can be bothered) and even their own audience. In the end, none of it matters, as we had a good run and a lot of fun, and we gave as good as we got.

A typical example were these replies to questions about 'My Brilliant Year' in 1986's Christmas issue of one of the music rags. My album of the year was our own, *God's Own Medicine*. My wally of the year was myself, Wayne Hussey. I wanted a blood transfusion as my Christmas present, and would give Prince a blow job for his. Are you a goth or a hippie, I was asked? I'm a 'goppie', I replied.[9] And the thing I wanted most to see happen in '87 was New Year's Eve. I think right there in that exchange is exactly who I was in 1986, as commercial success first hit.

Right, that's enough bitching about the British music press. You shan't hear a peep more from me. Except to say that all the rags that were around in the mid-Eighties have all gone the way of the dodo, apart from the *NME*, which is today limited to an online presence only. And The Mission still exist and flourish. Just saying.

It's difficult for me now, as I write, to fully comprehend just how well known, infamous if you like, we were in the second half of the Eighties. The memories I have are like watching old news reels of someone else. The person I have become and am now feels a million miles away from the media pop tart I was back then. I'd feel very uncomfortable playing that game now, as I do every time we release a new album and I have to dip my toe back into that particular ocean. I have changed, inevitably. Success changed me. As has failure. And just as success is relative, so is failure. We don't enjoy the chart hits anymore, haven't done so for a long time, or the attention from the media that was once lavished on us. But more than 30 years on we, *I*, still exist and still make music and still have a fervent worldwide audience. I don't consider that to be failure. In the interim many of my contemporaries have fallen by the wayside and changed career paths, some are tragically no longer with us, while a select few have gone on to become massive global brands. Like we do, most still trade under the same name as they did in the Eighties, nostalgia being our chief commodity. Regrettably for some, nostalgia is all they have to look forward to. I do persist with releasing new music and I am constantly writing new songs, but it's a frustrating fact of my life that everything we, *I*, now do is compared to what we did 25 or 30 years ago. Fortunately we, *I*, enjoy an audience that on the whole welcomes new music – with a caveat; that it doesn't stray too far from the accepted perimeters of what they expect from us.

Endnotes

1   Somehow I've ended up with numbers 1 and 2 of the 'Stay With Me' limited-edition single, and both are unsigned, which is a rarity in itself.

2   The midweek chart position was based on sales for the first part of the week, the information usually being made available to the music industry on a Thursday or Friday, with the 'real' chart to follow being announced on the Sunday evening. If a record was struggling then a record company could give it a push over the weekend to try to get it higher. For a band like us with a very partisan audience, the midweek chart position was usually higher than where the record would eventually end up, by virtue of our audience going out and buying said platter in the first few days of release. Record companies would try all kinds of marketing ploys to sustain the sales throughout the week. The highest midweek position we ever achieved for a single was 'Butterfly On A Wheel', which was number 4. It ultimately entered the chart at a disappointing number 17. On sales it was enough to get us straight into the Top 5, but we were penalised for the number of formats we had available – two CDs, two 12-inchers, a 7-incher, and a souvenir collectible box in which to house all the various formats. I believe the rule was that you were only allowed to have five formats available in any given week. And we had six. Heads rolled at Phonogram for that boo-boo. Of course it was too bloody much, but everyone was at it in those days.

3   The Eskimos were so named when a group of our fans were stopped at a German border crossing. Among the dishevelled rabble was Ray Ramone, a likeable Scouser with an eye on the main chance and a gob that could guide ships into harbour during a storm, who looked, shall we say, slightly Inuit. 'Eskimo' was the only word they could discern the German-speaking border guards saying while pointing at Ray and laughing. Of course, the weary travellers themselves found this hilarious, and that very night the

cry of 'Eskimo' went up in the mosh pit between songs for the first time, and from there the legend grew.

4   A stamped, addressed envelope. Circa prehistoric.

5   Being very busy, flying around doing promo and playing shows, we didn't get the chance to approve the final cover for the album. When it hit the stores, the cover read 'Gods Own Medicine'. An oversight. The absence of an apostrophe gives the title a wholly different meaning.

6   The fabled, and apocryphal, Led Zeppelin biography, written by Stephen Davis and published in 1985.

7   In the late Seventies the *NME* featured a photo of Freddie Mercury on their cover with the headline 'Is This Man A Prat?' In 1990 they put a photo of Craig and I on the cover and tagged it 'The Mission: Britain's Stupidest Band'. A framed copy adorned my office wall for years.

8   While researching for this book I unfortunately came across this particularly spiteful piece, written by the little twerp who masqueraded as 'the kid from a fanzine' just to get an interview with me. He has subsequently gone onto a long and successful career in journalism, which tells you an awful lot about the dubious conduct of some within this particular profession. There are others, however, that practise journalism with integrity, intelligence, empathy, and a genuine desire to inform but with very few exceptions – and they know who they are – in my experience most so-called music journos I've had the misfortune to encounter are a far more degenerate, immoral, narcis-sistic, disingenuous, unprincipled, dishonest bunch than any musician I've ever known.

9   Being such a huge admirer of The Beatles film *A Hard Day's Night* (1964), I remembered, when asked if he was a mod or a rocker, Ringo's quip that he was a 'mocker'.

CHAPTER 5

All Over This Wasteland

PLAYLIST:
1. The Christmas Song – Nat King Cole
2. Wasteland – The Mission   3. Wishing Well – The Mission
4. Highway To Hell – AC/DC   5. Need You Tonight – INXS
6. Achilles Last Stand – Led Zeppelin
7. Aqua Marina (*Stingray* end titles) – Gary Miller
w/ The Barry Gray Orchestra

VIDEO PLAYLIST:
1. Wasteland – The Mission
2. Holiday – Madonna (*The Tube*)
3. Relax – Frankie Goes To Hollywood (*The Tube*)
4. (Full performance) – The Mission (*The Tube*)
5. Shelter From The Storm – The Mission (*The Tube*)
6. Severina – The Mission

One evening just before Christmas, 1986, we found ourselves sat celebrating at the bar of an almost deserted beachside hotel. It had been a meteoric 12 months for us. Cocksure and full of ourselves, we were riding high on the euphoria of having the top-selling independent single of the year in 'Serpents Kiss', hitting the UK Top 30 for the first time with 'Stay With Me', a Gold-selling album with *God's Own Medicine*, sold-out tours both at home and abroad, and ending the year by topping the readers' polls in both *Melody Maker* and *Sounds*.

We were in Brean Sands, Somerset, to shoot the video the following day for our next single, 'Wasteland'. There was an open log fire blazing away in the corner of the room, with a Christmas tree standing erect just off to the side decked with twinkling fairy lights, various coloured ribbons, tinsel and baubles, and topped with a dazzling white angel. The winds outside were soughing in from the Bristol Channel with the constant pitter-patter of rain against the darkened windowpanes decorated with fake snow. Nat King Cole's *The Magic Of Christmas* was playing quietly on the stereo. The only guests staying at the hotel were ourselves and our film crew – and a young honeymooning couple sat cosying up together in front of the fire. I don't think they quite bargained for us heathens as company when they booked their quiet couple of days for nuptials in this out-of-season and off-the-beaten-track establishment. Feeling as if we were intruding on their amatory idyll, I bought a bottle of champagne from the bar and, moseying on over, presented it to the love-birds on behalf of our entourage, along with a rueful apology for our rowdiness. A look of acute consternation was clearly evident on their faces as they peered up to be confronted by a gothic Jeff Spicoli[1] lookalike, dressed all in black and donning a bolero hat and Ray-Bans, looming over them proffering a bottle. They graciously accepted the champagne as reparation and very soon were retiring to their room. But as they passed us at the bar on departure, a conversation took place.

'So, are you guys a band?' the bride enquired.

'Whatever gives you that idea?' Mental Mick said, smirking.

'Yeah, what gave it away?' was Slink's retort.

'What's the name of your band?' the recently espoused hubby asked.

'U2,' deadpanned Craig.

'Five Star,' said I.

'Ah, you won't have heard of us,' said Mick, laughing. 'The Sisters Of Mercy.' Oh, he was a wag, was our Mick.

Tony Van Den Ende (TVE), our video director, clarified, 'Ah, don't listen to 'em, they're having you on. These boys are The Mission, the hottest band in Britain at the moment!'

The couple looked blankly at each other and shrugged. 'Nope, sorry. Never heard of you,' they chorused and off they trotted to their matrimonial bed with the bottle and two champagne flutes in hand.

An old adage about wind and sails springs readily to mind.

Shot among the desolate dunes on a bitterly cold and blustery slate grey day, when we weren't striding purposefully across the sands, for the video we had to stand around *pretending* to be mean and moody, all of which was filmed from the helicopter flying above us. As shooting videos ordinarily goes, it was a long and tedious process, exacerbated by the fact there was nowhere to take shelter from the freezing wind that was howling in from the coast, the hotel being quite the hike back up the beach. While we were shooting close-ups and stills, TVE sent the helicopter off to film the nearby Glastonbury Tor. For its return flight, four large standards, one for each of us, were erected in the dunes by which we had to stand guard, patiently waiting for the helicopter to fly over. This was the opening sequence of the video and all I can tell you is that it seemed an eternity stood there exposed to the elements, waiting for the all-clear that the shot was complete to the director's pleasing. At the end of the afternoon it started to drizzle so TVE took pity and called a halt to proceedings. The two-man helicopter crew mentioned there was room for one person to fly back to the hotel with them, rather than have to trek the best part of a mile in the wind and the rain across the dunes back to the hotel. Being *primus inter pares*, I pulled rank and bagsied the spot amid grumbles of 'bloody singer gets all the perks' from the other three. It was my first time in a helicopter. We were swooping so low in and out of the dunes, and what with it being a glass-bottomed cockpit, I felt like I could just reach out and touch the sand at times. All I needed was a 9mm pistol in hand and I could imagine myself as James Bond on my way to Pussy Galore. Of course, I was nice enough to wave to the other three and the camera crew as we flew over them, only to be rewarded by a flurry of Vs in return for my thoughtfulness.

Interspersed with footage filmed at our previous autumn show at Aylesbury Friars[2], the 'Wasteland' clip is a big step away from the fun, frolics and humour of the 'Serpents Kiss' and 'Stay With Me' videos, and only served to confirm the ever-growing popular misconception that we did tend to take ourselves too seriously. I have to confess it's not a favourite of mine, but it did its job in helping to break the band internationally.

With a few days off over the holiday period I went to spend the time with my family in Yate, near Bristol. While there I booked myself into a small local 16-track recording studio run by family friend Ray Markham. It was located in the Ridgewood Community Centre, a short walk from the family home. Over the course of a couple of days I recorded demos of half a dozen or so new songs I had on the go. The tapes only came to light again in 2020, after they were found hidden away in the attic of Mr and Mrs Adams, Craig's mum and dad, and how they got there no one knows. Hearing them afresh again today is interesting inasmuch as they include the very first versions of later Mission songs 'Tower Of Strength', 'Kingdom Come', 'Beyond The Pale', 'A Wing And A Prayer', 'Heaven On Earth' and 'Bird Of Passage', and it's striking how very close some of them are to the arrangements that ended up on later Mission records.

While in Yate I did look at houses to buy in the vicinity, having started to earn the first decent money of my life from my publishing income. The idea was to find a fair-sized house away from the hustle and the bustle, which had a granny cottage or an annexe where I could live, while my parents and siblings would live in the main house. The idea being because I was away from home most of the time it would make sense to have someone living there to look after the property in my absence. We did find a lovely, ideal place just on the outskirts of Yate, as it was at the time, but then I had second thoughts. I wondered how inhibiting it would be to my hedonistic lifestyle having my parents so close by, so ultimately decided against it. It broke my poor mum's heart and it is a regret of mine that it did so, but I do believe it to be the correct decision in the end. I wouldn't have liked my parents or one of my brothers or sisters walking in while I was in the middle of an orgiastic drug binge.

I arrived back to my home in Leeds early in the new year, 1987, to find I'd been burgled once again. I was still living in Ashville Grove with Stevie Sex-Pistol, but by this time Gilly, my landlady, was with child and had moved out to live back at home with her parents for the duration of her pregnancy. In her stead a young, brash scamp from Wakefield had moved into her room. Along with an irrepressible demeanour, a bag full of black clothes and a crateful of records, Dave Beer moved in and brought with him an air rifle. Dave had been a sometime roadie for The Sisters Of Mercy before and during my tenure with the band. We shared a landing, my room looking out over the dustbins at the back of the house, while Dave's looked out over the street and into the houses opposite that were rented out to students. Early one afternoon I arrived home and clambered up the stairs to find Dave skulking down behind the windowsill in his room, with the air rifle in his hands.

'What the hell're ya doing?' I reasonably enquired.

Giggling furiously to himself, and obviously more than three sheets to the wind, Dave replied, 'I'm shooting out the windows of the bedrooms across the way. Wanna try?'

'Bloody right, gisago then,' was my instant response. And so we spent the next half an hour taking it in turns to fire the gun and wait for the breaking of glass before diving down beneath the sill in fits of hysterical cackles. Our mirth knew no bounds when the students, having arrived home from uni, came knocking on our door to complain that all their windows were smashed and to ask if we'd seen anything.

'Nada, sorry,' we both replied, trying desperately to keep a straight face.

Dave, as history would prove, liked a good night out like the rest of us and, on the odd occasions I was at home, we'd traipse down to the Warehouse on quiet nights during the week. Upstairs in the cocktail bar, we'd start in on the 'Gangrenes', a potent lurid green mixture of Bailey's Irish Cream, crème de menthe and Midori that went down as easy as mother's milk. A couple of those and I'd be leaning against the bar or the person stood next to me to stop from falling over. One night, and one Gangrene too many, I was feeling a trifle queasy in the taxi. We barely made it home in time. I dived out the cab, leaving Dave to pay the fare, and threw up all over the low stone wall outside of 27 Ashville Grove. The rains soon came and washed the vomit away but, no word of a lie, that green stain was ingrained in the stone for years, through all seasons and all weathers. People coming to the house would ask, 'What's that green stain on the wall outside?' 'Oh, that's where 'Ussey threw up his Gangrene.' There should be an English Heritage blue plaque up there by now.

One morning I woke up, went downstairs to the living room, threw open the curtains and there in our front garden stood a four-foot high wishing well. It definitely wasn't there the night before. The Mission had not long been going, and we had started playing a cover of Free's 'Wishing Well' in our live sets. Some joker, obviously knowing I lived in the house, had thought it an amusing caper to leave a wishing well for me. Very kind of them. Except it was obviously stolen from someone else's front garden. Nonetheless, there it stayed in ours for months, the mystery of its provenance remaining unknown to us. Until one evening, that is, when Dave, while under the influence of a *truth* drug, confessed that it was, indeed, he and a mate who had nicked it from some posh garden in Wakefield. After loading it into their car, they'd driven it over to Leeds in the middle of the night to deposit in our garden, for us to find the next morning.

In the Nineties, Dave Beer, who's passport occupation once read 'Purveyor of good times', went on to become a notorious nightclub promoter, earning the nickname 'King of Clubs' by establishing his own *Back To Basics* night as a UK institution. Now legendary in club circles, when he lived with me he was a bratty, noisy kid with a penchant for air rifles and an aversion to students. Like the rest of us though, he wasn't particularly wicked or malicious, just a bit naughty and mischievous, and certainly liked to be the life and soul of the party. It seems he never changed.

So, yes, I'd been burgled again. Maybe it was karma at work for my part in shooting out the students' windows. More likely, it was the perfidy of some petty villains who used to come to our house to score their speed, and they knew we'd be away. As Stevie Sex-Pistol was now employed by the band as our on-tour 'procurer and enter-tainments manager', and with Dave very often staying in Wakefield with his long-suffering girlfriend, Jill, the house would sometimes lay empty for weeks. Easy target. By the beginning of 1987 I had been burgled two or three times. Each time my newly purchased TV and stereo would be stolen along with other sundry replaceable items such as toasters and kettles. The scoundrels very considerately never stole my records or guitars or anything that was clearly of sentimental value to the inhabitants of the house. Honour among thieves, eh? It was obviously someone in the know. I have my suspicions as to whom. Works in vice now for the police.

I managed to grab a couple of nights at home in Leeds before we were due to head south to The Smoke to start work again. I ended up in Le Phono one night and met T. She was one of the first people who'd made the effort to befriend me when I'd moved to Leeds. T had once been a girlfriend of Craig's and their union had produced a daughter, Jessica. Anyway, as I was fairly sloshed, T, owning a car and taking pity on me, offered to drive me home. She ended up staying the night but, like a phantom, had disappeared by the time the sun had risen. When I awoke there was a pile of bangles – not mine – discarded on my bedside table and, bit by bit, a vague recollection of the previous evening's escapades came back to me. I nabbed the best bangles for myself and added them to the armful I already sported, and later that day travelled down to London, not thinking too much about what had happened the night before. Adventures of this kind seemed to be happening to me all the time.[3] But this particular night would bring a consequence that would prove seismic and lifelong.

I believe it was this trip home to Leeds and having been burgled yet again, AND the fact that when I wasn't working I was spending almost all my free time staying at the Columbia Hotel, that I decided to move out. The house in Yate with my parents already dismissed, I bought a place in London. Our manager Tony Perrin was selling his ground-floor flat at 33 Ellison Road, Streatham Common, just a 200-yard walk from the station. Ever the aspiring yuppy, Tony, now flush with managing two soon-to-be successful bands (us and the Eves) was moving upmarket and buying a house in Purser's Cross Road, Fulham. He'd bought the flat in Streatham a year or two previously for £30,000 and was now asking £50,000 for it. I'll have it, said I, sight unseen. Because there were no estate agents involved and consequently no commissions to pay, Tony – my manager and very good friend, lest we forget – knocked a bit off the price for me. Not much, mind; just £500, tight git. After the contracts were signed and I moved my exiguous belongings down from Leeds – basically a bed, a few clothes, and my records and books (no TV or stereo, remember) – I spent one night there and didn't stay there again for the next two years, preferring to carry on living at the Columbia in Lancaster Gate.

Ever since my days with Dead Or Alive, whenever I was in London and when I could afford it – if someone else was footing the bill – I had stayed at the infamous Columbia Hotel, staggering distance across Bayswater Road from Kensington Gardens and The Serpentine. The hotel of choice for a certain kind of musician, i.e. not quite yet in the money and not too fussy, the Columbia could hardly claim to be luxurious. Besides its reasonable rates and convenient location, what most attracted musicians was that the staff turned a blind eye to most goings-on. The bar, usually tended by a squat Spanish man nicknamed Franco, who would ask 'Wad ya wanna drin-kie?', would stay open as long as there were people wanting drinks, right through to breakfast if you so desired. There were always other bands there at all hours of the day or night, some wary and suspicious of us, some more friendly. Very rarely saw any of 'em at breakfast though. The only time *I* made breakfast was when I'd been up all night and we just moved from the bar into the breakfast room when they started serving kippers at 7 a.m. One memorable night we came back from a show to find a happy throng crowded around the piano in the restaurant, with Noddy Holder sat there banging out old Slade hits and everyone singing along. Of course we joined in.

You could bring as many guests as you liked to the bar or even to your room. No one batted an eyelid. The rooms were high-ceilinged and tall-windowed and varied from the size of a small bus shelter that could barely take a single bed to rooms as big as a bus that accommodated four or five people. All the beds were covered in a gruesome, grubby Gangrene-vom green bedspread mottled with ciggie burns and dubious stains, and off-white Bri-Nylon sheets that could give you friction burns if you turned over too quickly in your sleep or became too passionate while in the throes of *l'amour sauvage*. The wallpaper was originally a white with a brown stripe affair, that with age and cigarette smoke had transmogrified into an ugly homogenous shade of taupe. Each room had a couple of pieces of generic scuffed furniture – a bedside chest of drawers, a chair, maybe a table, and a wardrobe if there was enough space. Anyway, whoever hangs their clothes up in a hotel? No musician I know ever does. The TVs were all small and fuzzy-screened, useless in the bigger rooms, some with wire coat hangers hanging off the back as an aerial, and with no remote control it meant you had to get up to manually change the channel to the other one – yeah, two channels worked if you were lucky. Room service was limited to drinks and sandwiches that you could order from your room, but then you'd have to go downstairs to the bar to fetch it yourself. Calling it room service was a bit of a stretch if truth be known.

But I always felt comfortable at the Columbia. For eighteen months or so I lived there when we weren't touring, recording or away on promo trips. Until I got asked to leave and was banned, that is. My crime? One night I was entertaining a roomful of people, most of whom I didn't know, and party supplies were running low. I knew that Stevie Sex-Pistol was in the room overlooking the main entrance to the hotel. And he was holding. Rather than contact him via conventional methods – you know, by telephone or actually just taking the short walk down the corridor and knocking on his door – I decided to show off my best Spiderman impersonation. My room was on the first floor, a fair height up, facing Bayswater Road. I climbed out of my window onto the one-foot-wide ledge that wrapped around the building. With my guests trying their best to dissuade me from this lunacy, but being so full of chemicals and bravado, I ignored them and gradually made my way around the side of the hotel to the front, passing the windows of several rooms en route. As I passed I knocked on the windows and the inhabitants of the rooms would pull open their curtains to see me grinning maniacally. Some laughed, some were aghast, but an older American tourist couple woken from their slumber took umbrage. They called reception to complain about the long-haired bloke wearing sunglasses and crawling along their window ledge. Of course, the night porter instantly knew who they were talking about. I made it to Stevie's room and clambered onto his balcony and knocked on his window. No bloody answer, was there. The bugger had gone out. By this time the night porter was outside the front of the hotel in the driveway, calling up to me, 'Hussey, you stupid sod, get yourself back inside before you fall and break your bloody neck.'

'I can't, me mate's not in his room. I'll have to climb back to mine,' was my less than clever suggestion.

'Don't you bloody dare. Wait there, I'll get a pass key and let you in', was the night porter's response, born more out of fear of a damaging headline rather than concern for my well-being, I reckon. A few minutes later the window to Stevie's room opened and I clambered inside.

'Now get back to your room and stay there. I don't wanna hear another peep out of you tonight, okay? We'll deal with this in the morning', he reprimanded.

The morning came along with a phone call from reception. 'Ah, Mr Hussey, can you please vacate your room today and please don't come back. Thank you.'[4]

In the early days of The Mission we used to stay at the Columbia so often that we'd hide our drugs under the carpet on the back stairs whenever we were leaving to travel abroad. At the opposite end of the hotel to the reception, the main stairs and the lifts, the back stairs were very rarely used, there ostensibly so that the hotel met fire regulations, as far as I could ascertain. This was before security cameras or CCTV were installed. A couple of times, when I'd been sharing a room and wanted a degree of privacy, I had used the back stairs, between floors two and three, for trysts. I had never once been disturbed. An ideal place to stash the stash, it was surmised. Four steps down, on the left-hand side, the carpet was pulled up at the edge and our drugs were deposited with the underlay. We'd arrive back to this sceptred isle, and if we were staying at the Columbia we'd have a stash ready and waiting for us on arrival. If we were travelling on to somewhere else, we'd make a detour to the Columbia en route, stop off for a quick pint in the bar, and then one of us, usually Mick, would surreptitiously pick up our speed and dope. The drugs were always there. I wonder if there's still any there that we'd forgotten about? I wonder if they've changed the bloody carpets.

'Wasteland' was released on Monday, January 5, 1987. The second single from *God's Own Medicine*, it entered the UK singles chart at number 24 the following weekend, our highest chart position yet. Still, Auntie Beeb was resistant to our charms, neither A-listing it at Radio 1 nor rewarding us with an ever-elusive performance slot on *Top Of The Pops*. We were, however, scheduled to appear on the popular Channel 4 music show *The Tube* the following Friday evening, the 16th.

Hosted by the sardonic and droll Jools Holland and the ebullient and flirty Paula Yates, *The Tube* was broadcast live, just after *The Chart Show*, with bands playing live (as opposed to miming), interspersed with interviews and 'magazine' features. By January 1986, it was well established as a prime show for the youth of the nation, second only to the perennial *TOTP*. An arbiter of the alamodic, an appearance on *The Tube* could make or break new bands and artists, having had a hand in, among others, Madonna's and Frankie Goes To Hollywood's rise to fame.

We'd been in Europe earlier that week fulfilling promotional duties and arrived back to Heathrow to find the country at a standstill under a heavy blanket of snow. There was considerable doubt that we'd be able to catch a flight to Newcastle, where *The Tube* was filmed and broadcast from. Certainly the truck carrying our backline would have major problems on the roads. They set off a day earlier than originally scheduled to try to make it on time. Fortunately for us, they did. The record company called in a favour and got us on a flight the day before the broadcast.

These four photos were snapped by Sandy (Ball) Holden in Stevie Watson's bedroom in Leeds, over the winter months of 1985/86. Photos from these sessions (although not these particular ones) ended up on the back cover of our first single, *Serpents Kiss*, in May 1986. © Sandy 'Ball' Holden

This is from our very first band photo session in late '85 or early '86. Taken by Sandy (Ball) Holden at Headingley Bear Pit, Leeds, just around the corner from where I lived in Ashville Grove. © Sandy 'Ball' Holden

This is another very early photo shoot, early 1986, this time outside the 'infamous' Columbia Hotel in Lancaster Gate, London. © Adrian Boot

The Sisterhood. Our first ever 'gig' at Alice In Wonderland on Dean Street, London, on 20 January 1986. © Maria Moore

'Gi' us a song, Addo!' Craig showing off his unique, three-handed piano style somewhere in Europe during The Cult tour, 1986. © Wayne's personal collection

'You and me, we are blood brothers'. Me with Ian Astbury early one morning at Berlin Airport, as The Cult flew home and we took the bus, Feb 1986. © Wayne's personal collection

Essential reading in the Flying Turd – Slink, me and Mick. © Craig Adams

Me with Tim, Julianne and Andy from All About Eve in late 1986, celebrating their signing to the same publishers as The Mission. © Nic Duncan

Appearing on the *Joan Rivers Show* in May, 1987. We gave her a bouquet and a bottle of Blue Nun and she gave me a bottle of black nail varnish. She was sacked about 10 days after our appearance for falling viewing figures. We didn't help much. © Craig Adams

The V's in the world of singers, as everyone knows, is 'can you turn my vocal up, please?' © Simon 'Sparky' Parker

Craig in just his underpants and Spinal Tap 'skeleton' T-shirt entertaining the masses at the Hollywood Palace before our ill-fated lunch-time show for 'the world famous KROQ', southern California's biggest 'modern rock' radio station. May 1987. © Simon 'Sparky' Parker

Rehearsing on stage at the Hollywood Palace. Our sound engineer, Pete Turner, was filling in for Craig, who had 'gone berserk and run amok at the Hyatt Hotel' and been sent home for his own good as well as ours. May 1987. © Simon 'Sparky' Parker

Chris 'Surf' Bocast, who we met in San Francisco and who ended up joining the band and taking over from Pete, who had taken over from Craig, for the remainder of our 1987 North American tour. The date stamp on the photo is 27 May 1987, the day after my birthday. © Simon 'Sparky' Parker

'Hi, I'm Jim, you're Wayne, right? I love that first line on your album, "I still believe in God but God no longer believes in me".' My first meeting with Iggy Pop backstage at the Bizarre Festival in Berlin, 10 July 1987. © Jez Webb

Me slaving over a hot notebook, writing lyrics for our second album, *Children*, in the Capel-Y-Ffin monastery in the Black Mountains, Wales. August 1987. © Nic Duncan

Me endlessly practising the newly scribed 'Black Mountain Mist' in the same location, wearing a pair of my mum's old leggings, enough to scare off any wildlife. August 1987. © Nic Duncan

Team Mission before a charity five-a-side competition in August 1987 at Loftus Road, London. Back from L to R: Watson, Adams, Brown, Perrin. Front L to R: Gregory, 'Ace' Hussey, Hinkler, Webb. We got knocked out by eventual winners The Housemartins. © Nic Duncan

On the day of the show we arrived at the TV studio to find a large horde of our followers had braved the weather and had somehow made it to Newcastle. As *The Tube*'s regular audience was a little thin on the ground due to the inclement weather, the producers of the show agreed to let all our people into the studio to swell the audience numbers. And I bet they wished they hadn't. Remember, this show was broadcast live from 5.30 p.m. until 7 p.m. We weren't due on camera until about 6.50. All through the show, from start to finish, when 'Mr Smug' or 'Mrs Smutty'[5] were trying to introduce another band or conduct an interview from the studio floor, chants of 'Eskimo' and 'Mission' and 'Jools is a knob' could be heard on air on every TV tuned in throughout the land. They did us proud.

Generally with live TV, bands sound terrible – thin and overly compressed, and with the vocal mixed far too loud. We wanted it to sound as close as possible to how we sounded live. One thing we'd had the foresight to ensure was to take our regular live sound engineer, Big Pete Turner, to oversee the studio sound and to make sure the echo cues on my voice were in the right places. It worked. It sounded very live and dynamic. And it looked great, too, for TV. We'd taken in our stage set from the tour as well as our lighting designer, Phil Wiffen, to again oversee proceedings. Perhaps a little brighter than we were used to when playing live, it worked as exciting TV, because our followers helped make it the spectacle it was. More a live show than a stilted studio performance, The Eskimos ripped up newspaper and threw it in the air, like confetti at a wedding, at strategic moments during the first song, our *hit* single 'Wasteland'. They moshed, they built towers, they sang along and gurned into the cameras; it was as much their show as ours. And they deserved it for the effort they'd made to get there to support us. Thousands of teenagers around Britain watching at home, seeing The Mission for the first time, must've thought to themselves they wanted a part of this. There was no other band around at the time doing quite what we were, and looking and

105

sounding so good and having so much fun doing it. I know if I'd have been a teenager in January 1987 I would've fallen in love with The Mission and wanted desperately to be an Eskimo. We also played The Stooges anthem of nihilism, '1969', and *The Tube* rolled their closing credits over us as we rocked like a bastard with 'Shelter From The Storm'. What the viewers at home didn't get to see was us carrying on playing for a good 20–25 minutes after the show had gone off air, much to the irritation of the TV studio technicians. They daren't try to stop us, though. *The Tube* did broadcast 'Shelter' in its entirety on a later show due to popular demand. We may have looked like anachronisms, although I would personally argue that point, but watching the clip again while researching this book, I'm struck by how much more akin we were to the spirit and energy of punk rather than the excesses of early Seventies rock that so many critics derided us for. Those excesses would arguably come later, but they certainly weren't apparent in January 1987.

One disappointment, though, was our midweek chart position. 'Wasteland' was predicted to go down. Oh well, no time to get despondent: we were travelling out to Germany the next day to begin the second leg of our World Crusade tour.

A couple of days later, Tuesday 20th, we arrived in Berlin, having travelled overnight from Bielefeld through the snow and the East German corridor, to be greeted by Big Pete waiting for us in the hotel lobby. 'Okay, lads. A couple of pieces of news. You want the good or the bad first?'

'Bloody 'ell. Best give us the bad first then,' happy Craig Adams replied.

'Dub's artic[6] has been stopped on the way into the city and he's had to unload all the gear for inspection by customs. He ain't gonna make it for tonight's show,' he informed us.

'What can we do about it?' Slink asked.

Pete explained. 'Well, tomorrow is a scheduled day off, so we postpone tonight's show to tomorrow.'

'Ah, that sounds sensible. We'd left tomorrow free just in case the single had gone up in the chart and we might have been offered *Top Of The Pops*,' Mental replied, sagely.

'What's the bloody good news, then? We could do with a bit,' I asked.

Pete unfurled a telegram he was holding in his hands and started reading. 'To The Mission. Stop. Congratulations. Stop. Wasteland number 11 in the UK singles chart. Stop.'

We all started cheering and giving each other big hugs.

'Wait, I haven't finished,' Pete went on, '*TOTP* want you. Stop.'

We all started cheering and giving each other big hugs. Again. At last, we'd be on *TOTP*. The holy grail. The barometer by which success was measured by my parents and siblings, my uncles and aunties and cousins, old school friends, by the average man and woman on the street, if not by all my peers. This was it, big time here we come. A moment later a realisation dawned.

'Hang on, Pete,' I reasoned, 'we can't move tonight's show to tomorrow because *TOTP* is filmed on a Wednesday. We'll have to fly to London tomorrow to film it. We have to play tonight with hired gear.'

'Um, there's a bit more bad news, lads,' giant Pete murmured, obviously quaking in his size thirteens at the prospect of having to impart it.

'Go on,' Mental urged.

'Well, you were on the road and no one could get in touch with you and a decision needed to be made pronto. I've spoken with Perrin and he's been in touch with the TV department at the label and, between us, it was decided to tell *TOTP* you're not available this week.'

Me, with encroaching psychotic desperation: 'Why the fuck not? *TOTP* is always filmed on a Wednesday and broadcast the day after. We purposely left Wednesday as a day off just in case this 'appened.'

Pete: 'Unfortunately, for the first time in an eon, *Top Of The Pops* is gonna broadcast live this week on Thursday evening. You can't do it unless you cancel the gig in Hamburg.'

'Bollocks. That's just rubbish, innit?' Simon added, not so slinkily.

'The Beeb have promised they'll show a couple of minutes of your video and then when the single goes up again next week into the Top 10 you can go on the show then.'

Mental Mick, man of the people, responded. 'That seems fair enough. We can't cancel a gig just to do bloody *TOTP*. It's not fair on the fans who've bought tickets and have made plans to travel.'

We all grumbled assent, despite our bitter disappointment. The following week our midweek chart prediction was number seven. When the chart came out, as well as 'Wasteland' slipping down to number 13 our chance to perform on *TOTP* had also slipped away with it. I must confess, when we received the news, I got completely wrecked on the tour bus that day and cried my eyes out like the baby I was. Silly sod. Number 11 was as good as it ever got for us in the UK singles chart – we were never to reach those heady heights again, although we came close when we later hit number 12 with both 'Tower Of Strength' and 'Butterfly On A Wheel'. We did, however, make it into *The Guinness Book Of Records* in the mid-Nineties as second only to the mighty AC/DC as the band with the most Top 40 hits in the UK but without ever having a Top 10. AC/DC did enjoy a number four in 2012 with a reissue of 'Highway To Hell', so they no longer qualify. I dunno where that leaves us today.

Talking of bands from Down Under, one day around this time, while I was in Phonogram, I picked up a couple of albums by INXS. The Antipodeans were starting to get the big record company push. I took the albums back to the Columbia and Mick saw me arrive with the records under my arm. 'Ah, you've got the inks album.'

'Inks? What're y'on about?'

'Inks. You've got their album there in your hand.'

'You mean in excess?'

'In excess? That's inks, innit?'

'Read it, Mick, In. X. S.'

'Oh, bugger. I've been hearing about this band called in excess and reading about this band called inks, and I thought they were two different bands.'

'No, Mick. It's just the one,' I informed him as I walked away laughing.

Mick was far from thick, though. I don't think he left school with many formal qualifications, if any, not that that is an indication of intellect.

Academic accomplishment doesn't automatically confer intelligence. It just means you can be taught and retain information. Some of the most stupid people I've come across have spent years in further and higher education and have come out of it with degrees and doctorates. And yet they don't have a bean of common sense. Hearing Mick speak in his broad, Yorkshire accent, his language littered with curse and slang words, it'd be easy to jump to the conclusion that he isn't very clever. You'd be so wrong in your assumption. Mick was one of the smartest people I've ever known. He may have come across sometimes as vulgar and uncouth but that masked a razor-sharp wisdom and a warm and ready wit. He got on with everybody, and everybody loved him. Mick would take the mickey out of everyone – none more than himself – within his orbit. Nobody was sacrosanct; no band member, no crew member, no fan, record company exec, or journalist – no one. The only people he didn't have time for were the fake, the poseurs, the disingenuous; those he considered to be putting on airs and graces or, as he would say, the hoity-toity. It was never a case of tolerance for Mick, as tolerance implies a lack of understanding and empathy. Mick had empathy and understanding in droves and was the least prejudiced and judgmental person I knew.

Like me, Mick was born and raised working class, he in Leeds, to parents who were well into their thirties when the bouncing baby,

Michael John, came along. One story he liked to iterate was, when he was in his teens and had just left school, he couldn't find a job at first. So he used to spend an extra few hours in bed of a morning. After all, what was there to get up for? One day, his mum, crying, came into his bedroom, pulled open the curtains and started shouting, 'Come on, Michael. I don't want you lounging around in bed all day anymore, get up and look for a job, will you? It's a disgrace you being on the dole. You're the black sheep of this family.' And then she stormed out the room, leaving Mick thinking to himself, *but hang on, how can I be the black sheep? I'm the only child.*

Mick did find a job eventually, as a forklift truck driver in a warehouse in Leeds. It wasn't long, though, before he was back on the dole. Being the new boy, Mick was constantly being picked on by his bully foreman, undoubted acts of territorial pissing. With the end of his tether finally breached, Mick drove his forklift truck through the wall of the foreman's office – the office being a prefab construction – and pinned him against the back wall within its forks. He turned off the engine, climbed down and started to walk away. 'Brown! Let me out of here. Brown, you're sacked. Sacked!' screamed his trapped boss. Mick glanced over his shoulder and replied, 'No one talks t'me the way you do, fucker, and gets away with it. You can't sack me, I quit!' And away Mick walked, leaving the man ranting and raving at his back as he did so.

Mick was much-loved by the ladies, too. He was an absolute charmer and, once he got his hair cut short, very good looking. He was definitely one to have a different paramour waiting for him in most cities. I remember one time we had just arrived at the Marriott Hotel in Bristol city centre. We exited the bus to check in. 'We've got 10 minutes before we have to leave again for soundcheck,' instructed Stevie. We all rode the lift up to our rooms, Mick with his regular girlfriend at the time (he'd split up with Sandy by this point) in tow. Ten minutes later we were sat in the hotel lobby,

110

waiting for the bus to arrive to take us to the Colston Hall, when the lift opened and Mick walked out with a completely different girl on his arm. Craig, Simon and I looked at each other, astounded and awed at Mick's impeccable timing, and I don't mean his drumming. In the short time we'd been in our rooms Mick had said goodbye to his girlfriend, who was leaving to catch the train back to London, and welcomed his other girlfriend, who had travelled down from Nottingham to be with him. The two girls must've passed each other in the lobby. Another example of why he was called Lucky Mick.

There was an after-hours club that Mick and I went to a couple of times, just off the bottom of the Queensway, a short walk from the Columbia. To enable it to stay open until sunrise it remained unlicensed, meaning that it couldn't legally sell alcohol. That inconvenience, however, could be bypassed by bringing your own booze. Or by nipping across the street to the enterprising Greek restaurant that used to stay open, long after it had sold its last kebab for the evening, just to sell beer and wine at extortionate prices to us Cimmerian[7] creatures. One night in the club we met a couple of girls, Nic and Karen, and as the sun was coming up and it was time to leave, they invited us to their flat in Kennington. Never ones to turn down a party, we jumped in the back of a hackney carriage with them. I was snuggling up to Karen and Mick was paired off with Nic. En route, Karen asked the taxi driver to stop outside a newsagents.

'You three stay here, I'll go,' Karen instructed. 'Is there anything you want?'

'Yeah, get us a couple of packets of Silkies. Here's a fiver. Ta.'

A few minutes later she climbed back in the car with the ciggies and a couple of soft-porn mags – *Fiesta* and *Club International*, I think it was. Mick and I raised eyebrows at each other.

'Worra've ya got there then, luv?' asked Mick.

'Oh, I thought you'd like to see these. I'm in both of these mags this month,' she replied, beaming proudly.

111

She leaned into me and, placing the first magazine in my lap, opened it and flicked through a few pages until she found what she was looking for: photographs of herself in various provocative poses garbed in stockings, suspenders and heels. Karen then opened the second magazine and showed us more semi-naked photos of herself. 'Phwar,' was Mick's subtle response. I was busy pushing my tongue back into my gob while trying not to drool all over the pages.

When we arrived at their flat we sat around drinking and smoking for a while until Karen led me to the bedroom with the two magazines in her hand. 'Okay, 'andsome. I want you to shag me while you're looking at these photos of me. *Capiche?*' With that, she lay both magazines on the bed open to her photos and then we got down to it. Every time I turned my head to look directly at her, Karen, between swoons and sighs, would demand, 'Not at me, the pictures.' As Mick and I were later crawling into a taxi to take us back to the Columbia, Karen came running out of their flat and insisted I take the magazines as souvenirs. 'You might want these for later,' she said with a smirk. Was she calling me a wanker?

I realise that this episode may seem quite tame compared to the goings-on of today, what with Tinder and Grindr and other hook-up apps, and people exchanging photos of various intimate parts of their anatomy, along with the easy accessibility to porn that the internet now affords. In 1987, though, soft porn was only available from the top shelf at newsagents, wrapped in cellophane (and there was never a dick in sight). Or via mail order. Not that I ever did that; I was quite happy with the high street newsagents' fare. The more hard-core stuff could be searched out in specialist shops in Soho and the red light districts of Amsterdam and Hamburg and other big cities. Did it objectify women for me? Probably. But I could very easily differentiate between a photograph and interaction with a real live person. I wasn't numb to the human experience because I looked at photographs of naked bodies. If anything, it made me value the experience even more. I dunno. In a way that the internet has devalued music by making it more easily and instantly available, so it's done the same for porn, I reckon. I rarely *watched* porn. Even though most back-street video rental stores would have a cordoned-off area where porn videos could be rented, I was always too shy and embarrassed to go behind the curtain for fear that someone I knew might see me. And maybe this fusty viewpoint has more to do with my encroaching years, but hasn't porn gotten more abusive, violent and graphic too? Or do we just have access to more of it? Where's the romance, the tenderness? I know, it's porn, it's not an amoret. But I've always liked a little back-story to my pornography. You know: boy meets girl in the launderette, he asks to borrow some of her Daz. They flirt a little and then they go for a walk in the nearby park while their smalls are tumbling in the shared dryer, and end up bonking in the bushes, that kind of thing. I do wonder what message our kids are getting with the easy accessibility to today's porn. Is it healthier than the repression of impulses that I contended with as a young teenager? Does watching porn educate you as to how bodies respond to touch and stimulation or is it better to learn for yourself with innocent youthful gropes and fumbles? I reckon it's gotta be through your own, unique experiences, rather than watching 'actors' faking it, hasn't it? Exposure at increasingly younger ages to hardcore pornography that normalises abuse and misogyny during sex must confound young, impressionable minds. Some kids can't help but grow up believing this is the acceptable way to behave with their sexual partners. And that just ain't right.

My first encounter with just nudity, even, was the sensational nude Vivien Neves advert in *The Times* newspaper in 1971.[8] I'd never seen a naked female before, certainly not one over one or two years old – sisters and cousins I hasten to add, before you jump to any errant conclusions. I ripped that page out of the newspaper and kept it hidden away in my LFC annual for months, enthralled and appalled

113

in equal measure, amused and confused by my illicit treasure. That spring, Vivien Neves became the focal point of my 13-year-old sexual fantasies. The launderette featured, as did the daydream wet-dream that Ms Neves was one of the customers on my mum's Avon round, whose weekly payments, by riding my bike around the neighbourhood, I collected on mater's behalf. Ding dong – Avon calling. There were a couple of quite coquettish ladies on the round, who were 'playful', shall we say – MILFs, I guess they'd be disparagingly called today – that would send me on my way with their weekly dues, a biscuit and, unwittingly, a hard-on. A smile, a ruffle of the hair, a wink, a kindness, a flirty innocuous compliment, such as 'and how's my handsome lover this week', a tantalising glimpse of heaving décolletage, a slight grazing of hands as she handed over her Avon money; all acts interpreted as amorous advances, as seduction, in the fertile, febrile imagination of a hormonally berserk pea-brained sex-centric teenager. Most males, in my experience, grow up sharing the same delusion. One look, one word, even just an acknowledgement, and it's 'she fancies me, she does'. We do grow out of it though, most of us. Thankfully.

When I was a kid – and being raised as a Mormon from an early age made it even more pronounced – there was never any open dialogue about sex. Not in our house there wasn't, anyway. I learnt 'the facts of life' from other boys talking about S, E, X, at school. It was all perceived as smutty and dirty and the work of the Devil. Christ, I was even embarrassed by the word 'pregnant' because the implication was that someone, somewhere, had had sex. We were told that touching ourselves 'down there' was a sin against God and we'd go to Hell if we indulged in masturbation, a crime just shy of murder in the eyes of the church. That was cruelly conflicting to me when teenage hormones and testosterone started kicking up a ruckus. It *felt* so good to have a fiddle, but then I'd be ravaged with guilt once it was over, and quickly down on my knees by the side of the bed in prayerful contrition, vowing never again. That residual guilt stayed with me until I was well into my twenties and, even then, I don't consider that I developed an entirely healthy attitude to sex until I hit my early forties. And it wasn't for the want of trying. Ever since I understood what the word meant I considered myself a sensualist, and dedicated myself to its pursuit through whatever means possible. With the benefit of hindsight, it's clear to me that it was validation through others – *amour-propre*[9] – that I was striving for, never realising that the only validation I really needed – *amour de soi*[10] – comes from within. I can just as easily be a sensualist keeping my own company as I can with others. What was that about being a wanker?

It's a complicated time for us to be living in, a veritable minefield, I would imagine, for the dating singles among us. I've been married for 20 years now, so I've not had to contend with this quagmire, but sex today, this casual hook-up culture, seems to me to be more about transaction than interaction, based on an online profile with photoshopped photos, swiping left or right, rather than good ol' fashioned courting, as my mum would call it. The art of flirting, of seduction, is being lost, becoming a dying art, now construed as being tantamount to coercion by many. At what point does flirting become seduction become coercion? Casanova would be seen as a serial sexual predator these days and locked up. It's a major debate, coming more and more to the fore, and quite rightly so, and too contentious to really go into any depth here, but it does make me wonder how single people, and teenagers primarily, navigate the perils of courtship with any degree of confidence and certitude. When and how does one know when it's okay to make advances, to kiss or to hold hands without it being deemed inappropriate behaviour or regarded as sexual harassment? Okay, I totally understand what rape is, and what *no* and *consent* mean; I also understand the subtle difference between coercion and seduction. But what if you're a clumsy flirt, not a very good reader of signals, shy and gauche – and,

115

let's face it, there must be a lot of us about – it's then that I can appreciate the appeal of 'the dating app' to dispense with all the possible ambiguities and complexities inherent in the sexual landscape of today. Where is the romance in that though? Can sending someone flowers constitute sexual harassment? Valentine's cards? Love letters? Do young people actually do these things anymore? Or is it more likely to be a text or a WhatsApp message? Me, I always liked to seduce, and be seduced. Seduction turned, *turns*, me on. As long as the desire to play was mutual, consensual, I liked the game, the romance, the candles, the wine, the sweet-talk, if you want; the feeling that you have to 'work' for the pleasure. Using your mind, your intellect and gift of the gab rather than any skill you may possess for online negotiation.

I like to hold doors open for women to go first, to walk on the outside of the pavement if I'm walking with a female, pull the chair out for them when sitting down at a table. Are my values just old-fashioned? Is this patriarchal conditioning? Is this behaviour sexist? Or good manners? I understand equality and support it wholeheartedly, whether it's based on gender, religion, sexual orientation, race or an unconventional lifestyle choice. And it shouldn't be something that is just tolerated but something we should actively encourage in our society. Let's not forget that, whether we are male, female or gender fluid, we are all different. And that difference should be acknowledged and celebrated, and, most of all, respected.

Taking a mid-tour break for a couple of weeks at the beginning of February, amid promotion and a trip to NYC, we filmed a video for our next single, 'Severina', my homage to Zeppelin's 'Achilles Last Stand'. Despite the musical influence being plainly evident 'Severina' did end up sounding unmistakably like The Mission, and was a damn fine pop single. It was a two-day shoot with our now director-in-residence, TVE. The first day was spent in a large, empty warehouse on the outskirts of London, miming to the song as wind machines blew back our hair, and with yours truly flaunting and flouting, taunting and pouting, for *all* I was worth. The video is the zenith of our poptastic glamorous period with all of us, with the help of the genius make-up girl, looking as pretty as we ever had and would ever again. Simon and I kiss on camera towards the end of the song, which caused a small frisson among certain factions of our audience. Of course, while it was a spontaneous act, we knew it would. Hardly the stuff of outrage, in 1987 it was still considered risqué by the record company, and we had to stand our ground to keep it in the final cut. Outside of our audience it barely caused a murmur and, quite rightly, went unmentioned in most quarters. We were right and they were wrong. Ner-ner-ner-ner-ner.

For the second day of shooting we had to travel to Sunningdale, a village on the Surrey–Berkshire border. The scene where I am lured into the waters by a most comely siren (in my mind she was Aqua Marina from the Sixties TV show, *Stingray* – that was my brief to Julianne for her vocal on this song – *be Aqua Marina!*) was filmed in the famous indoor pool at Orchard Manor. It'd been the home of Diana Dors and her partner, Alan Lake, and venue for her notorious sex parties, for many years, up to her death in 1984 from cancer and his, driven to suicide by grief, five months later. I only had to shoot one scene that day, the one at the end of the video when I walk into the water and embrace the water nymph. As we came together, she swung me around and pulled me down under the water. I resurfaced moments later coughing, spluttering and bedraggled, to watch my hat floating off down to the other end of the pool amid cheers and applause from the technicians and the rest of the band. In the final edit, I made sure the scene was faded well before my embarrassment.

117

Endnotes

1   Jeff Spicoli was the stoner character played by a young Sean Penn in the 1982 classic American high-school film, *Fast Times At Ridgemont High*. There were some among us who were convinced that I looked like Penn playing this character, with some of his traits very similar to mine. This was another favourite film of ours on the tour bus for a while.

2   Released later in 1987, *Crusade*, so named after the tour of the same name, was our first long-form film. The complete live show as it was at the time, it hit number one in the music video chart on release and featured high in the year-end readers' polls. For me, although it stands as a decent arte-fact, it doesn't quite bear true testament to the fervour and pandemonium of our live shows during this period.

3   One time, early days, when we were playing at Nottingham Rock City, I spied, scrawled on the wall outside the front door, the legend 'Hussey Is A Sex God'. Underneath it someone had added 'No, he isn't. I've had him and he's crap'. Ouch.

4   I did indeed stay at the Columbia again, in the mid-Nineties, and was welcomed back with open arms. 'Wayne! Where have you been? We've missed you!', the girl on reception enthused as I was checking in. 'I was banned, don't you remember?' I reminded her. 'Ah, that was a long time ago. It's all forgotten now. Anyway, we've had that Oasis in here recently and they're far more trouble than you ever were,' she consoled me. I believe Oasis soon thereafter joined the ranks of legends by also being banned from the Columbia.

5   Jools Holland = Mr Smug, and Paula Yates = Mrs Smutty, as deliciously branded by DJ Andy Kershaw.

6   Dub was the driver of the articulated truck that all our backline, guitars, PA and lights, catering and the band's wardrobe was being conveyed around in during this tour. By this time we'd progressed to using two tour buses

– one for the band and one for the crew – and an artic. Gone forever was The Flying Turd. By the way, the band's wardrobe was so huge that we couldn't get it into most backstage areas of venues we were playing, having to go out into the car park and the back of the truck to choose what togs we'd don for that evening's performance. We each had a big drawer and a large hanging communal area where all our stage clothes, mostly mine I have to confess, were hung. At the end of the tour, when the wardrobe was returned to our warehouse, on opening, along with the stench of stale sweat, all that was found in Mick's drawer was a dirty pair of his drumming shorts, a grubby headband and an empty vodka bottle.

7   From Greek mythology, a member of a mythical people living in perpetual mist and darkness near the land of the dead.

8   The full-page ad for Fisons Pharmaceuticals appeared in *The Times* on March 17, 1971. The advert, which featured the tagline 'What's a nice girl like you doing in a firm like this?', caused a sensation; it was the first time a woman had appeared naked in a broadsheet newspaper, and it brought Neves instant international attention and notoriety. Thereafter she was a regular Page 3 girl in the repugnant *Sun* newspaper, until her retirement from nude modelling in 1973. Sadly, Neves was diagnosed with multiple sclerosis in 1979 and died, aged just 54, on 29 December 2002, after contracting pneumonia.

9   A self-esteem that depends upon the opinion of others. A concept in the philosophy of Jean-Jacques Rousseau.

10   Self-love, or self-esteem, which does not involve seeing oneself as others see one, being self-contained. It's primal, and is compatible with wholeness and happiness.

CHAPTER 6

Coming In On A Wing
And A Prayer

PLAYLIST:
1. Our Summer – All About Eve
2. Lady Moonlight – All About Eve   3. Severina – The Mission
4. Tomorrow Never Knows (Amphetamix) – The Mission
5. Wishing Well – The Mission
6. Watching The Wildlife – Frankie Goes To Hollywood
7. Respectable – Mel & Kim
8. America Is Waiting – Brian Eno & David Byrne

VIDEO PLAYLIST:
1. Severina – The Mission (*Top Of The Pops*)

Reaping the dubious benefits of our patronage, during the same mid-tour break as the 'Severina' video shoot, Simon and I also produced the All About Eve single 'Our Summer'. We booked into a small basement studio in west London for a few days, enlisting 'ar Mick to play the drums, as the Eve's didn't have a drummer of their own at the time. We recorded two songs, the aforementioned 'Our Summer' along with the dreamy 'Lady Moonlight' (a song Crazy Rachel claimed was written for her). Maybe, in hindsight, the level of input from Simon and I was a little overpowering, as 'Our Summer' could, lyrics and vocals aside, quite easily have been a Mission song. It certainly bears clear evidence of our involvement. It incorporates a fair few of the trademark Mission constituents of the time, such as the arpeggiated guitars, thumping bass and clattering drums. Tim Bricheno – lovely, beautiful man – was a more than able guitarist and went on to develop his own unique sound and style, but all I hear on this record is him sounding like me and Simon. The same with Andy Cousin, the bass player. Not quite as beautiful but just as lovely as Tim, and destined to be my roomie in the Nineties when he was in The Mission for a few years, Andy sounds like Craig. And with Mick on drums, the imposition of the Mission sound on the Eve's was complete. Needless to say, and quite rightly so, they didn't ask us to produce their next single. When 'Our Summer' was released in April of that year, 1987, the Eves, who had just completed a British tour as our support, reached number two in the UK Independent chart while peaking at number 87 in the national chart. Nae bad for a first crack at it.

Late one night, towards the end of the week we were working with the Eves, I was in my hotel room at the Columbia when the phone rang. 'Hello, is that Wayne?', a male voice enquired.

'It might be,' was my wary reply, 'why, who's this?'

'My name's Bernard. My sister, T, asked me to call you. I've been trying all week to get ahold of you but you seem to keep strange hours.'

'Well, maybe that's something to do with being a musician, eh?' I proffered. 'Anyway, how'd you know where I was?'

'An educated guess.'

'Yeah, well done. So? How can I help you, Bernard? Is T okay?'

'She's pregnant. Again. With your child this time.'

Oh, bugger me, I wasn't expecting that. After picking both myself and the phone up off the floor, I asked the question that all men ask who don't know what to say in this situation: 'Is she sure?'

'Yeah, she's absolutely positive. You remember when you were home in Leeds for a night or two in January and T drove you home from Le Phono and stayed the night? It happened then, apparently.'

'Oh. Yes, I remember.' Blurrily.

So. That was that then. I was going to be a father. I freaked out a little. Well, a lot actually; I wouldn't leave my hotel room for a couple of days, shacking up with a bevy of Blue Nun and a pile of white powder, not answering my phone. I left Simon alone to mix the Eve's single, not being able to face the cold, harsh light of day. It took Tony Perrin to come knocking on my hotel room door to talk me round. I'd spoken to T on the phone over those couple of days and, being Catholic, she confirmed that she was indeed going to have the baby. I'd come to grips with her decision pretty quickly and easily, and was, in fact, already beginning to look forward to being a dad. My bigger concern was how the hell was I going to break the news to Craig? Craig and T had produced a daughter together, Jessica, just two years previously and were even engaged to be married for a little while. Craig could be a little volatile, shall we say, and I wasn't sure how he'd take the news. The Mission tour reconvened in Oslo on Thursday 19 February, but it was almost a week later before I summoned up the courage to tell him. We were in Ghent, Belgium, and I asked him if I could have a word. So we found an empty room backstage.

'What's up?' he asked.

'T's pregnant again. And I'm the father,' was my tremulous response.

Craig looked me straight in the eye and held my gaze for a beat or two. And then just burst out laughing. Hysterically. 'You silly sods, both of you. She should've learned her lesson with me. As so should've you. Why didn't you use a johnny?'

'Well, T's Catholic and the church doesn't believe in contraception, you know that. And anyway, I didn't have any,' I petulantly argued.

'They also don't believe in sex outside of marriage either but that didn't stop you though, did it? Jeez. The Catholic church has a lot to answer for. Ah well, Jessica's gonna get a little brother or sister then,' said Craig trying, for a change, to see the upside.

Hannah, my daughter, was born later that year in Leeds. Despite my foreboding, Craig seemed to accept the news far better than I'd anticipated and, in actual fact, as close as we already were, I think we became even closer after this episode. It certainly bound us as being 'family', albeit once removed, even during the years when Craig and I were later estranged. Family gatherings would bring our parents together, as both families were very involved with T and the infant girls. Despite their dads being feckless and dissolute and mostly absent, Jessica and Hannah were raised with a strong family support system in place and were, and are, much loved by all. Credit where it's due, T made sure of that.

Speaking of families, like a lot of other bands we were very close with our touring crew, most of whom we'd brought with us when Craig and I had left TSOM. As well as Dave Kentish, who in the early days drove us around in The Flying Turd and was, in effect, the band's tour manager/minder, there was our front of house sound engineer Big Pete Turner, cruelly nicknamed Fatman Turner Overweight by his best mate, and our lighting designer Phil Wiffen. Both hailed from Bridlington on the east coast of Yorkshire[1], as did Nipper Bayes, who along with Jez Webb looked after our backline. Yaron Levy was our original onstage monitor engineer but he defected to The Cult when we took him along on our first tour as their support. Bad move. He didn't last long with them, unsurprisingly, Billy Duffy notoriously dispensing short-shrift and P45s to stage crew as regularly as Liverpool were picking up trophies at the time. Eds Barlow, who only ever ate McDonald's, took Yaron's place and stayed with us for years. We employed Stevie Sex-Pistol to look after us as our, ahem, entertainments manager. A little further down the line and additional crew were drafted in for various tours, some working with us for several years while others just couldn't take the pace. Adam Stevenson – Squeak, as he was rechristened – helped Phil with the lights. Andi Watson came in a couple of years later as we started playing arenas and needed even more light crew. Andi, who has been Radiohead's genius lighting designer for the last 25 years or so, was once sacked from a Cure tour because Andi kinda dressed like Robert Smith – and was prettier. That's how I heard it anyway. Others, too – Adam Birch, affectionately known as Baldrick (after the lovable but gormless *Blackadder* character); another Adam, Booker, rebranded as Igor because he walked with a limp after suffering meningitis as a young 'un; Dave 'Milky' Milward, Rob Coles, Big Joe, Hippy Nige, and Tom Lesh, who wore his hair in the shortest ponytail I've ever seen; Jet Doll and Zara, our on-tour caterers; 'Old Woman' John and Howie were the bus drivers while Dub and Frank drove the equipment artics. A tour or two in and Harry Isles became our tour manager and brought some order, organisation and discipline to proceedings as well as wisdom and seniority. Christened the 'Dog's Bastard Crew' by Mick, most of them went on to bigger and better things after they left our employ. I'd hire most of 'em again in a heart-beat but we wouldn't be able to afford 'em now, such is their standing and respect within the industry. They'd have to slum it a bit and I couldn't ask that of them. But I know that whatever they've gone on to do, all of them have a fair degree of fondness for their time in our service and I am still in touch with most of them, a few to this day I consider to be very good friends.

During the European leg of our World Crusade tour, the morning after a particularly chaotic show in Vienna where the deranged audience had completely mangled the barriers in front of the stage (it was a miracle no one was seriously hurt) we had to rise early to catch a flight back to Heathrow to appear on that week's *Old Grey Whistle Test*. We performed two songs: our soon-to-be-released single 'Severina' and a typically Mission-esque version of the Beatles' psychedelic classic 'Tomorrow Never Knows'. When asked why we recorded that one, my smart-ass riposte was, 'I love The Beatles and I wanted to cover one of their songs. In the Beatles songbook it was only one chord. That was the song for us. Nothing complicated. We added two more chords of our own, that's how brilliant we are.' Of course, as per usual, only a few saw the tongue I had firmly planted in my cheek while my words were taken too seriously by most. Silly people. Julianne and Tim from All About Eve joined us on the show, Julianne adding her ravishing Aqua Marina vocals while Tim played guitar on 'Severina' to free me up to be the prancing, preening ninny for the TV cameras. I looked every inch the mid-Eighties pop star, almost beautiful even. Becoming ever more the diva, I made a costume change between the two songs, black coat for 'Severina', white one for 'TNK' – replete with the previously mentioned painted-on love heart on my cheek and a shade of fiery red varnish for my fingernails. Along with the ever-present black wide-brimmed hat and dark glasses, it was a look I was beginning to see more and more among our audience. Fans were copying the way I dressed! How weird that was but also strangely thrilling. I took to wearing ever more outrageous outfits to stay one step ahead, sartorially speaking, of our audience, preferring to do my shopping in places like Chelsea Girl, Miss Selfridge and the girls' departments of Top Shop and French Connection. And if I was in London then I'd always visit markets Kensington and Camden. For a while there I even took to designing some of my own clothes and having them made for me. Let's just say I was never a threat to Vivienne Westwood or Katharine Hamnett. What all this meant, however, was that I developed my own look, without the help of stylists or personal shoppers. No one to blame but myself. In truth, my look was a hotchpotch of the fashions of the day, ideas nicked from sources old and new, that added up to a style that was, while not cutting edge or innovative, unique. Much like the music that we produced. It's easy now to look back, and I do, at the Eighties and think, *What the hell was I wearing? What on God's earth did I look like? What in tarnation was I thinking?*, but the truth is it was a time when young people seemed more inclined to express themselves through what they wore and how they looked. Naturally, young people still do this today but fashions seem more conservative and uniform to me now. There were youth movements back then too, of course, and ultimately each tribe could be discerned by what they wore, but I remember there being more individuality, more colour, more creativity than what I see on the streets now. The worst thing that ever happened to fashion, as far as I'm concerned, was the rise of sports clothes in the Eighties as fashionable attire ('baggy' wasn't far behind, mind). And the international franchise clothing brands that now have outlets in every shopping mall in the world. I can buy the same shirt in Bristol as I can in São Paulo or LA, just another symptom of an encroaching global conservatism.

This particular tour, World Crusade in spring of 1987, was perhaps the zenith of our *pop stardom*. There was pandemonium at every show – screaming, fanatical teenage audiences, and always small crowds waiting for us at stage doors and back at the hotels. To ensure *some* privacy we took to using pseudonyms to book into our accommodation – mine was Albie Singer, Craig was Marlon Karpov, Mick was Curtis Mamon, and Morris Shootingbrake was Simon's *nom de guerre*.[2] In Paris we turned up for soundcheck at La Locomotive, next door to the Moulin Rouge, where we were playing that night, to find a sizeable throng waiting for us armed with bouquets of roses and various other gifts. Not an altogether unusual occurrence by this time, except that on this occasion we were surprised to find the crowd were predominantly pretty young boys as opposed to the more typical pretty young girls. Made a nice change, much like having fish on a Friday instead of the meat I'd eat every other day. Not that I eat either anymore, having been a veggie now for nigh on 20 years. (God, the euphemisms flying around in that last couple of sentences!)

On the day after our *OGWT* appearance, Friday, March 6, the same day we flew back to Bologna to reconvene our Euro tour, we released the 'Severina' single, otherwise known as *V*. Coupled with 'Tomorrow Never Knows' on the 7-inch, and the additional rather-too-faithful-to-the-original-for-my-liking cover of Free's 'Wishing Well' on the 12, the single sneaked into the UK chart at number 32, one place above Frankie Goes To Hollywood's stodgy and tuneless 'Watching The Wildlife': a feat, remembering Holly's recent invective towards me, I took no small delight in. This time we were picking up substantial airplay from BBC Radio 1 – John Peel aside – and we even, God forbid, enjoyed a few decent reviews for the single in the stinky inkies. Nonetheless, we didn't anticipate the single going much higher in the following week's chart, since it was the third one to be taken from *God's Own Medicine*. But, love me tender and call me Elvis, when the next chart was announced, 'Severina' had climbed to number 25, our third Top 30 hit in a row. And we were invited, at long last, to appear on *Top Of The Pops*. My long-held dream was about to come true.

Or was it? Our UK tour was due to kick off at a sold-out Sheffield City Hall on the day of filming at the BBC studios in Shepherd's Bush. How could we film our *TOTP* performance and then make it to Sheffield in time to play? We'd be finished at Auntie Beeb by about 6.00 p.m. and then due onstage in Sheffield at 8.30. It could just about be done but we'd have to forego soundcheck, a decision not taken lightly seeing as this was the opening night of our biggest UK tour so far and we were using a yet-to-be-tried, brand spanking new PA system. Phonogram came up with a solution: they'd throw us in a couple of big black cars immediately upon getting the all-clear from the *TOTP* director, which would rush us through the north London traffic to a small airfield just outside of London where an eight-seater plane they'd hired would be waiting to fly us to East Midlands Airport, the nearest one to Sheffield at the time. From there, there'd be two more big black cars waiting to hasten us to Sheffield City Hall.

Filming *TOTP* itself was, inevitably, a disappointment. A day of tedium spent mostly just hanging around doing nothing, with very little fraternisation with any of the other acts on the show. In fact, the only ones to give us the time of day were Mel & Kim[3], who were at number two that week and on their way to number one with

127

the effervescent 'Respectable'. The only thing to do was to sit in our bare dressing room whiling away the hours, drinking, snorting and playing the board game Frustration. Playing Frustration while whizzing was fraught, tense and fiercely competitive – not recommended for children over 21. Thereafter, whenever we got the call to appear on any TV show, Frustration was the first thing to be packed.

With Julianne again in tow, we did a few run-throughs miming to the song while the studio crew sorted out their camera angles and positions, and then we were told to go to make-up and then wait in our dressing room while they let the audience in. The make-up girl didn't blanch one iota when I asked her to paint the big love heart on my cheek: she'd seen it all before many times over, I'm sure. Togged out in my favourite purple crush-velvet long coat over black, I once again played the prancing buffoon for all I was worth. I was getting well practised at buffoonery.

As soon as we were done we were out of there and into the waiting cars and driven to the waiting plane. It was a dismal evening, raining and windy. Not the most ideal weather for flying in a tiny eight-seater. On arrival at the airfield we all clambered in and took our seats.

The flight itself was horrendously turbulent. We were tossed about like a feather in the wind in that little plane. A few screams were emitted, mostly by Craig[4], and a few muttered petitions were sent heavenwards, but the pilot was always confident. Confident enough, even, to let our sozzled, speeding drummer have a go at the yoke. Mick was sat in the pilot seat, looking back at us, with his thumb aloft, grinning maniacally. 'Keep yer eyes on the road, ya twat,' shouted someone, possibly the green-around-the-gills Tony Perrin. I was sat in the back, holding on for dear life to Nicky from the TV department at Phonogram, who had been tasked to look after us. Poor girl.

Less than an hour in the air and we landed bumpily at East Midlands Airport. Off the plane and straight into more waiting cars, and then rushed at 100mph up the M1 to Sheffield. We arrived only a little late for the show. Still in our *TOTP* clobber, a quick line and a hearty guzzle of the ol' Freira Azul, and 'Dambusters' was already blasting out over the PA. Straight on and into 'Tomorrow Never Knows', our new opener. Not having soundchecked, the onstage sound was dreadful and we all struggled to hear ourselves and each other. Plagued with bad sound, faulty cables, drunken musicianship and my rapidly fading voice, it was a surprise it took as long as 40 minutes before the tether of The Adams finally snapped and he pushed his amps over, threw his bass guitar to the floor and stormed off in a tantrum which couldn't have been more impressively dramatic if it had been choreographed. He was closely followed by Slink and Mental. Having been deserted by the rats fleeing this particular sinking ship, as captain I was left with no alternative but to try and entertain the gathered legion on my own. Grabbing my Ovation 12-string acoustic from Jez, our guitar tech, I then proceeded to stumble through a hitherto never before performed version of 'Love Me To Death'[5], at the end of which the place erupted, it being the moment which turned a show that was heading towards unmitigated disaster into a slender victory. Rejoined onstage for the next song by my compadres, we then stormed through the rest of the set with aplomb, if not surgical precision. There's one thing I must contend about us as a live band – we could, on certain nights, be the best live band in the world bar none, but we could also be absolutely dreadful. There were very few nights where we were just plain average. The longer we've stayed together, through various line-up changes, the more consistent we've become. Rarely are we as ramshackle as we once could be and, conversely, rarely do we touch heaven as we once could either. This may also have something to do with the consumption of less to no drugs and temperance in our pre-show alcohol intake...

We arrived at Glasgow Barrowland on a Saturday afternoon to find Sauchiehall Street completely blocked off to traffic because of a huge crowd waiting for our arrival. Getting from the tour bus to the backstage door was an ordeal in itself. Still being fairly new to the game, we didn't yet have our own security – just Dave Kentish and Stevie Sex-Pistol. We sent Craig and Mick out first as unwitting decoys with the instruction to head for 'that door over there where the venue security are waiting to let you in'. While the attention of the heaving horde was momentarily diverted by Craig and Mick, Simon sneaked off the bus with Stevie Sex-Pistol looking after him, shortly followed by my good self under the protection of Dave. I was pushed and pulled all over the place, my hair was tugged, my clothes got ripped, and my person was groped in various intimate places. I loved it; it was exhilarating. I'd always dreamed of this happening to me. It felt like I was in *A Hard Day's Night*. Eventually, Dave got me into the dressing room reasonably unscathed where Simon was already waiting, also intact. Neither of us had ever experienced anything quite like it before and excitedly compared experiences. After a while we realised we were still short a bass player and drummer. Where's Craig and Mick, we wondered, they should be here by now? Stevie went to look, and found them still stuck outside the venue, cornered by a slavering gathering in a closed and locked doorway. They had gone to the wrong entrance and, despite bangs and shouts, weren't let in. They weren't best pleased when they appeared flustered and dishevelled in the dressing room. 'You can get off the bloody bus first next time, 'Ussey,' moaned the ever moaning bass player.

Mind you, Brownie got his own back a week or so later when we were scheduled to make an in-store appearance at HMV in London. I begged off, citing tiredness or some such pathetic excuse. The other three trundled off to stand behind the shop counter for a couple of hours to pose for photos and sign singles, albums and posters for a long line of waiting and expectant fans that snaked down Oxford Street, while I enjoyed a couple of extra hours in bed. When one fan asked Mick, 'Where's Wayne today?', the best drummer in the world shouted for all to hear, 'Ah, he's gone to the clap clinic. He's got a dose.'

That night, and for the next few days, fans would be asking me how I was and was it cleared up yet. I had no idea what they were on about until I finally asked one of them what they meant, and he told me that it was common knowledge among The Eskimos that I had VD. Mick had told them so. Bastard. I don't know if I was just plain lucky or the gods were looking out for me but, just to clarify, apart from the crabs I'd caught from Craig (see *Salad Daze*) I've never, ever contracted any STD.

Just because I am not, for once, regaling you with tales of non-stop on-tour hi-jinks and debauchery please don't assume that we were being goody-goody-two-shoes and tucked up in bed by midnight. Well, some nights we may have been but if we were then we weren't alone. It just gets tiresome to rabbit on about the sex and drugs and booze. Please take it as said that there was plenty of transgressive and diabolical behaviour afoot during the World Crusade tour of 1987, with the most decadent still yet to come. America was waiting.

Endnotes

1   One of the interludes on *The Mission II* 12-inch, performed on bottleneck slide guitar by Big Pete Turner, was entitled 'East Coast Lament' in honour of the east Yorkshire seaside town of Bridlington, from whence Pete came.

2   Alvy Singer was the name of Woody Allen's character in *Annie Hall*. Being a huge fan of Woody Allen's films then and now, I took that idea and changed Alvy to Albie. If you don't get it, just try saying the name out loud. Try doing the same with Billy Duffy's, which was Mike Hunt. Ha ha bloody ha. Of course, after a while some sleuths among the more zealous and enterprising of our fans found out our aliases and so, after receiving middle-of-the-night phone calls and, even on occasion, uninvited late-night knocks on the doors

of our hotel rooms, we had to change them again. My next one was Alexander Pope, the English poet who had originally written the line, 'Who breaks a butterfly upon a wheel?' (in 'Epistle to Dr Arbuthnot', 1735). Craig, at that point, and taking the piss out of my pretentiousness, became Archie Bishop. Later still I reverted to an expansion of my first pseudonym – Albie Mischenzingerzen. Again, for best effect, it needs to be read aloud. Mick got his Curtis Mamon from a Cheech & Chong film, as in 'Curtis, my man!' Simon was booked in as Tom Jones for a while, until he received flowers, a fruit basket and a fawning letter from management at the Hotel Elysee in Frankfurt, from someone mistaking him for a certain Welshman of the same name, at which point Simon thought it best to come up with a name that couldn't be confused with anyone, hence Morris Shootingbrake.

3   Sadly, Mel was to die of cancer at the tragically young age of 23 in 1990.
4   Craig has endured a lifetime of aviophobia, or fear of flying. He's tried all kinds of cures – hypnotherapy, various pills and tinctures, a doctor's note to visit the cockpit in-flight (pre 9/11), acupuncture, but he swears nothing works as well as getting falling-over sloshed. Personally, I think it's yet another excuse to exercise his excessive bibulous tendencies.
5   I shoulda mentioned this earlier but forgot: When we'd finished mixing *God's Own Medicine* it transpired that we had too much music for the vinyl album. CDs were a fairly new innovation at the time and with none of us owning a CD player and as CDs weren't selling anywhere near the quantities of vinyl, the latter was far more important to us as an artistic statement. With 20–22 minutes per side of the 33rpm 12-inch vinyl the optimum, we overran our proposed side 2 by a few minutes, so the record company suggested we lose a track. We held a band vote and t'other three all voted to lose 'Love Me To Death'. I wasn't having that – that was one of my favourite songs on the album. In a fit of diva-ish proportions I threatened to quit the group – so much for band democracy (never works anyway) – if 'Love Me To Death' was omitted. Tim Palmer then stepped in and said he could edit a bit off a couple of tracks and if we removed the long intro to 'Love Me To Death' we'd lose none of the proposed songs for the album. Crisis averted. N.B. The original long version of 'LMTD' was eventually released as God intended on a 2007 remastered version of the album.

CHAPTER 7

Dreams Don't Come Easy Without Any Sleep

PLAYLIST:
1. White Lines (Don't Do It) – Grandmaster Flash & The Furious Five
2. I Wanna Be Your Dog – Iggy & The Stooges
3. Blitzkrieg Bop – Ramones   4. Kick Out The Jams – MC5
5. Roadhouse Blues – The Doors
6. Sweet Jane – The Velvet Underground
7. Roadrunner – The Modern Lovers   8. Psycho Killer – Talking Heads
9. Mother Of Earth – The Gun Club   10. Rip Her To Shreds – Blondie
11. Back Street Luv – Curved Air   12. Roxanne – The Police
13. Light Of The World – Balaam & The Angel
14. Kingdom Come – The Mission

Once the British tour had culminated with a sold out 6,000-capacity Brixton Academy show on Saturday, March 28, it was only a matter of days before we were preparing to fly to NYC to fulfil some promotional obligations, before later heading out on our first North American tour. This was when the real insanity began. Up to now, the craziness and excesses had been, believe it or not, comparatively restrained.

The night before we were due to fly we were once again in the Columbia Hotel (I'd not yet been banned). I dropped acid with a friend of mine, Karen, and we ended up on our backs in the nearby

Kensington Gardens, watching stars disappear into the dawning blue sky of morning. When Karen left for work I returned to my hotel room and packed my bags and gobbled the rest of the acid, enough to re-kickstart my trip and keep me awake to get me through check-in, boarding and the flight. We arrived at JFK just as I was coming down, surreally navigating my way through customs and immigration without giving myself away. Or maybe I did but they just didn't care then. *These goddamn limey punk-ass drug-addled rock stars. They ain't no threat to the Stars and Stripes.* Couldn't get away with it now, I'm sure.

Starting as we intended to carry on, we were in NYC for a few days conducting interviews – radio, press, TV – face to face and by phone. But first up there was the small matter of a meet and greet to navigate, with record company execs and employees in the conference room at the Phonogram offices. Left on our own, sat at a huge wooden table waiting for our guests to arrive, Mick suggested a sniff-sniff top-up. He quickly chopped out four hefty lines, Craig, Simon and myself instantly availing ourselves of the proffered refreshment. With one line left on the table, Mick snatched the rolled-up dollar bill from my hand and stuffed it up his nostril, bending down over the table just as the double doors flew open and in walked 30–40 record company personnel. Caught in the act, Mick coolly looked up and, in his broad Yorkshire accent, said 'Ah, bugger it, in't fa' penny, in't fa' pound. 'Scuse me a moment, please,' and proceeded to hoover up the white line while the astonished throng watched on. Lesson one to young bands on how *not* to endear yourselves to your American record company, with plenty more lessons to follow, rest assured. Exacerbated by the moral climate of the 'Just Say No' movement, the thing about record company personnel in those days was that they were all at it too but couldn't be admitting it or seen to be doing it. We had no such reserve.

Because success had come to us quickly and relatively easily in Britain and Europe we went into the US thinking they would follow suit. Like so many bands before us and since, we presumed all we had to do was turn up and play the game the same way – and America would fall to us. Nuh-uh. No way, José. Because America is so vast there was very little nationally syndicated media. Apart from a few TV shows, and a couple of magazines, it was all mostly regional. Every city had its own newspapers and cultural magazines; its own TV shows; its own college, modern rock, classic rock, pop, black, soul, oldies, dance, funk, blues, country, jazz, and classical radio stations, each specialising in their own chosen genre. The four of us could spend a whole morning on separate phones talking to different radio stations, in Chicago say, and still only hit a fraction of them. To compound matters, the record company weren't quite sure as to which specific audience it would be best to promote us. That's the thing with the US, they like to put you in a category. Woe betide if you don't fit easily and comfortably into one of them. And we didn't, we fell between the cracks. And that was, and still is, a big part of our problem across the pond. We were not quite alternative enough for the college and modern rock stations, not quite rock enough for the hard and classic rock stations, and not quite pop enough for the pop stations. We did enjoy a bit of college play with 'Wasteland', the later 'Deliverance' fared well on both rock and modern rock stations, while 'Butterfly On A Wheel' picked up some pop action. But that was about it. Stone-wall Mission classics such as 'Severina', 'Tower Of Strength', 'Like A Hurricane' and 'Beyond The Pale', while minor hits throughout Europe and elsewhere in the world, were all but ignored by US radio. These days, Eighties flashback weekends, or lunch-hour, or drive-time, when only records from the Eighties are played, are huge on American radio. Craig, who now lives in Maryland, tells me he quite often listens and we – and TSOM, for that matter – are NEVER played, while every other band under the sun from that period is. Most are one-hit wonders, but the airplay enables them to tour the US regularly, sometimes as part of an Eighties package. God forbid, you won't catch us doing that. Well, you might.

In contrast, the omnipotent BBC Radio 1 was essentially a Top 40 station but with more alternative and esoteric music being played in the evenings and at weekends. Being a national station, it had the power through airplay of somewhat dictating whether a track became a hit or not. A way of bypassing radio play was to go out and play live and build an audience, an audience big and partisan enough to chart your records on their first week of release. A lot of bands, us included, initially infiltrated the UK charts by this method. Because of its vastness, not so easy a route in the US. Texas alone is almost three times the size of the UK. To tour the UK and cover most areas could take you three to four weeks, maybe two if you only hit the big cities. Multiply that by 50 states and you begin to appreciate how much touring is necessary in the Land of the Free to cover just the major markets. Radio play was imperative for any stateside success. You might be getting 'break-out' radio play in San Francisco but nada in Boston. You might have a radio hit in LA but no one's heard of you in Nashville. You might be 'in with a bullet' in the college town of Columbus, Ohio, but dead as a dodo in nearby rock'n'roll Cleveland. A whole new vocabulary had to be learned just to converse with US radio pluggers and programmers, a bit like watching football there – which isn't even called football, it's the 'S' word – with US commentators describing the play using a language that sounds nothing like English to me.

TV helped, of course, in breaking a band, as it does everywhere. In NYC we appeared on MTV's *120 Minutes*, a programme dedicated to alternative bands, and while our videos received an airing or two it was not the rotation we'd hoped for or expected.

Needless to say, to crack America takes a colossal amount of work; work that we were neither totally prepared for nor did we wish to do. Our self-belief came across as arrogance and, to a degree, we did expect success without having to do all the legwork other bands had to. All we were really interested in was getting fucked up and shagged.

That was all America was good for, as far as we were concerned. We declined invitations, against the advice of all around us, to visit the local pressing plants where they manufactured our records, or key record stores and local record company offices in towns where we were playing, for example, believing that all beneath us. We were to get our comeuppance, though. Lesson two: Listen to the local record company Bobbi Flekmans and Artie Fufkins; they know their markets a lot better than you will.[1]

That first visit our promotion schedule was relentless. We spent all day every day for the best part of a week sat in an office, talking on the phone to interviewers of radio stations, newspapers and magazines from all over the US. Because we were the latest trendy import from the UK, the initial interest was overwhelming. We recorded thousands upon thousands of IDs for radio stations around the country that might wanna play our record – 'Hi, this is Wayne from The Mission UK.[2] Why aren't you out bird-dogging and banging beaver instead of listening to us on K-R-O-Q' and 'Hey, dudes, this is Wayne from The Mission UK on K-U-S-F telling ya that if you wanna good time then come and see us on tour. Bring yer drugs and we promise we'll do 'em with ya.' That kind of thing. Funnily enough, I never heard a single one of our radio IDs on the air. Lesson three: A simple, succinct 'Hi, this is Wayne here from The Mission UK and you're listening to New York's finest, W-A-N-K 106.7 FM' will suffice and ensure that the station will, indeed, play your record. Please excuse the local vernacular, but the radio stations don't like you getting creative on their asses.

During this time I met and was interviewed by the legendary Danny Fields for the first, and not the last, time. Danny managed Iggy & The Stooges and the Ramones for a while and had worked in some capacity or other with the MC5, Jim Morrison, The Velvet Underground and The Modern Lovers. I also met Tina Weymouth, the bass player from one of my favourite early NY punk bands,

137

Talking Heads, at a radio station. She was being interviewed at the same time I was. When the interviews were over we found a nearby bar and sat drinking and talking music for hours. She was great fun and I think it safe to say that, at this time at least, she wasn't particularly fond of Talking Heads front man David Byrne. I still rate her bass playing on the first three Talking Heads albums as seminal. We were also interviewed for the biggies – music mags *Rolling Stone*, *Creem* and *Circus*. But, just as in the UK, suspicion largely persisted within the print fraternity as to how our rise had been so inexorable and meteoric.

It was during this trip I first met Jeffrey Lee Pierce, too. Jeffrey fronted The Gun Club, the quite brilliant US punk/rockabilly/country blues band whose *Fire Of Love*, *Miami* and *The Las Vegas Story* albums I adored and still do. We spent a night sharing a bottle of brandy and several packets of cigarettes in a hotel room, talking life and art, surrendering to the senses, old guitars and amps, and Japanese literature, with both of us also giving full vent to our mutual loathing of Andrew Eldritch. TSOM had supported The Gun Club on a UK tour in April 1983, not long before I'd joined the band, and Jeffrey had, seemingly, not taken to the 'Dritch one jot. His chief beef was the way Andrew had been cosying up to bass player Patricia Morrison during the tour, trying to persuade her to leave The Gun Club and start a new band with him. I wasn't around at the time so can't vouch for the veracity of Jeffrey's claim but let's just remind ourselves that when Craig and I left TSOM in 1985, the first person Von called to join the new line-up of the band was, you've guessed it, Patricia Morrison. I was to meet up with Jeffrey a couple more times back in London and he was, despite bemoaning the plight of his stalling career, always a great raconteur. One evening around this time, while I was in my room at the Columbia, the telephone rang. It was Debbie Harry on the other end of the line. She explained that she and her partner in Blondie and in life, Chris Stein, were good friends of

Jeffrey's and that, as they were in London for a few days, they were trying to get hold of him. She'd heard I may've known where he was. I didn't, but of course passed on the telephone number I had for him. I sincerely hope they managed to hook up, as Jeffrey was very fond of Debbie and Chris and would wax lyrical, fanatically and for hours, about the early Blondie albums. The last time I saw Jeffrey was in the late Eighties and again we sat up 'til sunrise drinking and talking, and it was on this occasion he decided it was his best idea ever for me to produce his next solo record. Who was I to disagree? Sadly it didn't happen, it being one of those brilliant notions born out of a bottle that seem so obvious at the time while inebriated but are then forgotten about the very next day. I never saw Jeffrey again. He tragically died of a brain haemorrhage on March 31, 1996, at the age of just 37.

Our booking agency in the US was Ian Copeland's Frontier Booking International (FBI). Cool name and a cool roster, boasting bands such as The B-52's, R.E.M. and The Cure. Ian, one of the Copeland music mafia, was maybe ten years older than us and, after serving a stint in the US army in Vietnam, he'd been around the music business since the early Seventies, starting off in London as tour manager for Wishbone Ash. By the time we met him he was based in NYC and had flown to London a couple of times to see and court us, even claiming at one point that he could get *me* into films if we took him on as our agent. Yeah, right, watch out Tom Cruise. Missed that opportunity, didn't I? Ha. I liked Ian though, once I put my bullshit filter on. Great company, another brilliant raconteur, he told great rock'n'roll stories. His girlfriend at the time, who he brought backstage at one or two of our shows, was a young actress who'd featured in the recent Bruce Springsteen video 'Dancing In The Dark'. Her name? Courteney Cox. We all came to know her a few years later as Monica Geller in the hit TV series *Friends*. Ian's older brother, Miles Copeland III, formed the IRS record label in the late Seventies and released early records by bands including R.E.M., The Bangles, Berlin, The Cramps, Dead Kennedys and The Go-Go's. His younger brother, Stewart, had been the drummer in Curved Air, a band fronted by the delectable Sonja Kristina. They'd enjoyed a number four hit single in 1971 with the stellar 'Back Street Luv', but by the time I saw them at the Bristol Colston Hall in late 1975 they'd gone through several line-up changes and were on the skids, eventually splitting up the following year. Stewart then went on to form a new band in 1977 with a Geordie school teacher named Gordon Sumner. They both got their hair slashed into the punk style of the day, bleached it peroxide blonde and, with Gordon changing his name to the more rock-star-sounding Sting, named their new band The Police. The rest, as they say, is garbage.

Ian booked a five-week US tour, with us naively insisting that we didn't want any days off. We didn't like days off; they were boring and just usually led to us getting more mashed than we would on a show day. Ian tried to persuade us otherwise, as touring the US with such huge distances between shows would be too much even for road warriors such as we considered ourselves. We should've listened to Ian. We also insisted on shipping our entire production – PA, lights and backline, and the crew we'd toured Europe with – at huge expense. We hired two big sleeper buses[3], one for the band and one for the crew, along with an artic to carry the gear. No 'in-the-back-of-a-transit-van-roughing-it' for us. We'd just come off a UK tour where we'd been playing sold-out City Halls and Apollos, and here we were in America turning up to play, in some cases, small bars, where we couldn't even get the truck or the buses anywhere near the venue. I believe we're still paying for this tour even now. There was a small demo studio installed in the back lounge of the band bus with the idea that I could bash down new ideas for songs as they came to me. Did I ever use it? Did I heck. The back lounge was used primarily as the shagging room and was claimed by whoever had guests to entertain that particular night. We ran up an $8,000 bill in the first couple of weeks on 'miscellaneous', which was essentially our communal tour drug stash. It was ridiculous excess. It's easy now to apportion blame to Perrin and claim weak management for letting us get away with the excesses but the truth is we were bloody-minded and wouldn't listen to reason, whoever it came from. And as long as Phonogram were subsidising the tour, why should we worry? We didn't consider at all that we'd ultimately have to pay back the money they were spending on our behalf. That being said, I look back at this time now and I have no regret. We toured America in a fair degree of comfort and luxury and had a brilliant time. We could have done it with the band and a skeleton crew in a minibus, using hired amps and house PAs and lights, and staying in cheap motels that would've possibly enabled us to financially break even, but where was the fun in that? That was just too much like hard work.

We kicked off the tour in Toronto at the RPM Club on April 16 and worked our way down the East Coast. Our record label top-nobs came to see us in Boston so what did Simon, Craig and Mick do? They all dropped acid before we went onstage. Sensible, that. Somehow we managed to hold it together and finished the show on the same beat and chord. Simon later claimed that he couldn't look at me at all during the show, as he swore I was wearing a yellow Zoot suit and he didn't recognise me. Hmmm. The meet and greet with the record company execs after the show was, uh, interesting, with no doubt some nonsensical conversations taking place. At one point one of the execs walked into our dressing room uninvited, just as Mick was chopping out four chunky lines of speed. 'Oh, I'll have one of those if you don't mind,' chimed our over-familiar visitor. Mick, ever willing to oblige, chopped out a fifth. The dollar note was passed around and the lines were snorted. 'Whoa, what the hell is that, dude?' exclaimed the stranger in our midst. 'It's whizz,' Mick informed him. Sniffling and snuffling, the record company man complained, 'I was expecting coke! Why didn't you tell me it was amphetamine?' 'You didn't bloody ask,' our drummer blithely replied. About a week later our management received a fax from the US record company hierarchy complaining about our behaviour. 'They openly use drugs, they are rude, unco-operative, unwilling to fulfil their promotional obligations, and to top it all they spiked one of our employees with amphetamine. The poor man has not been able to sleep since. We feel it our duty to inform you that unless your clients show more compliance and co-operation then we will have no other recourse but to withdraw our support of their North American tour.' This wasn't a good start; we were making more enemies than friends on the other side of the pond. Lesson four: Don't ever offer your record company employees drugs. On the other hand, if *they* offer by all means accept, but be on your guard. As much as they might argue otherwise they are not your friends and never will be. Just like journalists.

A couple of days after Boston we played a sold-out show at The Ritz in NYC and I met up with Sandra, an old friend of mine from Liverpool. My friend Brian Brain Damage[4] was also in attendance, and after the show the three of us dropped acid and decided to hit the town. You see, I may have deservedly earned a reputation for dissolute behaviour but there were occasions when I did recognise my responsibilities and exercised self-discipline. Unlike t'other three in the band, I waited until *after* the show to drop my tab.

We cruised around town, went to a couple of different clubs, the Danceteria and the Limelight I remember, and outside one of them I bumped into Nigel. Nigel was from Birmingham, England – not Alabama – and he was the proprietor of a bootleg merchandise crew. You know the sort, the ones that hang around with the ticket touts outside of venues and sell unofficial band T-shirts and the like. For bands these crews are a nuisance because they are pretty impossible to control and they take away income from selling official merch inside the venues. Early on we decided we'd try something different to combat the bootleggers. First, we had our own line of bootleg merch that was sold outside of venues by our own people, and second, we did deals with the other bootleg crews for a small share of their profits. Obviously there was a large degree of trust involved in an arrangement like this because, come on, no one kept accounts. It was quite a lucrative business all around so they wanted to keep us sweet and we wanted to keep them on our side too. We'd allow them to sell, free of aggravation, in return for them policing other crews and either running them off site or doing a deal that cut us, the band, in on a percentage of their sales as well. Anyway, Nigel was in NYC and looking for me. He had $1,000 in cash he wanted to give me which I'd earned from bootleg T-shirt sales of yours truly in the US so far. And wouldn't you know it, he gave it to me that night while I was tripping and out clubbing. Not having anywhere to deposit that thick wad of notes, I asked Sandra if she'd look after it in her handbag and then thought no more of it. We carried on with our evening.

Bored with the more conventional clubs, Brian took us to a vet's club that he sometimes frequented (as in veteran, as in ex-military – not a club for animal doctors). On arrival we were greeted by a black metal door with a little hatch at eye level. We rang the bell, someone pulled back the hatch and shared a few words with Brian, then the door was opened and we entered. There was a sign that read 'No guns or knives allowed. Please check in any weapons at the cloakroom'. We were patted down and after it was confirmed that it wasn't a .44 Magnum stuffed down my trousers, we were allowed to continue into the club. It was dark, just a few table lights scattered around, and the walls were painted blood red – at least I hope it was paint – with rows of recessed booths and alcoves on either side of the dance floor. I looked around and saw that most of the clientele were indeed seemingly war vets, some of them hideously maimed, several in wheelchairs with leg stumps, some without arms, or an eye, and others with horribly disfigured faces. It was an arresting procession and the strangest club I'd ever been in. I do have to remind you, and myself, however that I was tripping, so I wouldn't swear to the veracity of what I remember seeing. We didn't stay there long because the music – fast, hard, heavy and at tortuous volume – was just too damn loud to have any kind of conversation. By this time the night sky was just beginning to be tinged by the first blushes of morning light and, as we had a show that day in Washington, DC, Sandra and I caught a cab back to my hotel. She stayed for a while and as she was later leaving she remembered the $1,000 of mine she had in her purse. Me, being so out of it, insisted she keep it. 'Treat yourself to a trip back to Liverpool,' was apparently my exhortation. She left with the money but, bless her, she returned to the hotel later that morning when we were scheduled to leave for DC and found Stevie Sex-Pistol, explained where the money had come from and handed it over to him. Of course, I had no recollection of anything when Stevie gave me the cash later that day. I stashed it away in my suitcase and again completely forgot about it until I found it some 18 months later, stuffed in a sock at home.

It had been a custom of ours to allow a bevy of interlopers to invade our dressing room after every show. We didn't mind at all – it was a good way to meet our audience – but this open-door policy of ours would end after our show in DC at the 9:30 Club. After the show we entertained the usual large throng of revellers wanting autographs, photographs, kisses and more. At the end of the night when we eventually cleared the dressing room and were getting ready to vacate the venue, Simon realised his camera had gone missing from his bag. Of course, we jumped to the conclusion that it had been stolen by one of our visitors. 'Right, that's it,' it was decreed, 'no more people in the dressing room after a show unless we personally know 'em'[5], and we carried on our not-quite-as-merry-as-before way, putting the episode out of mind.

Some months later, back home in England, we popped into the MWIS office one day and we were all handed a pile of mail that had been building up for us while we were away on our travels. Among Simon's there was a small package with a Washington, DC, postmark. Upon ripping it open, he found it contained photographs – of us on our tour bus, in dressing rooms, at the airport, and in hotel lobbies and the like across America. And one of a vaguely familiar young couple gurning into the camera. Weirdly, Simon wasn't in any of the photos. It took him a few beats to realise what these were – they were the photographs he'd taken on the stolen camera. The couple that had filched it had the decency to send the photographs, including one they'd taken of themselves, to Simon once they had the film developed. No names, no note, no return address – nonetheless, jolly decent of them to post the images.

After the Philadelphia show a party was held in one of our hotel rooms. It was a big city centre hostelry, proudly flying the Stars and Stripes on a 20-foot long flagpole above its entrance. Someone in the room mentioned that they'd like to take a US flag home with them. As we were on the same floor as the roof, and being ever eager to oblige, at sunrise I took it upon myself to climb out of the window and proceed to rein in the flag flying over the front of the building and steal it. I obviously encountered difficulty doing it on my own as there is photographic evidence of Slink helping me commit what would amount to a treasonable offence today. I don't know how we got away with it; maybe the early hour helped, with none of the other guests yet awake. Knowing what I now know and how sacrosanct the flag is to the American people, I realise that we could well have been put straight up against a wall and shot, certainly at least kicked out of the country and never let back in again. Where did that flag end up? In Leeds, decorating someone's living room wall.

Pittsburgh was an early show, about 9 p.m., which meant a younger audience and no alcohol on sale in the venue. No problem for us, we had our rider. If I wanted to drink onstage, however, my ever present bottle of Blue Nun did have to be decanted into what looked like a hospital specimen bottle. 'Last time I saw one of these was when I went to the clap clinic,' I proudly announced to the audience. 'Positive, right?' shouted a wag. 'Nah, I was pregnant. Are you enjoying it up there?' I shouted to the row of faces on the balcony. 'Ah, you're sitting down, you must be the fucking press!' How to charm America.

A few days later at the Phantasy in Cleveland we all celebrated Jez's birthday. Jez Webb had been a guitar tech for us when we were in TSOM and we'd brought him with us when we started our new band. Calling Jez a tech at this time is perhaps a little bit of a stretch; he was more a mate that we liked having around. I remember one time turning up for soundcheck and asking him, 'Have you restrung the Starcaster, Jez?'

'Yes, mate,' was his insouciant reply.

Picking up my guitar, I asked: 'So how come it's only got five strings?'

To be fair, he was very willing to learn and now knows how to restring and tune guitars among many other skills, and has become a much sought-after tech working with, among others, Depeche Mode, The Cure, Massive Attack, Björk, Sigur Ros, Robbie Williams and, most recently, Queen as Brian May's guitar tech. Everybody loves Jez. Anyway, it was his birthday and we'd arranged an after-show party for him in the venue. We had cake, champagne... and a stripper. Being the sweet talker I was, when the party had finished the woman who removed her clothes in public for a living came back to the hotel with me. We went straight to my room and she re-enacted her striptease just for me. After we had rolled around for a bit, with me fully expecting her to stay the night, she said 'I have to go now.'

146

'Why? Why don't you stay, give me five minutes and we can have another go?' I replied, not quite begging.

'Sorry, I can't, my husband's waiting in the car outside.'

'Ah, okay. See you then,' I said, promptly opening the door for her. And with that she gave me a quick kiss, handed me her knickers as a keepsake and left the room.

The next night we were at the Isis in Pontiac. It was a late stage time, as many of these club shows were, and we ended up getting back to the hotel which was by Detroit Airport at around 4 a.m. Not so bad, except we had to check out just two hours later to catch a flight to LA. We'd been invited to appear on *The Late Show Starring Joan Rivers*. Picked up at LAX on arrival and driven straight to Fox TV studios in Hollywood, we then spent the rest of the day cooped up in a small but plush dressing room. There was eight of us in our party – the band, of course, plus Jez, our sound guy Pete Turner, our light guy Phil Wiffen, and our manager Tony Perrin. Our confinement in the dressing room was occasionally relieved by rehearsals and run-throughs for the camera and sound crews. We'd brought Pete to oversee the sound and to do the vocal delay cues and Phil to oversee the lights. We had a bathroom in our dressing room with a toilet and small sink/mirror area. At one point Jez excused himself and went to the loo. After a while someone piped up, 'Jez has been in there a long time, hasn't he? Should we check on him?'

Someone else shouted through the door, 'Hey Jez, you alright, mate?'

'Hang on, I've had a bit of an accident, I'll be out in a minute.'

While speculating among ourselves as to what kind of accident had occurred, Jez appeared sheepishly in the doorway. 'I had a dump and then flushed the bog and it blocked up and overflowed. There's shit all over the place. I did try to stop it but I couldn't.' Of course, we all started rolling around, laughing hysterically, which further added to Jez's discomfort. 'It wasn't even that big of a poo, just a normal one. Oh, come on, what am I gonna do?' With the toilet starting to reek, Big Pete took control of the situation and went to find one of the assistants, bringing her back to the dressing room. 'Yeh, this young chap here,' pointing at Jez, 'had a mishap in the restroom[6] and the toilet overflowed,' he explained.

'Oh, let me take a look,' replied the assistant, not quite realising what she was letting herself in for. A few seconds later she came back and, to a blushing Jez, said, 'Yeh, that is quite the mess. How does a little chap like you block up the john? What DID you have to eat last night? Let me get one of the janitors to come and clean it up.'

The rest of the day went without any more *shit* happening to us and we played 'Severina' and 'Wishing Well' to a live studio audience and millions of homes across America. On air, Joan Rivers presented me with a bottle of black nail varnish while Simon and I presented her with a bouquet and a bottle of Blue Nun. Lucky Joan. All a bit tacky, to be honest, and our appearance didn't seem to do our profile much good in the US – nor Joan Rivers, as she was fired just two weeks later and replaced by Arsenio Hall.

A few days later we were in Nashville, playing at a bar the size of my downstairs toilet called the Exit-In. We'd made the long drive from Chicago the day before and were looking forward to an evening off. What did we do? Go and explore the city, see the sights, take in the local colour, catch some authentic country music? Of course not, we convened to one of the rooms in the hotel and all dropped LSD. Eds, our monitor guy, had never done it before, his drug of choice being a Big Mac, as evidenced by his sallow and spotty complexion. He'd only ever read one book in his life and that had been *The History Of McDonald's*. He loved McDonald's and that is ALL he ever ate. Anyway, he was persuaded this particular evening to join us and partake. With the party in full swing and the acid in full effect an hour or two later, somebody came in and started chopping out lines of cocaine. Eds was encouraged to snort his first ever line and as he was tripping he was game for anything. A communal cheer went up as he stuck the rolled-up dollar bill up his nostril and inhaled. A few minutes later, he uttered the immortal words that were to become our tour mantra: 'Coke is shit, I'm gonna stick to acid.' Fair comment.

As I mentioned before, the venue in Nashville was tiny, with the entrance down a small alleyway. The buses and truck couldn't get any closer than half a mile away, which presented a problem for even getting the backline there. Amps and flight cases had to be rolled through the streets to the venue. I don't know whether it was the comedown from the acid trip the night before or because we only attracted a handful of people despite it being a free gig, but it was the nadir of our touring experience to date. Usually under such circumstances we'd find some reserve of energy somewhere and make the most of it. But not tonight. We were rubbish, the venue was rubbish, the audience spartan and unresponsive. The only saving grace was there was hardly anyone there to witness it. If I told you that we've never been back to the 'Country Music Capital Of The World' since then you may get some idea as to just how bad it was. Back at the hotel after the show I was bemoaning our lot to Tony Perrin and telling him I was thinking of packing it in and going home. I didn't see the point of travelling all the way there to play to no one. I went to bed that night very despondent and as low as I'd been since we'd started the band. And woke up the next morning not feeling much better. I boarded the bus and found a seat away from the others, wanting to be quiet and… sulk. Perrin came to sit next to me. Not wanting him to I asked, 'What do you want?'

'Do you want some good news?'

'What, we're leaving Nashbloodyville?'

'I received a call this morning from Martin Horne.[7] U2 want us to support 'em in Leeds and Edinburgh in the summer.'

'What? I mean, how? Why?'

'Apparently Bono really likes *God's Own Medicine* and has person-ally asked for you.'

'Wow, that's great,' I replied, cheering up rapidly, 'that's summat to look forward to – but why only the two shows?'

'Because Larry Mullen and The Edge *don't* like *God's Own Medicine*.'

'What about Adam Clayton?'

'He doesn't get a vote.'

Within minutes my demeanour had changed from desolation to euphoria. Moody bugger. Watch out Atlanta, we were on our way.

A few nights later we find ourselves in New Orleans. This was my first time in the 'Big Easy' and in the afternoon before soundcheck we trawled the bars of Bourbon Street and ate gumbo. As you do. We were in the city less than 12 hours and Mick had befriended the local chapter of the Hells Angels and gotten us all invited to their clubhouse after our show. Again, we dropped acid and Simon and I ended up in a cage on the dance floor, simulating gay sex. Think about that for a moment. We were in a Hells Angels clubhouse being watched by Hells Angels simulating gay sex. It took an awful lot of persuasion on Mick's part to get us out of there in one piece. 'Ah, they can't take their drugs, them two. They don't mean any harm, they're just stupid,' he explained as he hustled us out the building. Back in town at the waiting bus, Simon and I then took it upon ourselves to jump up on the bonnets of parked cars and run over the roofs before jumping off the back onto the bonnet of the next parked vehicle. A police car pulled up and once again Mick had to talk them out of carting us off to the local nick for the night by explaining that we had to be in Houston, Texas, the next day for a show. They told us we had exactly 20 minutes to get everyone on the bus and be outside the city limits. They followed us out of town to make sure we were.

The tour rolled on through Texas, mayhem accompanying our every step.

In Houston, I got asked to leave the hotel in the middle of the night and had to go and sleep on the bus – having to wake up our bus driver, Archie, who was not best pleased – after a noisy 2 a.m. skinny-dip splish-splash in the hotel pool with a few invited stragglers from the gig. In Dallas, the club was raided for underage drinking while we were onstage. Nothing to do with us really on this occasion but nonetheless we were hurried offstage mid-set, straight out the back door into a getaway car and driven directly to our hotel, where we were told to stay in our rooms with the doors locked until the coast was clear. In Austin, I accidentally poured half a vial of poppers, amyl nitrite, up a poor girl's nose when my arm slipped while in the service of Venus. Fortunately, after extensive showering of her nasal passages, we didn't have to take her to A&E but *le contretemps* certainly put a dampener on our evening together.

Then followed a 36-hour drive on the bus through the desert from Austin to Phoenix, Arizona. For this journey Mark Morris from our support band, Balaam & The Angel, travelled with us. Balaam were/ are a three-piece band made up of Scottish-born brothers – Mark, Des and Jim – who hailed from the Birmingham area. One of several strange things about them was that all three had different accents, Mark being broad Scottish, Des being pure Brum, and Jim a hybrid of the two. Another not-so-strange thing was that they fought all the time, very often resulting in real fisticuffs. The Gallaghers had nothing on the Morrises. I seem to remember during the tour that all three of them turned up for soundcheck at various times with black eyes, a direct result of them smacking the hell out of each other. Man for man they were lovely lads but you had to keep them apart. So, their tour manager asked if Mark could travel with us for the drive to Phoenix. As Mick loved driving trucks and was promised a turn at the wheel by Farley, our truck driver, he wasn't on the bus so we had a spare bunk. 'So yeah, sure, Mark can come with us.'

On the afternoon of the first day of our drive we were all sat in

151

the front lounge of the bus watching films (we had some tour faves, *Spinal Tap*, *Up In Smoke*, *Fast Times At Ridgemont High*, *Repo Man* among them) and of course most of us had dropped acid yet again to while away the endless hours of desert as our only vista. Mark, who like his brothers was not a druggie in the least (boozers, they were) chirped up after a while and demanded, 'Let's watch some porn!' We ignored him but on he kept. Let me explain something here. On a tour bus with entertainment systems there's usually a pretty extensive library of viewing and listening choices. It was VHS in the olden days, followed by DVDs and Blu-rays and nowadays it's all on streaming. Films, TV series, documentaries, music, and of course always a bit of porn. Now, you may not believe this but, being such avowed tour animals, we never watched porn. Certainly not together. Maybe if one of us had commandeered the back lounge for a night we might watch a bit if we were on our own but it was most definitely not a thing we did collectively. Never. Until this fateful day. With his persistent haranguing and our resistance being that of tripped-out acid-heads, we eventually acceded to Mark's demands and let him put some on. And we all got horny. Of course we did. Now, we should have just slunk off to our bunks and taken care of the business in hand ourselves but some bright spark came up with the idea of pulling in at a truck stop and picking up a prostitute. We knew that Archie, the bus driver, availed himself of this roadside service regularly and knew all the places to stop on the interstates. And wouldn't you know it, there was one coming just up ahead. He pulled in, parked up and disappeared. A few minutes later he climbed back on the bus with a Native American woman following him. 'This here is Crybaby. She'll look after you. Treat her good as she's a buddy of mine.' Quite why she was called Crybaby we were never to ascertain. Crybaby looked around at us one at a time. 'What can I do for you boys, then?' No one immediately answered – I think we were all in shock at this actually happening. Being 'Our Glorious Leader', though, I took control of the situation and explained to Crybaby our predicament. And struck a deal for $10 apiece. Crybaby would ensconce herself in the back lounge and we'd all go in one at a time. As I'd done the talking and brokered the deal, I went first. One by the one everybody else on the bus followed me in and out. Except Mark, the twat that had started all of this. He chickened out. Or, more to the point, he saw sense. Once her business was concluded, Crybaby gathered up her pile of tens and exited the bus. No one said a word for hours afterwards. It was either such a great film we were watching or we were all stunned into silence as we were coming down from the acid. The thing is, I know damn well that if Mick had been on the bus with us he would not have let it happen. Without him around we were just numbskulls destined to get into trouble.

We arrived in Phoenix the day before the show with an afternoon off, which most of our party spent hanging out by the hotel pool in searing heat. There were some sunburned bodies that night, I can tell you. I braved the blistering sun for about five minutes before retiring to my hotel room to write 'Kingdom Come' about our escapade in the desert. 'Desert rat, cry me wolf, shedding skin upon your lips...'

Ian Copeland flew in from NYC to join us for a few days. He'd been receiving reports from the various promoters across the South about our ever worsening behaviour and had come to try to talk us back from the precipice. To compound matters, we also had a lunchtime radio show, for KROQ in LA, coming up in a few days that we were threatening to cancel. The task of persuading us that it would be tantamount to ending any hope we harboured of cracking America if we did so had fallen upon Ian. Lucky man, good luck with that.

After the hottest ever show in a packed venue with no AC, where the outside temperature was in the high nineties, we all climbed onto the bus for the overnight drive from Phoenix to southern California. Now the madness that ripped us apart and almost finished the band was really about to begin.

Endnotes

1   Bobbi Flekman and Artie Fufkin are two fictional Polymer record company employees in the classic rock-band-in-America spoof movie *This Is Spinal Tap*. It gets so close to portraying how truly ridiculous touring the US can be that if not for the laughter it'd be a very uncomfortable watch. Ruth Polsky, our dear departed friend and the Sisters' US agent, took the Finnish band Hanoi Rocks to see the film on its release in the US. They all thought Spinal Tap was a real band and on exiting the cinema wanted to go immediately to the nearest record store to buy their *Smell The Glove* album.

2   We'd had to include the addendum 'UK' to our name to avoid confusion with a by-then defunct black funk band out of Philadelphia, named Mission. Later, a couple of times when I flew into the US I was met at the airport by a limousine driver holding up a placard with 'Hussey MUK' printed on it. I'd like to think it was some wag at the record label exercising their sense of humour but I doubt it was – in my experience, Americans generally don't do subtle.

3   US tour buses were a big step up in luxury compared to British ones. They're bigger and plusher, designed for bands to stay on the road for literally months, even years in some cases. They have essentially the same facilities, though: bunks, lounges with TVs and video machines, a small kitchenette area and a toilet. Bus etiquette, however, decrees that you can only use the bus toilet for a number one. A number two is an absolute no-no. If anyone uses the toilet for a number two then the driver refuses to move until someone confesses, then fines the culprit and makes them clean out the septic tank. If no one confesses then the unenviable task usually falls to the tour manager. Much bitching, pointing of fingers, accusations and suspicions usually ensue and the bus becomes a toxic environment for a few days. You soon learn. To circumvent getting caught short while on a long journey with no services or truck stops for miles

Craig and I devised what we call a 'Poo-Kit'. Basically, it's plastic bin bags and wet wipes. What you do is you lift the toilet seat and stretch out a bin bag across the bowl, lowering the seat to hold the bin bag in place. You sit and do your business, using the wet wipes to clean yourself *après* poo, dispensing said dirty wet wipe in the bin bag. Once finished, you lift the toilet seat and take the bin bag and tie a knot in it and then deposit it somewhere secure on the bus (under your pillow is not a good idea) until you get to the next services and find an outside bin to drop it in. You're welcome.

4   Brian Brain Damage, so christened for his propensity to take a lot of drugs. Please see *Salad Daze* for full explanation.

5   This new policy of ours, of course, wasn't to last long, but we did learn to hide away personal belongings and valuables before we allowed the horde access to our dressing room.

6   I've never fully understood why Americans call a toilet a restroom. I mean, does anyone go there to actually rest? I know some spend quite a time on the porcelain throne − our dear Mr Adams, for one − but that's in the sanctity of his own home or hotel room or even a dressing room. But you can hardly call it a rest, can you? He and I have a code. 'I'm off for a Sudoku,' one of us'll declare, alluding to the fact that we both like a good game of Sudoku while perched on the Armitage Shanks. 'What level? Is it an easy, medium, tricky, fiendish or diabolical?' the other'll enquire, and by the answer we know how long to expect the restroom to be engaged.

7   Martin Horne, our UK agent at ITB, just in case you'd forgotten.

CHAPTER 8

I Felt The Heat
In The City Of Angels

PLAYLIST:
1. Hymn For America – The Mission   2. Hymn For America – The Mission
3. Hymn For America – The Mission   4. Hymn For America – The Mission
5. Hymn For America – The Mission   6. Hymn For America – The Mission
7. Hymn For America – The Mission   8. Hymn For America – The Mission
9. Hymn For America – The Mission 10. Hymn For America – The Mission
11. Hymn For America – The Mission 12. Hymn For America – The Mission

After the overnight drive from Phoenix we woke up on the bus parked outside a strip mall in Orange County, south of Greater Los Angeles. We were due to play a club named Confetti that evening. The general atmosphere on the bus was one of escalating psychosis coupled with exhaustion exacerbated by prodigious amounts of drugs. A combustible formula with touch paper doused in lighter fluid just waiting for the ignitive spark. We were on the verge, the powder keg was bound to blow at any moment. And, in truth, it could well have been any one of the four of us. The crew, travelling on their own tour bus, by this point dreaded us even turning up for soundcheck not knowing what state or mood we'd be in. The thing is when I got shitfaced I usually got silly, reckless, amorous and sometimes obnoxious. But I was always a bigger danger to myself than I was to others. Same for Simon; he

156

could be arrogant, patronising and superior, and silly too if egged on, but would never knowingly hurt anyone. I can only ever remember seeing Slink lose it twice and neither occasion was particularly down to consumption of drugs or drink. The first time was when a member of house security at a notorious Midland venue allegedly sexually molested his passed-out girlfriend. Justified. The other occasion was in the dressing room in Toronto the evening he left the band and walked out on us after the first show of a scheduled three-month tour of North America. On that occasion he wasn't justified (we shall come to that later). Mick wouldn't really change with any amount he'd consume; maybe the worst thing he was guilty of would be chewing your ear off spouting a bunch of suspect philosophies. With Craig, it was a darkness that would fall that quite often precipitated violence. Who would you've put your money on to crack first?

One night a little earlier in the tour, Neil 'Spud' Perry of *Sounds*, one of our rare journalist friends, was visiting from the UK and bunking down in the spare bed in Craig's room. Spud, the next day, relayed the story that with each line of cocaine Craig was getting more and more paranoid, convinced that Mick, Simon and myself were in one of the adjoining rooms plotting against him. He had a glass up against the wall trying to listen to our conversations. Eventually conceding that all he was hearing was snoring, he decided then to deal with a small wart he'd had in his ear for years. He disappeared into the bathroom and a few minutes later came back into the room with blood pouring from his ear and down the side of his face. He'd cut out the offending wart with his penknife. 'Got the bugger,' he proudly declared.

Craig absolutely hated the idea we'd be doing any of the drugs without him, to the extent that he'd use the old James Bond trick and pull a hair from his head (so that's where it's all gone), moisten it with his tongue and tie it around the wraps of coke that were stashed away on the bus. He'd do the same across the door of the cupboard where we hid the drugs. If he saw the hair had been broken then he'd know somebody had been in the cupboard while he wasn't around. The same with the wraps. And then all hell would break loose.

This is the scenario Ian Copeland walked into when he arrived in Phoenix. Ian would later write in his autobiography: 'The bass player, Craig, was so strung out that he reminded me of some of the crazier fuckers I'd known in Vietnam.'[1] If only we'd heeded his advice and scheduled a few days off here and there during the tour then maybe we could've avoided what was about to happen. I doubt it though, as we spent our days off in much the same state, if not worse, as our days on.

Tony Perrin had also flown in for the southern Californian shows, meeting us in Orange County. The afternoon before the Confetti show we had a pow-wow on the bus. We were scheduled to play a lunchtime show the next day at the Hollywood Palace for KROQ-FM, followed by a sold-out *normal* evening show at the same venue. We'd agreed to the matinee show because we'd been asked to be in the next Dudley Moore film – *Like Father Like Son* – for which they were gonna film us at the Palace. KROQ had been playing 'Wasteland' on heavy rotation as well as co-promoting the evening show and giving away tickets for the lunchtime matinee for weeks now. A few days, maybe even as much as a week, before the show, the film company cancelled – I can't now remember the reason why – and with our logic being twisted the way it was we decided we didn't want to play the KROQ lunchtime show. We didn't see any point. Their tagline was 'the world famous'. Not with us it wasn't, we'd never heard of it. The fact that we were being told it was Southern California's biggest alternative/modern rock radio station, as well as being a major arbiter of what was *cool* for the rest of the States, held no sway with us. Perrin had informed Phonogram that we were pulling the show, citing exhaustion, and they in turn informed KROQ. Needless to say, the show's producers were apoplectic, threatening not only to never play our records again but also every other artist on PolyGram. Corporate weight was brought to bear on Perrin and Copeland, who were being called at all hours by top brass from both the US and UK record labels, threatening all sorts – 'they'll never work again', 'we'll pull all support for the tour and all future releases' and 'we'll kill the band off if they don't play this show', and so on. We were adamant though. So, that was why both Perrin and Copeland had flown in, to persuade us we were making a huge mistake.

We held a fractious meeting on the bus that afternoon. Voices were raised, grievances aired, accusations made, blame apportioned, with poor old Copeland unjustly getting the brunt of it. At one point our usually unflappable agent was ordered off the bus with Craig right up in his face screaming at him. That left the four of us on the bus with Perrin who, close to tears, was pleading with us. We were very close to him at that time, and would generally listen to and take on board what he had to say. With the promise of an ounce of cocaine to get us through the ordeal, we took a band vote – it was three to one in favour of playing the matinee. Guess who voted against? The touch paper was being lit.

The Confetti Club in Orange County was another hot, sweaty and late show, with us getting out of the venue at about 3.30 a.m. In an act of appeasement for what I considered a crummy perfor-mance, from the stage I offered to put everyone that wanted to come to the show the following night in LA on our guest list. Dave Kentish, our tour manager, took about 200 names while Perrin and Copeland just stood there shaking their heads in exasperation. We all climbed onto the buses and drove the hour or so up to Hollywood and checked into the Hyatt Hotel on Sunset Boulevard. It must've been 5.30 in the morning by the time we got to our rooms.

The Hyatt on Sunset is one of the most fabled rock'n'roll hotels in the world. Nicknamed the 'Riot House' in the late Sixties and Seventies, the hotel's proximity to the Strip and such popular dens of iniquity as the Whiskey A Go Go and The Roxy made it the favoured hostelry in LA for touring bands, most notably Led Zeppelin, The Who and The Rolling Stones. John Bonham was rumoured to have ridden his motorbike up and down its corridors; the two Keiths, Moon and Richards, both threw their TVs out the window. The Riot House has seen all kinds of shenanigans occur within its walls. We lasted about eight hours before we were ejected. But I'm jumping the gun here.

The crew dropped their bags in their rooms and went directly to the Palace to set up the gear for the soundcheck, which was scheduled for 9 a.m. I maybe got a couple of hours' rest before I had to be up and out again. I know Craig and Simon did a 'througher' – just kept going, fuelled by gak and Jack Daniel's. Lobby call was 8.30 a.m., showtime at midday being broadcast live on KROQ. We arrived at the venue with everybody, band and crew, on the brink. We basically drank and snorted our way through the morning running up to showtime. The whole shebang was careening out of control. The place was jam-packed to its capacity of 1,500 by 11.30, so Simon and Craig took it upon themselves to entertain the waiting throng by dancing onstage – in just their underpants and T-shirts. Not the coolest of introductions to the Hollywood glitterati.

Perhaps surprisingly, the show itself went off without incident. We were, after all, well-practised at playing in advanced states of intoxication and more often than not pulling off blinders.

With the matinee over and with KROQ and PolyGram being kept sweet, at least for the time being, it was time to get back to the Hyatt and try to get some rest before that evening's show. With the buses staying parked up at the venue, I climbed into one of the first taxis taking us back to the hotel. On arrival, I got into the lift with Little Richard, who was famously a resident of the hotel for many years. A little small talk later and after exiting on my floor I was soon in my room. I quickly showered and then climbed into bed, looking forward to an afternoon of slumber. My head had just hit the pillow when the bedside telephone rang. I contemplated ignoring it but its ring was persistent. 'Hello?' It was Kentish. 'Huss, there's been an incident in reception. Craig has been arrested and we're being kicked out of the hotel. The police are coming around to all of our rooms one by one and escorting us out of the building. Get dressed and packed and get rid of any drugs that might be lying around.' Just as I was putting my toilet bag back in my suitcase there was a knock on the door. I opened it to see two police officers standing there, one of whom said, 'I'm sorry, sir, but you and your party are being asked to leave the hotel. We've come to escort you downstairs to the lobby.' In the lobby I found the rest of our touring party all standing around or sat on their suitcases, looking disarrayed and ashen-faced. 'What's happened?' I asked someone, anyone. I eventually got the story. Apparently, Craig had come back in one of the later taxis and by all accounts was completely deranged. He had gone to the reception desk and asked for the key to his room. In his befuddlement he'd forgotten his room number, in fairness an easy thing to do when you're staying in a different hotel room every night. The receptionist had asked his name. Craig refused to give it, instead taking off his boots and throwing them at her. He'd then started screaming and shouting abuse at all and sundry. I'd seen this kind of behaviour from him before – and since – and I knew that you just had to let him vent until he was spent and collapsed. The worst thing you could do was try to placate him. But the hotel security had bundled Craig outside. And the police were called. Tony Perrin, who had just laid down to take a nap himself, heard the sirens screaming down Sunset Boulevard. He knew instantly they were heading for the hotel and that something had gone awfully wrong. He jumped up to the window in his room, which overlooked the lobby, and saw Craig standing shoeless in the middle of the Strip, ranting and raving. He watched

161

in horror as the first police car to arrive on the scene spotted Craig obviously out of control and drove straight into our madman bass player, knocking him to the ground. Tony flew down the stairs and out into the street to see Craig lying motionless, half under the police car. He was dragged up onto his feet by two of the police officers, handcuffed and thrown into the back of the second squad car. Tony described the scene, 'I'll never forget his face as he sat there, it was the most terrible expression I've ever seen on any man. He just looked like a wild animal, feral, his eyes were completely crazed.'[2] Sentiments echoing Ian Copeland's earlier observation of Craig. Tony then had to use all his diplomatic skill to convince the hotel manager not to press charges and the police to let Craig go. The manager acceded to Tony's persuasion with the proviso that we immediately, with the help of the police, vacate the hotel. All rooms we occupied were phoned and everybody warned, as I was, that the police were on their way up, which led to a mad scramble; the biggest drug deal of the tour was going down in one of the rooms, and a few of the lads were *entertaining* and told to get rid of their consorts as well as their drugs, pronto. There were some very grumpy Englishmen gathered in the lobby that lunchtime, I can tell you. And that's how The Mission were kicked out of the notorious Riot House within eight hours of checking in.

Taxis were flagged down on Sunset and we made our way back to the Hollywood Palace, where we were still due to take to the stage that evening. By this time the news of our expulsion from the Hyatt had gotten out and KROQ were running hourly bulletins about us alongside their regular news; the *LA Times* was frantically trying to get a statement from Perrin, as were the weekly inkies back in the UK. Even in this pre-internet era the news was spreading fast. Tonight's show was a big one. Sold out, an over-extended guest list full of record industry bigwigs, all the LA media (radio, press, TV) – and David Bowie. And not to mention the 200 people I had invited the night before. There were hordes of people hanging around the car park outside the venue and we had to be smuggled onto our bus to avoid them. We thought we'd gotten through the worst of the day but as soon as we were safely on the bus, Craig was drinking and snorting coke again. By this time, and with the evening show fast approaching, Mick, Simon and myself had sobered up somewhat and, along with Tony, we tried to talk with him, but he was so far gone that conversation was impossible. One of us made a flippant comment and Craig flew into yet another rage, demanding his passport and his exit from the band along with a flight ticket home – NOW. When nobody made any immediate move to accommodate the request of our psychotic bass player, he growled like an animal, slammed his right fist into the window, causing serious damage to his hand[3,] and then stormed off the bus. We took notice of him then. Mick turned around to the rest of us and deadpanned with no hint of irony, 'I guess that means tonight's gig is off.' Perrin followed in pursuit of Craig. When he caught up with him, he gave him his passport, put him in a taxi along with a bunch of cash to buy himself a flight home from LAX, and by the end of the evening Craig was on a plane back to Heathrow.

With queues snaking around the block we had no other recourse but to cancel that night's show, minutes before the doors were due to open. KROQ had the dubious pleasure of breaking the news on air to people listening in their cars en route to the venue and a notice was posted at the entrance to the Palace for those that missed the announcement. We kept our heads down and stayed out the way as best we could. We had the pressing urgency of having to find another Hollywood hotel for the night. But first we held a band and crew meeting in the back lounge on one of the buses and, amid tears and contrition, unanimously decided to carry on with the tour. We only had a week-long run up the West Coast to fulfil before the first leg of the tour was finished, but then we had been invited to open for The Psychedelic Furs in arenas a few days after our last scheduled show in Seattle. And, with all of us huge fans of the Furs, that was something we all dearly wanted to do. With or without Craig. Our man mountain sound engineer Big Pete Turner was an accomplished bass player and agreed to step in for Craig until we could find a more suitable replacement. Dave 'Milky' Millward, who was travelling with us as Pete's PA babysitter, took over front-of-house duties. Seamless. We were due to play in Long Beach the following night but decided to postpone that show so we could rehearse with Pete at the Hollywood Palace which was, amazingly and fortuitously, available. The plan was for us to get up early and spend the day at the Palace going through the songs that could get us through the next few days. But fate was to make one last effort to derail our tour.

After a couple of hours spent calling around the hotels of Hollywood seeking vacancies to accommodate our travelling party, Dave Kentish eventually found one, a couple of miles up on Sunset Boulevard. It was late, around 2 a.m., when we eventually arrived and checked in by which time I had somehow found myself some company for the night. I had met Marilyn and Darcy earlier in the day when the turmoil with Craig was unfolding. They'd followed us in their car and had parked in the hotel's underground car park. Having cosied up with Marilyn earlier, she came with me to my room while Darcy slept in the car. It had been a long, hot, sweaty, stressful day on the bus and I badly needed to shower again. I took off my shirt, my boots and socks and was on my way to the bathroom when I perched myself on the edge of the bed to talk with Marilyn. We were sat apart just talking, Marilyn fully clothed and I had kept my jeans on. I don't recall for how long we were like that, maybe a minute, maybe five, when there was a loud banging on the door. I stood up and asked, 'Who is it?'

'It's the police, open up, please.'

Oh bollocks, here we go again... what now? I undid the latch and started to pull the door open, barely an inch or two, when it was shoved all the way, forcing me to stumble back on to the bed. Two police officers stomped into the room and addressed my guest.

'What's your name?'

'Marilyn.'

'How old are you?'

'Seventeen.'

'Right, stand up and turn around please and put your hands behind your back.'

One of the officers handcuffed her while the other went through the paraphernalia scattered around the room – ciggies, some wine, plectrums, other bits and bobs, but fortunately my drugs were stashed away in a dirty sock. I had no idea what was going on and why they'd handcuffed this poor young girl. What had she done? Marilyn started crying. I stood up and wiped the tears away from her cheeks and then felt an almighty thump in the stomach. One of the cops had whacked me with his ASP[4] and I was doubled over, winded and in some pain. 'Keep your goddam hands off her,' and with that I was pressed hard against the wall, my arms pinned behind my back, and also handcuffed. I still had no shoes or socks or shirt on when we were both led downstairs to the hotel lobby where there were more police waiting for us. Tony Perrin and Dave Kentish were called and woken and told to get downstairs, pronto. Marilyn was sat on one side of the lobby in tears while I was sat on the other with this cop that kept coming up to me and saying, 'You're gonna get at least a year for this.'

'For what?' I thought was a reasonable enquiry.

'For having an underage girl in your room, you scumbag.'

'But she's seventeen', I whimpered in reply.

'That's underage in this state, buddy, and you're gonna get at least a year for this.'

And I remember distinctly thinking, *if I go down for a year then at least I'll have time to write the next album.* I must confess, I was scared witless while sat there handcuffed, shirtless and shoeless, with all these

165

cops buzzing around and a couple of squad cars parked outside, blue lights flashing. It had been barely 24 hours since we'd come offstage in Orange County yet so much had happened since. The thought that maybe we had brought this on ourselves with the acceleration of our debauchery since we'd arrived in the Land of the Free did cross my mind and I remember making the resolution to myself that if I got out of this jam then I'd change my ways. Was it a prayer? Or just fear talking? Isn't prayer born out of fear anyway? I looked across at Marilyn and we exchanged wan smiles. She looked terrified, too. Eventually, we got the story that the father of a young girl had called the police and reported his daughter and a friend had taken his car without permission, and driven to Hollywood to go and see an English band called The Mission. She was 17 years old, had not been to school and not seen since early morning the previous day. The police had gone to the Palace and, not finding the two girls there, had used their uncanny powers of deduction and elicited the information as to our whereabouts. When they found Marilyn in the room with me they'd called the father, saying, 'Come and pick your daughter up, we've found her.' The father arrived at the hotel and parked in the underground car park. The lift opened in the lobby and out he stepped with Darcy.

'I found her; she was asleep downstairs. I recognised the car when parking and took a peek inside and there she was, fast asleep,' he proclaimed.

'So this one here,' the officer pointing at the handcuffed Marilyn, 'is not your daughter? Who is she then?'

'She's my friend,' chimed in Darcy, helpfully.

'Ah, when I phoned I gave both the girls' names. They must've gotten mixed up,' Darcy's relieved father said.

'So, do you wanna press any charges?'

'Nah, no one's gotten hurt and the girls are safe and shall be dealt with at home,' the father coolly, and thankfully, reasoned.

166

Eventually the situation was resolved and the two girls went home with Darcy's dad and I was released from my handcuffs. And then we were asked to leave the hotel – again. The second Hollywood hotel in just over 12 hours we had been ejected from. I was allowed to my room to quickly dress and get my things together, while Perrin and Kentish had the unenviable task of phoning all the rooms and informing everyone in our party that they had to vacate *this* hotel immediately, at about 5 a.m. by this time. I wasn't very popular, I can tell you.

I know the cops had certainly entertained the idea of charging me with *something*, as Marilyn was only 17 and she was in my hotel room in the middle of the night. The fact that we were just talking when the cops burst into my room didn't seem to matter, as it was surmised that if something hadn't already happened between us then it was likely to later. It was kind of accepted and expected that musicians behaved in an extremely immoral and irresponsible way, more so than even movie stars or footballers, and we willingly followed in the footsteps of a long lineage of morally degenerate rock stars. I look back at my promiscuity now, and while I find it hard to regret most of my behaviour – I met some amazing people and enjoyed some fantastic intimate experiences – I do now realise that there were occasions where I very much walked a moral tightrope. The lines were often blurred and with any amount of alcohol and drugs in my system I wasn't always the most discriminating in my choice of partners. All comers were generally welcome and I was usually game for anything and everything. That's not to say, though, there wasn't sometimes a degree of regret in the harsh light of the morning-after, but regret is a consequence, not an action. None of this is an excuse and, as I look back at these incidents today, not something I am proud of.

My awareness of what is right and wrong has changed through the years and with experience.

So, with word having gotten around town of our second expulsion from a Hollywood hotel in less than 24 hours, we were personae non gratae. With no sleep, our bass player missing in action, and no rehearsal with Craig's stand-in, we had no choice but to get the hell out of town. We had taken LA by storm and made quite the noise but not quite in the way any of us – the band, management, record company – had hoped.[5]

Our next scheduled show was in Encinitas, half an hour north of San Diego. We managed to get some rehearsing done with Pete on the bus and during an extended soundcheck. I had an interview to take care of with a local San Diego alternative radio station, so I left Mick, Simon and Pete onstage going through some tunes and I took up a position in the back lounge of the bus, as it was the quietest spot around, and waited for Kentish to collect and bring the interviewer to me.

'Wayne, this is Juna[6] from 66.6 FM Grave-Wave Radio,' Dave said. I stood up to shake her hand but she ignored my mauler and instead lent in and kissed me on the mouth. Okay, so if that's how they do things down here I wasn't complaining, especially as Juna was quite the striking raven-haired beauty. We sat down and she set up her tape recorder but before we started the interview she asked, 'Do you mind if I lock the door while we do the interview? I'd hate to be interrupted.' There was a lock on the door of the back lounge that Juna got up and turned. She set her tape recorder to record. We talked for a bit, with obviously a large portion of the interview dedicated to what had happened in LA over the last couple of days. Once we were finished she turned off the recorder, stood up and, without a word, came and sat astride me and we started kissing. Within minutes we were having unbridled sex. In a moment of quiet there was a tentative knock on the lounge door. It was Kentish. 'Juna, your husband is wondering how much longer you're gonna be?' What!!!?

'Tell him five minutes more, we're just finishing up here,' my entwined paramour casually replied. And without missing a stroke she quickly brought our entanglement to its natural conclusion, after which she straightened her clothes and hair while explaining that she had come to the venue with her husband and daughter and they were both waiting outside for her. And then she left. Wow!

I'm not particularly good looking in the traditional sense, I know that – although I can look good but that is something entirely different – and I am ordinarily quite shy and reserved in normal social situations, believe it or not. Hence the drugs and the drink. It's always been a form of Dutch courage for me. Much like Clark Kent nipping into a phone box and transforming himself into Superman, so it was always the way with me before a show or public appearance – 'Tonight, Matthew, after I've guzzled this gallon of Blue Nun and snorted this hefty line, I'm gonna be Wayne Hussey.'[7] You put someone like me – or pretty much anyone, if it comes to it – on a stage and all of a sudden we're conferred with charisma and an attractiveness, a presence, that doesn't exist if you were to pass us in the street. I remember around the later *Carved In Sand* era, Phonogram employed a stylist to smarten us up – yeah, like we needed it, bah. She asked me who I thought I was most like, my response being Woody Allen. Not for me Clint Eastwood or Sean Connery or any other fine specimen of super hunky, confident, handsome, masculine, 'kill 'em dead with a smoking gun' kinda guys. No, I saw myself more as the neurotic, insecure, obsessive, self-absorbed, pseudo-intellectual, thin-lipped, stick-thin runt with a pigeon chest. But, with a bit of bluff and shades, a big hat and the ingesting and imbibing of ego stimulants, I could transform myself into the 'rock star' some saw me as. I get it; I've always understood and was never under any delusion that I was special. I've always felt preordained to be doing this for a living but never felt special because of it. Lucky maybe, deserving arguably – but special? Nah, not really. There have been times, though – as there have been for all of us, I'm sure – when I've got carried away with myself, usually fuelled by an overindulgence in alcohol and/or illicit substances, with the comedown, the hangover, even more pronounced when I realise what a tosspot I may well have been while under the influence.

I'm sure a fair proportion of the people that were nightly offering themselves to us sexually were no doubt at another show the following night wearing another band's T-shirt and behaving in much the same way. There's no way any of us would've been as sexually magnetic if we weren't in a successful band. We knew that, understood the deal, and as a consequence generally shied away from the more openly aggressive 'groupies'. What a horrible, denigrating thing to call someone anyway, although the term is probably preferable to 'band rat', which was what groupies were called during the big band era. I guess the term 'groupie' covers a lot of descriptive ground, and in the true sense of the word it should mean someone who likes to hang around with groups, bands (which makes me a *groupie*), but it's become synonymous with the offering of sexual favours for the dubious privilege of doing so. I can't imagine anyone deriving any pride in being called a groupie. Unless your thing is notches on your bedpost or writing kiss-and-tell memoirs. We were young lads away from home and let off the leash and finding ourselves in a land o'plenty with all kinds of carnal and narcotic delights readily available to us. Of course we were tempted, and very often gorged ourselves on the proffered fruits. Fame, whether real or relative or even imagined, is a very powerful aphrodisiac.

The show at the El Cortez that night, with Pete on bass, was a raving success. We made him grease back his hair like a Teddy Boy and wear dark glasses, and instructed him to stand at the back of the stage next to the drum kit and not move. It no doubt looked incongruous with Pete being so much taller and larger, and older, than us, but the audience loved it and were fully aware and appreciative of the circumstances. Pete received the loudest cheer of the night when I introduced the band and you could see by his beaming smile that he was lapping it up. Bless.[8]

170

Endnotes

1   Ian Copeland's memoirs were published by Simon & Schuster in 1995 as *Wild Thing*. Not sure of the veracity of some of the things he wrote about us but nonetheless it was a rollicking read. Ian sadly died in 2006, at the age of 57. The last time I saw him was in the early Nineties when he was living in LA and I was invited to a Ride after-show party at his house.

2   As told by Tony Perrin to Neil 'Spud' Perry and taken from *Names Are For Tombstones, Baby*, the Mission biography co-authored by Neil with Martin Roach.

3   When Craig eventually made it back home to the UK it was determined that he had actually broken several bones in his hand right hand during this episode.

4   The ASP is a collapsible baton that is about 7 inches long collapsed and 21 inches extended. These are very nasty pieces of equipment.

5   The LA episode was chronicled in the song 'Hymn For America' on our next album release, *Children*, following this tour. Lyrics reproduced by kind permission of me:

I've felt the heat in the city of angels, dust up on high and the worse for wear
I've seen the lights going down on Sunset, madmen running loose, there's
    murder in the air
So this is America
Love colder than death, working the streets, love doesn't come cheap, so I
    learn how to steal
Religion for sale, buy my way into heaven, sell my soul for a trick, it's not
    worth a great deal
So this is America
I remember her smile and her virgin heart, I remember her tears tearing me apart
I remember my hands, helpless and tied, as they led her away I remember I cried
I've put my life in the hands of a Scream, small-talked and less with legends
    to be

But I carried a torch for the child forbidden, when the heat closed in, they crucified me

So this is America

Dreams don't come easy without any sleep, laid wide eyed and weary on this damned bed of nails

I hit the freeway and step on the speed, head for the desert when madness prevails

So this is America

6   Marilyn, Darcy and Juna are not their real names. In a rare act of chivalry on my part, I've changed them because I want to protect their true identities. And my lawyer advised it.

7   Contestants on the early Nineties TV talent show *Stars In Their Eyes*, at that time presented by Matthew Kelly, uttered the immortal catchphrase 'Tonight, Matthew, I'm going to be...' right before they strode through the sliding doors and clouds of dry ice to 'transform' into one of hundreds of musical stars, including Whitney Houston, Dolly Parton, Elvis Presley and the like. I remember a contestant mimicking Julianne Regan one Saturday evening. Hoots and guffaws resounded in the Hussey household that night, as I'm sure they also did in chez Regan.

8   There are conflicting memories regarding the day and night following the Hollywood fracas. The account here is how I remember it. Some claim we played the Palace the day after with Pete on bass, and that's why we postponed the Long Beach show. I remember postponing the Long Beach show because we needed the day as a rehearsal, and Pete's first show being in Encinitas. I'm not sure after all these years if there is a definitive truth, so in its absence I prefer to recount how I hazily remember events rather than rely on the likewise decidedly dodgy memories of anyone else.

CHAPTER 9

I Still Believe In God But God No Longer Believes In Me

PLAYLIST:
1. Oh, Well – Fleetwood Mac   2. Autobahn – Kraftwerk
3. Master Of Puppets – Metallica   4. Dream On – Aerosmith
5. More Than A Feeling – Boston
6. American Girl – Tom Petty & The Heartbreakers
7. (Don't Fear) The Reaper – Blue Öyster Cult
8. I Want To Know What Love Is – Foreigner
9. Pretty In Pink – The Psychedelic Furs   10. With Or Without You – U2
11. Nightclubbing – Iggy Pop   12. Bullet The Blue Sky – U2

After Pete Turner's debut in Encinitas we boarded the buses for the long overnight drive to San Francisco. I love San Francisco, perhaps my favourite city in the USA, and I've been lucky enough to have spent a little time there over the years. On this occasion, though, we arrived and checked in to the hotel and were then hurried off to a reception thrown for us by the local radio station, Live 105. Not content with shaking some hands and then retiring early to our hotel rooms to lick our wounds and take stock of the momentous events of the last few days, of course we 'partied like it was 1999' and a civil afternoon reception turned into an all-night roister-doister.

173

Among the people who came to pay homage that day were Metallica's Kirk Hammett and Lars Ulrich, who were apparently big fans of *God's Own Medicine*. Their *Master Of Puppets* was a big hit on our ever-expanding bus playlist, Mick being particularly fond of it.[1]

Our show at Wolfgang's in San Francisco the following night is memorable only for the fact that Kirk Hammett joined us onstage for a rampage through The Stooges' '1969' and our own 'Shelter From The Storm', Kirk giving me a piggyback around the stage without missing a note. What a pro.

We became pally with the Metallica chaps over the next couple of years, bumping into them a few times at festivals and rehearsal studios, but James Hetfield was always a little standoffish. Bloody singers, eh? Apart from one time, when we played Nottingham Rock City the evening before they played Donington Festival. An evening off in the city and the whole band came to see us, with James being his usual aloof self pre-show. As soon as we'd finished onstage and gotten back to our dressing room James burst in and exclaimed, 'Fucking hey, man, you rock.' No finer accolade have I ever received.

A couple of nights later we found ourselves at Starry Night in Portland, Oregon. A strange gig inasmuch as halfway across the room a rope-chain was strung out from the stage to the back of the hall, separating one half of the audience from the other. We wondered what it was for since we don't condone segregation at our shows. It transpired that the show was an 'all-ages show' and those under the age of 21, the legal age to consume alcohol in the state, had to stand on one side of the rope, while their elders were to congregate on the other side of the rope, where the bar was stationed and booze was served. Come showtime and one side of the hall was more or less empty while the other side of the rope was rammed. I'm sure you don't need a university education to work out which side was which. There were a few couples holding hands across the divide but essentially Simon was performing to an empty room while big Pete, Craig's substitute, was having the time of his life, hamming it up for the drunken hordes. Me, I was the typical Gemini dual personality that night.

The following night, we finished the first leg of our debut US tour at the Moore Theatre in Seattle. We weren't quite done with the USA just yet, though. We'd been invited to open for The Psychedelic Furs for a slew of shows they were performing in support of their latest album, *Midnight To Midnight*. After Seattle we had more or less a week to kill before we were to join up with the Furs in St Louis. We travelled back to Hollywood to hole up for the duration at the Franklin Plaza Suites. We were, perhaps unsurprisingly, finding it difficult to locate any conventional hotels in the city that would take us, so we were checked in to what were essentially short-lease apartments, each chalet having its own bedroom, living room, bathroom and kitchen area. I loved it, and we were to stay there on subsequent visits to LA over the next few years. Situated on Franklin Avenue crossed with La Brea, just a block north of Hollywood Boulevard, and literally just around the corner from the famous Grauman's Chinese Theatre[2], it was an ideal location for easy access to the freeways – and the sins of Hollywood.

While we'd been in San Francisco and hobnobbing with future dark lords of the thrash-heavy metal scene we'd also met a genteel, young and pretty guitar player by the name of Chris Bocast. Chris boasted that he could also play bass and so it was decided he would replace Pete, who had replaced Craig, for the Furs tour. Chris joined us at the Franklin Plaza and we spent our days ensconced in one of the chalets, teaching him our songs. Speedily christened 'Surf Dog' because of his long blond locks and Jeff Spicoli stoner demeanour and presumed affection for surfing, Chris learnt the set chop-chop, aided by a heap of white powder. We'd then spend our evenings in the niteries of Hollywood, rubbing shoulders and small-talking with fellow celebrants and aspiring legends. On 26 May I celebrated my 29th birthday at the Franklin Plaza. Craig phoned me to wish me a happy birthday, which was the first time any of us had heard from him since he'd freaked out and done a runner back to England. I thought it was a lovely gesture, until I arrived home in Leeds myself a few weeks later to find that he'd been staying in my room and had used my phone and the call had been billed to me. Oh, that Adams.

We'd spent the previous evening at Scream³, and I'd invited all and sundry to the Plaza party. By late afternoon my chalet was chocka and the celebration was in full swing. While I was dragging the mattress from my bed into the living room to make a more comfortable lying area, in walked three of the most beautiful creatures I'd ever seen. I was flying on acid at the time so that may well have had something to do with my perception, but I swear I was dazzled. Brightly coloured clothes with red ribbons tied into their long flowing locks, exotically made up, lipstick, blusher, eye-shadow – one a blonde, another a redhead and the shorter and not-quite-so-pretty-almost-ugly one, a brunette. They found somewhere to sit and I went and sat with them, welcoming them to my temporary abode, thinking I'd hit pay dirt. Then they opened their mouths and spoke... and shattered my illusions. Out come these deep male Welsh voices. I wasn't expecting that. They introduced themselves and it transpired this was my first meeting with Jay and Michael Aston and James Stevenson from Gene Loves Jezebel. I couldn't get over these heavy Welsh accents coming from such luscious, pouting, kissable lips. James is a cockney, but in my addled state I confused him as being Welsh too. I would be put straight a few years later when I met James again and was taken by surprise by the fact he didn't have a Welsh accent at all. Bloody drugs, eh?

Surf Dog made his debut with the band at the hastily rescheduled Fender's Ballroom show in Long Beach on 27 May.⁴ Long Beach is 'just down' the 405 freeway from Hollywood but we made the mistake of leaving for soundcheck just as rush hour started and spent three hours in bumper-to-bumper traffic. We made it just in time for showtime sans soundcheck. It took just 20 minutes to return to the Franklin Plaza after the riotous show.

The following day we made our way to St Louis to join up with The Psychedelic Furs tour. All of us were fans of the band (*Mirror Moves*, their previous album, was another band bus favourite) and we'd crossed paths several times over the years appearing alongside them at a couple of European festivals, their guitar player John Ashton also having produced the Sisters Of Mercy single 'Alice'. By this time the John Hughes film *Pretty In Pink*, named after the Furs song and featuring a re-recorded version of the track, was a big hit, and so the band were riding the crest of a particularly high wave. Obviously, our on-tour exploits had reached the ears of the Butler brothers – Richard, one of the *coolest* front men/singers and a brilliant wordsmith, and Tim, the bass player – and we'd been warned we'd have to behave ourselves or we'd get kicked off the tour. To be fair to the Furs themselves and having supported other bands with American crews and tour managers over the years, it is my observation that, generally, American tour managers, and crew, do like to exercise their *Hitler* tendencies by needlessly throwing their weight around while, mostly, the bands themselves aren't aware of the draconian measures that are being imposed in their name.[5]

Anyway, Richard Butler was trying to abstain from or at least moderate his on-the-road excesses so his tour management implemented a policy for us of NO open drug use anywhere backstage and alcohol to be imbibed only in the privacy of our own dressing room. Of course, at that time we were never ones to abide by rules and such forbidding only added to the fun of partaking. Now… having communicated with Richard while writing this section of the book he does remember the Furs, himself aside, 'carrying on merrily carousing as before' with no such restrictions in place. And this is the problem with how the memory works after 35 years because I remember it differently. I *remember* the lecture we received in our dressing room from their tour manager on arrival at the first show in St Louis and the law being laid down. I can only surmise that perhaps Richard wasn't aware of his tour manager doing so and it was an attempt to keep Richard on the straight and narrow. And I remember the rest of the Furs being very sensitive to Richard's desire to keep temptation at bay. So much so that each member of the band alone – excepting Richard – would join us in our dressing room at various times throughout the day for a surreptitious alcoholic and/ or pharmaceutical top-up, whichever was their fancy. Guitarist John, sax player Mars (who would join us onstage a couple of times over the ensuing years when we hit NYC) and keyboard player Roger O'Connell would leave our inner sanctum suitably refreshed.

Roger was a strange duck. He'd just been offered the keyboard job with The Cure and so these were his last shows with the Furs before he toddled off to join up with Robert Smith and cohorts. His heart really wasn't in it anymore, and he was voluble about it, to the extent that I seem to remember him wearing a Cure T-shirt on stage on occasion. If he'd done that to us, he'd have been unceremoniously booted off the tour bus in the dark on a godforsaken back road in the Middle of Nowhere, Wyoming. Not that I'm the vindictive type or 'owt. I would get to know Roger a bit better in later years, while he was playing with The Cure, and we ended up getting on just fine, but my first impression of him was of being a Judas, I must say. I think my memory may have been coloured by how I felt at the time – despite my own track record of jumping from band to band, I always wanted to be in a group that was the proverbial last-gang-in-town, where we all had each other's backs, where we all lived together like The Beatles did in their film *Help*, where we'd all go out clubbing together, and believed we were the best band in the world. That *was* The Mission in 1987.

Surprisingly, or not, I have very little memory of this particular leg of the tour. I do remember being warmly welcomed by the Furs and their entourage, albeit receiving the anti-drug lecture in our dressing room upon arrival.

There were a couple of things that stood out. Earlier on the tour Mick had bought himself a Harley-Davidson motorbike, which was being shipped back to the UK with all the PA and lighting equipment we had stupidly brought with us. During the Furs dates, Mick had found a nearby Harley-Davidson shop and bought himself a few biker accessories. Returning to the hotel, he excitedly tried on his new clobber. Picture this: I was in my hotel room relaxing, maybe watching a bit of TV or reading a book. There's a knock on my door. I open it. There's no one there. 'Tada!' Mick jumps out from behind the door in front of me. He's stood there in the hotel corridor with a Harley-Davidson-monogrammed leather cap atop his head, sunglasses, long black leather Harley gloves, a pair of white socks and his newly purchased black leather Harley underpants. He looked more like a member of the Village People, if truth be known, than the hardened motorbike-riding road-warrior he aspired to be. 'W'orr you think?' he asked. Speechless, I was. With that, Simon, who was in the room opposite to me, opened his door to check what all the kerfuffle was and, seeing Mick, just started laughing. As you would. But when Simon had opened his door a cross breeze had been created and the door to Mick's room, which was next to mine, had slammed shut. 'Oh, fucking 'ell, I've been locked out. Can one of you go downstairs and get me a new key card?' he pleaded. Me and Si looked at each other, smirked, and both shut our doors on Mick, leaving him stranded in the corridor. 'Oh come on,' he was begging, 'I can't go down to reception dressed like this, ya twats.' Needless to say, neither Simon or I felt inclined to rescue Mick from his embarrassing plight and he did, indeed, have to venture down in the lift to reception, looking like an extra from Al Pacino's 1980 film *Cruising*.

Another prevalent memory was that Surf Dog used to *run* onto the stage and wave at the audience at the beginning of our show while Simon, Mick and myself would casually saunter on, affecting nonchalance. We put it down to him being American and us being Brits. I think Americans are so much more adept at *playing* the rock star than us Brits, who feign slight embarrassment at so much fuss being made of us. We love it really but can't be seen to. And, to totally contradict myself, another prevalent memory I have of that tour is Simon and I completely trashing our dressing room at Radio City Music Hall in NYC. We were playing two nights at the fabled venue and inexplicably we took it upon ourselves to *wreck the joint* after our first show. I remember us doing it gleefully, not through anger or frustration or disappointment, just downright wilful, giddy vandalism. We were laughing at each other as we did so and egging each other on to even greater acts of destruction. Stupid idiots. We deserved to be kicked off the tour for such wanton hooliganism but after some delicate negotiation with the powers that be, we were allowed to play the second night, with the proviso that Simon and I were only allowed into the building under escort five minutes before showtime and had to leave as soon as we came offstage. The stuff you can get away with when you're in a band. Any other occupation and we'd have been quite rightly thrown in jail for such behaviour.

We played our last show with the Furs in Columbia, Maryland, on 17 June and bid them fond adieu before boarding a flight back to the UK. We had been in the US for just over two months. We were bloodied and bowed and one man down, but we'd defeated the odds, and the gods, and we'd made it. It was the stuff from which legends are hewn, fables are honed, brands are forged and *careers* are made. Not for us though – America never really forgave us. We'd 'raped and pillaged' – figuratively speaking, I hasten to add – our way across the Land of the Free at a time when conservatism was perhaps at its zenith. 'Just Say No', they preached. 'Just Say Yes, and lots of it, please', said we. Within a year or so a new 'hair' band from LA called Guns N' Roses broke big, expounding essentially the same life philosophy as ours, only they were greeted as saviours of American rock'n'roll. Again, I tell you, we were ahead of our time.

We dragged Surf Dog back to Britain with us as we had some fairly big shows coming up and we weren't sure what state we'd find Craig in on our return. However, during his time lolling around at home while we were toiling away in the States, he'd put himself back together somewhat. Most strikingly he'd had a haircut. Gone were the unkempt, manky locks and in their place was a neat, short and tidy middle-aged hair do, which only really served to accentuate his thinning pate. He also had a healthy tan, having been to Greece for a couple of weeks of sun and ouzo with Stevie Sex-Pistol. He'd also sworn off the white powders, which didn't last long but it's the thought that counts. Of course, he was welcomed back with open arms and poor ol' Surf Dog had to sit around for a week or so watching us rehearse, perhaps hoping that Craig might fall off the wagon again. We did try our best to test Craig's resolve but he held firm, at least for the time being. We also briefly entertained the idea of keeping Surf Dog in the band as a third guitar player, alongside both Simon and me, but we soon realised that four was the perfect number for us as a band. We weren't Blue Öyster Cult. So, Surf Dog returned to San Francisco, no doubt disappointed that his time with The Mission had come to an end so soon, but we kept in touch with him, and he would always turn up when we played in the Bay Area and it was always lovely to see him.[6]

Now back on our home turf, first up for us, on July 1, was supporting U2 at Elland Road, Leeds United's football stadium. This was a huge moment for us all but particularly for Craig and Mick, who were natives of the city and bonkers-mad supporters of 'super' Leeds United getting to play at the stadium they'd seen their team play at on many an occasion. It'd be like me playing Liverpool's Anfield, or the Gallagher brothers playing Maine Road,[7] Manchester City's famous old stadium before they moved to the soulless Etihad Stadium. Monumental.

U2, of course, were perhaps the biggest rock band on the planet at this time, having recently released *The Joshua Tree* (in March 1987) – their first album since their headline-making appearance at the Live

Aid concert held at Wembley Stadium, London. *Joshua Tree* was the album that took U2 from contenders to the stratosphere and it's since sold in excess of 25 million worldwide. I was one of those 25 million. I ended up making 'With Or Without You' my single of the year in one of the annual music paper polls. I had never really been a fan of U2 and wouldn't count myself as one now, but I do like some of their singles and having seen them for the first time at Brady's in Liverpool and then next time at the Liverpool Empire and then several times at stadium level, I have to admit they've always put on a mighty show. So, we were supporting U2 in front of 40,000 people, our biggest show to date. How did we prepare? How else; we got drunk in the Dragonara hotel bar before we boarded the bus to the stadium.

As we were pulling into the stadium someone spied a street vendor with a life size cut-out of me. 'Come an' 'ave yer photo taken wi' Wayne 'Ussey, only 50p,' he was hollering. 'Stop the bus, stop the bus!' hollered I. I clambered off, borrowing 50p from Tony Perrin en route, and walked up to the guy. He looked at me, looked at his cut-out and grinned. I handed over my 50p and he said, 'Yer kiddin'?' I wasn't. I had my photo taken with the cardboard *me* outside of Elland Road, with crowds milling around and gawping. I wish I still had that Polaroid but I don't – it was lost somewhere in the mists of time, like so much memorabilia and ephemera that has disappeared over the years.

Sandwiched between The Fall and The Pretenders, our show was – as expected, considering our early afternoon inebriation – a shambles, but I felt comfortable and in my element up on that stage in front of that huge crowd. I wasn't cowed at all by the size of the audience, never really have been, although I was sickeningly nervous before we went on. But the same can be said whether I'm playing in front of 40,000, 4,000, 400 or 40. Even more so in front of four, probably. *I could get used to this*, I thought, as I trod the same boards as Bono, Chrissie Hynde and Mark E. Smith that day. After our chaotic performance – which seemed to go down pretty well judging by archive footage that was discovered in recent years in Craig's parents' attic ('Hey mate, was that Polaroid up there by any chance or my long-lost letter from Kate Bush?') – we were led to a backstage ligging area, where I was introduced to John Paul Jones. I shouldn't really need to tell you this but I will just in case you've been living in a cave with no communication with the outside world for the last 50 years. JPJ, as we affectionately called him, was bass and keyboard player in the almighty Led Zeppelin, a favourite band of mine in my youth and with whom I had fallen in love again around that time, when it started to be cool again to like 'em. JPJ had been suggested to us by Charlie Eyre, our A&R gadgie at Phonogram, as the possible producer for our next album. In fact, a few suggestions had been thrown at us, but none that took our fancy – that is until JPJ was mentioned. We had previously met up with Charlie's favourite, Peter Collins, in a studio in Toronto where he was producing the new Rush album, and while I did like him – not Rush, mind you – the death knell was sounded for our prospective collaboration when he suggested we routinely get up early each day and work in the studio from 10 a.m. to 6 p.m. Did he not know us? That *really* wasn't our style and we all found the idea deplorable. In hindsight, overlooking Tim Palmer, who had co-produced *God's Own Medicine*, was perhaps not our best move and certainly not fair on Tim. While our snub certainly didn't hinder the trajectory of Tim's musical career I know from speaking with him since that he was hurt he wasn't considered for our sophomore album. I don't blame him, but we did return to Tim a few times later on down the line and he and I are still good friends to this day (at time of writing, 23/3/22 if you're asking), 39 years since we first met and worked together at Utopia Studios. In our defence we were being offered the chance to work with one of our musical heroes from our youth and at that time I was enamoured with meeting my heroes. Still am. Anyway, I was introduced to JPJ for the first time and the first words out of my mouth were, 'What about Willie Dixon then?'[8] JPJ just quietly laughed, and despite my best efforts to sabotage our relationship from the off we ended up getting on fine and promised to meet again to discuss him producing the band.

While The Pretenders were onstage entertaining the masses, I went out to one of the stands where my mum and dad were sitting; they'd travelled up from Bristol to proudly watch their son drunkenly cavort around the stage in front of 40,000 people. Once I'd said my hellos I then made to make my way backstage to our dressing room. Uh-oh. I didn't have my pass on me. Like royalty who never carry cash, over the years I had developed the habit of rarely carrying my backstage pass. Arrogance, I suppose, assuming that most people working at the venues we played should know who I am. I only ever ran afoul of this conceit once or twice, and this was one such occasion. Argue and cajole as much as I could, the two man-mountains guarding the entrance to the backstage area wouldn't let me pass, claiming I was a Bono imitator. I've had many insults hurled my way over the years but that one was perhaps the cruellest and still hurts deeply. Smirk. Stevie Sex-Pistol was with me, supposedly looking after me, and he remonstrated on my behalf too and showed them his own pass. But try as we might, they could not be persuaded. A crowd of people started gathering around asking for autographs and suchlike and began beseeching the security guards on my behalf. 'Don't you recognise him, he's just been onstage. He's the singer in The Mission,' they chorused. Nada. In the end Stevie had to leave me, rush backstage, pick up my pass[9] and then come back and rescue me from the ever-growing surrounding throng. That taught me another valuable lesson I later chose largely to ignore.

I did watch a bit of U2 that day and was impressed. They were perhaps at their most potent during this period, when taking that next step from arenas to stadiums. They still had the hunger for it. I saw them again in the São Paulo Morumbi Stadium many years later and by then they had been playing stadiums for a couple of decades and had the whole thing down pat – it all felt very staged and rehearsed and was slightly boring. But not in 1987. Very few bands can success-fully make that transition from indoor venues to stadiums; most lose some edge the bigger they get. Some of the bands that, in my opinion, have succeeded are, of course, U2, Radiohead, Queen, Depeche Mode, and, on their good nights, The Cure. Some that haven't are… shouldn't go there, should I, if I wanna keep my friends.

After the show we made our way back to the city-centre Dragonara, where we were greeted by family and friends who'd come back to the hotel for an après-show tipple. I was in the lift, which was already full with my very own little entourage, and just about to hit the 'close doors' button when I heard this voice from across the hotel lobby shouting, 'Please, hold the lift, I want an autograph!' Being the ever-obliging sort and fancying a little bit of adulation in front of my folks and friends, I held the lift doors open for the young lad to scamper across and join us before we ascended. He made it, his hands shaking as he handed me a pen and a programme from that day's show, and asked, 'Can you please sign this for me?'

'Yeh, sure,' I replied.

'Aw, great, can you make it to Peter please, Bono?'

Now, in normal circumstances I wouldn't have done it but because I had an audience I grabbed the pen and programme and, in my best Irish accent (which is really not very Irish at all), said, 'Sure thing, kiddo', and scribbled '*To Peter, keep the faith, love Bono. x*'. When the lift stopped at the hotel reception the young lad exited, beaming and thanking me profusely, 'Thank you, Bono, that was a great show today.'

'Aw, ta,' I replied. 'May the road rise up to greet youse, la.'

The lift doors shut and we all burst into laughter. My mum often reminds me of this incident when I'm at hers and moaning about having to sign a pile of new albums or photos. 'You should be thankful that somebody's interested enough to want it. Remember that time you pretended you were Bono to cover up your embarrassment at

185

not being recognised as you?' Mmm, mother always knows best, eh, and there's no pulling the wool over her eyes. I've often wondered since if that young lad ever came to know that it wasn't Bono that signed his programme that day? I hope not. And where does this idea that I'm imitating bloody Bono come from? It's the other way round, I'll have you know.

We played a bunch more festivals over the month of July, including closing the Orange (main) stage at Roskilde following The Pretenders, Iggy Pop and Echo & The Bunnymen. I ended up staying on for the next day to see our ol' muckas The Cult perform and I joined 'em onstage to play guitar on a couple of songs. It was only halfway through the second song that I looked down at the borrowed guitar and realised I wasn't even plugged in. No wonder I couldn't hear myself. Bastards.

Then we played the inaugural Bizarre Festival in Germany over two days: the first in Berlin and the second at one of my favourite festival locations, Loreley. Craig and I had previously played there with TSOM in 1984, sixth on a bill of seven which included Frank Zappa, Rory Gallagher, The Waterboys, and Blancmange! The Loreley amphitheatre is situated on the top of a steep slate rock on the bank overlooking the River Rhine in the town of Sankt Goarshausen. The backstage area boasted spectacular views across the Rhine Valley. The Mission were third on the bill this time, to headliners Siouxsie & The Banshees and Iggy Pop. There was a strong ex-Liverpool contingent there that day as I got to meet up with Budgie, the drummer with the Banshees, and Julian Cope, who performed before us, both of whom I had known from my Liverpool days. As good as it was to catch up with them though, it wasn't them I was dying to meet. It was Iggy Pop. I've been a huge fan since I first saw him at the Bristol Colston Hall in the mid-Seventies. Iggy has always been such an energetic and intense performer and, being very close to the lip of the stage that night, I was within striking distance as he smashed up a chair. I suppose it seems quite tame now compared to some of the stuff I've witnessed since, but at the time I was an impressionable youth and the energy that rolled off that stage was terrifying as well as immense. I first got into his two Bowie-produced albums – *The Idiot* and *Lust For Life*, two classics in my opinion and both released in 1977 – which led me to investigate his back catalogue with The Stooges. Life altering. Punk was changing the guard and Iggy was at the forefront as one of the few, along with Bowie and Bolan, still highly regarded by the new wave, and so out went my Barclay James Harvest and Wishbone Ash albums and in came Iggy & The Stooges, Television, Talking Heads, Blondie, etc. We'd already played with Iggy at Roskilde and shared a backstage area, but saw hide nor hair of him. Some people might think backstage areas are one big lig where everybody is socialising with everyone else but that's mostly not the case. There are areas *outside* the dressing room area where the liggers – personal and business guests and the media – congregate, but there's no access to the inner sanctum unless you have the correct specific pass. I very rarely left the dressing room area at festivals after the U2 Elland Road debacle and if I did, I made sure I had my pass. When we first started playing at festivals we did like to arrive early and hang around thinking that we might be able to meet up with the other bands but in my experience not an awful lot of socialising goes on backstage at festivals, certainly not as much as you might imagine. Or maybe it was just other bands didn't like us and tried to avoid us. Most bands keep themselves to themselves and tend to hide away in their own Portakabin, maybe popping their head out the door when they're smoking a fag, or you might bump into someone coming out of the portaloo you're waiting to go into. And the headliners very often have their own secluded area, which none of the other bands have access to. None of that mixing with the riffraff. In fact, we quickly learnt that hanging around backstage at a festival is actually very tedious and dangerous for your health, so the higher up the bill we were, the later we'd arrive, sometimes timing it so we'd arrive just before we were due onstage, and then getting away as soon as our show had ended and the audience were still cheering for an encore. All the big bands do it.

So... we were backstage at the Bizarre Festival in Berlin and Craig and I were stood facing Jez, our guitar tech, with me imploring him, 'Can't you get one of Iggy's roadies to see if we can go and meet Iggy?'

'Dunno, mate,' replied the little sod, a gleam in his eye and a smirk on his face. With that I felt a tap on my shoulder and turned around to face the outstretched right hand of Iggy Pop. 'Hi, I'm Jim, you're Wayne, aren't you? I love that opening line of your album, "I still believe in God but God no longer believes in me".' Bloody 'ell, Iggy Pop knows who I am and has heard our album!

There are photos of that first meeting, probably taken by Jez – I'll try to find one for this book. A rabid conversation and a friendship ensued. I spotted Iggy the next day at Loreley, his dressing room caravan next to ours, and watched while he worked his way through his pre-show exercises and stretches. 'Hey, Wayne, how's it hanging?' he asked me.

'Err, not as well as yours, mate, by the looks of it. Do you do this for every show?'

'Yeah, man, gotta prepare.'

That man has boundless energy and puppy-dog enthusiasm, and really *prepares*.

Jim and I stayed in touch with the occasional phone call and annual exchange of Christmas cards for a few years, and he would come and see The Mission when we played in NYC and I would, of course, go and see him when he was in town. He came to see us when we played at The Ritz in early 1988. We had an evening off the following day, so he and his lovely wife (at the time), Suchi, invited me to their apartment. On arrival Jim, with evident great pride, proceeded to show me his paintings – a recently newly taken-up leisure time activity – which were a bit Van Gogh-like if memory serves, a visual representation of Iggy himself as I knew him, great slabs of vivid, vigorous colours teeming with exuberant life. While I was sat on his couch he grabbed an acoustic guitar and, bouncing on his haunches in front of me, proceeded to play and sing me a song he'd just written. Sadly, I can't remember what it was and I didn't recognise it on any of his albums that followed over the next few years, but imagine that scene, will you? Iggy singing a new song for an audience of one. Me. How thrilling that moment was. We then went out for dinner at a local favourite restaurant of his and Suchi's. Great company – so warm and funny and so many great stories.

Perhaps the next time I saw Jim was when he was playing at Brixton Academy, just before Christmas 1988. I went along and loved the show, and afterwards made my way upstairs to the after-show bar at the venue. I was stood there chatting with some folk when a burly security guard tapped me on the shoulder and asked me to follow him. Him being twice the size of me, I wasn't about to argue. He led me through the horde that was clamouring to get backstage and into a quiet corridor. We stopped at a black door that had a white star painted on it and he gently knocked. The door opened an inch or two and an eye appeared in the gap. 'Oh, come in, Jim is expecting you', as the door was flung open by Chrissie Hynde. The security guard bade his farewell and made his way back to his post, keeping the hoi polloi at bay. I entered the dressing room. The only people there were Chrissie, Suchi and Iggy, attired in a white dressing gown with *Jim* monogrammed across the breast. He bound across the room and gave me such a big welcoming hug. I do love that man. So generous with his spirit.

I'd met Chrissie a couple of times previously, the first being when the Ded Byrds[10] supported The Pretenders at Eric's in Liverpool in 1979, and our paths had crossed again when we'd played with U2 and at Roskilde. By 1988 she was well on her way to being the legend she is, Iggy already having that status conferred on him.

And, I don't wanna go all *Wayne's World* on you, but I was sat there feeling *I'm not worthy.* Now, I guess there must come a moment in each *successful* musician's life when you feel like you *belong* at that top table. I can't claim that has ever happened to me. I was sat there with Iggy and Chrissie and the thought kept going through my mind: *This is rarified air, I don't belong here, I'm only here by invitation.*

We chatted for a bit, just the four of us, and then it was time for me to leave and head out into the cold December night and flag down a taxi to carry me home. The next morning *Melody Maker* and *Sounds* published the results of their annual readers' polls and me and The Mission completely swept the board. Again. Just saying.

After the Bizarre festivals in Germany we played a few more shows before ending our summer sweep through Europe at the Murrayfield Stadium in Edinburgh on August 1, again in support of U2. It wasn't quite the drunken, shambolic performance we'd put on at Elland Road – we were maybe a little more moderate in our pre-show drinking – but nonetheless we seemed to nicely warm up the multitudes patiently waiting for the newly crowned Irish rock deities. After our show we were sat in our backstage Portakabin dressing room, enjoying a celebratory drink, smoke and line, when there was a knock on the door. Stevie Sex-Pistol opened it and some chap handed him a piece of paper and in a gentle, sing-song Irish brogue said, 'This is for Wayne from Bono.' Stevie handed me the note, an invitation for me to join Bono and U2 in their hotel later.

We didn't hang around until the end of the U2 performance that night, leaving as they played 'Bullet The Blue Sky'. We were learning that it was better to get out of there before the mass exodus that could get you caught up in traffic for hours after a show of that magnitude. All the big bands do it.

We went back to our hotel and freshened up before Stevie and I caught a cab over to where U2 were staying. The security at their hotel was draconian. They'd completely block-booked the hotel, so only U2, their families, friends and crew were staying there that night. There was obviously a throng of waiting fans outside, who roundly ignored me when I arrived, hoping for a glimpse of our Irish brethren. So much for that Bono lookalike notion. We showed our passes (I remembered mine this time) and we were permitted to enter the inner sanctum. Then we were led through to a large bar area, where-upon entry Bono spotted us and came over to introduce himself. He took us around and introduced us to several more people, including other members of the band, The Edge and Larry Mullen Jnr. Both were very polite and gracious, although conversations were brief. Adam Clayton wasn't there, apparently entertaining in his room. We ended up sat in a corner away from the noise of the revellers and we got Bono all to ourselves for the next hour or so. He was attentive, warm, smelt rich and was very generous with his time, I have to admit, and sitting there with 'the biggest rock star in the world' we got the full-on Bono charm offensive. I liked him, and my memory of our meeting always salvages my opinion of him whenever I see or hear him being the patronising public persona *Bono* that he often chooses to show to the world. From the little time I spent with him, I'd say that underneath the bluster and bore beats a genuinely kind heart. We talked for a while, about what I have little recollection, but things started to get a little weird when the acid started kicking in. Both Stevie and I had dropped tabs in the taxi on the way there. The two of us decided that we should leave before we started crawling around licking the carpet and making fools of ourselves. That just wouldn't look good, would it? We bade our farewells, with a peck on the cheek for me from 'the greatest living Irishman'. Rather than head for the safety of our hotel, we instead found a club to patronise. Presenting our U2 passes, we got in for free and were shown to a booth in a roped-off VIP area and a magnum of champagne was brought to our table. 'With compliments of the management. Will the rest of the band be joining you this evening?' chimed the waiter.

191

'No, it's just the two of us,' replied Stevie. 'Well,' the waiter said, looking directly at me, 'we're honoured to have you here this evening, Bono.' Bloody hell.

Endnotes

1   It's a strange phenomenon, but some records which made no sense to us back home in Blighty came to life when played at brain-crushing volume on a tour bus speeding along US freeways and interstates. A bit like Kraftwerk's 'Autobahn' – makes perfect sense when travelling through Germany. Not so much when wending your way through the Yorkshire Dales. Our US playlist started to include cassettes and CDs we'd pick up cheap from the bargain bins at truck stops – Aerosmith, Boston, Tom Petty & The Heartbreakers, Blue Öyster Cult, Foreigner et al. Among my new favourite songs was the new-to-us 'Dream On' by Aerosmith, which we started mucking about with in soundchecks.

2   The historic Grauman's Chinese Theatre is situated on the Hollywood Walk of Fame. The paving blocks in the forecourt bear the signatures, footprints and handprints of famous movie stars from the 1920s to the present day. (Thank you again, Wikipedia.) I have indeed put my hands in Marilyn Monroe's handprints. They were tiny.

3   Scream was an underground LA music venue – very trendy in the summer of '87.

4   We were originally scheduled to play at Fender's Ballroom on May 15 but decided to postpone so we could rehearse at the Hollywood Palace with Craig's stand-in, Pete Turner. The promoter of the Fender's show threatened to sue us so we agreed to rearrange the show for the 27th to avoid a lawsuit on top of all the other shit we had brought down on ourselves.

5   Perhaps the most tyrannical we encountered was the despot that was in charge when we supported Alice Cooper on his 2017 UK arena tour. We were there as a *favour* to help sell tickets, not because we *needed* the

exposure, and because we were all big Alice fans as young teenagers. Imposing a mere half-song soundcheck, none of our guests allowed backstage, not being allowed in catering when Alice or any of or his band were scoffing, and with us being absolutely prohibited anywhere near Alice's backstage area, the restrictions were stringent in the extreme and soured somewhat what should have been a groovier experience. I'm sure Alice himself wasn't aware of any of this and we did at least get to briefly meet the great snake-charmer - even though we had to make an appointment to do so.

6   On his return to San Francisco Chris eventually became involved in ambient music, among other things, and released several lovely albums of that ilk. Chris later gender-transitioned to Chrys, but sadly passed away in early January 2022 after losing a fight with colon cancer.

7   Oasis famously played two nights at Maine Road in April 1996.

8   Led Zeppelin were sued several times for plagiarism. Zeppelin had a tendency to steal riffs, melodies and lyrics and even on occasion entire songs, most notably from Willie Dixon and other old, relatively unknown blues artists, and claim them as their own compositions. Not that I'm one to talk on that score. For evidence of my own culpability of 'borrowing' compare Zeppelin's 'Achilles Last Stand' and The Mission's 'Severina'. For further reading of Zeppelin's pilfering you can go to: https://liveforlivemusic. com/features/just-how-much-of-led-zeppelins-music-was-stolen/

9   You might be wondering why Stevie didn't just let me use his pass and then I'd send it back to him with someone else from the crew once I was safely ensconced in the dressing room. I can't remember why. Maybe they were photo passes; some of those bigger shows sometimes are. But more than likely, in our state of mild inebriation we just didn't think of it.

10   Ded Byrds were a late Seventies Liverpool band I played with – see *Salad Daze*.

CHAPTER 10

To The Manor Born

PLAYLIST:
1. Beyond The Pale – The Mission   2. Tower Of Strength – The Mission
3. Heaven On Earth – The Mission
4. A Wing And A Prayer – The Mission
5. Black Mountain Mist – The Mission
6. Shelter From The Rain – All About Eve
7. School's Out – Alice Cooper
8. *Blankety Blank* Theme – Ronnie Hazlehurst   9. Jeepster – T.Rex
10. Mama Weer All Crazee Now – Slade   11. No Quarter – Led Zeppelin
12. Hellhound On My Trail – Robert Johnson
13. Fabienne – The Mission   14. This Corrosion – The Sisters Of Mercy

Llanthony is a hamlet in the Black Mountains. Hay-on-Wye lies eight miles to its north with Abergavenny some 14 miles to the south. Laying on the outskirts of Llanthony is the Capel-Y-Ffin Monastery. Built in the late 1800s, by August 1987 the monastic orders had long since disappeared into the mists of time and the monastery had been converted into spartanly furnished holiday accommodation. A tall white statue of the Virgin Mary welcomed you with open arms as you arrived at this secluded sanctuary. Just beyond lay the ruins of a church, no roof but parts of the walls remained. A gate where once the church doors had been, opened on to the burial place of Father Ignatius of Llanthony, founder of the monastery. A set of decrepit steps led up to the alter area, now in fascinating disrepair. To the right of the church was the monastery itself. A narrow path curled round its side, past tangles of wild foliage and on past the door of the little chapel, which still held occasional mass, to the exclusive very black back entrance to our temporary abode. The interior was perfectly representative of its ascetic past – all old wood and narrow windows, creaking stairs and doors, low wood-beamed ceilings, small, austere single beds, and a big old wooden table with wooden benches either side, the centrepiece of the downstairs area. The place was reputedly haunted and you could very well believe it. Even on a bright, sunny afternoon, you close your eyes and you could almost hear the monastic voices, 100 years old, chanting down from the hillside into the valley below. There was no telephone, no television, and for entertainment I had only brought a pile of books, a bunch of cassettes with my cassette/radio blaster to play 'em on, and an acoustic guitar. And for company, Stevie Sex-Pistol Watson. Of course, Stevie came stocked up with *supplies* for the duration. We'd spend our days with me working on the new songs and writing lyrics while Stevie kept house, took walks, read his books and popped down into Llanthony every couple of days for wine and groceries – essentially bread and Heinz Toast Toppers – and to call Perrin's office from the local phone box to let 'em know we were still alive. In the evenings we'd crack a bottle or two, share a line or two, smoke, listen to T.Rex or Iggy and play Scrabble. Stevie invariably beat me, the shame of it, being a lyricist an' all...

After the insanity and chaos of the last few months I needed a place to go and repair and, before we started new-album rehearsals later that same month with John Paul Jones, to piece all the bits and pieces of songs together I had accumulated since the release of *God's Own Medicine*. While on tour I had got into the habit of recording our 'jams' at soundchecks. Once soundcheck was done we'd very often start jamming on a riff or a chord sequence one of us would come up with and Pete, our sound engineer, knew to record these jams onto cassette. By the end of the tour I had quite the pile of tapes to sift through. Most of it was just unlistenable, directionless cacophony. We weren't great at jamming. However, there were one or two snippets I thought had something that could be developed into songs. I remember the main guitar riffs of 'Hymn (For America)' and 'Child's Play' coming to us this way. I already had a half dozen songs at various stages of being written, songs that had been demoed in Bristol the previous Christmas, along with further demo sessions in New York when I'd had a spare couple of days, and with Craig and Mick in Berlin when we were there for a few days between shows during the summer (Simon had decided to fly back to the UK for a few very welcome days in the new home he'd just bought, Sunny Cottage in Sheffield). It was a productive period at Capel-Y-Ffin Monastery, honing such songs as 'Beyond The Pale', 'Tower Of Strength', 'Heaven On Earth', 'A Wing And A Prayer', and of course the newly composed 'Black Mountain Mist'. I had to, didn't I, giving full vent to my Zeppelin proclivity. I drove Stevie mad with playing the song over and over, trying to perfect the finger-picking acoustic guitar part. Do a line of whizz and play 'Black Mountain Mist' for three hours. Fun only for me.

It was also absolutely necessary to spend some quiet time ruminating on the events of the past 18 months or so, coming to the conclusion that I, and we as a band, needed to heed Iggy's advice to *slow down a bit*. The band set out on this road with no long-term plan – just a desire to make the music we liked and be able to tour, record a couple of singles, perhaps even an album and, like a shooting star, shine and dazzle brightly before burning ourselves out. Well, that almost happened. We'd almost spontaneously combusted over the last few months, very nearly split up and seriously jeopardised our collective and individual sanities. And once we realised how close we were to the whole damn house of cards collapsing we remembered that, above all, we loved making music together. And wanted, *needed*, to carry on doing so. Everything else was a by-product. For 18 months or so we were being written about, with perhaps a little justification, as the new 'wild men of rock' and, in a way, feeling we had to live up to that notoriety. But by mid '87 I had a child on the way and we had a group of people in our employ, dependent on us for putting food on their tables. We had to take responsibility as a band, to care and look out for each other and the people that worked with us. We had to dial back our excesses if we were to survive another album release and attendant touring commitments. Good intentions an' all that.

After two weeks spent in the tranquil, magical, ancient, transformative Black Mountains we had the pressing urgency of putting together a 6-a-side football team to take part in a 'celebrity' charity event being held at Craven Cottage, Fulham's famous old stadium in west London. I attempted to enlist, as a ringer[1], the Liverpool footballer Craig Johnston. Sadly, he phoned me at the Columbia Hotel a few days before the tournament to inform me that Liverpool's manager, (today Sir) Kenny Dalglish, had forbade his appearing on The Mission's 6-a-side team on the grounds that LFC's injury insurance wouldn't cover him. Bugger. *There goes our chances of lifting the trophy.* As it happens, we narrowly lost to Frankie Goes To Hollywood, drew with the cast of *Coronation Street*, beat Brown's Nightclub, which was a mostly female team, and got hammered by The Housemartins on their way to winning the tournament. We were kitted out in all-black (of course we were) – shirts, shorts and socks, and I wore black woolly tights under my shorts, as it was a bit of a chilly day, if memory serves. Most of us wore sunglasses, too. While the other teams were running through their more 'professional' warm-up routines, we limbered up with smokes and pints. We could use any number of substitutions, which we took full advantage of. We'd run about like crazy men for two minutes before being subbed off, coughing and spluttering, to sit in the stand and smoke a 'recovery' cigarette and take a slug or two of rejuvenating Blue Nun, before being subbed back on to replace another of our ailing teammates. Craven Cottage, at the time, boasted a plastic pitch, very unforgiving if you were to fall down. Nearly all of us came away with what amounted to minor but very sore carpet burns with Tony Perrin coming off worst. At one point Tony was running down the wing with the ball, got tackled and went skidding along the surface on his face. Of course we all fell around in great mirth, but poor ol' Tony had those burn marks on his forehead and the tip of his nose for a good couple of weeks. We played another 6-a-side tournament the following summer at Loftus Road, home of Robert Smith's favourite team, Queens Park Rangers, and fared just as dismally. They were a lot of fun though, those days, and we got to play footie, albeit pretty badly, in proper football stadiums.

On Thursday, August 27, 1987, the day *Melody Maker* hit the streets with my fair countenance once again gracing its front cover, we played a secret warm-up show at The Marquee on Wardour Street supporting our compadres All About Eve. I even joined the Eve's onstage for a strum and a holler through 'Shelter From The Rain', a song to which I had contributed backing vocals in the studio when they'd recorded it, with their producer, ex-Yardbird Paul Samwell-Smith, berating me with 'Could you please be less of a vocal hooligan and tame it down?' Damned with faint praise, but I must confess I was quite proud of that.

Anyway, I was introduced by Julianne as I entered the Eve's stage at The Marquee and was greeted by equal amounts of cheers and jeers, the jeers being mostly good natured and ironic (I hope). I was handed an acoustic guitar and Andy Cousin, their bass player, told me the song was in A minor. I came in with a big strum at the proper moment but was horrendously out of tune. I looked at

Andy who was doubled up with laughter while Julianne looked quizzically at me over her shoulder. Fortunately, being the, um, consummate musician that I am, within a bar or two I had worked out that the song was, in fact, in B minor. After the show Andy admitted he had told me A minor 'to mess you up and make you look stupid'. Tough luck, matey, I can do that all on my own without any help from you.

The next day we headlined the Friday night at the Reading Rock Festival. We'd played the year before as third on the bill to Killing Joke and I hated it and vowed never to play the festival again until we headlined. Well, here we were just a year later. Status Quo headlined on Saturday with Alice Cooper closing the event on Sunday. We were invited to Alice's end-of-festival party but snubbed him. It wasn't like us to turn down a chance to party and particularly with someone that was a musical hero to us when we were young teenagers, so something had to be afoot. That's all I can remember about the 1987 Reading Rock Festival.

Over a free weekend earlier in the summer we'd recorded a version of new song 'Heat' with Tim Palmer. This one weekend was the only break in our schedules where we could get together. I'll let Tim tell you in his own words what happened:

'The studio on Queensway (London) where we recorded 'Heat' was called Marcus, and um, it was a great studio that moved later, but that was its original location. I recorded Robert Plant's *Shaken 'N' Stirred* (1985) there and I was in the middle of recording the basic tracks for *Now And Zen* (1988), which I co-produced for him. It was a weekend, and we sneaked in and used the room I was using to record Planty's album to record 'Heat', and it was a really pressured thing for me because Robert used to want us to take a weekend off. He'd say "Everyone go home and chill out and relax", stuff like that, and of course I was using *our* studio to record with you guys and so it was all very under the radar. And then of course you brought in about a 100 fucking people, partying and drinking, and I was getting more and more freaked out. And of course the worst thing happened. Robert decided to pop by and collect a jacket or something he'd left behind and sees me in the studio with all these people hanging out, and I'm supposed to be on a weekend off so he was really miffed with me. He was fine after a couple of days but yeah, he thought I was taking advantage. And,' laughing, 'anyway you didn't use 'Heat' and ended up recording the album with John Paul Jones, so yeah, it was funny times.'

That was the first time I met Robert Plant, but of course he was quite curt with us, since he thought we were stealing his producer and using his studio time. We were to bump into Robert a fair bit once *Children* was released, more of which later...

The album pre-production rehearsals were held at Nomis Studios in Sinclair Road, Kensington, London; a purpose-built facility just behind the Olympia, set up by Simon Napier-Bell and first opened in the late Seventies. This was pure luxury compared to some of the cramped, grotty rehearsal rooms we'd experienced in earlier days. State-of-the-art, air-conditioned, spacious, well equipped, with sparkling clean toilets and showers, and a fabulous canteen – we were moving up in the world. Paul Weller was in the room to our right and our buddies from San Fran, Metallica,[2] were to our left. I'd love to claim that we got loads of work done while we were there but I do remember there were a couple of days when we turned up and just had breakfast in the canteen and then went back to the Columbia Hotel to sleep off the hangovers from the night before. Other days, when we did turn on the amps and plug in the guitars, we'd spend hours working on our versions of the *Blankety Blank* or *Looney Tunes* theme tunes, or banging through glam rock classics such as 'Jeepster' and 'Mama Weer All Crazee Now'. Of course *some* work was done when John Paul Jones was in attendance. I remember us working with him on 'Beyond The Pale' and getting the arrangement together, complete with the

'No Quarter'-ish intro that made it onto the album. Aerosmith's 'Dream On' was another one we honed ready for recording. After a couple of weeks of the 'Blankety Blank Theme', we were primed and ready to adjourn to The Manor, in Shipton-on-Cherwell, just north of Oxford, to record *Children*, our sophomore album.

Purchased by Richard Branson in 1971 and set up for artists signed to his fledgling Virgin Records label, The Manor[3] was put on the map due to the huge success of Mike Oldfield's *Tubular Bells* (released by Virgin in May 1973) and was soon in high demand among those artists and producers looking to get away from it all and make their music in quiet seclusion. Built sometime during the late 16th century, The Manor and its outbuildings are Grade II listed, and consisted of a two-storey grand stately country home boasting four reception rooms, one of which housed a full-size snooker table, another a ping-pong table, and yet another a grand piano; a dining room that was serviced by a huge wooden banquet table and benches carved from the hull of a shipwreck; a communal living room with a big open log fire that featured ornate French doors which opened out onto the swimming pool area; and eight or nine bedrooms, some with en suites (I bagsied one), which was certainly enough for the band, our two man studio crew, Jez and Nipper, JPJ, and our engineer Mark Stent each to have their own room. There was also a gym which, unsurprisingly, barely got used during our three-month tenure. There was a large kitchen and a wonderful staff to take care of our every whim. The studio itself was situated in a long, low one-storey outbuilding adjacent to the house. And all this set in 26 acres of beautiful gardens and parkland featuring a man-made lake and go-kart track. The property backed up to the River Cherwell, where Ian the gardener lived on a houseboat docked just behind the house. On pleasant evenings you could stroll along the riverbank to the local pub. Not so easy stumbling back in the dark while three sheets to the wind.

Mick and I had been to The Manor previously when All About Eve were there recording their debut album. Mick had played drums on a few of the tracks before they found a drummer – Mark 'Hovis' Price[4] – of their own. And I'd been there to do backing vocals, as mentioned earlier.

When we arrived, we'd parked up outside on a grass verge but, the place being surrounded by a high stone wall, we couldn't find a way into the property, except via a pair of tall, locked gates at the end of the driveway. So we jumped 'em and started walking up the long gravel drive towards the house when Mick nipped my ass and barked 'woof-woof' in an attempt to scare me. 'Ey, Wayne, this looks just like the kind o' place where they'd have big dogs running round,' he opined. And with that, two Irish wolfhounds the size of small horses came bounding down the driveway at us, howling and growling. We spun round and made a mad dash back to the gate and managed to clamber over just before the dogs could sink their fangs into us. We weren't sure they weren't large enough to jump the gate, so we dived into the car and slammed the doors shut, before catching our breath. They were up on their hind legs against the gate, making a right din, when up walked a tall, middle-aged, dark-haired man wearing green Wellington boots and one of those green all-weather gaberdine jackets that gardeners and farmers and Land Rover drivers seem to favour. 'William! Bowser! Get down and be quiet,' and with nary a whimper the two hounds from hell retreated from their attack position and lay prone at his feet.

'Hello, can I help you?' the kindly wild dog tamer enquired. 'Don't worry about these two, they're all bark and no bite, soft as ice cream left out in the midday sun, they are.' Could've bloody well fooled us. We exited the car and warily approached the still-locked gates and introduced ourselves, explaining that we were there to visit our friends, All About Eve. He introduced himself as Ian. 'I'm the gardener and odd-job man around here. There's a small door up there,' he said, pointing up the road, 'with a bell and an intercom next to it. Ring that and someone'll let you in.' And indeed, William and Bowser were to prove perfect canine companions during our stay at The Manor but always caused a terrifying commotion when anyone new turned up.

The pace of recording was the diametric opposite to that of *God's Own Medicine* with Tim Palmer. *GOM* was recorded in a blizzard of amphetamine and 18-hour days in the studio, and all done and dusted within five weeks. It had helped that we'd been playing most of the songs live for six months or so before we recorded them. With *Children* we didn't have that same luxury, even though we had started dropping in several new songs – 'Heat', 'Child's Play' and 'Kingdom Come' – during the summer festival shows. We had played 'Tower Of Strength' at our Reading Festival headline appearance and at our warm-up shows which, as well as The Marquee with the Eves, included our annual fan-club all-dayer, that year at Nottingham Rock City. 'Tower Of Strength' was initially met with a muted response, which disappointed if not surprised us. I remember JPJ explaining: 'It's the same for all bands when they start playing new songs: the audience are mostly not interested. They wanna hear songs that they know. When we first started playing 'Stairway To Heaven' the audience couldn't care less and were shouting for 'Immigrant Song' or 'Whole Lotta Love'. It was only after the album had been released and out for a while that people began to accept it.' Other words of wisdom imparted to us by the metal guru JPJ were, 'Always start your shows with a couple of songs the audience know and love to get 'em on your side and then you'll be able to play what you want.' As it's me that decides the set-lists on a daily basis[5], usually an hour or so before we hit the stage, it's advice I have mostly heeded through the years. The few occasions when I haven't and chosen new or lesser-known songs as openers, it has always felt like an uphill battle thereafter to win over the audience. Occasionally I relish that challenge but most of the time I prefer to go onstage and bask in the immediate adulation that comes with the audience recognising the opening guitar motif of 'Beyond The Pale' or 'Wasteland'. It's like going 1–0 up in the first minute.

So, we took our time recording the new album, playing live together in the studio to lay down the basic backing tracks, JPJ insisting we play together to try and capture the 'true essence' of the band, and then spending days and weeks and months overdubbing. We experimented with guitar sounds; along with our own ever expanding collection of guitars, JPJ brought with him an array of 4, 6 and 12-string acoustic and electric guitars, mandolins and various other stringed instruments. I was playing his vintage six-string Martin acoustic on 'Black Mountain Mist' when he casually dropped into the conversation, 'Ah, Jimmy used that guitar on 'Stairway',' or messing around on his mandolin, 'I played that on 'Battle Of Evermore'.' Every instrument JPJ had brought along had its own unique Zeppelin story and pretty much all of them ended up being used on *Children*. One he didn't own was the Danelectro Coral Sitar[6], which we rented in. Simon played it on 'Hymn (For America)' and I used it on 'Beyond The Pale' and loved it so much I ended up buying it from the rental company. We used it again on the following album, *Carved In Sand*, on tracks such as 'Sea Of Love' and 'Deliverance', before I eventually got bored of it and sold it to Adrian Utley of Portishead (the band not the place). I've never been one to get sentimental or too attached to guitars, selling them on when I no longer have a use for them. They are, after all, merely tools of the trade and if I ain't using 'em then what's the point in keeping 'em? Mind you, I still have over 40 guitars, which takes some re-stringing, but is nothing when compared to the likes of, say, Martin Gore's or Billy Corgan's collections. I believe Billy, at last count, has somewhere in the region of 250 guitars. But then he employs people to re-string 'em for him.

We had problems getting the drums *just* right and to JPJ's exacting standard for 'TOS', with Mick struggling to play to the rigid drum machine beat that drives the song. The same for Craig with the rolling bass line. In the end, the drums were programmed using JPJ's brand new Apple Macintosh computer (we'd never used or even seen one before) and MOTU's Performer[7] MIDI sequencer software program. JPJ and Mick took two whole days just doing that – the same amount of time it took to record the entire first EP. The drums that ended up on the record sound realistic enough to fool pretty much anyone. Even Youth, when he came to remix 'TOS' a few years later, was stunned when he received the multi-track tapes and realised the drums were programmed and not played. Some of the big drum fills were happy accidents, as Mick believed he was programming the drums at normal tempo but, when run alongside the song on tape using SMPTE[8] time-code, the programmed drums played back at half speed, making the fills bigger, slower, longer and *monumental*. Likewise with Craig, he was having problems playing the rolling bass line, so JPJ ended up playing the basic riff himself, just once, sampling it and triggering it via MIDI. Craig then overdubbed the other sections of the song. A painstaking process, which bored senseless anyone sat in the control room not directly involved in the process. We took up conkers[9] to ease our tedium.

Mark Stent was a 22-year-old recording engineer who had just turned freelance after working at Jacobs Studio in Surrey for several years. He was selected by JPJ and we first met him when we arrived at The Manor. Mark, a friendly, confident chap, was a sedulous worker but when he laughed, which he did regularly, he'd guffaw unapologetically. During the first few days at The Manor, Mark got his hair cut into a short, spiky style. Rather than trying to remember the names of a whole new cast of characters (never been good with names), I christened him 'Spike'. It stuck. Charlie Eyre, our A&R manager at Phonogram, was never happy with our choice of engineer for *Children*, feeling he was too young and inexperienced, and constantly griping, 'Spike's not good enough, we need a world-class engineer.' But JPJ put his foot down.

During the first few weeks of sessions Charlie would drive up from London every now and then and have a listen to how we were progressing, always making comments and suggestions that he considered constructive, but that we saw more as interference. And always with the admonition as he left, 'We need a world-class engineer,' which only left us with a renewed determination that Spike was *one of us* and would finish the record *with us*. In the end, about four or five weeks in and after yet another visit that ended with us feeling unsettled once again, JPJ banned Charlie from visiting until we'd finished the record.

Week by week we were bunkering down even further with a developing siege mentality that most visitors found hard to penetrate. Even Perrin would visit and complain we were becoming too insular. Of course, having JPJ at the helm encouraged this state of mind as that was how Zeppelin had worked, with absolutely no outside meddling. And it was absolutely how we preferred it. We were a tight, very close band of brothers during those three months or so at The Manor, probably more so than we had ever been before and definitely more so than we'd ever be again. Still, Charlie persisted with the 'world-class engineer' poppycock, right up to when we were mixing the album at the Townhouse Studios on Goldhawk Road in Shepherd's Bush. So much so that, in an act of bloody-mindedness on my part, when it came to putting the album credits together I added "World Class" engineering by Mark (Spike) Stent'. And who is it that has enjoyed a long and wildly successful career in the recording business? Mark Stent has used that same 'Spike' appellation on every record he has been involved in since and he's been involved in many. You name 'em, he's worked with 'em, from Madonna to Oasis, Massive Attack to Ed Sheeran, and on and on... so in a really roundabout desperately-clutching-at-straws six-degrees-from-Kevin-Bacon kind of way, I have also contributed to all of those releases. Ho hum.

As occurred on *GOM* and recording with a string quartet, it'd been a long-held ambition of mine to work with a Celtic harp. A track on the new album, 'Black Mountain Mist', was the perfect opportunity. In came renowned harpist Skaila Kanga – among her many credits are The Beatles – who left me friable with how wondrous she made the track sound. Well, alongside Julianne Regan's backing vocal, that is. Of course we asked Julianne back to decorate both 'Beyond The Pale' and 'Black Mountain Mist' in her exquisitely melliferous way.

We sent our recording assistant, 'Master Of Atmosphere' Michael Ade, a young lad fresh out of school who'd been assigned to work with us by The Manor hierarchy – to the local Woodstock Primary School. He was to record the children playing in the playground, two minutes of which appear at the start of the album along with other sound effects and a snippet of 'Serpents Kiss' being played in the distance and Michael himself playing violin. We also invited a group of about 20 eight-year-olds from the school to the studio one afternoon to record the well-known 'Fee-Fi-Fo-Fum' nursery rhyme, which we used as an intro to 'Hymn (For America)', and to get 'em to *la-la-la* some backing vocals. We had to clear away any tell-tale evidence that may have been lying around as well as all the valuable guitars and instruments. There were two teachers in attendance, but have you ever tried to control 20 eight-year-olds running around a recording studio? It was bedlam and perilous, but I have to say the results were exactly as I had imagined and hoped. They did us proud and I daresay they enjoyed a memorable afternoon away from the classroom. In lieu of a session fee we bought new kits for the school's football and netball teams – all black, of course.

On our second EP release – 'Garden Of Delight'/'Like A Hurricane' – we had recorded musical interludes to go between the tracks. Craig recorded his smoking-60-tabs-and-drinking-a-bottle-of-whiskey-per-day-voice version of the Woody Guthrie standard 'Vigilante Man', which always leaves him spluttering and croaking. We have persuaded him on occasion to regale our audience with said version at live shows. He has to be in the right mood to do it. In other words, inebriated. You should also hear his 'Nutbush City Limits' version sometime, too. Anyway, I digress. Pete Turner played an acoustic bottleneck blues we entitled 'East Coast Lament' in honour of Bridlington, his northern English seaside hometown. And we recorded Jez sucking and blowing on his harmonica and, after turning the tape over and adding a huge reverb, named it 'Gleaming Dome' in tribute to one of his favourite Seventies Derby County footballers, the follicly challenged Terry Hennessey. Jez was credited as composer and the song was registered with PRS.[10] But for Jez to become a member of PRS he needed to have at least two published works, so once again during the *Children* sessions he got his gob-iron out and gave it another huff and puff. While he was recording I was in the room with him taking photographs and, in his nervousness while trying to say 'camera shy', he came out with a phrase I pounced on. 'That's it, that's the title for this piece, and we'll spell it s-h-a-m-e-r-a k-y-e so it looks and sounds more Celtic,' I pronounced. Again, we turned the tape over, added a bit of violin from young assistant Michael and tons of reverb, registered it with PRS and Jez became a member. His first cheque arrived a few months later, the same time as we were expecting a bumper payout from 'Wasteland' featuring during a car chase on then ultra-popular crime drama *Miami Vice*. He received £50 or so while the four of us made about 11 pence each for *Miami Vice*. Oh, how he lorded it over us.

Working with JPJ was a dream come true; only a dozen or so years older than me in human time, he was decades older in terms of experience and wisdom. His favourite attire at the time was brown corduroy trousers with a woolly green pullover worn over a T-shirt, topped off with a pair of brown Hush Puppies. That memory may well be errant but I remember him as an avuncular, unfazed and very cool elder statesman, and him dressing accordingly. Nothing seemed to raise his ire (well, perhaps certain record company personnel); he was a devoted family man with a brilliant knack of subtly keeping us in our place. We might be boasting about playing seven nights at the London Astoria (see Chapter 12) on our next tour and he'd casually drop into the conversation, 'Yeh, that's pretty good but we played 15 nights at Madison Square Gardens in NYC.' Oh, alright then. JPJ had seen and done it all; nothing we did could impress him. We'd be talking about on-tour shenanigans and he'd just raise an eyebrow and say, 'I did tour with Robert Plant, Jimmy Page and John Bonham, you know, and they were no saints.' Really? I never knew.

JPJ is also a masterful multi-instrumentalist, having played on umpteen hit records[11] as a session musician before Led Zeppelin formed. Jimmy Page was also a much-in-demand session guitarist and the twain met when they played on many the same session. When Page was putting his new band together his first call was to JPJ.

JPJ played all the keyboards on *Children*, as well as the string arrangements on 'Tower Of Strength' and 'Heaven On Earth'. He also played some bordering-on-the-lunatic harpsichord on the joyfully ludicrous 'Fabienne', a song destined to be the B-side of the 'TOS' single. One time, I was sat in his producer's chair behind the mixing desk. We ran the song down to him and he played his part but some of his timing was a little off. 'Mmm, JP, could you please do it again? I'm afraid it was a bit sloppy,' and I remembered thinking to myself as I sat there, how did I get the nerve to tell the great, almighty John Paul Jones that his playing wasn't up to scratch?

Of course we didn't give up *all* of our bad habits, and there were nights where we'd sit up and watch the sun rise. One time JPJ, Mick and I were sat up late, sharing a bottle or two of some dark liquid with high alcohol content, and we got talking about Led Zeppelin. And Mick and I started playing our favourite Zep tracks, while JP reminisced about the good ol' days. Of course the conversation eventually turned to John Bonham, the colossus Zeppelin drummer who died at the tragically young age of 32 in September 1980, from pulmonary aspiration – choking on his own vomit – after a day of particularly heavy drinking. It was JPJ and the band's tour manager who found Bonham and were unable to rouse him. As JPJ was telling us the story the tears were flowing all around. He was evidently still absolutely devastated by the death of his band mate. 'There was no way we could carry on without Bonzo, we'd never be able to replace him, and if we did it would, could never be the same,' he explained as he wept.[12] I think Mick and I were crying as much in empathy as sympathy with JPJ, as we realised that if someone was to leave The Mission, by whatever means, it would signal the end for us. We were *that* close as a band at that time. Sadly though, for one reason or another, that kinship was to disintegrate over the ensuing years.

Whenever we spent any length of time locked away in a recording or rehearsal studio we'd start suffering from cabin fever and feel the need to get out and kick up our heels a little. With just the promise of a crate of Blue Nun and a small pile of white powder we could be had. During our time at The Manor, we took a night off to secretly support Balaam & The Angel and All About Eve at the Birmingham Hummingbird. Another night off and we played a charity show for Mencap at nearby Oxford Poly. Both nights ended up with us inviting a crowd of folk back to The Manor and the party continuing. In the three months we were there we built up quite the coterie of local doxies and paramours we could phone when we had an evening free and desired company. Such were the dubious advantages of being a *rock star*.

While we were recording I was still refining the lyrics to the songs. I would lock myself away in my room with a work-in-progress mix on cassette and play it repeatedly until I felt the lyrics were ready to be committed to tape. The subject matter for the songs on *Children* was a little broader than the love, sex and drugs that framed the songs on *GOM*. There was still plenty of that, mind, but, for example, 'Beyond The Pale' was a political song, perhaps the only one I've ever written, although so oblique that no one ever understood it. Apart from Stevie Sex-Pistol. 'A Wing And A Prayer' was about the seduction of fame and the damage it can wreak, along with the loss of equanimity that came with the constant touring we were doing at the time. 'Heaven On Earth' was written for Hannah, my daughter that was soon to be born. 'Kingdom Come', affectionally re-christened 'Condom King' by our crew, was about a blow job in the desert. 'Heat' was more sex and drugs in the Arizona desert. 'Child's Play' was a night of amphetamine and lust in Berlin. 'Fabienne' was a night of no sleep I enjoyed with a Belgian photographer. You get the picture. I was having a lot of sex with a lot of different people. No way would that have happened to me in the normal course of events. From an uptight, hick, virgin Mormon boy to an unfettered, libidinous, debauched rock'n'roll animal within the space of a few short years. I'm not complaining, absolutely not, and you'd think that would've been all the validation I'd need, wouldn't you, but no, I was riven with insecurities and doubts and fears. Of course I largely kept it to myself and blustered my way through it all with the aid of personality-altering drinking and drugging. But there were days when it did get to me, days that were darker than others, days where I wanted out. Chief among my anxieties was the feeling I wasn't good enough, I wasn't deserving of the success we were enjoying, an omnipresent suspicion that I was 'getting away with it'. I reckon most musicians must feel the same way – with the possible exception of Morrissey and Liam Gallagher, both Mancs coincidentally. Just like their football teams and supporters: full of themselves.

I was sat on my own in the studio one day, perched on an amp and feeling a bit blue, when Jez walked in and asked, 'What's up, Mr Huss, why so glum?'

211

'Aw, mate, I dunno if I can do this anymore, I don't feel cut out for it. I don't feel like I'm good enough to be doing this, I don't deserve it. I think I'm gonna give it up and go back to just being a guitarist,' I bemoaned.

And Jez, being the cheerleader type, replied, 'Come on, Mr Huss, you can't give up now. There are loads of people out there that love you and love what you're doing. Think of all the people that come to the shows and buy the records. You're a tower of strength to them.' And with that exchange I had the title for the pivotal song on the album as well as the pep talk I needed. 'Tower Of Strength' was written for our audience at a time when I really needed them.

As I mentioned earlier, we had a far more leisurely paced working routine at The Manor compared to how we'd previously worked, of perhaps 11 a.m. to 10 p.m., with an early evening break for communal dinner in the banquet room. Along with thick egg, bacon, and sausage sandwiches slathered with ketchup for breakfast, and plates of tuna and sweetcorn sandwiches throughout the day (and a lot fewer 'diet-aid' drugs than previously), some of us even began to put on a little weight, God forbid. Every Thursday after dinner we'd take a mandatory break to watch *Top Of The Pops* followed by *Blackadder The Third*, which starred Hugh Laurie as the hysterical oaf, the Prince Regent. During the six weeks the series was being aired, *Melody Maker* took to running a weekly comic strip with Andrew Eldritch cast as the thoroughly self-serving, conniving, ever-ready with an invidious put-down Edmund Blackadder, and me as his gormless but affable side-kick, 'I have a cunning plan' Baldrick. Mmm.

Towards the end of September, early on in our stint at The Manor, Eldritch and The Sisters Of Mercy released the single 'This Corrosion', their first release since Craig and I had left the band in autumn 1985. Their previous single, 'No Time To Cry' (it should've been 'Marian'!), released while Craig and I were still in TSOM in spring the same year, barely scraped into the Top 75. It could be argued that in the interim, the best promotion the Sisters ever had was the inexorable rise of The Mission. As a result, and the fact that 'This Corrosion' really was a staggeringly good single, it flew into the UK Top 40 at number 13 and reached its zenith, number 7, the following week.

The first time I heard the track, I was tripping one night with Mick in The Manor's TV room when the video was shown on a late-night TV show. I was astoundagasted and immediately felt the pointedness of the song, which was aimed directly at me. I have to admit that I was shocked at first but, ultimately, all it did was raise my competitive hackles and made me more determined that *Children* would be the best album we could possibly make. 'This Corrosion' was the precursor to the Sisters' *Floodland* album, which came along in mid-November and entered the UK album chart at number nine. Some of the tracks I recognised from the skeletal demos I worked on with Von in Hamburg in September 1985. There were some good songs on the record – as well as 'This Corrosion', the singles 'Dominion'/'Mother Russia' and 'Lucretia My Reflection' were the standouts – but, and I know I will irk the ire of *the legion* with this, to my ears it was generally one-dimensional, the work of one man as opposed to a band or even collaborative. Nothing wrong with that but, for me, it lacked musical depth. Of course, lyrically it was once again peerless wordplay from the 'Dritch. The git. One thing was clear, though – by this time, The Mission and the Sisters had evolved into two very different bands, even though we had both come from the same place, *First And Last And Always*.

On October 12, 1987, my first daughter, Hannah, was born in Leeds. A Monday child, fair of face just like her ol' dad. A few days after she came home from the hospital I was driven up to Leeds by Mick to visit mother and baby. It is ineffable for me to say how it felt when I first saw and held Hannah in my arms. Far better writers of prose than me have described the experience but most anyone who has sired progeny will know what I mean when I say that holding Hannah for the first time made me want to be a better man. I left Leeds completely overwhelmed that I had contributed, albeit unwittingly and admittedly with little effort, to bringing new life into the world, and full of resolve to *be a good dad* – whatever that means. Again, best intentions an' all that. Maybe that should be the subtitle of this book – *Best Intentions An' All That.*

Every few weeks JPJ would take a weekend off from recording and travel back to his family home in Devon to spend time with his wife, Mo (Maureen), and their three teenage daughters. While Mo did come and stay at The Manor once or twice, their daughters never did, I suspect primarily because JPJ did not trust us one jot around his begotten.

One such weekend, a few weeks after Hannah was born, and as we weren't working, we decided to invite all our parents to visit, along with T and her daughters, three-year-old Jessica and newborn Hannah. (Remember, Jessica is Craig's daughter and Hannah is mine). It was the first time all the band members' parents had met and certainly the first time my parents had met T and Hannah, their first grandchild. Craig's parents already knew T and had been active, doting grandparents to Jessie, as mine would become to Hannah. The unusual situation no doubt initially raised the eyebrows of Simon's and Mick's parents, who were a little older than mine and Craig's, but everybody got on fine and I know the parents exchanged Christmas cards for years afterwards, even after the band had split up. We set up a marquee in the grounds and arranged for a firework display and enjoyed a huge banquet prepared for us by the very accommodating Manor staff. We each gave up our rooms to our respective parents and found a spare room for T and the girls, while we – the band, Jez and Nipper – all bunked down in Jez's room, blankets and sleeping bags on the floor. Six of us in a tiny room. We'd all gone to bed at the same time and were settling down for the night, and with Jez's room being next to Simon's, we were trying to keep the noise down so as not to disturb his folks. Much whispering and stifled laughing ensued until Mick let out a loud fart followed by, in full voice, loud enough to be heard in the room next door, 'Simon, do you have to mate? That stinks!' Of course we were all tittering now, that is apart from Simon, who was pleading, 'Aw, come on, me mam and dad are next door,' which just made us all laugh even more. How old were we? In our mid to late twenties... It's an observation I've made over the years that no matter how old you are, whatever the situation, farts always make you laugh, easing any tension there may be, whether they're your own or somebody else's.

Anyway, farting aside, the weekend was a success and all the parents had a great time – they got to stay in a beautiful stately home for a couple of days and see how well their lads were doing.

Jez's parents couldn't make the weekend, sadly, but Roger, his dad, did come down to stay on another night. He was a sales rep and happened to have an important business meeting early the next morning in Oxford, so rather than stay in a hotel he came to The Manor. And he certainly got into the rock'n'roll spirit, throwing back the port and brandies all evening, and he was even spotted at 3 a.m. skinny-dipping in the outdoor swimming pool! He was woken the next morning more than two hours later than his intended departure time and ended up being several hours late for his meeting. But, like son, like father, Rog had the gift of the gab, and after explaining he'd been up all night partying with *international rock stars*, the people he was meeting with were suitably impressed and he was instantly conferred with an air of *cool*, his tardiness immediately forgiven and forgotten.

The Lord of the Manor, Richard Branson, also popped in once or twice to say hello and see how we were getting on, despite us not being on Virgin Records. A few years later, I had just boarded a Virgin flight from Heathrow to LA and settled into my seat when

Branson came up and asked how I was and if there was anything I needed. He then proceeded to the rear of the plane to sit with the flight attendants on a jump seat for take-off and landing and most of the flight. And he owned the airline. Not for him a first-class seat at the front of the plane, away from all the plebs. Richard Branson, man of the people. That's not something you hear said about him very often, is it? I know he often comes across as being a bit of a toffee-nosed twerp but I must admit I was impressed he would take Virgin flights sitting with the riffraff.

Come the beginning of December and it was time to leave The Manor and adjourn to the Townhouse Studios on Goldhawk Road in London's Shepherd's Bush, to mix the album. We were sad to leave – we'd been treated royally and I look back at that time with fond memories. One of us, though, was leaving with something more than just memories. While we were there, Spike had gotten friendly with Tracy, one of the girls who worked in the office. They ended up getting married and are still together today, with Tracy having been Spike's manager all these years. We do like a happy ending, don't we?

The Townhouse was also owned by Branson/Virgin and I had recorded there previously in Studio One with The Walkie Talkies back in 1979. This time we were in Studio Two – Queen were in Studio One, they'd been there for yonks. I met Brian May and Roger Taylor in the communal recreation room, hanging out as Freddie recorded vocals, apparently. Both were reasonably down-to-earth considering they were *Queen*, Taylor whipping me good 'n' proper at pool several times over. Queen were, and are to this day, one of the very best bands I have seen live. I saw them at Bristol Colston Hall in December 1975 the week that 'Bohemian Rhapsody' hit number one. I didn't meet Freddie (or John Deacon as it happens), but I did nod hello to him. Studio One was at one end of the building while Studio Two was at the other. The toilets were in the middle. One night, quite late, I decided I needed to pee so tottered off to the loo. Walking up the narrow corridor, I saw Freddie walking towards me, obviously going to the loo too. I was dumbstruck, and as I neared the entrance to the toilet I carried on walking as if I was going to reception, and as I passed Freddie I nodded and he said 'hello'. That was it – just 'hello'. I carried on walking towards reception until I heard the bathroom door close behind me and then turned around and raced back to our control room. Breathless, I blurted out to JPJ, 'I've just seen Freddie in the corridor and he said "hello"!'

'Did you speak with him?', he asked.

'No, I was too scared. He was going to the loo,' I replied.

'Why not? He's a lovely chap.'

'Ah, I couldn't go in the loo with Freddie. I couldn't small-talk with him while standing at the urinal having a pee, and what if he'd gone into a cubicle? I didn't wanna hear him having a poo. That would've just blown it for me – he's Freddie Mercury,' I reasoned.

We were at the Townhouse for four or five weeks, but sadly I didn't get the chance to nod at Freddie in the corridor again.

The mixing was painfully slow, 'TOS' alone taking a week and the album itself taking as long to mix as it took to record *and* mix *God's Own Medicine*. A couple of times I overheard JPJ and Spike in quite heated arguments regarding the amount of reverb JPJ was wanting on the vocals in particular, and everything else in general. Spike said it was too much. It's easy to be wise in hindsight and say yes, there's too much reverb on *Children*, but it was what we wanted at the time, it was the record we wanted to make. Certainly we were willing to defer to JPJ's experience and expertise, but there was nothing on that album we didn't want on it. Like with all art – and music is of course art as well as a commodity – music is subjective. If we were to record the album again today it would no doubt sound very different. I don't believe it would be imbued with the same confidence and swagger – and, yes, to a degree naiveté – that we possessed back then. If we

217

had recorded the album with Tim Palmer, for example, it would've been a totally different beast – perhaps more direct. But, as good as Tim is, we would have missed JPJ's musical contributions, which were immense. I was and still am inordinately proud of *Children*, as flawed as it is. It is The Mission at their commercial peak and most bombastic, melodramatic and grandiloquent, with 'Tower Of Strength' proving to be the band's evergreen anthem for the ages. Other highlights for me are 'Beyond The Pale' and 'Heaven On Earth'. It is an album made by a band stretching their wings for the first time, full of whims and flights of fancy, with some very evident indulgences throughout. And that's what makes it unique, both at the time of its release compared to what else was around at the time, and in the canon of The Mission's recorded works. Perhaps with a more commercially minded producer some of the excesses may have been reined in a little but JPJ, and Spike, encouraged us to be creative, expressive and to make the record that *we* wanted to make rather than the one that was expected or hoped for by any external parties. It is the work of a band unified and defiant. *Children*, to me, is an album that was aiming for the stars... that it only made the moon is no small feat in itself.

Flawed but beautifully so...

Endnotes

1   In this context, 'ringer' means a player entered into the competition under
     fraudulent representation as to identity or ability, i.e. as a member of The
     Mission or our crew or management team. Don't think we would've gotten

away with it though; pretty sure someone would've recognised Craig Johnston, even kitted out in all-black and wearing shades.

2   Metallica played a 'secret show' at the 100 Club on London's Oxford Street during the period we were rehearsing and, with them being next door at Nomis, we'd blagged our way onto their guest list. They were chuffed to bits that we managed to persuade JPJ to indulge in a rare night out by dragging him along with us to see them.

3   Formally known as Shipton Manor, The Manor was closed as a recording studio in 1995, when Virgin Records was bought out by EMI.

4   Mark Price came to All About Eve after playing with the Nik Kershaw band and then went on to play with Del Amitri after the Eve's folded. He got his nickname 'Hovis' because he'd starred in a Hovis advert as a boy in the Sixties. Sadly, he wasn't the iconic 'boy on a bike', though he was directed by then up-and-coming director, now Sir, Ridley Scott.

5   I like to change the set every night, even if just a little; it keeps the band and crew on their toes and is interesting for those in our audience who come to see us more than once during a tour. And there's a fair few of those maniacs, lovable as they are. If Craig and Simon had their way, they'd play the same 12 songs every night in the same order. Craig maintains that when he was with The Cult they played the same 12 songs every night for five years! He reckoned he could be in any state of inebriation, and he wouldn't get lost. Mind you, Billy Duffy apparently told him on joining, 'If you do get lost at all just hit a D and you won't ever be far wrong.' You oughtta see how many pieces of paper with scribbled notes Craig has at his feet during rehearsals, even for songs we've been playing for 30 years! Me, I've got it all on a foot-controlled iPad mounted on my mic stand these days.

6   The Danelectro Coral Sitar became all the rage in the late Sixties. The traditional sitar, India's national instrument, was popularised in the West most notably by George Harrison and his teacher, Ravi Shankar. The sitar itself is regarded as a very difficult instrument to play and certainly to master. I had one myself for a while and can attest to that fact. Hence session guitarist Vinnie Bell came up with the genius design for all the guitarists that liked the sound of the sitar but couldn't be bothered to learn to play it. The Coral Sitar is a standard six-string guitar and fretboard with a flat metal plate bridge under the strings that give it its unique

sitar-like sound. It also features a set of strings that aren't actually played but can be tuned to resonate in sympathy. It's been heard on thousands of recordings since and is still in use to this day.

7   The MIDI protocol, introduced to the world in the early Eighties, enabled electronic equipment such as drum machines, sequencers and synths to communicate and play in sync with each other. Initially thought of as a fad by many, MIDI quickly became industry standard and alongside computer-based recording systems, samplers and sequencers, it came to revolutionise the business of music-making. Mark Of The Unicorn's Performer was one of the earliest commercial software sequencers and certainly the first for Apple's Macintosh system.

8   SMPTE is the standardised time code in hour:minute:second:frame protocol that would usually be recorded to track 24 on a 24-track recording machine, which when played back into external computers, drum machines and synthesisers would enable the whole system to play back in synchronicity. Due to technical advancement and more integrated recording systems being used 'in the box', SMPTE is now largely redundant in most recording studios. However, as I understand, the protocol is still widely used in film and video production.

9   You've played conkers, haven't you? The game is played by two players, each with a conker threaded onto a piece of string or a shoelace, who then take it in turns to whack the other's conker until one of 'em is smashed to smithereens. It's a game that demands to be played in the spirit of absolute honour and probity but there was some surreptitious cheating going on by certain members of our party, not naming names (okay, Mick and Jez), who were caught baking their conkers in the oven to 'harden' them. If you were caught cheating then punishment was meted by having your conker disqualified and ceremoniously stomped to a mushy pulp by all the other players. While researching conkers for this book I came across some amusing, but ultimately useless, facts: The first World Conker Championship took place in Ashton, Leicestershire, in 1965. It still takes place on the second Sunday of October every year (don't forget to put *that* date in your diary). In 2004 the tournament attracted an audience of over 5,000 to watch more than 500 competitors from all over the world. All I've gotta say on the matter is there's a word that begins with B and

rhymes with conkers that perfectly sums up those that take this pastime that seriously. But, hey ho, each to their own.

10   PRS (Performing Rights Society) – these days known as PRS For Music – is a publishing income collection agency set up to collect song royalties from around the world for radio and TV airplay, which it then distributes to its members – songwriters, composers and publishers – every 3 or 4 months. But in the age of internet radio shows and social media, it's become largely impossible to police and enforce. Television and film is the pay-dirt, though. Except *Miami Vice*, it seems.

11   Between 1964 and 1968, JPJ worked on hundreds of sessions, often up to three a day, six or seven days a week, with a long list of artists, including The Rolling Stones, Dusty Springfield, Rod Stewart, Donovan, Tom Jones, Lulu and Nico. 'I can't remember three-quarters of the sessions I was on,' he said years later. By 1968 he'd run out of steam: 'I was arranging 50 or 60 things a month and it was starting to kill me.' And then he received a call from Jimmy Page.

12   The band announced in a press release on December 4, 1980: 'We wish it to be known that the loss of our dear friend and the deep respect we have for his family, together with the sense of undivided harmony felt by ourselves and our manager, have led us to decide that we could not continue as we were.' It was signed 'Led Zeppelin.'

CHAPTER 11

Gypsy In My Blood And I Lie Where The Myth Is Sold

PLAYLIST:
1. It's Alright, Ma (I'm Only Bleeding) – Bob Dylan
2. Georgia On My Mind – Ray Charles
3. Only The Lonely – Frank Sinatra
4. Tower Of Strength (radio edit) – The Mission
5. Tower Of Strength (Bombay Mix) – The Mission
6. Song To The Siren – Robert Plant
7. Song To The Siren – Tim Buckley
8. Song To The Siren – This Mortal Coil
9. Beyond The Pale (Armageddon Mix) – The Mission
10. Tadeusz (1912–1988) – The Mission   11. Forevermore – The Mission
12. Wicked Game – Chris Isaak   13. Dominion – The Sisters Of Mercy

VIDEO PLAYLIST:
1. Tower Of Strength – The Mission   2. Beyond The Pale – The Mission
3. Beyond The Pale (Armageddon Mix) – The Mission

The Mission were and are a very good band, particularly live, a quality I don't believe we've ever *quite* captured on record. Two very separate mediums, anyway – one shouldn't inhibit the other. What I mean by that is, very often what works in the studio may not work on the stage and vice versa. We *have* made some good records though, and some not quite so good, shall we say. But each is a testament to where we were as a band, and where I was personally at the time of making a particular record. We never set out with the aim of making a duff album – the intention is always to do our best – but oft times our best is determined by what is going on in our lives. And like everybody else in the world, musicians have good days and bad days.

It's perhaps a strange admission but I'm not sure I'd be a fan of The Mission were I not in the band. I'd like some of the songs, of that I'm certain, but I wouldn't love us with the same fervour as some of the more zealous members of our audience, or with the same passion I have for artists such as The Beatles, Radiohead, Massive Attack, Bob Dylan et al. I don't sit at home listening to Mission records; I hear 'em enough to last a lifetime when we're making 'em. The only time I listen is when we have a tour coming up and I need to remind myself of what to play and sing. Sometimes I even need to watch YouTube clips of budding guitarists who've posted videos of themselves playing Mission songs. They're all just a little bit different (I won't say wrong) from the way I play them, but it is usually enough to kickstart my memory. Some songs, though, I NEVER have to listen to, as they're ingrained in my psyche, part of my DNA – songs such as 'Wasteland', 'Tower Of Strength' and 'Butterfly On A Wheel'. It might be a year or more since I've performed them but as soon as I start playing, like a reflex they're there, almost like riding a bike. In fact, if I think about it too much I'll quite often mess it up. And if you've ever seen us live then you'll know I am prone to messing up the lyrics, particularly on newer songs. I had problems with remembering 'Severina' for years to the extent that I always taped an A4 prompt sheet to the floor monitor in front of me onstage. It was supposed to read something like:

Clouds
Stars
Dream
Wind
Moonchild

And so on. Except Jez quite regularly would throw in substitute lines like: 'Diddley sky' or 'blancmange or jelly' and even sometimes a list of his favourite 1970s Derby County footballers:

Kevin Hector
John O'Hare
Alan Hinton
Terry Hennessey
Roy McFarland
Colin Todd

And so on. (Yes, Jez is a Derby County supporter if you hadn't guessed by now.) I would even attempt to sing the names in front of me rather than attempt to remember the correct words. Oh, we enjoyed some jolly japes. That's why these days I have all my lyrics on an iPad attached to my mic stand with a small foot switch connected via Bluetooth that enables me to turn the page. Isn't technology brilliant? There's a lot of bloody lyrics to remember, I can tell you. We rehearse upwards of 40 songs for any given tour, many more if it's a solo tour, and my memory ain't quite what it once was, so I'll take all the help I can get. But those early songs, the ones we've been playing for decades, are branded indelibly.

Back to my thoughts on the band, I think my biggest problem with The Mission would be Wayne Hussey. I'd like him even though he could be a bit of a dick, in much the same way as I like a lot of front men and women. Guitarists have it way easier. They can look cool without having to open their mouths, without having to betray themselves with idiocy. It was so much easier being the *cool* guitarist in a band – TSOM, Dead Or Alive, Pauline Murray & The Invisible Girls – as opposed to being the singer of The Mission. I consider myself a far better guitar player than I am singer/lyricist, or rather, a far more *unique* guitar player than vocalist.

I believe I'm The Mission's strongest asset as well as its weakest.

I can sing – in fact, I've become a very good singer – but I don't have a *great* voice. By that I mean I don't have a unique voice in the same way as, say, Morrissey or Björk or Robert Smith or Kate Bush or Siouxsie or John Lydon or Neil Young. You think of all the greats and they all have unique and singular voices. Marmite voices, you might even say – you either love 'em or detest 'em. Some of them aren't particularly good singers technically, but that matters not a whit if you are unique. Any technical deficiencies you can wave away as style. Take Bob Dylan, for example. So many people abhor his voice and I can understand why. It's not a *pretty* voice, it's got a nasal quality. He sings with his head rather than his diaphragm and he does that idiosyncratic thing where he slurs the notes 'up' at the end of lines. But when you hear Dylan, it's unmistakably him and no one else. Personally, I love Bob Dylan and believe *he is* technically as good a singer as pretty much anyone else. Except perhaps Ray Charles or Frank Sinatra.

I've been blessed/cursed with a voice that is perfectly adequate and over which I have some measure of control, but I do so wish I had something in my voice that sets it apart. Technique and control can be taught, but uniqueness can't; it's innate and a priceless commodity. Note, I'm not disparaging the Mission audience by writing this (I think some of 'em would maybe even agree with me), and I'm not looking for any 'shucks, how can you say that?' validation. I'm very conscious of my own strengths and weaknesses and I genuinely feel The Mission would've been a more successful band if it had a singer with a more distinctive voice. But likewise, The Mission would not have existed in the first place or survived all these 30-plus years we've been around without me at the helm. I am the one that has driven the band, guided the sound, written the vast majority of the songs, worked the long hours and had the casting vote in any decisions that weren't unanimous. As Simon once said, 'Wayne always asks everyone's opinion and then turns around and does what he wants anyway.'

I don't *quite* see it that way but I also don't believe a band can function by committee. There is always one or sometimes two people that push and pull everyone else along. And while decisions were often made whimsically and without much deliberation, they were decisions I or, in the early days at least, *we* made as a band. No one else made those decisions. We could and would listen to advice but advice generally, particularly regarding the music business, seems to be loaded with an agenda of self-interest. One thing I have learned is to stick with my own instincts, since they've usually ended up serving me better than someone else's. The only decisions I've truly regretted have been when I allowed someone else to make those decisions for me. If a decision is to be made then I like to be able to only blame myself if it's the wrong one, and no one else.

With *Children* finally mixed, mastered and ready to go, January 1988 was spent preparing for its release. 'Tower Of Strength'[1] had been selected as the first single from the album, all 8 minutes plus of it. It was whittled down to a more radio-friendly 4 minutes 39 seconds, a bastardisation in my opinion but, hey ho, we wanted it to be played on the radio so we had to play the game. There was also the 'Bombay Mix' by Mark 'Spike' Stent, which came in at a majestic 11 minutes 36 seconds. The definitive version though, in my not so humble opinion, is the album version. 'Fabienne' was the B-side with our version of the sacrosanct Aerosmith classic 'Dream On' as the extra track on the 12-inch.

During the recording of the album I had one night watched the Ralph Bakshi-directed 1978 film version of *The Lord Of The Rings*, decades before the later Peter Jackson trilogy. While I enjoyed it I was particularly struck by how the film *looked*. It used a process called rotoscoping, an animation technique in which live action scenes are first filmed, and then each frame of the motion picture footage is coloured by hand. It's a lengthy and costly process but I got it in my head that I wanted the video for 'TOS' to look like this. We were hooked up with Ian Emes[2], who had actually worked on *The Lord Of The Rings*, and together we came up with the idea of creating a modern-day fairy tale set in a dystopian world for the video. With the band cast as the Magnificent Four (as opposed to Seven[3]), we were on a – please forgive me – mission to rescue a little girl who has been abducted by a demon and is being held captive in the tower of a derelict high-rise building. Attired in all-black, with long coats, hats, fingerless gloves, five-day stubble and me sporting a clerical collar to symbolise that I am the 'glorious leader' of our gang, we looked like we'd just walked off the set of *The Good, The Bad And The Ugly*.

The video starts with me riding a white horse across not Tower Bridge, but the more prosaic London Bridge. Never having ridden a horse before (I don't think you can count the donkeys on Weston-super-Mare beach), I had a couple of horse riding lessons beforehand while we were still at The Manor. I wasn't a natural. All I can say is that my bony little ass was very sore afterwards. Those opening scenes of the 'TOS' video were filmed indecently early one winter's morning, with passing cars and buses full of commuters staring with mouths agape at the strange apparition of a long-haired, shades-wearing, behatted 'vicar' riding a white horse across London Bridge. My initial brief was to ride at a gentle trot from the south side of the river to the north. The first time I attempted it the horse, sensing I was a terrified novice and not in control, sped up, first to a canter and then broke into a full gallop. By the time we reached the other side of the bridge I was barely hanging on for dear life. Concerned they were gonna lose the singer of the band to the freezing, churning River Thames below, it was thought prudent to use a stand-in to film further takes. So, the horse trainer borrowed my clothes and hat and donned a wig and a pair of sunglasses, and voilà. You'd never know, would you? It wasn't all jiggery-pokery, though; there was one shot used of me atop the white stallion before the bugger had put my life in jeopardy, and I was also filmed dismounting. That bit was easy, and a relief.

As for the single's cover, we chose an illustration of a double-headed eagle. We also wanted one of those in the video but it was a devil of a job to find one. Smirk. So we filmed a *normal* eagle and the clever video animators added an extra head on the bird. The eagle lands upon an arm that appears to be mine but it's not mine; it's another stand-in, this time the falconer. And my fingertips didn't shoot lasers either, more's the pity. That particular skill would've come in handy at times in my life when faced with certain adversaries. All this magic was conjured up in the animation studio. Anyway, needless to say we zap our way through zombies and ogres and save the little girl. She didn't really want to be rescued, though. When I picked her up I had to coax her to tickle me under my chin, as she was certainly more wary of me than any of the monsters she'd been playing with. And who could blame her?

The little girl's name was Taryn, found through a children's modelling agency. She was so pretty that we ended up using her face on the cover of *Children*, too. Mick had made the original cover image out of plasticine during our time at The Manor but the face he had sculpted looked more like Gollum than the angelic cherub we were after, so we superimposed Taryn's face onto the artwork.

The budget for the 'TOS' video was an eye-watering £60,000, a far cry from the £2,000 it cost to do 'Serpents Kiss'! Admittedly, small potatoes for the likes of bands like Duran Duran, but we could've bought a house each in Leeds for that amount. It's by far the most we ever spent on a video, our budget usually being around the still excessive £20,000 – £25,000 when we were on the Phonogram label. More fool them for spending so much. Mind you, we're still paying off our debt to them, so more fool us in actuality.

'TOS' was released the first week of February, and late afternoon on Sunday 7, while rehearsing at Nomis Studios, we broke off to gather around a radio and listen to the Top 40 chart run-down. Because it had only been released the preceding Friday we didn't have a midweek chart position so had no idea how it'd been selling. We were expecting it to be a new chart entry, hopefully between 40 and 30, even up to 25 if we were lucky. 40 to 30 came and went and no mention of us. 28, 27, 26, 25... still nothing. 24, 23... 'Ah, bollocks. Turn it off, let's get back to making a racket,' one of us suggested. We hadn't even made it into the Top 40. Disheartened, we turned the radio off and went back to rehearsing with that sinking feeling of 'what's the soddin' point?' A little while later Perrin walked into the room with his ever-present briefcase in hand and a smile on his face.

'What've you got to be so bloody happy about?' I barked.

'You didn't listen to the chart run-down?' he replied.

We informed him we'd given up by number 22, 23. 'Why, what happened?' one of us asked.

'You were the highest chart entry this week at number 20 and you're on *Top Of The Pops* again this week. *And* you've been added to the Radio 1 playlist!'

And with that he whipped open his briefcase and pulled out a bottle of champers and a little paper wrap. 'Right, Jez, get some glasses from the kitchen and Mick, chop 'em out', our manager demanded, 'let's celebrate.'

And thus began a hectic period of promotion – flying around Europe to appear on television and radio shows, press interviews and all that malarkey, with 'TOS' making an appearance, admittedly mostly the lower reaches, in the pop charts of several countries. In attendance was Sian Thomas from Phonogram's International department, assigned to look after us and make sure we got from A to B, and on time. Sian was originally from the valleys of South Wales and, as she was a couple of years older than us, she'd been in the music business for a good few years and was working her way up through the ranks, eventually becoming head of Phonogram. Sian would travel with us on many occasions over the next couple of years or so, to Mexico, South America and Japan as well as all over Europe, and was to become a much-loved and integral part of the extended Mission family.[4] One time, early on, we were away in Sweden or somewhere Scandinavian and the local record company had thrown us a reception in a nightclub. As we were leaving the hotel for the shindig, Sian gave us all a condom each. 'What's this for?' Simon asked. 'Oh, just in case you get lucky I want you boys to be safe, okay,' she advised. We all looked at each other with raised eyebrows. The next morning as we were ferried in a big black car to the airport, Sian salaciously asked, 'So, did any of you get to use your condom last night?' Much like his drumming, without missing a beat Mick replied, 'Yeah, I had a posh wank.'

Another time, on arrival at our hotel in Paris for a round of promo, we were handed a fax at check-in. Remember them? It was actually addressed to the local record company rep, who the hotel receptionist assumed was among our party. It read, 'Dear Sébastien. The Mission will ask you for drugs as soon as they arrive. If you want them to do their job properly, please don't give them any. Just tell them you can't get anything. They are nice boys, really.' When later confronted with this incriminating evidence, Sian giggled and confessed that she had sent out similar faxes to all territories that we were due to visit for promo duties. No wonder our reputation preceded us.

It was during the promo for 'TOS' that we bumped into Robert Plant and his band a couple of times, appearing on the same TV shows. We ended up getting pally with them and I remember an occasion in a pub near Olympic Studios in Barnes, London, and while I was sat with Robert and our producer pal Tim Palmer, we overheard a conversation between Mission drummer Mick and Chris Blackwell, Planty's much respected regular drummer at the time. It went something like this:

Chris: 'So Mick, what kind of drumsticks do you use?'

Mick: 'The biggest bleedin' pieces of wood I can find.'

Robert Plant was great. *Is a great.* He was everything I wanted him to be; the quintessential rock star. He was friendly and sociable, down to earth, a fount of musical knowledge, and he loved a natter about football. He was also a total babe magnet. Just being sat with him I'd look on in absolute astonishment and awe, and a teeny-weeny bit enviously if truth be known, at the number of stunning women that would parade past him, blatantly giving him the come-on. And he loved it, revelled in it. Of course he bloody did. Who wouldn't?

Much later, in October 2012, I went to see Robert play in São Paulo. I hadn't seen him for a good few years, probably since the late Eighties, but I managed to finagle myself a place on the guest list with after-show passes. I took Cinthya, my wife, who, it must be said, is not a fan. She's an Eighties kid – loves The Cure, The Smiths, Depeche Mode, the Cocteau Twins, that kinda thing. She dismissed Zeppelin as she pretty much dismissed most music from the Seventies. I've tried to educate her but she's not having it. 'I just don't like the sound,' she opines. Fair enough. Anyway, she came with me to see Robert this night, the first of two nights he was playing at the Espaço das Américas. And while I can't claim that she loved the show and was converted, it did reduce her to tears when Robert performed his shatteringly moving version of Tim Buckley's 'Song To The Siren'. Of course Cinthya knew the song primarily as sung by Elizabeth Fraser as part of the This Mortal Coil project. The song is so beautiful that I've included all three versions in my playlist at the head of this chapter. Take yer pick, they are all goosebumpy. After the show, we went backstage and stood in the outer dressing room area chatting with the lads in the band, a couple of them Bristol lads (as am I) who'd also played with Massive Attack and Portishead, when Robert came out of his dressing room and made a beeline straight for Cinthya and me. 'Wayne, me old fruit. I haven't seen you for years. How the devil are you?' he asked, while warmly taking my hand and giving it a rigorous shake. And before I could reply, 'and who is this ravishing beauty?', he went on with a twinkle in his eye. He then proceeded to chat to Cinthya for the next 20 minutes or so while I barely got a word in edgeways. Cinthya received the full Robert Plant charm offensive and was absolutely enchanted by the old Lothario. By which time the tour manager was trying to clear the dressing room and get everyone ready to leave. 'Are you coming tomorrow night?', Robert asked. 'Come and watch the show from the side of the stage.' Unfortunately, or maybe fortunately for me, Cinthya couldn't make the next night. She's an actress and was busy rehearsing a new play, so I went on my own. Robert's disappointment was palpable when he saw I was there alone. 'Where's that lovely wife of yours?' he lamented. I did watch the show from the side of the stage that night. It was another cracker, and with the privileged view it was a lesson in stage craft and presence. The old boy still has IT, the intangible IT, that is. After the show, as I sat with the boys in the band, I watched Robert saunter out of his dressing room, a cursory wink my way, and then head straight for the most striking woman in the room. He is a rascal. You have to tip your hat to him though, whether or not you're a fan. Planty is a genuine icon, arguably one of the best front men that rock music has ever seen. He has stuck to his guns and forged his own path since the Zeppelin split, and apart from the few occasions the band have got back together and performed at charity events, Robert has thus far resisted all entreaties to re-form with Page and JPJ for one final bumper pay-day. I often wish I'd been brave enough to make those kinds of artistic decisions but then I don't have the financial cushion that I assume Robert sits upon. That being said, as The Mission these days we do generally get to choose what we do and when we do it. I still enjoy, every couple of years or so, making a big ol' noise together with the other chaps in the band and bringing in a little of the ol' filthy lucre for my dotage.

We were very busy in February 1988. This was our schedule for the month:

Addo with one of our mates, Kirk Hammett from Metallica; four gentle, shy, quiet lads from San Francisco in August 1987. One of the nicest things anyone ever said to me was when James Hetfield once proclaimed, 'Fucking hey man, you rock!' I was so proud. © Nic Duncan

'Tonight, Matthew, I'm gonna be Wayne Hussey!' John Paul Jones from Led Zepplin dressing up as me during a night of revelry at The Manor, while recording our second album, *Children*. October 1987. © Nic Duncan

JPJ as 'our favourite uncle'. October 1987. © Nic Duncan

All of us together at The Manor. November 1987. © Nic Duncan

Me with my newly born daughter, Hannah, at The Manor. November 1987. © Nic Duncan

Overdressed for dinner at The Manor. November 1987. © Nic Duncan

L to R: the 'world class engineer' Mark 'Spike' Stent, me and JPJ. The grafters hard at work in The Townhouse Studios, Goldhawk Road, London, December 1987, while mixing *Children*. © Nic Duncan

T'lads on the set of the 'Tower of Strength' video, December 1987. © Nic Duncan

One (daft) lump or two? Mick and me taking a camel ride at San Diego Zoo in Feb 1988. Wouldn't do it now for many reasons, but primarily because I've come to hate zoos. © Craig Adams

At Niagra Falls, Spring 1988. L to R: me, Adam Stevenson, Pamela Burton, Stevie, Slink, Mick, Ann and Harry Isles and on the end, unknown. © Craig Adams

Me getting some much-needed beauty sleep on the tour bus somewhere in America May 1988. © Craig Adams

A fine figure of a man – Craig Adams poolside in Arizona. May 1988. © Wayne's personal collection

Living the dream. Mick in the pool and me in the jacuzzi, Arizona. May 1988. © Craig Adams

Stevie and Slink, poolside, with Mick treading water in the background, Arizona. May 1988. © Craig Adams

Me trying to persuade drivers-by to come to tonight's show in Dallas, Texas, June 1988 while on tour opening for Robert Plant. 'Tickets available'. © Craig Adams

Here we are in the cable-car on the way up to the Corcovado in Rio. Please note the open windows and those sat on the left (as we look at the photo) had the 'closer' experience with the 'wanking man'. September 1988. © Stevie Watson

The universally loved and much missed Stevie 'sex-pistol' Watson on the balcony of our hotel on the Copacabana Beach, Rio, in September 1988. © Wayne's personal collection

Mick and Slink at the Sugarloaf. September 1988. © Wayne's personal collection

At the Corcovado in Rio, September 1988. L to R: Stevie, Harry 'the bastard' Isles (our tour manager), Mick, Slink and me being all posey and pouty. © Craig Adams

Craig showing us all up with his dance moves with Selma at Ronnie Biggs's house. Note woman whispering in Ronnie's ear in the background, 'I'd get rid of this lot if I were you, Ronnie, fraternising with them is gonna ruin your reputation.'
© Stevie Watson

A very drunken photo shoot we did with Peter Anderson for *Sounds*, late 1988. We ended up using this photo as our fan club Christmas card that year. It sums up 1988 very nicely for us.
© Peter Anderson

Mon 1: In Livingston Studio remixing 'Beyond The Pale' with Spike for next single.

Tues 2: In Livingston Studio recording 'Forevermore' and 'Tadeusz' as B-sides.

Wed 3: In Livingston Studio recording and mixing 'Forevermore' and 'Tadeusz' as B-sides.

Thu 4: Promo in London.

Fri 5: 'TOS' released. Tour rehearsals start at Nomis Studios.

Sat 6: Tour rehearsal (or band practice, as Mick liked to call it).

Sun 7: 'TOS' enters UK Top 40 at number 20. Tour rehearsal.

Mon 8: Fly to the Netherlands for promo and appear on Dutch *TOTP*.

Tues 9: Drive to Belgium for more promo.

Wed 10: Fly back to the UK in the a.m. Film *TOTP* at BBC Studios, Shepherd's Bush.

Thu 11: Secret warm-up show at Leeds Warehouse. 'TOS' aired on *TOTP*.

Fri 12: Secret warm-up show at Leicester University.

Sat 13: Another secret warm-up show at Norwich University of East Anglia.

Sun 14: Fly to Los Angeles. Film for the 'Beyond The Pale' video. 'TOS' up to number 13 in UK Top 40.

Mon 15: Promo in LA.

Tues 16: Show at the Bacchanal, San Diego.

Wed 17: Show at the Coach House, San Juan Capistrano.

Thu 18: Show at Hollywood Palace, LA.

Fri 19: Fly to NYC. Record company reception and party.

Sat 20: Show at The Ritz, NYC.

Sun 21: Day off. Went to Iggy Pop's for tea and then out for dinner with him and Suchi. 'TOS' up to number 12 in UK Top 40.

Mon 22: Promo in NYC.

Tues 23: Promo in NYC. Fly the red-eye from NYC. First time in business class. Pop go the champagne corks.

Wed 24: Arrive early morning at Heathrow. Film the second appearance for *TOTP* at BBC Studios, Shepherd's Bush.

Thu 25: Fly to Germany for promo. 'TOS' aired on *TOTP* for a second time.

Fri 26: Fly back to the UK in the a.m. Radio 1 interview and session in the p.m.

Sat 27: Production rehearsals at TourTech, Northampton.

Sun 28: Production rehearsals at TourTech, Northampton.

Mon 29: Travel to Dublin. *Children* is released.

Tues 1 March: Children Play world tour kicks off at the Olympic Ballroom, Dublin.

The month started with us in Livingston Studio in north London, remixing 'Beyond The Pale' as the follow-up to 'TOS'. With World-Class 'Spike' as the man in charge, the 'Armageddon Mix' was the result. It remains one of my favourite extended mixes of one of our songs. We also edited the track for the now-becoming-standard more-radio-friendly shorter version. We also needed a couple of new songs as a 7-inch B-side and 12-inch extra track. The first of these started life as a tune that Craig and Simon began messing about with in soundcheck and in rehearsals, as at that time they were both playing keyboards onstage for a couple of songs. Entirely written – or should I say composed – and performed by Craig and Simon, over time it evolved into quite the epic, moving piece of music, so we decided to record it. Slink asked if he could name it in memory of a neighbour of his who had recently died, an older Polish gentleman whom he was particularly friendly with and fond of. So we called it 'Tadeusz (1912–1988)' in his memory. I have to say it is an exquisite piece of music that I really didn't wanna sully with my hollering on top of it – so we kept it instrumental. My only regret is that we didn't have the budget to record it with an orchestra, it being recorded entirely with synthesisers. Mick and I had no input on 'Tadeusz', aside from encouragement, but we both loved it and it became the band's walk-on music on the Children Play tour, superseding 'Dambusters'.

The second track we recorded during those sessions was one of mine, 'Forevermore'. I always liked to tinker around on the piano in studios that had them, never really getting a chance otherwise. And with Simon and Craig both busy in the control room, I came up with this piece in the studio and immediately recorded it with no click track or rhythm keeping time. I scribbled some lyrics down on a bit of paper, sang 'em, added some string synth, and got Mick to somehow play drums to my somewhat erratic piano playing over the outro fade. All done, and mixed, within the space of a couple of hours. And it ended up being one of my favourite songs that I've written. Entirely spontaneous and in the moment. I love it when creativity comes as a gush and I have no option but to surrender to it. I've often been asked who I wrote the song for, the truth being no one in particular. By this time I had split up with Crazy Rachel and was ardently footloose and fancy-free. I would 'give myself to' pretty much anyone who asked.[5]

To prepare for the tour we played a couple of warm-up shows in Albion, the first at the Warehouse in Leeds on February 11, the club from which I'd been banned a couple of years previously. Ha, I'm back! Mick, alongside his mum and dad, was interviewed for the Yorkshire TV evening news, and when his dad was asked whether he liked The Mission he replied, 'Aye, they ain't bad. Not sure I'd like 'em tho' if our Michael weren't playing drums for 'em.' Any of our parents would probably have said the same.

Anyway, it was supposedly a *secret* gig but word had got out[6], and with 'TOS' flying high in the charts there were hundreds of people who couldn't get into the venue that evening.

After a couple more warm-up shows we found ourselves on a flight to LAX with Tony Van Den Ende, our video director, and a small film crew in tow, who were shooting our trip for the 'Beyond The Pale'

235

music video. While I spent a day holed up at the Franklin Plaza Suites doing interview after photo shoot after radio ID after interview, t'other three were being filmed bombing around Hollywood in a hired pink convertible, trying their hand at baseball in a batting cage, dodgem car racing, eating burgers at Johnny Rockets, shopping for hats, and generally having the time of their lives. All while I was trying to fathom the inexplicable meaning of *Children* for journalists who really didn't give a monkey's and were asking questions by rote. Interview after interview, the same questions. The only way to get through it all and to retain any sanity was to start telling fibs and making up stories to entertain myself, and just to see how much of the crapola I could make 'em believe. And most of it they gobbled up with relish.

Rightly or wrongly, when bands start to taste a little success, it's the singer who generally gets singled out for more attention. We would, however, and particularly in the early days, try to do as much of it as we could together as a band. And if that wasn't possible then the others would take it in turns to accompany me, so as to always try to reiterate that we were a band. But inevitably, as time wore on I ended up doing more and more of the promo by myself, not by choice I hasten to add. Well, if there was a choice involved then it would've been the choice of t'other three. And who can blame them? Even if they were sat next to me in an interview situation 95 per cent of the questions would be addressed to me. Who wants to just sit there and be my side-kick with their only contribution being the occasional grunt of affirmation to something I say? So, yeh, the band started bailing out on interviews and leaving me to it. And with practice, I became a lot more adept at handling the media than they were anyway. I think they'd all agree that none of them were entirely comfortable with a camera or a microphone being stuck in their face. As a natural consequence I did begin to feel a little alienated from the rest of the band. I think it's a feeling that every singer in the world experiences at some point. It's why singers gravitate towards each other; we know what we have to go through. I mean no disrespect to my fellow band members as I write this, but none of them have ever experienced that degree of scrutiny. Nor would they want to. I'm making it sound like it's a cross to bear; it's not. It can feel intense at times but there are plenty of perks to compensate, I can assure you.

San Diego was our first show in Southern California of this whirlwind promo trip, and during the day we took the opportunity to visit the world-famous zoo, where we were filmed watching the animals. Mick and I rode together on a camel, Mick wearing a Hunter's Club[7] T-shirt with the legend 'God Sent Us' emblazoned across the back. Indeed.

Next stop was the Coach House[8] in San Juan Capistrano, a quaint town on the coast between San Diego and LA, famous for its annual migrating swallows and home to the oldest in-use building in California – the Serra Chapel, part of the 18th-century mission. The area is also the site of both the first vineyard and first winery in California. God bless those missionaries.

We pulled up at the venue in the early afternoon, ready for soundcheck. There was already a sizeable throng waiting for us, among whom I spied a very pretty hippie girl with long red hair, wearing a big floppy purple hat and a smile as sharp as a blade with lips stained a shade I call panic-button-red. It's fair to say she stood out from the crowd. Once safely ensconced in the building I asked Stevie Sex-Pistol to go and ask the girl if she'd like to come in and watch the soundcheck and meet the band. Jeez, I shudder now at the transparency of it all, I couldn't even do my own dirty work... Anyway, long story short, she did come in and Stevie introduced her as Sheryl. She and I got chatting and soon hit it off. Sheryl was to become my long-suffering girlfriend for the next almost two years.

The following night we were at the Hollywood Palace, the scene of the previous year's debacle in which Craig and I both had dust-ups with local law enforcement in separate incidents and we had to cancel the show. Of course, we weren't to get out of LA this time either without *something* happening.

During the show I was swinging my microphone around onstage, à la Roger Daltrey, a practice I didn't engage in very often and for good reason. I wasn't very good at it, which made it bloody dangerous for the rest of the band and the front row of the audience. So, this particular evening I was swinging the mic around with gay abandon when the cable slipped out of my hand and the microphone disappeared into the audience, followed by a loud thud. Jez scrambled onstage and grabbed the microphone cable and started reeling the mic in as if he had caught a prize pike, and on retrieval handed it to me and on with the show we carried. We finished the encore and as we came offstage there were two police officers waiting for me. Oh my scunnered snout, here we go again. They led me upstairs and took me into one of the dressing rooms, barring entrance to anyone else (all caught on camera and appearing in the 'Beyond The Pale' music video). Inside they asked me to empty my pockets, which was a bit pointless as I was only wearing a pair of black leggings and my long black coat that I'd slipped on after coming offstage having discarded my top in the throes of performance. Finding nothing except ciggies in my coat pocket they then informed me that the venue paramedics had called them, something that they were obliged to do, when someone in the audience had been injured by my flying microphone. Utterances of criminal negligence and lawsuits followed, and another nightmare involving the LAPD looked to be unfolding. They said the microphone had struck a girl in the head, causing her to need medical attention, but before the police could proceed further and she be taken to hospital for further tests, she had asked to see me. I was led downstairs, again by the two police officers, and into a small room adjacent to the first aid station. There sat a voluptuous dark-haired beauty with an Elastoplast affixed to her forehead. I apologised for hurting her and asked if she was okay to which she replied she was fine and apologised in return for causing all the fuss. It really was no fuss at all, as I was starting to contemplate a night of torrid fornication with her instead of damage limitation or even possible incarceration. Such is the mind of men. We chatted for a short while until one of the police officers interjected and advised that she now leave for the hospital for further tests and a check-up. And then he asked her if she wanted to press charges. She looked at me with what I interpreted as regret, but really could well have been relief, and replied 'No, I'd just like a hug and a kiss before I go.' Ever the gentleman I was more than willing to oblige. And then she disappeared into the night and from my life forever, although the meeting is immortalised on celluloid.

The next day we flew out of LA to NYC, to play a sold-out Ritz show at which John Paul Jones joined us onstage to play keyboards on a couple of songs. JPJ had flown in for a few days to help promote our upcoming *Children* release. It was my turn to be sidelined in interviews, as most of the questions were addressed to him and after a few initial cursory queries about his involvement with our album the rest of the time was spent interrogating him about a possible Led Zeppelin reunion.

A couple of days of me being put in my place later and we then caught the late-night flight back to Heathrow, arriving early morning, just in time for another appearance on *TOTP*. After we'd appeared on the show for the first time when 'Tower Of Strength' was at number 20, the single had climbed to 13 the following weekend. And then again up to 12, the same week The Sisters Of Mercy entered the chart at number 17 with 'Dominion'. The Mission and Eldritch in the UK Top 20 at the same time… it didn't have quite the same seismic cultural effect of, say, a couple of years later when The Stone Roses and Happy Mondays appeared on *TOTP* on the same day. For our second 'TOS' appearance we roped in Jez, our roadie, to bash away on the congas. Sadly, it must've been his appearance with us that led to 'TOS' slipping down the chart to 18 the following week. No elusive Top 10 for us.

A few days spent fulfilling yet more promotional duties back in Blighty followed by a couple of days of production rehearsals in Northampton and we were off to Dublin to kick off the Children Play tour, which would take us to 25 different countries, including our first visits to Japan and South America, over the course of the next nine months or so. Oh, and *Children* was released on Monday, February 29.

Endnotes

1   While researching for this book I came across a fair few 'experts' online who expounded with absolute conviction that 'Tower Of Strength' was written with the DADGAD tuning on a guitar. That contention, I can confirm here and now and once and for all, is erroneous. It was written by moi in standard guitar tuning, EADGBE, and is played by using the bottom E string as the drone while playing the chord changes moving the same shape – 1st finger at the E/7th fret position on the A string, and 3rd finger at the E/9th fret position on the G string, damping the D/3rd string (it doesn't matter if you hit the open B and top E strings as they both work harmonically with the droning bottom E) – up and down the fretboard. Try it, preferably on a 12-string acoustic, it's so easy. And thereby endeth today's guitar tutorial.

2   Award-winning British artist and director Ian Emes made a name for himself through his pioneering and experimental film techniques and installations. In the early Seventies he came to the attention of Pink Floyd, who commissioned him to produce the legendary animated concert film for *Dark Side Of The Moon* in 1974. Since then, he has worked with some of

the biggest names in rock and pop, including Mike Oldfield and Paul McCartney, and his work has featured globally in a number of major exhibitions and live music tours. For more info on Ian's work see https://www.ianemes.com/.

3   *The Magnificent Seven* (1960) is a Western starring a dazzling list of Hollywood's leading men, including Yul Brynner, Steve McQueen and Charles Bronson, as a group of gunslingers hired to protect a Mexican village from bandits. Not to be confused with the travesty that is the 2016 remake of the same title.

4   Sian's mantra to me was, 'You only get to make a first impression once, Wayne. Remember that when you're opening your big gob in interviews.' Words that I've always remembered but rarely heeded.

5   This comment alludes to the chorus lyric of 'Forevermore' – 'I give myself to you, heart and soul, flesh and blood, for ever more' (lyrics by kind permission of me).

6   Maybe it was the pseudonym we were using that day – Three Anteaters & A Helmet Head – which gave the game away. Lots of people in the city of Leeds knew the members of The Mission in the biblical sense. It wouldn't have taken much sleuthing to work it out. (And no, I'm not gonna tell you who the Helmet Head is – you'll have to ask someone who lives in Leeds.)

7   The Hunter's Club were a greebo band out of Leicester in the late Eighties.

8   The Coach House was also my local venue when I later lived in Orange County, and I saw many shows there, my favourite being Chris Isaak attired in a dazzling silver lamé suit.

CHAPTER 12

The Only Meat That Will Touch These Lips Of Mine Is Human

PLAYLIST:
1. Wishing Well – Terence Trent D'Arby
2. Sign Your Name – Terence Trent D'Arby
3. I Wanna Be Adored – The Stone Roses
4. Weekender – Flowered Up   5. Strawberry Fields Forever – Candy Flip
6. Love Like Blood – Killing Joke
7. Walking In My Shoes – Depeche Mode
8. Heaven Knows – Robert Plant
9. Dream On – Aerosmith   10. Dream On – The Mission
11. Hit The Road Jack – Ray Charles   12. Burn The Witch – Radiohead
13. Rain – The Cult   14. You Was Born To Die – Blind Willie McTell
15. Blind Willie McTell – Bob Dylan   16. Grotesque – The Mission
17. Meat Is Murder – The Smiths
18. Kingdom Come (Forever And Again) – The Mission
19. Love – John Lennon

VIDEO PLAYLIST:
1. Kingdom Come (Forever And Again) – The Mission

Friday 4 March, 1988, and I was in my hotel room in Newcastle city centre preparing for that night's sold-out show at the City Hall. On the TV in the background was that week's *Chart Show* on Channel 4,

242

featuring the album chart run-down. *Children* was the highest new entry, straight in at number one. The album had shipped Silver (60,000 sales) and had been certified Gold (100,000 sales) within four days of its release. It was also number one at midweek in the BBC's chart. 'Tower Of Strength' was spending it's fourth week in the Top 20 singles charts, too. Three days earlier in Dublin we had just kicked off our biggest – and completely sold out – tour to date. We were on top of the world. A scummy, anachronistic, much-derided rock band who originally hailed from Leeds had defied all naysayers, including such self-appointed arbiters of taste as John Peel and the changeable on-a-weekly-basis opinion-shaper, the hag-rag *NME*. The slight disappointment of 'only' making it to number two when the 'official' album chart was released that Sunday (*Introducing the Hardline According to Terence Trent D'Arby* beat us to the top spot[1]) was tempered by taking to the stage in front of a rabid audience of 3,000 that night at one of the best venues in the world, Glasgow Barrowland.

The tour passed in a blur of frenzied adulation, mostly Apollos, city halls and universities, and on any given night I could look out from the stage into the seething mass and see a host of Wayne Hussey lookalikes, both male and female. Still, it was a flattering if surreal experience. I've seen Wayne Hussey dolls, toilet roll holders, teddy bears. I've seen my face adorn many a leather jacket and even tattooed on arms and backs.[2] The extent of some fans' fervour is mind-boggling. Of course, all bands have followers who are as zealous as The Mission's, many even more so. Some are quasi-religious in their fanaticism. The Sisters Of Mercy have always boasted a core audience who are as fanatical as any, and among whom I have been long regarded as the antichrist. I've always gotten a kick out of that. Of course, the degree of zealotry has tapered off over the years, what with the changing of fashions, but mainly due to our audience getting older and having more pressing concerns in their life than what shade of nail polish I'm currently wearing. But it still amazes me the lengths some fans go to when following the band, some travelling from as far as Australia, New Zealand, Japan, and North and South America when we tour in Europe. Which indicates that they must have better-paying jobs than mine to be able to afford to do so. Thousands have been bigger, brighter and far more aeonian than me, but in spring 1988 I was what I had always dreamed of being since I was a kid and first watched *A Hard Day's Night*: a rock star.

The Mission were perhaps at their zenith during this period in terms of popularity and commercial success. Certainly in the UK. But the winds of change were blowing. I remember being on the platform at Crewe train station later in the year and seeing two teenage girls wearing the baggiest jeans I'd ever seen (not a good look in my opinion, but what did I know, sporting my black leggings under a skirt) and colourful T-shirts, 'The Stone Roses' splashed across the front. Never 'eard of 'em. I would soon enough, though.[3]

I have very few stand-out memories of our European tour of spring 1988, our excesses being a little more restrained than previously. Don't misunderstand me – we still had our moments, but I think we chose those moments a little more judiciously after the experiences of our first US tour the previous year. As I write it's a strange realisation that the more sober I was the less I remember. Or, more likely, it was just that less memorable things happened to me the more I tempered my indulgences.

Our tour bus was broken into outside of the Manchester Apollo and my briefcase (yeh, I owned a briefcase but in my defence it was purchased on Haight-Ashbury in San Francisco and was covered in a paisley pattern) was stolen, but not before the thieves had dumped its contents, mainly notebooks and a sheaf of papers containing lyrics I was working on for the next album. Personally I was mightily relieved, although I know there are some in our audience who wish they'd stolen the lyrics, too.

We got to play at Bristol Colston Hall for the first time on this tour, which was a landmark for me as I was there all the time as a teenager to see my favourite bands. Our guest list that night was jam-packed with family – uncles and aunts and second cousins I didn't even know I had. Even both grandmas! I spotted them sitting in the front row on the balcony overlooking the stage. During our encore of 'Shelter From The Storm', I climbed the PA stack – with poor ol' Stevie following to prevent me potentially falling and breaking my neck – and up onto the balcony to give both my beaming grans a hug and a kiss and introduce them to the audience, who roared their approval. Both of them got mobbed and asked for autographs when they went to the toilets after the show, an incident they boasted about for years after at family gatherings.

Our agent and management had tried to persuade us to play Wembley Arena, or at least a couple of nights at Brixton Academy, but we thought it a better idea to schedule seven consecutive nights at the London Astoria[4] instead, all sold-out shows (a record that still stood when the venue finally, and sadly, closed its doors in 2009).[5] By now, climbing the PA had become a bit of a 'thing' for me, especially as the venues we played got bigger. I liked to make sure that the people upstairs were having as much fun as those down on the floor in front of the stage.[6] Each night I ventured further and further up and into the balconies and with a radio microphone – not on a cable – I could still contribute to the noise that was emanating from the stage. By the last couple of nights I ended up in the bar and was surprised to find guests of mine stood drinking and socialising and not watching the show at all, including Paul Raven, bless his cotton socks, from Killing Joke[7] and the comedian Alexei Sayle. Imagine their surprise when I turned up with a mic in hand, the band still hammering away at 'Shelter From The Storm'.

'Err, hello Wayne, what're you doing here? Shouldn't you be onstage?' stammered Raven.

Holding up my mic I replied, 'I am still onstage. I'm on a wander.

Thought I'd see who was in the bar, and then kick 'em off the guest list for tomorrow night.' I laughed as I informed the audience who I'd found skulking away in the bar.

On the last night at the Astoria we were joined onstage again by John Paul Jones playing keyboards. 'Shelter From The Storm' was recorded that night and edited down to a scant 9 minutes 26 seconds – God knows how long it was before – and later released as an extra track on a 12-inch single. Most notable, while listening today, is how hoary and self-indulgent this song had become compared to the no-meat-on-the-bone, energised version we'd performed on *The Tube* just over 12 months previously. That's what extensive touring in the US can do to you. And the sickly icing on the ever-fattening cake was JPJ's keyboards – a horrendous Eighties synth brass sound played in a jazzy fashion. Can't particularly blame JP for it, as it was where the band were at that time – living up to the critics' accusations of musical excess and increasing irrelevance. We continued ending our shows with 'Shelter' for the remainder of the year but it was becoming apparent we needed to replace it with something more slimline, though just as audience-involving.

After finishing up the UK leg of the tour we went on to mainland Europe with All About Eve as our support, their first jaunt abroad. Julianne Regan had previously embarked on a relationship with Simon, which dissolved early on during the run of shows. I saw Julianne suffer through the break-up but could do nothing to help. Slink was alright; he had Saskia at home, as well as occasionally finding comfort in the arms of strangers, as we all did, Craig aside. Night after night I'd watch Julianne pour her heart and soul into her singing and performance. It was cathartic for her, and during the course of the tour I started to see her heal and regain some of her lost spirit.

Julianne and I have enjoyed a friendship now for 35 years or so and I love her dearly. There's been times we've been very close and others where we haven't communicated for a couple of years. But it's a relationship that doesn't need constant communication. It's never been one of those high-maintenance friendships; you know the kind, where the 'friend' complains if they haven't heard from you in a few days, or you fail to reply to their email or WhatsApp message within minutes, or, God forbid, you miss their birthday. That's not real friendship anyway. True friendship isn't based on dependence. Sometimes I don't see some of my friends for years but as soon as I do it's like no time has passed and we pick up from wherever we left off. They know where I am if they need me and I know where they are if ever I'm in trouble. That being said, my attitude is slightly changing as encroaching age brings the realisation that I may never see some of these friends again, so a little more effort is being made these days to stay in touch. It's easier now, though, what with email, WhatsApp, Skype and all that t'interweb gubbins.

However, one huge regret I have regarding distant friends is when Jez messaged me in August 2019 to let me know that Stevie 'Sex-Pistol' Watson had died. I hadn't seen Stevie for a good few years; every time I was in Leeds I promised myself I'd go, but always found some feeble excuse not to. And then all of a sudden he's gone and I don't have the chance.

Stevie and I were very close for many years, living together in Leeds when I first moved there in late 1983. One of the very few people I felt completely safe and comfortable with, as well as working for the band and touring with us, Stevie also accompanied me on my writing excursion to the Black Mountains, as he did on a holiday we took to Italy in the summer of 1990 – a few days in Rome, which was primarily spent trying to score some drugs, and then when we did, holing up in our hotel room for the duration. The Vatican? The Colosseum? The Trevi Fountain? Forget it. I've got a better idea, let's shovel a pile of bugle up our beaks and stay in with the curtains drawn closed, listening to music and watching Italian TV. Apart from the Italian TV we coulda done that in Leeds and it would've cost me a lot less. We did make it out one day and climbed up the Spanish Steps, leaving both of us wishing we hadn't as we coughed and spluttered our way back to the sanctuary of our hotel. (I've since come to adore Rome and can quite happily walk for hours and days around the Eternal City now. But not in 1990.)

After a few days, I had arranged for us to travel to Firenze to go and stay with a mother and daughter who always turned up to our shows in Italy and kept inviting me to visit them at their home. On the day we planned to leave Rome, there was a train strike. So, like the rock star I thought I was, we took a taxi. From Rome to Florence. It cost me something like a million lira, the exchange rate being around 5,000 to the pound. I could be exaggerating – I've been known to – but I seem to remember the journey costing me the equivalent of around £250, which was a lot of money back then. Mummy and daughter lived high on the hill across the river, a beautiful spot with gardens and a pool overlooking the picturesque city of Firenze. I'm sure, knowing how my mind worked back then, I accepted the invitation to visit because of the prospect of a bit of mother-daughter carnal action but it transpired that possibility was never on the agenda. It soon became evident that mummy was trying a bit of chaperoned matchmaking. Stevie and I rode it out for a day or two, lounging around the pool supping on cold beers and chilled wines, before making our excuses and catching an earlier than scheduled flight back to Blighty...

So, back to Julianne and witnessing from close quarters her emotional hurt and then recovery led me to writing a song for her. That song? 'Butterfly On A Wheel'.

The inspiration behind the title is well-documented. When Mick Jagger and Keith Richards got themselves arrested and convicted for drug possession in 1967, the *Times* published an editorial by William Rees-Mogg called 'Who Breaks a Butterfly on a Wheel?' The piece was deemed instrumental in swaying public opinion in favour of the two Rolling Stones and helped grease the wheels of British justice during the successful appeals of both sentences. Rees-Mogg had himself borrowed the phrase, from Alexander Pope's 1735 poem 'Epistle to Dr. Arbuthnot', which alludes to 'breaking on the wheel', a particularly barbaric form of torture during which victims' bones were snapped by an iron bar while bound to a breaking wheel. To me, at least, the quote suggests heavy-handedness is being employed in a situation that really requires sensitivity.

As moderated as they were, there was yet more excesses – carnal, pharmaceutical and musical – on the European leg of the tour. It's not easy to resist the enticements put in one's way when touring with a successful rock band. As I live and breathe, and with all the best intentions in the world, many with far hardier resolve than me have succumbed to the temptations of life on the road. As Depeche Mode's Martin Gore wrote, 'Try walking in my shoes.' It's not a *normal* life. Every whim, every caprice, is catered to and indulged. And the bigger and more successful you get the more detached you become from *normal* moralities, *normal* societal behaviours and etiquettes, and *normal* responsibilities. There are people paid very good money to keep the 'artistes' sated and insulated from the mundanity of the real world. Of course it turns your head, how can it not? I've never known anyone to experience a degree of fame and not be affected by it. You'd have to be a megalomaniac sociopath not to be. Most famous people just learn to live with it – they have to – but *real fame* is not a state of being I would wish on my worst enemies and I fail to understand its allure. In the words of John Lennon, 'I don't intend to waste energy and time in an effort to become anonymous. That's as dumb as becoming famous in the first place.' However, I didn't experience fame wide or long enough to ever really get used to it, my 15 minutes lasting about 2 and a half and then really only in our metaphorical street.

All that being said, I was enjoying myself in 1988. One blot on the landscape was when I woke up in my empty hotel bed in Lund, Sweden, after a night of bacchanalia with a couple of blonde-haired buxom Vikings from Copenhagen to find my wallet and cash, my Dictaphone (on which I recorded ideas, both lyrical and musical, for songs), a few trinkets of (cheap) jewellery, and a couple of items of clothing had all disappeared in the night as I slept, along with the thieving minxes. They, like the villains in Manchester, left behind my lyric notebooks.

The tour rolled on through Europe and we played our final show at the Zénith in Paris on April 30. Within a day or two we found ourselves on a flight to the US again. We embarked on a short run of our own club shows up the East Coast and into Canada before joining up with the Robert Plant *Now And Zen* tour, our first show being at Poplar Creek Music Theater in Hoffman Estates, Illinois. Never heard of it? Nah, neither had we but it was a 25,000-capacity *shed*. A shed, as we know it in Britain, is a little wooden hut at the end of the garden in which the 'man of the house' keeps his gardening tools, lawnmower, homing pigeons, fishing tackle, golf clubs and football paraphernalia that he's not allowed to keep in the house. It's where he slinks off to for a sneaky smoke and, in the olden days, for a quick browse through his stash of well-thumbed *Fiestas* and *Club Internationals*, hidden away on the top shelf behind the big jar of odd screws, nails, nuts and bolts. There's something mucky about the British garden shed, isn't there? Hands up who's not had sex in a shed? Unlike a Mission audience when we play 'Tower Of Strength', I don't see many hands raised.

A *shed* in the US, on the other hand, has also no doubt been host to many grubby sexual indiscretions, but its main purpose is acting as a large, covered, outdoor music venue, usually with uncovered banks of grass rearing up at the back where the less affluent could bring their blankets and spread 'em on the ground upon which to sit and watch the show from afar. A bit like Wimbledon's Henman Hill. The 'cheap seats', we call 'em. Being as we were a late addition as support act for a swathe of shows down through the Midwest, that's where the Mission people were mostly situated in the sheds on the Plant tour. Many of

250

the seats directly in front of the stage, bought early by eager Robert Plant fans, were mostly empty or occupied by people who either greeted us with moue-faced distaste or, even worse, total indifference. I soon came to realise three things when playing to this audience:

1. The vast majority of the audience hated it and booed us when we performed our version of the Aerosmith song 'Dream On', regarding it as an act of desecration akin to Ozzy's pissing on The Alamo.[8] Once we realised this fact, we made sure to include 'Dream On' in the set every night because at least then we elicited a response. (It's better to be booed off than face the apathy of 'Oh, they've finished and left the stage? I didn't realise.')

2. As I said before, most of the people who came to see us were up on the hill, so I took to leaving the stage with my radio mic and navigating my way through the stalls up to 'our people'. One night on my way back to the stage, with the band still thundering away, I got stopped by a burly security guard and asked to show my ticket. I just showed him the mic in my hand and made a joke to the audience. Luckily, he saw the funny side of the situation and, laughing, he let me through. Note to self: always carry a microphone with you at gigs; in most cases it can get you into anywhere in the venue.

3. It's nothing to do with him personally, but I didn't have a great time supporting Robert Plant. Simon agreed with me. After our experiences supporting The Cult, The Psychedelic Furs and U2, and playing festivals where audiences were a lot more receptive to us, having to play in front of an audience as partisan as Robert's was really quite dispiriting at times. I'm not convinced it did us much good, that tour, in the long run. I've since read on forums and gig-lists some Plant fans claiming we were the worst opening act he ever had. That's another accolade I'm proud of. At least we're remembered, I guess, even if it's for the wrong reasons – I

can't remember who supported Be-Bop Deluxe in 1976 or even Depeche Mode in 2019, can you? We've had many support bands over the years that I have absolutely no recollection of. Nah, we preferred to play *our own* shows in small, sweaty clubs to *our own* audience, playing for as long as we liked. Craig and Mick quite liked the tour, though, because it meant we could turn up for soundcheck later than usual and only have to play for 40 minutes, then we'd have the rest of the evening free to get hammered.

Complaints aside – and I'm not really complaining – it was a great experience getting to hang out and watch Robert Plant and his band every night. Couldn't mention John Paul Jones, though; there didn't seem to be any love lost between those two. Don't ask me why, it was never explained by either. Maybe it was just banter in the same way as someone asking me how Craig is and me replying, 'What, that ol' curmudgeonly moaning Minnie?'

We arrived in New Orleans the day before we were due to play. We'd been invited to a party being thrown by the Atlantic Records boss, Ahmet Ertegun, for Robert and his tour entourage – which included us. The venue was a dinky, dark club just off Bourbon Street. There was a small, low stage, in front of which were a number of chairs in which we all sat rapt as we were entertained by an old, blind, black blues singer performing with just a beat-up acoustic guitar and a burnt, deep, gnarled rasp of a voice. Craig remembers him being led onstage and sat down on the stool by his wife. Sadly, neither I nor any of my compadres can remember his name but being blind he was called 'Blind something or other', as all old blind blues greats seemed to be.[9] I know Robert, who is a life-long blues aficionado, was mightily impressed that Mr Ertegun had arranged for this particular blues legend to perform privately for us that evening. I knew very little about Delta blues back in 1988, only getting into it some years later, so I really wish I could remember who it was we were entertained by that night. One amusing incident took place during the evening, though. I'll let Simon tell you what happened: 'I remember it was a typical blues/jazz club with tables and chairs facing the stage. The booze was flowing and everyone was dancing in their seats and having a great time. I felt my chair being rocked about from behind me and I thought, Ho ho! Exuberance! Then the rocking was with hands on my shoulders and I thought 'alright, alright... calm down.' Then the hands went under my arms, onto my chest, and started pinching my nipples. So I turn around to say, 'what the fuck!?' and it's Ahmet. The look of horror on his face told the whole story when he realised I was a long-haired man. He immediately stood up and left, looking embarrassed. I told Robert about it the next day and he laughed his socks off.'

By the end of the night I found myself with a couple of our crew in a drag bar making friends with some of the locals. That was fun. Crawled into bed as the sun was rising to sleep it off before that night's show.

Not all the venues on that tour were *sheds*. There were a few indoor arenas, too, places that usually played host to basketball or, even on occasion, ice hockey games. One such place was the Lakefront Arena, home to the men's college basketball team the New Orleans Privateers. Our dressing rooms were the team's changing rooms, with the shared toilet and shower facilities in between having access to both dressing rooms. After the show I was in a toilet cubicle enjoying the ministrations of a female friend, Jodie from Salt Lake City, when I heard whispers, titters and tell-tale moans from the cubicle next to ours. I decided to investigate. I stood on top of the toilet and peeped over the top.

'Hello, Wayne, fancy seeing you here!' said Robert Plant, looking up at me in much the same position as I had been just seconds before.

'Oops, sorry to interrupt, Robert, looks like you're having fun so

I'll leave you to it,' and with that exchange I jumped down from the toilet and carried on where I had left off with Jodie.

A few nights later and we were in Tempe, Arizona, our last show on the *Now And Zen* tour. We walked onstage and I casually sauntered up to the microphone and announced, 'Ah, it's great to be here tonight at the Arizona State University' and the whole place started booing, and this was *before* we'd even played a note. It was a most perplexing moment, one from which we never really recovered. You oughtta have heard the razzing when we played 'Dream On'! It was only after the show that I was told we were actually at the *State University Of Arizona*, Arizona State University being their arch-rivals and based in Phoenix. How was I supposed to soddin' know that?

The night did take a turn for the surreal after the show, however, and ended up being memorable for an entirely different reason. We were sat backstage in our dressing room, bemoaning our poor response from the audience – perhaps the worst on the entire tour – when Pete Turner came in and said, 'Wayne, there's a young lady at the back door who says she knows you and wonders if she could come and say hello?'

'What's she like?' I enquired, lasciviously.

'It's hard to tell as she's dressed in a long white bridal gown with a matching veil hiding her face.'

'Oh, go on then, bring her in, this could be fun,' was my instruction.

A few minutes later and in walked the girl, dressed as Pete had described.

'Hi, do you remember me?' she asked, as she lifted her veil to reveal her rather pretty face.

Frantic with a quick rifling of my memory banks – much like a scene from a film where an Interpol computer scans through a million faces in seconds, trying to find a match – I had to concede defeat. 'Mmm, could you give me a clue?'

'Oh, we were married about a thousand years ago,' was her deadpan reply.

Quick as a flash I countered, 'Aw, right, it's coming back to me now. How're the kids?'

We did end up consummating our 'marriage' that night, albeit a thousand years or so after the ceremony, but there was a strange moment in my hotel room when she emptied her bag onto the bed looking for a lipstick or a cigarette lighter or some such item and out plopped a small handgun. With a gulp I asked, 'What have you got that thing for, is it loaded?'

She picked up the gun and, pointing it at me, looked me in the eye and then down to my crotch and replied, 'Is *that* thing loaded? It'd better be or I may be forced to use this on you.' Instantly my gun *was* loaded, cocked and ready to shoot. Later she explained she was a security guard and was licensed to carry the gun as part of her job, but I must confess that thoughts of John Lennon being gunned down by an obsessed fan did, at first, flitter across my mind before thoughts of perversion took precedence.

After the *Now And Zen* tour we ended our US jaunt with a run of our own up the West Coast which included an LA show where, for the first time, we managed to avoid any run-ins with the local law enforcement. We did, however, have one with the venue security.

The John Anson Ford Amphitheatre is situated at the foot of the Hollywood Hills, just off the 101 Freeway. It's a great outdoor venue for those warm summer nights (LA has several such places, most notably the historic Hollywood Bowl where I once saw Ray Charles perform, and later Radiohead) and the evening we played, Thursday 16 June, was no exception – a balmy evening about to get cauldron hot. The show was a sell-out and from the off the audience were well up for it, up and on their feet, dancing and having fun. Ten minutes into the show and I saw one of the beefy front-of-stage security gorillas openly punching a young man in the face. I immediately brought 'Like A Hurricane' to a shuddering halt and, pointing accusingly at the stage security, I shouted down the microphone, 'Yeah, you guys there in the yellow jackets, fuck off, we don't need you.' A thunderous cheer of approval rose from the audience. Visibly squirming and bristling, the bouncers initially refused to move. Several minutes of stand-off ensued and we refused to resume playing until security was removed. Eventually the Neanderthals realised that we were serious and they'd have a chaotic riot on their hands if they didn't acquiesce, and weighing up the odds – 1,500 irate punters against a dozen venue security – they wisely decided that discretion was the better part of cowardice and made their way to sit along the back of the stage for the rest of the show, their tails firmly between their musclebound legs. Every time I turned around to look at them – these fully grown, brutish-looking mofos – they were blowing *raspberries* at me. I could only laugh, which seemed to make them blow even harder. It was bizarre. With the retreat of the bouncers the first of many stage invaders clambered over the monitors to then hurl themselves into the night sky and back into the churning throng. It was left up to our crew and local friends to eject stage invaders who outstayed their welcome but mostly we were able to control the audience ourselves without the need for the venue's over-aggressive dumb-nut raspberry blowers. We raised the levels of noise and heat a little more when we brought on our mate, Billy Duffy of The Cult, who was by then a resident of LA, to join us on guitar for a raucous rendition of The Cult's 'Rain' and our own 'Shelter From The Storm'. One reviewer commented on the show, 'it was a risky decision (to get rid of the house security) but, in the closed confines of the gig, a genuine extension of friendship, and after last year's LA nightmare, a PR move worth a hundred radio interviews. Wayne Hussey does a lot of things onstage that he shouldn't, but he does some things so overtly well that he's beyond comparison.'[10] I like that.

After the tour concluded and before returning to Britain we found ourselves out in the desert of Southern California, in the middle of nowhere, miles from even the nearest road or trail let alone a gas station, shooting a video for what was proposed to be the third single from the *Children* album – 'Kingdom Come'. At one point in the early afternoon when the blazing sun was high in the sky, we heard some rinky-dinky jingle coming from somewhere, evidently getting closer by the second. And up and over a sand dune appeared the surreal sight of an ice cream van. We thought at first it was a hallucination, perhaps brought on by sunstroke, but no, it was real. It stopped at our base camp and we all bought 99s with Flakes or flavoured lollies and then, with its bells ringing their insistent tune, it disappeared back over the nearest sand dune. A few hours later and we first heard, and then saw, a motorcycle racing towards us across the sands. We'd hired a Harley-Davidson for Mick to ride during the shoot, but he was stood with us as the motorcyclist approached so we knew it wasn't him. The mystery bike pulled up, the rider, dressed all in black leather, dismounted and pulled the bike up onto its kickstand and then took off his helmet. Well, flibbertigibbets, it was only our mate, Billy Duffy. Again. Even out in the middle of miles and miles of desert we couldn't escape him. Of course we were happy to see him, although amazed he'd managed to find us.

While we were away on tour in the middle of April, 'Beyond The Pale' was released as a single in the UK. It had entered the singles chart at a disappointing number 36 and while it had shimmied up to 32 the following week, that was as high as it would reach, spending one more week in the Top 40 before quietly slipping away and into Woolworth's bargain bins. As we were out of the country at the time its poor performance hadn't particularly bothered us, but it had raised alarm bells at Phonogram, who had expected it to fare a lot better. Compared to the success of *Children* and 'Tower Of Strength', the three weeks 'Beyond The Pale' spent in the lower reaches of the Top 40 were regarded as a bit of a flop, and thus it was decided to save face by releasing no further singles from the album. Despite having filmed the video for it, plans to release 'Kingdom Come' as a single in Europe were shelved, although the US label did release a promo-only 12-inch vinyl to media outlets with another Spike extended mix on one side and the shorter, single version on the other.[11] We'd been playing around with a piano-led ballad version of the song in sound-checks and rehearsals and thought it was perhaps a good idea to record this new, stripped-down rendition as an interim single to kinda tide us over while we worked on new songs for the next album.

So, during the summer of '88 we booked into the big room down-stairs at the legendary and storied Olympic Studios in Barnes, London. Paul and Linda McCartney were working in the studio upstairs at the same time – sadly, I didn't bump into Macca at all on his way to the loo á la Freddie Mercury at the Townhouse – but because of their much trumpeted vegetarianism they demanded there be no meat or fish products on the premises while they were in residence. So, all meals and snacks provided by the studio had to be strictly vegan.[12] Now, I'm a veggie myself and have been for 20 years – this time round. I did flirt with it once or twice before but never for any real length of time. As with most things I liked that I knew were bad for me, my resolve was never strong enough to be able to resist the temptation for too long. My longest period of vegetarianism was in the early Nineties, although I was to spectacularly fall off the wagon. On this occasion I hadn't eaten meat in months and, having been at home during that period, it was pretty easy not to do so. Then, during the summer we were flying out to Europe somewhere to play a festival. Having not seen the crew lads for a while we had a few drinks in the bar at Heathrow to celebrate our reunion before boarding the plane. Of course, being slightly soused I got the hunger. En route to the gate there was a McDonald's and I stopped and bought a Super-Big-Mac, or whatever they're called, and boarded the plane, McDonald's bag in hand, and took my seat. I fell asleep before take-off but woke up as the drinks cart was being wheeled around for the first time. I was sat next to Big Dave – lovely lad and our onstage monitor engineer, later promoted to front-of-house sound as well as tour manager. Dave had given me a nudge and I asked for an alcoholic beverage of some description. With my drink I decided to tuck into my Big Mac, the first meat, if you can truthfully call it meat, to pass my lips in a long time. I was about halfway through the burger when one of the flight attendants came up with a meal tray in her hand and, checking the seat number, she quizzically asked, 'Are you Mr Hussey?' With my gob full of Big Mac I nodded affirmatively. Glancing at the half-eaten burger in my hand she said, 'Oh! I do hope I've got this right. Here's the vegetarian meal you ordered.' Busted! Big Dave stifled his laughter as I sheepishly took the tray from her.

And then I was back on the meat again until about 20 years ago, when Cinthya and I were staying with our very good friend, Claudia, in Brighton. Claude is a long-time vegan and at the time was working for PETA. We'd been out for a scrumptious vegan meal (never knew that beansprouts and twigs could taste so delicious) and had gotten around to talking about her work. When we returned to her house I asked to see some of the videos PETA had made covering the inhumane treatments of animals during meat production. Of course, I'd seen some of these videos before and was well aware of what meat was, but I could always quite easily disassociate what was on the dinner table from where it came from. But watching those videos that night, hideously cruel and monstrously barbaric, did it for me once and for all. From that day to this neither Cinthya or myself have ever knowingly eaten meat or fish again. It was difficult at first, after 40-plus years of meat being a staple part of my diet, the smell of sizzling bacon in the mornings being particularly hard to resist, but eventually over time any desire has long since abated, and now it doesn't ever cross my mind. Much like my use of amphetamines – daily at one point but I haven't touched the stuff in decades. One line would probably finish me off now anyway.

In our culture, we are blessed with ever-increasing options for veggies, and being on tour and able to specify our daily riders means that I and other veggies and vegans among our travelling retinue are always catered for just as well as the meat-eating barbarians, the rest of the band included.

By the way, while I've made the choice to be veggie I don't judge others who haven't. I'll call them 'cannibals' and 'savages', just as they will call me 'hippy-dippy' or Citizen Smith or other such light-hearted jibes. I'm not one of the hard-liner militants, like those who insist on no meat or fish backstage, and I have no problem sitting at a dinner table with people who eat it. I don't believe I have the right to impose my beliefs on those who don't share 'em, even if I am 'Our Glorious Leader'. I'm well aware of Morrissey's edict of no meat anywhere in the venue at his shows and it's laudable, but I do know that some of his crew members resent his demands and pop out during the day to chomp down on a Whopper or scurry off for an after-show kebab without the boss's knowledge. Alongside Johnny Marr, Morrissey's *Meat Is Murder* campaign is to be admired and certainly he has been instrumental in many a young Smiths fan converting to vegetarianism, and for that achievement alone he should be forgiven such sins as voicing contrarian opinions that don't tally with current popular (and trendy) thinking. And for releasing *Kill Uncle*. Of course there are other high-profile vegetarians/vegans, among them Chrissie Hynde, Joaquin Phoenix, Thom Yorke and Billie Eilish, who are just as vocal in their support of this particular lifestyle choice, but it's perhaps Morrissey that is the most celebrated, certainly in the world I inhabit. I heard a tale from a South American promoter that Morrissey's band and crew had flown into Santiago, Chile, to play a show. Morrissey was to arrive later. They'd all checked into their rooms at one of the best hotels in the city and some were resting up, sleeping off the jet lag, while others were out investigating the city. Moz arrived and was shown to his suite. He walked in and adorning the walls were various works of art. One painting depicted a scene of a lion with a dead bird clenched in its jaws. Upon viewing it Moz demanded that the entire entourage vacate this particular hotel immediately and the promoter check them into another of similar calibre post-haste. Most *normal* people would, without wishing to disturb the band and crew, simply ask to be moved to another room free of the offending art. But not Morrissey. I actually found the story quite amusing and pondered whether I might be able to pull a trick like that, soon realising that I'd just be told to bugger off by our crew and the rest of the band.

Back at Olympic Studios and we were ready to start recording the new version of 'Kingdom Come'. We'd been persuaded to work with producer *du jour* Julian Mendelsohn on these sessions. He'd recently been nominated as Producer Of The Year at the 1988 British Phonographic Industry awards for his work with Pet Shop Boys, Elton John and Dusty Springfield, among others. I found him to be the most passive producer I have ever worked with. Basically, he left us to do what we wanted while he sat on the couch at the back of the control room reading a newspaper and occasionally looking up and making a comment like, 'yeh, that's a good bass drum sound' or 'throw a compressor over the vocal'. Very little input or even inter-action, leaving all the technical whatnot to the engineer and the musical malarkey to us. I didn't dislike him, I just found him to be... uninvolved. Maybe he didn't like us or the song, I dunno, but the upshot was that none of us felt the new version – retitled as 'Kingdom Come (Forever And Again)' – warranted being a single, so it ended up as an additional track on the later studio outtakes album, *Grains of Sand*.

Sheryl, my new girlfriend who I'd met in San Juan Capistrano in February, flew over to the UK from her home in Orange County for a few weeks over the summer. We'd seen each other a few times during the US tour, and having a girlfriend around had calmed me down a little, if not curbed my philandering. I'd still sneak off for assignations while she was distracted elsewhere, possibly with assignations of her own. As much fun as I could be to be with (wink) I wasn't a particularly easy boyfriend, certainly not reliable, and nigh on impossible to tie down or control. But that was the way I was back then and I never made any secret of it; I never offered faithfulness or made promises I didn't intend to keep. If you could accept that then I was great company – make demands and then it was 'bye bye, ta for the memories'. And it was reciprocal. If I wasn't around then I didn't expect my partners to sit alone at home and pine for me. Go out and make jolly with other people!

Sheryl and I were always fine when we were together and we enjoyed being together, but when we weren't, neither of us were committed to a conventional monogamous relationship. The main difference between us, though, was that my dalliances were mostly with people I'd only just met and would very unlikely meet again. Not that I always wanted it that way but I was constantly on the move, and the only ways to stay in touch before the internet were by sending the occasional postcard or making the even rarer phone call, and calling from a hotel room cost an absolute fortune. Just ask Craig. He once made a call from his hotel room in Buenos Aires to Leona, his girlfriend, at home in London. He let the phone ring for maybe a minute or so but no one answered, so he returned the phone to its cradle. When we came to check out he was handed a bill for £80 for that unanswered call. He wasn't best pleased, still moans about it some 30-odd years later. For months after we'd jibe, 'Hey, Addo, does 80 quid ring a bell?' You can also ask Simon. He'd regularly phone his girlfriend in New York City from points around the globe. One night he phoned her and, being a little inebriated, fell asleep during the conversation, the call remaining connected all night. That was a hefty bill too, of several hundred dollars. My preferred means of communication was the cheaper trusty ol' postcard, and I'd quite often arrive home before the postcard was even delivered. 'I sent you a postcard from Paraguay, honest I did,' I'd say, pleading my case.

'You bloody liar, you just couldn't be bothered to write or call, eh?', the accusation would be tossed at me like a firecracker.

Imagine my glee when the postcard would finally arrive, weeks later. 'Have to make it up to me now then, doncha?' I'd gloat.

On the rare occasion when there was an unguarded phone in a venue production office we'd take it in turns to make quick calls home, all at the expense of the poor, unwitting promoter. All the bands did it, I'm sure. These days it's a doddle to keep in touch while away but the downside is that now we really don't have any excuse when we don't.

Sheryl didn't ask for or expect much from me, and neither me from her, and that suited us fine. I knew that she enjoyed liaisons while I was away but what I didn't know, at least not immediately, was that some of those affairs were pretty close to home with people I knew, friends of mine in other bands, and even on one occasion a member of my own band. But that wasn't uncommon. There were quite a few people with two or more Mission notches on their bedposts. One person, I believe, had all four of us, plus a number of our crew! I had no compunction about coupling with the partners of friends and, on occasion, fellow band members' girlfriends either. I don't think any of us did. What you get is what you give and what you give is what you get. Such was my notoriety at this time that a lot of people didn't like me, and I knew some just wanted to fuck Sheryl so that they could boast they'd shagged Wayne Hussey's girlfriend. And of course I knew that some people just wanted to shag me so that they could say they fucked Wayne Hussey. Well, join the club – a rather large one at that. There's all kinds of reasons to have sex; or you don't need any reason at all. Mostly though it's just fun and meaningless. A body function like any other. Of course, it can mean the world and be life-affirming, spiritual and transcendent, and an enriching manifestation of your feelings for each other when you're with someone you love. Likewise, some of the best sex I've ever had has been with complete strangers, some whose name I didn't even know. We all have our own definitions of what love is and, for me, sex isn't love and shouldn't be confused as such. Love is a far more precious state of being, a higher state of grace. Love can last a moment or it can last a lifetime. Ephemeral or eternal. Love is caring, is giving, is needing, is wanting, is respect, is truth, is being unafraid to show your true self and willing to stand naked and bare. Love is being willing to die for the ones you love, to put them first in all things. Love comes and it goes, it ebbs and it flows, on occasion it can feel more akin to hate, but above all else in my mind, love is simply feeling like I am, or want to be, a better person when I'm in their presence. No one's ever died from lack of sex but it is possible to die from lack of love. I was with Sheryl for close to two years so, yes, there was some genuine affection there between us and moments of real love, but love in the conventional, moral sense? I don't think I was capable of it at that time.

Sheryl and I spent a few days in Paris – it being her first time in Europe, I had wanted to show her one of my favourite cities. We visited all the major tourist attractions – the Eiffel Tower, Notre Dame, Montmartre, the Louvre, Musée D'Orsay, a boat ride down the Seine, and one day, a trip out to the Palace of Versailles. While we were there wandering around the gardens I was spotted by a group of about a dozen schoolgirls on a trip from Ireland, who started trailing Sheryl and me. 'Hey, look, those young girls are staring at you and following us!' said my new and impressed inamorata. Eventually the girls mustered up the nerve to approach and ask for autographs and photos. Of course I was more than willing to oblige, as much to impress Sheryl as anything else. 'Oh, thank you, Bono, we love you', they chorused. For fuck's sake.

Endnotes

1   In fairness, it was a mighty fine album, and to be held off the top spot by such an iconic record is no shame. I even bought it myself, graced as it is with at least two phenomenal singles in 'Wishing Well' and 'Sign Your Name'.

2   A girl in Italy once asked me to sign one of her breasts. Next time I saw her, she'd had my signature permanently tattooed and asked me to sign her other breast. I obliged, and she went and had that tattooed as well, an act I daresay she's probably regretted since and which I did advise her she would.

3   Pop music is ephemeral and movements come and go with predictable regularity. As I attempted to explain in *Salad Daze*, once a youth movement becomes popular it's infiltrated and corrupted by the mainstream and loses its potency. The more creative and forward-looking end up transcending their roots. Most don't. Few trends survive, and if they do, they are largely perceived as being hopelessly retrogressive (see Fifties Teddy Boys, Sixties mods and hippies, Seventies glamsters and punks, Eighties goths). I'm today reading that the skinny jean is OUT and the baggie jean is making a comeback! God help us. Who wants to look like Ian Brown or Shaun Ryder did in 1988/89? Come to think of it, who wants to look like anyone did in 1988, even Wayne Hussey (showing my age, aren't I)? And as I've bitched before, the very worst offender was sports apparel becoming *fashionable*. Bands appearing onstage in sweatpants, hoodies and trainers is just not on in my book. Call me old-fashioned but where's the glamour?

4   Located at 157 Charing Cross Road, right next to the junction of Oxford Street and Tottenham Court Road, the Astoria was built as a warehouse in the 1920s. Over time it was used as a cinema, a ballroom, and was eventually converted into a theatre in the Seventies. After further conversion it re-opened in the mid-Eighties as a nightclub, becoming one of London's most important music venues. In addition to the seven nights on the *Child's*

Play tour, we played there numerous times over the years, it being my favourite London venue to play. Sadly, the place was torn down in 2009 to accommodate the new Crossrail construction.

5   It was a great idea in principle, and the shows were increasingly blinding, but after a couple of days it began to feel like a residency and we didn't like it. Same venue, same trek to the top of the two or three flights of stairs to reach the same dressing room where the same rider was waiting for us night after night.

6   Reproduced with kind permission from Steve Sutherland, this is his piece 'Letter From America', which he wrote for a *Melody Maker* review of our show at The Ritz, NYC, appearing in the March 19, 1988, issue. I came across this again while researching for this book and it raised a titter. Hope it does the same for you.

'Right now, though, Wayne is writhing around the stage more like a kid in a sandpit than, say, Jim Morrison. He meticulously peels off his shirt and shoes and socks, accepts a cowboy hat from the crowd, tries it on and wings it back, and launches the band into 'Shelter From The Storm'. He's trying to lift the show, trying to force it, physically, into a higher dimension and suddenly it occurs to him to climb the speaker stack and head for the balcony. He clambers up with difficulty while the band integrate 'Light My Fire' and 'Hello, I Love You' into 'Shelter' – the old Bunnymen trick – and the first person he encounters is... me!

'Hello Wayne.

'Hello Steve,' he sings and hands me the mike while he scrambles up onto the balustrade. He's now precariously perched some 30 or more feet above the crowd and he grabs the mike and makes for the back of the hall singing Led Zep's 'Rock 'N' Roll'.

'Working his way around the precipice, he scrambles back down onto the stage with, for all I know, the grace of an angel. I missed this bit. You see, he trod on my balls on the way back and I spent the end of the gig in a foetal position blinking back the tears.

'I was a bit bloody dumbfounded when I met you on that balcony,' he says later backstage. 'Sorry I trod on your bollocks. Here, you can dangle them in here if you like.' Wayne's stripped to the waist and has his feet in a bowl of water. 'Cut me bloody foot. Gotta watch out for infection.'

'There are four girls on the bench next to him, all vying for his attention. One is breaking up a rose he'd earlier thrown into the crowd and dropping the petals into his footbath. He looks like a cross between a garden gnome and a grinning buddha. Someone comes in and says there's a girl crying outside because she can't get in to see him. Apparently she's English so Wayne says 'let her in.' The DJ meanwhile is playing 'This Corrosion'.

'I'll bloody kill 'im!' Wayne jokes as the girl appears and starts into this anecdote about how she once danced with Craig at some disco or other. The other girls are getting jealous and the boldest, the one in the All About Eve tee-shirt, climbs onto his knee and dangles her feet in the bowl too. Pretty soon there are six people paddling and no room at all for my poor balls.'

7   Bass player Paul Raven, known mostly for his stint in Killing Joke after Youth had left the band, was a top, top man – funny as fuck but somehow gentle. I bumped into him many times over the years, mostly backstage quaffing someone else's rider, usually ours. And he always had the most beautiful women with him who always seemed to be German. He asked to be considered as bass player when Craig left The Mission in 1992 and, as both Mick and I were, and remain, big fans of his playing, we took his offer seriously. However, we had no plans to tour and didn't really have a band as such at that point so Raven, in his inimitable way, immersed himself in a host of other projects, including work with Murder, Inc., Pigface and Ministry. It was a huge shock to hear of his death in 2007 from a heart attack at only 46 years old. Sorely missed. Another gone too early.

8   On February 19, 1982, the Prince of Darkness himself, Ozzy Osbourne, offended the entire state of Texas by taking a wee on The Alamo, the scene of a pivotal and bloody battle between Mexican and Texan troops during the Texas Revolution of 1836. Consequently, the site is a revered symbol of Texan, and American, pride. Ozzy, there for a promotional photo shoot, was taken short and needed a piddle. Rather than do what 'normal' folk would do and go looking for a 'rest room', in a prime example of rock stars thinking themselves exempt from 'normal' societal convention, he whipped out his todger and pissed – not on the walls of The Alamo itself, as legend has it, but against the Cenotaph. That was enough to get him arrested, although it's been claimed that had he pissed on the *actual* Alamo, the local police wouldn't have arrested him – they'd have beaten him to death. Ozzy was banned from playing in San Antonio after the incident, a ban lifted 10 years later after he donated $10,000 to the Daughters of the Republic of Texas, who maintain the monument. This story brings new meaning to the term 'spending a penny'.

9   Just some of the blind Delta blues artists: Blind Lemon Jefferson (1893–1929),

Blind Blake (1896–1934), Blind Willie Johnson (1897–1945), Blind Boy Fuller (1904–41), Delta Blind Billy (no birth records), and, my favourite, Blind Willie McTell (1898–1959), who plied his trade exclusively using a 12-string acoustic. Blind Willie McTell is also a fave of Bob Dylan's who, in 1983, recorded a tribute to the old blues legend entitled, strangely enough, Blind Willie McTell, and then inexplicably left it off the album he was recording at the time, *Infidels*. It was eventually released in 1991 as part of Dylan's Bootleg Series. It is arguably one of His Royal Bobness' finest songs. It is definitely one of my faves.

10 Our chum Neil Perry, for *Sounds*, July 30, 1988.

11 That 12-inch fetches a pretty penny these days in certain circles. I've got a couple stashed away for my emergency pension fund.

12 There was mutiny in our ranks regarding the McCartneys' 'no meat' regime. We complained to studio management that while we may not be as illustrious a client as an ex-Beatle, we were still paying for use of the studio, its amenities and catering just the same as the Maccas were, and therefore should be afforded the same courtesies. It worked. A compromise was reached and the McCartneys agreed that we could order in food from outside to be delivered, at Olympic's expense, as long as it was eaten in the studio where we were working and not in any of the social areas such as the dining room, kitchen, reception or TV/games room. Fair enough.

CHAPTER 13

A Man Can't Serve Two Masters, It's Either The Good Lord Or The Bad...

PLAYLIST:
1. Even Better Than The Real Thing – U2
2. Butterfly On A Wheel – The Mission   3. Into The Blue – The Mission
4. Martha's Harbour – All About Eve   5. Amelia – The Mission
6. Deliverance – The Mission   7. Belief – The Mission
8. The Grip Of Disease – The Mission
9. Grapes Of Wrath – The Mission   10. Bird Of Passage – The Mission

VIDEO PLAYLIST:
1. Martha's Harbour – All About Eve (*TOTP*)

So what is it with this Bono *thing*? We look nothing alike. Do we? I admit I may have an unfortunate passing resemblance to Geddy Lee, the bass player in Rush, and back in the salad days of back-combing my hair I heard the lazy accusation more than once that I was either a John Cooper Clarke, Robert Smith or Ian Hunter wannabe. But Bono? Come on. He did start wearing big hats when I came on the scene but his was more of a cowboy Stetson while mine was always more the gaucho-bolero sort. I'll leave it up to you to decide which is groovier. Mr Paul Hewson also took to wearing dark glasses a little bit later too and, while I'm not claiming that he started copying me, he even started donning dresses and make-up – and didn't he look scrumptious – around the time of U2's *Achtung Baby*, their best album for what it's worth. Bono even wrote 'Even Better Than The Real Thing' about me. Just take a moment for that to sink in. Okay? Of course, just in case you are now falling off your chair in disbelief at my self-absorption, let me make it perfectly clear – *I am joking*. Don't get me wrong, despite coming across as a sanctimonious twonk at times (but then who doesn't), I like him. What he does and what he says I believe is born of genuine good intention. And how can you dislike a man who once paid $1,700 to fly his hat first-class from Dublin to Italy for a show after he'd accidentally left it at home?

So, I've endured an adulthood where people have confused me with him. It's not been an everyday occurrence but enough to be perturbing and, as recounted here in this book, sometimes downright embarrassing. It still happens even now, although much more seldom. How? Although my mum and, I'd like to think, Cinthya would argue differently, I'll concede Bono is more handsome than me; but then, having money will very often confer comeliness on an average-looking man. I've got a bigger, more noble snoot and stand almost three inches (that's seven centimetres) taller than him – and *I'm* only 5 foot 8 inches (1.73 metres). Our voices, both singing and speaking, sound completely different; he can reach higher notes than me, but he can't get down as low as I can. He speaks with an, admittedly, lovely sing-song Irish lilt while my accent is more mongrel – a bit Scouse-Yorkshire northern but with a pronounced West Country burr when I've had a drink or two. He wears more expensive designer clothes and sunglasses but then he's got a lot more dosh than I have, and as another consequence of him being extraordinarily wealthy, he probably smells nicer too. He can afford more expensive soaps, shampoos and Eau de Cologne. *My* personal preference, for anyone that needs to buy me a present, is Hugo

270

Boss Man Eau de Toilette for the daytime, and, for evening wear, Acqua di Parma Colonia Intensa. Maybe it's a reaction to years of being a scruffy, scummy bugger but these days I even squirt a little of that on just before I go onstage. I think it's important to smell good when you're performing, although I'm not sure why. I don't really have to impress the rest of the band with how I smell, certainly not when you know how they smell. I guess it's for those times when I get down among the front rows of the audience. I like the idea that they think I smell nice when they get that close to me. I like them to go home after a show saying, 'That Hussey, he can be a bit of a twonk like Bono, but he does smell scrummy.'

I was introduced to Acqua di Parma by Gemma, Gary Numan's larger-than-life wonderful wife, when she bought me a bottle for my birthday a few years back and it's been a favourite ever since. Not sure Gary wears it though, as it's probably a little too effeminate a fragrance for him, he being far more manly than I. Not suggesting Gary wears Brüt or owt (and he does always smell nice, too), but he always smell like a man. If the perfumier is out of those two then I do also like Minotaure Paloma Picasso for those *special* occasions and, a more recent preference, the aptly named Black XS by Paco Rabanne, which is a good all-rounder. It's certainly a far cry from a brief period I went through around 1988 when I denounced all deodorants and perfumes as anathema and refused to wear anything, preferring my own Eau de Natural Essence. Of course, I showered and bathed, but a human stops being able to smell their own odour after a while as the receptors in our noses shut down after smelling the same scent for too long. That would explain how sometimes someone can sit down next to us on the Tube, or at the cinema or on a plane and they stink to high heaven. Don't be too judgemental, though, because most people obviously don't know they do and sometimes their malodorousness is due to illness. But maybe all it takes is a quiet word. I'd rather know I ponged than walk around in ignorant fetor.

Something along the lines of 'Excuse me, I hope you don't mind me saying, but I think you should know you whiff a bit' may get you a smack in the mouth, but it just might also earn you profuse thanks. Plus you'd be doing humankind a favour, saving others from having to contend with the same olfactory affront. It took Sheryl, Mick, Craig and Simon to sit me down one evening, much like an intervention, to tell me that my body scent wasn't as pleasant an odour as I assumed and that I needed to start using cosmetic fragrances again. That's what friends are for, to tell you that you stink.

Anyway, Bono... regardless of what you think of him (and I know a few that despise him – hi Milo!) I bet you odds on he smells more wealthy than you or I.

After our Paris trip I rented a cottage, again in the Black Mountains, to write new songs. Sheryl came with me this time and as she could drive we rented a car. We picked up the hire vehicle in central London and drove out into West End traffic. Being American, it was the first time Sheryl had ever driven a car on the left-hand side of the road so the first few minutes were a little hairy. As we approached a small roundabout, one of those that was a raised grass island in the road, I instructed her, 'Go straight across.' She took me at my word and drove straight across the middle of the roundabout, the car bouncing up and down the kerb and traffic coming to a standstill to let this mad woman pass. We received a lot of beeps with a bit of verbal abuse along with raised fists but miraculously we made it across without causing an accident.

'What the hell are you doing?' I screamed.

'You told me to go straight across the roundabout,' she reasonably argued.

'I meant follow the traffic *around* the roundabout and take the exit that was straight across, not just drive straight across the bloody thing,' I explained.

'Well, you should have said that then!'

I couldn't really argue with her logic.

She'd never seen a roundabout before, what with living in LA and her parents in Las Vegas. They don't do roundabouts over there, or at least very few. I remember there was one in the city of Orange when I lived there that always confused the locals. They also don't do 'em in Brazil either but that's because there's no road etiquette there as far as I can ascertain (I live in Brazil so feel qualified to make this observation), and there are pile-ups every day as no one gives a hoot about the rules of the road and it's every man and woman for themselves. Very aggressive drivers, they come at you from all angles and totally ignore any signals you may make. Every time I drive in the city I fear for my life. Have you ever driven in Rome or Napoli? It's worse than that in São Paulo. That's why I let Cinthya drive most of the time. She is fearless as well as being a very good driver, but I do have to shut my eyes sometimes with some of her manoeuvres.

So, Sheryl and I made it out to Abergavenny with no further life-threatening mishaps and, in a spare bedroom, I set up my new TEAC reel-to-reel 4-track recorder, an impressive upgrade from my previous cassette-based Portastudio. Along with my also brand spanking new Roland D50 synthesiser and Roland TR-626 Rhythm Composer drum machine, I'd brought with me a collection of guitars, and my by-now, and still to this day, trusty guitar FX processor, the Roland GP8.[1] And no, I wasn't being sponsored by Roland, more's the pity.

I set myself the task of writing at least one new tune a day. Generally I'd start with a guitar riff or a few chords thrown together or even sometimes a keyboard line. 'Butterfly On A Wheel' started that way. 'Into The Blue' started off with the ostinato rolling bass guitar part. Other songs I came up with in Abergavenny included 'Amelia', 'Deliverance', 'Belief', 'The Grip Of Disease', 'Grapes Of Wrath', an early version of 'Hands Across The Ocean' and a host of others. More than enough to be going on with for the next album. Poor old Sheryl was left to entertain herself for the most part while we were there but she did at least have the car so she could get out and about. And practice her navigation of roundabouts.

One day we took a trip to Hay-on-Wye, a small market town just north of the Black Mountains famed for its plethora of bookshops and hosting the annual Hay Festival of Literature & Arts. I bought boxes of used books, including several John Steinbeck[2] and Herman Hesse first editions, and Charles Bukowski's *Barfly* script, signed by the great man himself and the stars of the film, Faye Dunaway and Mickey Rourke.[3] This little excursion kick-started my passion for collecting first editions, which was curtailed when The Mission's star began to wane in the Nineties and money got tight. I still have a few, though, including a dozen Steinbecks.[4]

After Sheryl had flown back home to California and I was armed with a batch of newly written songs, I arrived to meet with my band mates at Stanbridge Farm, a residential rehearsal studio about 30 minutes north of Brighton. Owned and run by the genial Bob and Caroline Birthwright, and a lovely, tranquil location despite its proximity to the ever-busy A23, Stanbridge became a favourite of ours over the next few years, and is in fact the location where we were interviewed for the *Dusk To Dawn* video collection. Set in 15 acres of country gardens and open meadows, the rehearsal space is situated in a huge converted barn 100 yards away from the 500-year-old farmhouse, which is where we were accommodated. It was a fabulous place to get away from the distractions and temptations of the city to write and rehearse. Meeting up with the lads again after a few weeks apart was always a cause for celebration, the first evening usually drunkenly spent catching up. The next morning it was down to work.

No matter how confident I am of my new songs it's always a nervy moment playing my demos to the rest of the band for the first time, and not being sure they're liking what they're hearing. As the principal songwriter in The Mission my tunes were always gonna be the ones we'd learn, play and record but I was still insecure enough to want, if not *need*, their approval. Bugger the rest of the world; if I knew I had my homies behind me then I could face whatever barrage of abuse the media would be throwing my way. Playing a demo, though, can be a bit like showing a rough pencil sketch of two fingers reaching out to touch each other and then asking them to imagine the ceiling of the Sistine Chapel. It requires a degree of imagination, imagination that surprisingly few in the music business possess. That's why my demos were mostly already well formed by the time I took them to the band, with bass and guitar parts and drum patterns already written. The only thing left to write were the lyrics, which I would do over time. Even so, it made me very nervous playing them for the first time to t'other three. They were a hard audience to impress – perhaps the hardest.

It'd go something like this. We'd be sat around, usually chain smoking and drinking tea or coffee. I'd put the first demo on to play, all three of them would look away, at the floor in front of them or a far corner of the room, maybe sit with their head in their hands, avoiding eye contact with me and each other, their reaction impossible to gauge. I do it myself, too, closing my eyes and looking like I'm concentrating on listening to the music rather than being terrified of a negative reaction. Mick might be the only one to glance my way and give me a grin or a thumbs up if he was liking it, which wasn't always the case. When the demo finished playing I would occasionally get an 'it's alright, that' out of Craig or 'that guitar riff is nifty' from Simon. More often than not they'd say nothing or just emit a non-committal grunt. It has to be said that neither Craig or Simon were particularly demonstrative, certainly never effusive and encouraging in the same way Mick could be. I'd then go into an explanation of the song in question, explaining how I saw it progressing and, being a little synaesthetic (a condition that means I visualise colours when I hear music) I'd often confuse them with my instructions. 'I hear the guitar solo as kinda country-village-cricket-field green,' I'd suggest to

Simon and he'd nod as if to say 'yeh, mate, whatever'. And then on to the next song and the same excruciating process.

Once we'd gone through all the demos it would be time to start working on them one at a time. I'd play the demo again, and teach Simon the basic guitar parts, show Craig what I wanted him to play on the bass, and then explain to Mick how I heard the drums. Then we'd bash away at it for a little while until that alchemic moment when the song begins to coalesce and sound like *The Mission*. That moment, when it came, was always momentous and easily recognised by all of us, and a huge relief to me. Not everything worked, mind you; there are many demos that have fallen by the wayside or, even rarer, songs that have developed and evolved with the band playing 'em as to be almost unrecognisable from my original demos. Some we'd play around with for hours, even days on occasion, and nothing would spark. Save it for another day. 'Bird Of Passage', for example, I originally took to the band for the *Children* album, but we couldn't get it to work at that time. We came back to it for this next album and kicked it around in rehearsal for a bit and after suggesting Simon try playing the guitar part on piano, hey presto, as if by magic there it appeared.

Every band has its own processes and for us, at that time, this way worked, although Simon was beginning to show signs of resentment. He had brought a few ideas in for songs for the album but they were so complicated that, try as I might, I couldn't find any good vocal melodies within the music so they were nixed. In my experience, most guitarists have a tendency to play too much. They fill up any and all space in the music with yet more guitar parts, making the whole thing too complex sometimes, thereby leaving very little room to imagine a vocal. I'm sure previously that I was as guilty of the same inclination on some of my demos, but once I started having to write lyrics and vocal melodies too I soon learnt to *leave space*. And the easiest things to sing to are, in fact, sometimes the simplest and most widely used chord sequences. Once you have the basic song you can always tart it up afterwards. In hindsight, my rejection of Simon's tunes may have appeared a little offhand (I wasn't always the most tactful person in the world), and it was probably the beginning of his disaffection with the band, a situation that would only escalate during the recording of the new album.

(Side note: I hate chugging with a passion.[5] Always have done. A chugging guitar is for numbskulls and irrefutable evidence of a lack of imagination and creativity.)

We spent about a month at Stanbridge and it was during this period that All About Eve released 'Martha's Harbour' as a single. One evening after tea, we all gathered around the telly to watch them perform on *TOTP*. This particular show was being broadcast live – not recorded the day before like they normally were – and this was the infamous incident where Julianne and Tim (Bricheno) were introduced and the song started playing and they both just sat there and didn't even attempt to mime. My immediate reaction was that it was a deliberate, and brilliant, commentary on their part, to show up the pretence of miming on TV. It was only after the show had finished when Tony Perrin (remember, he was the Eve's manager too) called and told us it was all an Auntie Beeb shambles, and that Julianne and Tim hadn't been able to hear any playback of the track until about halfway through. It's unfortunate in many ways because that is perhaps how AAE are best remembered by the general public, much like I am for my drunken performance on the late-night James Whale TV show a couple of years later. We'll come to that in due course. In the meantime, as recompense, the BBC called the Eves back for another performance the following week, something they NEVER did unless you were number one, which helped 'Martha's Harbour' get up into the Top 10, something The Mission never achieved, and something Andy Cousin has never allowed me to forget – he's the Eve's bass player, and he didn't even play on the song!

We wanted to record the new album quite quickly again, like we had with *God's Own Medicine*, so we asked Tim Palmer to forgive us for forsaking him for John Paul Jones during the making of our sophomore album, *Children*, and to come back and produce this new one. Tim came down to Stanbridge and spent a bit of time with us doing pre-production work and helping us to arrange the new songs.

On August 25, at the end of our tenure at Stanbridge, we played our annual warm-up show at Champagnes in nearby Horsham, dropping a few of the new songs into the set: 'Deliverance', 'The Grip Of Disease' and 'Gone To The Devil'.[6] Champagnes was tiny, rammed with an audience well over capacity. There was a low stage at one end of the room but no dressing room. The backline techs, Jez and Nipper, were onstage with us, crouching down behind the small PA stacks either side but still visible to most of the audience. Just as we had done on a previous occasion with Speedy Keen, we'd invited Tim to join us onstage to play guitar on one of the new songs. I'll let Tim tell you what happened next.

Tim Palmer: 'The story of Champagnes was that in pre-production I'd played a little bit of guitar with you, you know, trying out new ideas, and out of the kindness of your heart [what, me? Ed.] you asked if I'd like to get up and play a song with you at Champagnes. And, basically, I can't remember what the song was, but you said, okay, you come on and you can play *this* part in *this* song, and I was secretly very excited to be honest, and thought the idea of getting onstage and playing with The Mission was great.

'So, when the gig came I was watching from the back and I realised how packed it was in there, and I could see Jez at the side of the stage and I knew that when I had to come onto the stage I had to come on from Jez's side. So I had a copy of the set-list and when you started playing the song before I was due to join you I knew I had to make my way up to the stage. It was crazy busy in there, sweaty goths everywhere [and what's wrong with that? Ed.], so I had to barge and push my way through the audience and managed to get to the stage and climb up next to Jez. Jez was ready and waiting for me with a guitar, which he put on for me and made sure the cable was wound round properly, and I began to get a bit nervous actually. And I was stood there at the side of the stage with most of the audience able to see me with a guitar hung around my neck, waiting to make my grand entrance onto the stage. The song before was just about finishing and Jez asked, 'Are you ready, mate?' and I said 'Yep', and before I had a chance to walk on you launched straight into the song and completely forgot about me. And you hadn't seen me either and so you just carried on, and as I wasn't just gonna barge onto the stage, I took the guitar off and passed it back to Jez, who just kind of shrugged his shoulders as if to say 'that's Mr Huss for ya', and then of course I had to climb back down off the stage and push my way back through the crowd, most of whom had seen me get up there and put on the guitar and then not get called onto the stage. It was a moment of huge disappointment for me, but more than that, embarrassment. Afterwards you were very apologetic but it was too late for that.'

Let it be said that this incident never really affected our relationship adversely but Tim's never really forgiven me, always harping on about getting up onstage with this or that band and how great it is. In my defence all I can say is that, despite Tim being over 6 feet tall, I swear I didn't see him make his way through the crowd and wait at the side of the stage with a guitar strapped on, so lost in the throes of my own performance was I.

The next day we flew out to Brazil.

One of the very best things about being in a band is the opportunity to travel. Before I started touring with bands the extent of my travel abroad had been a family holiday to Spain as a young teenager, and a trip to Paris in July 1981, taken primarily to avoid the grotesque nationalist fervour surrounding Charles and Diana's royal wedding (exile 'em all to the bloody Malvinas, if you ask me, but you're not so I'll keep schtum). Mind you, it was big news over there too but at least the news was in French, a language I barely understand. I'm a firm advocate of that ol' maxim 'travel broadens the mind'. It really does. Now… most of the time on tour is spent on a tour bus, in a hotel room, a venue dressing room and, of course, onstage. Unless you make the effort you don't really get to see too much more than that. But that is, more often than not, enough to give you a *feel* for a city.

On my very first European jaunts I would try to find time to have a wander around a town during the daytime, at least in the vicinity of the venue. After a show my favoured locale in a city would be the red light area, not because I was a randy sod as I never had enough money to indulge anyway (a £5 per diem might buy you a wink (here we go again – I said *wink*)), but more because they were the most alive areas, the beating heart of the city at night. I developed a fondness for being among the neon, the scuzz and the sleaze, appalled on the one hand and totally fascinated on the other by the sordidness of it all. Remember, I was raised a good Mormon boy and just a few short years previously I was an innocent – no, make that naive – West Country goody-two-shoes yokel. I was astounded, my eyes on stalks, to see for the first time scantily clad women sat in shop windows, beckoning me to enter as I passed by. I was too gauche to even make eye contact, scurrying on past with my head bowed. But being among all that colour, squalor, danger and life made *me* feel alive. And in a foreign place. And I've always loved that feeling, of being in a foreign place. Being exposed to different cultures, customs and traditions, different views on life and how to live it, new foods, drinks, humour, clothes, aesthetics, architecture, music, art, even the air. And where nary a word of English is spoken, where walking down the street it is a shock when you hear someone speaking English. A bit like Newcastle or parts of Wales.

Once my initial propensity for exploration while on tour gave way to debauched, narcotic and bibulous activities I'd barely see the light of day, the daily numbness and dumbness spent avoiding normality as much as I could. The whole day was geared towards the time performing onstage, that couple of hours in front of an audience the sole purpose of all my other routines and rituals, when I needed to be at my most cognisant and energetic. We call this pre-ordained hour 'Wine O'Clock', when the corks can finally be popped, years of experimentation teaching us that it is exactly one hour before stage time. The white powders and pre-show drinking honed the senses to razor-sharp points that peaked at the same time as natural adrenaline if you got the timing and the amounts exactly right. The trick was to be confident and fired up, to be in the state that was neither sober nor too drunk. If the stage time was delayed or brought forward after 'Wine O'Clock' had started then we were in trouble – a misplaced five minutes here or there could make all the difference.

Also part of the ritual for Craig and me was the pre-show vomit. It's exactly as it sounds. Both of us would need to pay a visit to the lavatory about 10 minutes before 'Dambusters' started to 'have a chuck' – brought on by nerves, we'd claim; nothing to do with the drink and drugs. This particular foible of ours went on for years although it is very rare for either of us to have to make that same mad dash to the loo before a show these days. Good job too, considering the amount of time Mike Kelly (a recent drummer) spent in there before taking to the stage. Not sure exactly what he was doing but it was a brave man that followed him when he was done. Anyway, enough of this toilet talk.

Another thing that will induce Craig and me to puke is eating too close to stage time. Some people can eat a full three course meal and then jump up and perform. How is that even possible? Through years of experience, and coming to know how my body works, I can't eat five hours or less before I go onstage; maybe a few peanuts or a hard-boiled egg but certainly not a meal. It's more or less the same for Craig, but with him being the consummate touring professional he always brings his Tupperware.[7] The first thing he does on entering a dressing room is to fill the various containers with all kinds of foods and snacks to scoff later on the bus or in his hotel room. He's nothing if not organised when it comes to his scran. His suitcase at the end of a tour is always full of pilfered bars of dark chocolate, stolen condiments and the more expensive bottles of wine that mysteriously disappear from our rider. In fact, he brings a spare, empty suitcase expressly for this purpose. Simon likes his tuck too so, believing Craig's use of Tupperware to be genius, he started bringing his own and filling up for an après-show nosh. Simon can and does eat at any time of the day and night, insisting on three full meals a day. He gets really cranky if he doesn't get to eat when he wants. When staying in hotels I have known Slink to go down for breakfast twice some mornings, often taking his Tupperware to stock up on bacon, bangers and beans for later in the day. It's actually quite smart, is that. Me? I did buy some Tupperware too but I always forget to take it into venues with me. And when I do I load it up with vegan lasagne or roast falafel or whatever veggie haute cuisine is provided for us that particular day, and then never fancy it after the gig, leaving it to sit in the fridge on the tour bus until it grows mouldy. Me and Tupperware don't get on. I have tried but I don't think the fault is mine.

I'm not gonna mither on about it because it's a privileged position I have found myself in for most of my adult life – to perform in a touring band – but so much of the preparation for a show is actually spent just *waiting around*. Charlie Watts once famously said, and I paraphrase, 'I've been playing drums in The Rolling Stones for 25 years, five of those years actually spent playing, the other 20 spent just waiting around.' And it's true. So much time is wasted just hanging around. And not just on tour but in life generally. Waiting for buses, trains, at airports, at the doctors, in line at Tesco petrol stations, for the wife or hubby to finish getting ready. There is waiting involved *everywhere*. And I hate wasting time. Now what I call wasting time and what you might call the same could be two very different things. For example, I consider being glued to your phone and social media all day a waste of time. Watching cute videos of dogs and cats, again, a waste of time – and I love cats and dogs. Mowing the grass – it always grows again so why bother? Watching documentaries about health or gardening, or brain-dead reality TV shows, or Britain's-Got-Talent-Strictly-Come-Dancing-Celebrity-Get-Me-The-Fuck Out-Of-Here-X-Factor and the like – all a waste of time. While Cinthya considers my watching football and listening to Bob Dylan a waste of time. I take her point sometimes with the football, particularly watching England or, on that rare occasion, when Liverpool lose, but how can she say that about Bob Dylan? But then again, I do have to put up with a lot of Morrissey. It's a wonder we're still together. Nah, we're lucky really because there are many things we like to waste time doing together, but listening to Bob Dylan? I'm on my own.

My tastes have changed over the years, my enthusiasm for red light areas has long since extinguished, as has my appetite for intemperance. My preference these days is for an amble around city centres during the daytime. As long as it's not chucking it down, so that's Manchester out then. Walking a great city can be a balm to the soul; it makes us engage on different levels, discover the new, rediscover the familiar, and in the process perhaps discover a little about ourselves. As I said, you can feel the spirit of a city from a flying visit, in and out in a day, enough to often make me wanna come back as a tourist. I love visiting art galleries, museums, famous landmarks and monuments; being the aimless flâneur strolling the avenues and boulevards, taking in the ambience in no particular hurry to reach any particular destination. My days off in international cities of interest are usually spent this way these days, although having a day off in, say, Belgium I'd probably prefer to have a long lie-in in a real bed (i.e. a bed that's not moving) reading a book.

As I mentioned before, I love reading books – novels, fiction and non-fiction, biographies and memoirs, classics, detective mysteries and true crime, rom-coms, history, erotica, *some* sci-fi, music. But not books about interior design or self-help psychobabble. Is reading a waste of time? I guess there are some people that might argue so, but they're generally moronic as a result. And that's obviously not you, as you're reading this. And not that I'm claiming to be the brain of England, but I do know a few things about a few things, most of which I read in books. God, I don't half witter on, dun I? Anyway, my point is it's always best to take a few decent books with you on tour, a few good TV series and films loaded onto your laptop, and lots of your favourite music too. Personally I spend most of my time on the tour bus in my bunk, entertaining myself and resting up. It's not that I'm anti-social, it's just that I value my alone, quiet time, and the only place you can get that on a tour bus is in your bunk. But don't forget the ear plugs for sleeping; there's an awful lot of noise on a tour bus at night – snoring, farting, groaning, moaning, people talking/ranting/arguing in their sleep, and there's always one twat who forgets to turn their phone off and their partner calls to check up on 'em at 3 a.m.

Endnotes

1   The Roland GP8 was first unleashed in 1987 and is basically a 1U FX rack unit that houses eight Boss guitar effects pedals – overdrive, distortion, compressor, dynamic filter, phaser, parametric EQ, digital delay, and chorus

– and each of them can be edited and all parameters saved to presets, which is then controlled by a foot controller onstage. Even though I have tried all kinds of other, newer amp and FX combinations I keep coming back to the GP8 through a Roland JC120 amp for my stage sound. It just works for me. You can pick up GP8s pretty cheaply on eBay these days – I have five, two in my studio and three in my rack for playing live – and for the budding guitarist I'd recommend it's worth having one in your FX arsenal.

2   The American author was my favourite, probably still is. Perhaps Steinbeck was regarded as a little passé by the late Eighties, certainly in the US, where some of his works had become part of the established school curriculum, and certainly among the trendy artistic intelligentsia. But sod them, anything popular is mostly perceived by those elitists as being poor art and that is just not the case. It becomes popular because people feel empathy towards it, whether it's a literary work, a film, a piece of music, a painting or any other work of art. Not everything that is popular and successful is about the lowest common denominator. There was a time when you could blind-fold me and pick any random Steinbeck from my shelf and read from any page and I would know which book you were reading from. I started with the classic *Grapes Of Wrath* and eventually worked my way through his entire oeuvre. I loved his writing: the humanity, and humour, the spirituality of it, with characters written in such a way I felt I knew them, even though they derived from completely different backgrounds, and eras, to mine. I need to start reading Steinbeck again.

3   Bukowski was another fave writer of mine, perhaps the antithesis of Steinbeck. I managed to pick up a few of the original Black Sparrow Press publications of his books in the late Eighties from a bookstore on Sunset Boulevard. Imagine my glee when I found the signed *Barfly* script in a second-hand bookstore in Hay-on-Wye. Mysteriously, this signed script disappeared in the aftermath of the failure of my first marriage, just a couple of years after Bukowski's death.

4   Also good for the ol' pension fund.

5   Chugging is a technique of palm-muting the strings on a usually distorted guitar tone and playing a rhythmic pattern with your picking hand. Employed most frequently in the various forms of metal (but sadly heard in all kinds of music), the practice gets its name as it sounds similar to the chug-chug of a

coal-driven train. My tip to aspiring guitarists: chugging to the guitarist is akin to hi-hats and cymbals to the drummer. There is ALWAYS something more creative you can play than chuggin', much like for a drummer there is always something better you can do than smashing bloody cymbals. If you can't come up with anything brilliant and must resort to chugging then learn to *leave space* and be confident enough not to play anything at all. The rest of your band will thank you for it, as will your audience. There is a little bit of a chug on 'Blood Brother' but that was intentional, as the song was written for Ian Astbury and is a bit of a tongue-in-cheek Cult pastiche. Other than that you won't hear any chuggin' on any other Mission records, although Slink has veered dangerously close to it on occasion. I've had to keep an eye on the boy but he has learnt and now knows better. I remember our producer, Tim Palmer, while recording 'Deliverance', once attempting to persuade me to put some chugs on the track by saying, 'If you want that big house in the country, Mr Huss, then you need to put some chugs on this song. Think of each chug as a brick.' That's a lot of soddin' chugs, Tim. I resisted his petty attempt at enticement and I still eventually got my place in the country. Admittedly it is in Brazil, where the property prices are a fraction of what they are in Britain or the US, but my dignity is intact. Well, as far as chuggin' goes, it is. And drummers: remember that tom-toms are always better than hi-hats and cymbals.

6   The working title for what was to become 'Hungry As The Hunter'.

7   I'm sure I really don't need to explain this but Tupperware is a home products line that has become genericised to refer to plastic or glass food storage containers with snap-close lids. Other examples of brands that have become genericised are Hoover, Xerox, Kleenex, Band-Aid and Q-tips.

CHAPTER 14

South America

We arrived in Rio de Janeiro early in the morning. Alighting from
the aeroplane, it immediately felt unlike any other place I'd been.
The sun was low and radiant in a clear blue sky, you could feel the
heat and humidity as soon as you stepped out and it was only 9 a.m.!
We were met by the record company welcoming committee, headed
by a cheery man who introduced himself with what we understood

as, 'Bon gee-ah and well commee The Miss-e-on. I am Clever and I am from Pollee gramma.' It transpired that his name was actually Kléber (pronounced Clebber, so our mistake was an easy one to make), but we ended up calling him Clever for the duration of our stay. He didn't seem to mind and we thought we were being clever calling him Clever. The simpleton mentality of bands on tour, eh? Anyway, the Brazilians got their own back as I was called Waynee everywhere I went. Still am to this day. At first I thought it was a cute nickname they'd given me but I was soon to learn that most Portuguese words that end with an 'E' are pronounced as a double 'E' – *ee* – so they extend the same principle to English words. As in, 'Would you likee a bitee of my cakee?' 'Hey, Waynee!' always sounds like they're calling the dog in from the backyard to me. Woof bloody woof. I have tried explaining to my Brazilian family and friends that my name is *Wayne* but, nope, I am still Waynee to them. Even Cinthya calls me Waynee when she wants to get my goat. I've even been known to resort to using Waynee myself when all else fails. Sometimes, like when I'm at the chiropodists or something, I say my name and I receive blank looks and '*Uh, não intendo?*' It's just easier to say Waynee and be done with it. 'Ah, Waynee. *O mesmo que* Waynee Rooney, *legal!*' Yes, the same as Waynee sodding Rooney. *Legal* in Portuguese (pronounced *lee-gal*), by the way, translates to cool. And Waynee bloody ain't.

After we'd cleared customs we were greeted by a sizeable throng of fans who'd gotten up early and made the effort to welcome us. This was to be a regular occurrence on the South American tour. I can only surmise the local record company weren't too secretive about our arrival and departure times or where we were staying. Obviously not looking or feeling our best after the 12-hour-long overnight transatlantic flight, we nonetheless obligingly posed for photographs, signed records and what-not, and allowed kisses to be planted on our cheeks. We were then herded into a couple of minibuses, the luggage and equipment in one and the band and crew in another, and then driven to our hotel, the Rio Othon Palace on Copacabana beach, where there was another group of fans waiting for us, among them many from the airport welcoming committee. How did they get there so bloody fast when it took us over an hour? We must've taken the gringo scenic route.

I checked into my room, which boasted a balcony overlooking the iconic beach. I sat there and smoked a cigarette and watched as a bevy of bronzed bodies in itsy-bitsy bikinis and teeny-tiny speedos paraded past. Don't see that in Weston-super-Mare. Some kids were playing beach football and others volleyball. Already at this early hour the beach was teeming with life. The seasons are in reverse in the Southern Hemisphere so the end of August is, in effect, the tail-end of the Brazilian winter. All I can say is that it was like the very best of summer days we occasionally see in Britain. To my left I could see the cable cars making their way up Sugarloaf Mountain, and to my right the bay curved out and around the bend, leading to the also-iconic Ipanema Beach. At the time, very few British bands had visited South America – to my knowledge only Echo & The Bunnymen and The Bolshoi from among our peers. It felt like we were pioneers, intrepid explorers, going where few (Nazi war criminals and felons on the lam not withstanding) had ventured. As well as Brazil, we were also due to visit Buenos Aires in Argentina and Montevideo in Uruguay, and we were gonna be the first non-South American band to play in Asunción, capital of Paraguay.

But first we had a few days' sightseeing and promotion to contend with. On a couple of occasions we combined the two, and we had a camera crew traipse up Sugarloaf with us. It's a double cable car ride to the top of Sugarloaf and Craig, being a bit of a pansy when his feet are off terra firma, was hanging on grimly to the safety rail, his complexion a whiter shade of pale and his eyes screwed shut all the way up. It does have to be said that once you're at the top the views are stunning. Rio is a beautiful place, as long as you don't look too closely. Having lived in Brazil for nigh on 20 years now, I've been to Rio many times. Every time a friend or family member comes to visit, we always insist they visit the 'Marvellous City', which boasts the world-famous Christ the Redeemer statue, his outstretched arms welcoming all pilgrims from atop Corcovado Mountain, one of the (new) Seven Wonders of the World.

But Rio is one of those cities; it looks fantastic from the top of the mountain but down below, amid a landscape scarred with favela after favela[1], there is abject poverty – and the danger and criminality that comes with such poverty. Down on the beach, tourists should avoid wearing watches and jewellery and carrying cash, mobile phones or anything of value, or you may well be robbed there and then in front of crowds of onlookers. It's been known for gangs of thieves to sweep the Rio beaches, and some have even gone as far as cutting off their victims' fingers to get to their rings. The beachfronts are generally safe, though, as long as you respect and adhere to the locals' advice. But ignore that advice at your peril. One or two blocks back from the beach and the streets start to get dirtier, grimier, darker. Shadowed shop doorways and alleyways look more sinister, passers-by more suspicious. I'm not doing much for the Brazilian tourist trade, am I? But the rule of thumb, as it is anywhere in the world, is respect the locals and their laws, etiquette, customs and traditions, and you should be fine. The more I got to travel, the more I was learning to not be a bolshie, pissed-up 'who-won-the-war' twat of a Brit abroad. There's already far too many of them without me adding to their number.

One fine day during the band's stay in Rio, we ascended Corcovado Mountain for a photo shoot. We decided to travel up by tram car to soak up some local flavour. Our party consisted of the four band members; Stevie Sex-Pistol; Tony Perrin; tour manager Harry Isles; Terry Staunton (the only decent *NME* journalist, in my opinion); photographer Derek Ridgers; Sian Thomas, our Phonogram

International rep from the UK; our UK agent Martin Horne; Pamela Burton, who was our new US manager[2]; and a couple of people from our Brazilian record label. We caught the tram car at the bottom of the mountain and we essentially had the whole thing to ourselves. It was a lovely, warm, sunny day – again. The car was painted yellow and green, the national colours of Brazil, with two-person seats either side of an aisle and open sides, meaning there was no glass or protection from the elements, not that it was the elements we needed protecting from, as you shall soon read...

Our tram car was navigating its way slowly up the narrow gauge railway track that girdled the steep incline flanked mostly by trees and foliage, and we're all sat there taking in the views, occasionally spotting marmoset monkeys jumping from tree to tree and feeling the warmth of the day and the company. About three-quarters of the way up, we passed a house that was evidently undergoing construction. Stood right next to the tram track was a man, presumably a builder, and he was having a wank – yes, I said wank. He was furiously pumping away and just as our tram car passed him, he ejaculated (funnily enough, Richard Hell & The Voidoids' 'Love Comes In Spurts' has just sprung to mind), narrowly missing the members of our group sat on that side of the car (luckily for me, I was sat on the opposite side). There was a few eughs and oh my gods and a little screech from Craig while the builder just looked at us and laughed. He had blatantly timed his release with our passing, obviously having practised this trick once or twice before on unsuspecting tourists. As Mick quipped, 'He were a big lad, too.' We're on our way up to visit Christ the Redeemer and we get jizzed on. Some might argue it was no less than we deserved.

At the top, we posed for band photos beneath the giant statue of Christ. Mick, Simon and I were attired in the prerequisite band uniform of *black*. The three of us looked like the rock gods we thought we were, or at least as though we were in the same band, whereas Craig looked like a tourist who'd accidentally ambled into shot, in khaki shorts and a short-sleeved shirt. He'd evidently missed the day's memo.[3] The photographs were so good, though, that once we returned to the UK we ended up paying a small king's ransom for someone to add the black to his shirt in post, years before Photoshop and the like.

I know I said earlier that the views from Sugarloaf are stunning – and they are – but compared to the views from the Corcovado, it's like watching a film on a tiny TV screen versus an IMAX. It's not regarded as one of the new Seven Wonders of the World for the Christ the Redeemer statue alone (although, as Mick might say, 'it is a big 'un'), there are statues of Christ all over the Christian world. We even have one on the hill overlooking our little town in the São Paulo countryside, not nearly as big as Rio's but nonetheless clearly visible from our home. No, the place is venerated as much for its location and the views it boasts, which really make it a wonder of the world. If you ever find yourself in Rio, make sure you visit the Sugarloaf first *before* the Corcovado, because if you do it the other way around, Sugarloaf is a bit of a disappointment. Got that? Sugarloaf first before Christ.

A block or so to the right of our hotel on the Copacabana was a nightclub called Help!. The band and the crew were all invited there by Clever and his record company lackeys the first evening we had free. Help! was a typical modern club with a big dance floor, flashing lights and loud disco music. We entered and immediately headed to the bar, where we ordered drinks and stood scoping out the lay of the land. The place was full of young girls and within minutes we were surrounded by a host of them, some being very forward and rubbing themselves up against us. My initial reaction was, wow, we must be really famous here in Brazil for all these girls to be coming on to us so strongly, promising a night of carnal delights. That is until I looked around and saw that the girls were coming on to every member of our entourage, including one tiny, mini-skirted Lolita, her feet off the ground and her arms wrapped around the neck of

Big Pete Turner, who had turned a flaming shade of crimson as he tried desperately to shake her off. Terry from the *NME* was stood there having his nipples tweaked and evidently enjoying it (he didn't include that fact in his article). Yes, Help! was a pick-up club, with the girls plying for trade, and unbeknown to us until much later, quite notorious in Brazil. As soon as the girls realised we weren't buying they left us alone and descended on a fresh groups of blokes who'd since entered the club and were more receptive to their advances. Not all the ladies there were on the game, though. I met one woman who'd travelled to Rio from Santiago in Chile expressly to see our shows. She didn't speak a word of English, nor me Spanish. Sometimes words are just not necessary and it's easier to communicate without them. And I didn't need to spend one cruzeiro real.[4]

In fact, while doing the promo in Brazil we soon learned that 'Severina' had been a sizeable hit there. We'd had no idea. Apparently Severina is a common female name in the north of Brazil, much like Jane, Julie or Sarah in Britain. Problem was, we'd stopped playing it live well over a year before.[5] So, our first soundchecks were frantically spent re-familiarising ourselves with our 'hit' song.

One day I asked how our record sales were doing in Brazil. We were told we were PolyGram's second biggest-selling international act in South America at the time, Bon Jovi being the biggest. Wow, we thought, that's good. So, how many have we sold? Oh, about 1,000 in each country. Is that all? Bloody hell, that doesn't seem like a lot. It was explained to us that Sting was the biggest-selling artist in South America, having just gone platinum with 6,000 album sales. So we weren't doing too bad. A visit paid to the PolyGram office in Rio should've provided a clue. In complete contrast to the plush foyers and high-rise, highly staffed offices of their British and American counterparts, the Brazilian headquarters, a small office manned by just a couple of staff, was reached by strolling first through a record shop (ironically selling bootlegs of our albums) and then through a small book store. There was, and still is, a lot of piracy in South America, mostly dictated by their generally very poor economies. Allegedly, groups of fans pool their resources to buy the album and then take it in turns to take it home to listen. The sharing of home-recorded cassette copies was also widespread. Personally, I never minded bootlegs, my reasoning being that I preferred people to be able to listen to the music than not. If they liked the music then we'd receive a pay-off in other ways, perhaps by them coming to a show, or buying a T-shirt, or passing on the music, or even just a recommendation to like-minded souls. I still feel the same way, although I do have a dislike for the likes of Spotify and YouTube; someone is making vast amounts out of streaming music and it ain't the musicians. It's made it very difficult for a lot of artists to make money from recording but that's an argument that has already been widely voiced and perhaps a conversation for another time. The Brazilian economy isn't too bad these days (can't say the same for the Bolsonaro government, mind) and, in the almost 20 years I've lived here, has been reasonably stable. But other South American countries, Argentina, for example, experience currency crashes fairly regularly. South America has vast and very rich natural resources but due to long-term mismanagement, widespread corruption, inept governments, and political volatility and instability the continent has remained mostly poor.

Our promoter for the tour was Phil Rodriguez, who was based in Florida, but with extensive links in South America.[6] Just a few days before we were due to play, I posed another question: 'how are the shows selling?' 'Oh, we haven't put them on sale yet, we only put them on sale the day before. If we put them on sale too early we'd lose too much money because of the rate of inflation.' The rate of inflation was something ridiculous like 800 per cent at the time so their method made sense. All shows sold out easily anyway, and some heavily oversold. In Rio, a 2,000-capacity nightclub called Caneçao was estimated to have crammed in over 4,000. Fire regulations be damned.

After a few days' promo in Rio we flew into Argentina's capital, Buenos Aires. Wide city avenues and faded, wasted elegance are a reminder of a finer bygone era and the city's fleeting belle époque of the late 19th/ early 20th century, when it was rich and promising and one of the world's prime cultural centres. The architecture conjures up images of black-and-white postcards of the old great and grand European cities – Madrid, Valencia, Rome, Napoli and the like, remnants of their Spanish and Italian heritage. Porteños (residents of the city) romanticise their city's past, revelling in their former glamour and glory days of yore, just like Norma Desmond does hers in *Sunset Boulevard*.[7] The national dance – the tango – is imbued with longing for the long-gone and elusive. Buenos Aires is, without doubt, my favourite South American city.

Sadly though, on our first visit we didn't have chance to see too much of it. As one of our party was heard to wryly observe, 'We're prisoners of our own success'. Everywhere we went we were followed and swallowed up by hordes of fans. We couldn't even walk out of the hotel because there were so many kids waiting for us at all hours of the day and night. We had security stationed at the hotel's doors to keep out the uninvited marauders who weren't hotel guests. In fact, I felt sorry for the other guests staying in the hotel, who were having to run that gauntlet every time they arrived or wanted to leave. When we did appear there was a mad, chaotic, screaming crush. I wanted to see the city but we were basically held captive until it was time to go to the venue for soundcheck, at which point we were smuggled out a side door and into a waiting minibus, and instructed to lie flat on the floor until we had at least got clear of the waiting throng. But some were super vigilant – they spied us sneaking aboard and threw themselves onto the moving vehicle as we attempted to make our escape. It was like a scene from *A Hard Day's Night*, and while it can all be a bit hair-raising it's also kinda fun when it first happens. But that level of fanaticism soon loses its allure. Mind you, from the safety of the stage it's another matter. We played two nights at the 4,700-capacity

Espaco Obras Sanitarias to an ecstatic audience that not only sang along with every word but all the guitar riffs too. It was really quite breathtaking, a level of reaction we'd not quite experienced previously. It has to be said that playing in Argentina, and Buenos Aires in particular, both as The Mission and solo, is always a highlight of any tour, the audience always elevating the show well above the norm. I suspect, though, that the Argentinian audience has the same response to all visiting bands, and their exuberance is not exclusive to us.

After the first show we were invited out to a club. Why not, we thought? I had two or three security guys assigned to look after me, with another couple looking after Simon and Mick. Craig didn't bother coming, preferring to go straight back to the hotel to ring Leona, his partner. We entered the club and within minutes I was being backed up against the wall by a heaving, crushing horde, desperate to get close. It was pandemonium and for a moment or two it really looked like it was gonna get out of hand with someone liable to get hurt, quite possibly me. Some of the club's security, along with my own, tried to hold back the crowd but the pressure was relentless and growing. Panicked, the security whisked out their mace guns and started spraying the manic mob while they bundled me out of a back door into a waiting car that sped me back to the relative safety of the hotel. Once past the gathered fans waiting outside, my only entertainment for the evening was to sit in the bar with Craig, who was lamenting the fact that he didn't get to speak with Leona. Just wait 'til he gets his bill on check-out; that'll give him something to really moan about. (Does 80 quid ring a bell, mate?) Simon and Mick arrived back some time later with a few of the crew lads who all said they'd had a great time at the club with absolutely no bother. Puh. Who'd wanna be the singer, eh?

The next day, we had a TV appearance scheduled so, again, we were surreptitiously sneaked out of a side entrance into the waiting conveyance. Again, we were spotted, but raced away before any of the fans could catch us. However, some of them set chase in cars and taxis, and as we raced through the back streets of Buenos Aires our driver took a right turn a bit too fast and we heard, and felt, a big thump. Our initial thought was that we'd hit a pedestrian, as we came to a screeching metal-on-concrete halt, we looked out the back window and saw a tyre bouncing down the street, narrowly missing a taxi full of our followers. The bloody wheel had fallen off our minibus, hadn't it, and we had shuddered to an embarrassing lop-sided stop in the middle of the road. Fortunately we were only a block or two away from the TV studio so we had to get out and walk the rest of the way, accompanied by the fans who had by this time disembarked from their taxis and were excitedly trying to talk with us in pidgin English.

Bless 'em. It's an arrogance we have, I believe, as a nation that when we travel around the globe we expect other countries to speak English and are surprised when they don't. In my experience most of Europe speaks English to a decent level, particularly my generation and younger. In South America, fluent English speakers are rare, most learning English from films, TV shows and the music they listen to, and thereby with a mostly American bias (*wadder* rather than *waughter*, *dienastee* over *dinastee*, *ay men* rather than *ah men*). In some ways the hardest nationality to communicate with is actually Americans, I have found. Sure, we supposedly speak the same language but communication is more than mere words. On a 2008 solo tour in the US with my very good friend, Miles Hunt from The Wonder Stuff, we stopped off at a diner on the road somewhere between Salt Lake City and Seattle. Being a veggie, my choices on the menu were limited. The only option for me, rather than order a full plate, was to order a few side orders. The waitress (is it politically incorrect to say that these days? Okay then, our server), maybe in her mid-thirties, took our order. I asked for a spinach quiche (pronounced *keesh*, as I'm sure you know), sides of mashed potato, peas and carrots. 'I beg your pardon, sir, can you please repeat your order?' I did as asked.

'I'm sorry, sir, I don't understand, what is keesh?' I showed her on the menu.

'Ah, you mean ku-ich.' It's easy to see how that *can* be confused, eh? And then she asked, 'And you want three side orders with that, sir?'

'Yes,' I explained, 'I'm a vegetarian and all the meal options are either meat or fish so I'm making up my own meal from the options available on your menu.'

'Aw, how cute, I've never met a vegetarian before,' she beamed. And I believed her. When my order arrived, it came on four separate plates – one for the quiche, and one each for the spuds, peas, and carrots. Why they didn't think to put it all on one plate is beyond me.

So, needless to say, I loved Argentina and the warmth of the welcome we received and have done every time we've returned since. Buenos Aires is only a relatively short hop of two hours or so from São Paulo, so Cinthya and I tend to go every couple of years for a visit. We even spent our 10th wedding anniversary in la Reina del Plata (The Queen of Silver), which was slightly marred by the fact that we had to go to a Morrissey concert during our stay. Ah, you know what, Moz always puts on a good show and he has oodles of charisma, so I didn't *really* mind. Plus he was a good mate of me ol' mucka Pete Burns, God rest his soul. And I have to confess that since being with Cinthya I have grown to quite like a tune or two of his, his 2004 album *You Are The Quarry* being a favourite in our home. I just wouldn't admit any of this directly to Cinthya. I'm convinced there's a few Bob Dylan tunes she secretly quite likes, too.

The day after our second BA show we made the short flight over to Montevideo in Uruguay. We were literally in and out in less than 24 hours. Each time I've been to Montevideo since it's been exactly the same: in and out, I see nothing. We arrived at our hotel, another overlooking a beach, this time on the River Plate, and it was one quick jaunt out for a radio interview and then onto the venue for that night's show.

The massive indoor arena El Cilindro was to play host to us, the previous event having been the South American basketball championship final in which Brazil hammered Puerto Rico 131–16, apparently. We soundchecked and it was a dreadful din, the sound clattering around like we were playing inside a cavernous, empty metal rubbish bin. None of us were looking forward to the show, with nerves getting the better of us and Craig enduring a particularly venomous pre-gig up-chuck. But then a miracle happened. We walked onstage and there was an estimated 10,000 people out there to see us. It sounded great, we played great, and the crowd screamed their heads off, giving us another small taste of what Beatlemania must've been like.

We did a runner after, with two big black cars waiting for us in the backstage drive-in area, engines running and doors held open for us as we dashed offstage, Stevie draping clean towels around our necks as we dived into the back seats. The gates swung open and in seconds we were out of the building and speeding away. One problem though. On our exit from the venue, our convoy made a wrong turn and we soon came up against a set of concrete bollards. Bugger. Reversing was out of the question as there was already a sizeable pack of rabid fans in hot pursuit, another Beatlemania experience that we could've well done without at this juncture. A quick shouted confer through the driver's windows and we were spinning off to the right and motoring across a park, everyone's bones being rattled as we bumped our way to escape. Anxious looks from the back seats were exchanged and we were all silently praying that we'd make it back to the hotel, wheels still intact this time. We did, thank the Good Lord. And then the four of us showered and changed and sat in the hotel bar (strangely named The Victoria Bar), on the top floor of the high-rise building, waiting for the crew and the rest of our entourage to arrive back. I stared out the window across the River Plate to where Buenos Aires lies, and down at Montevideo below, watching the cars driving the streets at this late hour, all looking like big Fifties American vintage cars to my eyes – none of this modern rubbish – and I felt transported back in time, like Marty McFly in *Back To The Future*.

We were up early with the lark the next morning to catch a flight back to more Rio madness. We were due to play the aforementioned show, where they crammed over 4,000 people into a 2,000-capacity venue. It was a sweltering, sticky gig, with another fanatical audience singing along to all the songs, even the brand-new songs we hadn't even released yet. How is that even possible? It amazed me they knew all the words. It's more than I do.

During the last song I grabbed a particularly zealous girl from the front row and pulled her up onto the stage and we danced together like long-lost lovers. We walked offstage hand in hand and I led her back to the dressing room, where soon we were joined by the band and Stevie Sex-Pistol. Within seconds the door of the dressing room violently flung open and in walks the head of PolyGram Brazil... demanding his daughter! Of all the girls in the front row I could've dragged up onstage it had to be her. As it happens, there was nothing untoward going on; she was just sat there drinking a guaraná or some such other non-alcoholic beverage (yes, we did have some of those on our rider, primarily for such occasions). The relief on the man's face was clearly palpable. How rude – what kind of rock star did he take me for? Anyway, no harm, no foul, with another international record company diplomatic crisis averted. Father and daughter soon left together, the father seemingly rather happier to do so than the daughter.

A few minutes later Ronnie Biggs and his wife, Raimunda, and son, Michael, were ushered into the dressing room. Ronnie, of course, is notorious for his role in the Great Train Robbery of 1963, receiving a 30-year sentence of incarceration at Her Majesty's Pleasure for the deed. However, he escaped from Wandsworth Prison in July 1965, after serving only 15 months of the sentence and, travelling via Paris and Australia, by 1970 he ended up in the relatively safe haven of

Rio de Janeiro. There Ronnie met Raimunda, a nightclub dancer who quickly fell pregnant, thereby invoking a Brazilian law at the time that did not allow a parent of a Brazilian child to be extradited. A cynic might speculate that Ronnie knew what he was doing by getting Raimunda up the duff, but the truth of the matter is that they eventually married in 2002 and remained together until Ronnie died in 2013, which would suggest their union became far more than a mere ploy to defeat the circling authorities. Though he was safe from extradition Ronnie's status as a known criminal meant he couldn't officially work, or visit bars or nightclubs, and a curfew of 10 p.m. was imposed. So, in the Seventies and into the early Eighties, he and his family hosted barbecues at his home in the hills of Rio where tourists, for a fee, could come and hang out and hear him spin yarns of his involvement in the robbery, his escape and his flight from justice that had taken him around the world to end up in Brazil. Of course, his fraternisation with Malcolm McLaren and the Johnny Rotten-less Sex Pistols only added to Ronnie's notoriety and even gave him a UK Top 10 single in 1978 as guest vocalist with the Pistols on the classless and lyrically repugnant 'No One Is Innocent'.

By 1988, Ronnie and Raimunda's son, 14-year-old Michael, had found fame and fortune himself as part of the Brazilian teen pop phenomenon Turma do Balão Mágico, a musical group borne out of a widely successful TV programme of the same name. They have, over the course of their career, sold over 13 million copies of their records in Brazil, a somewhat higher figure than us. It seems that young Michael was a fan of The Mission (and The Sisters Of Mercy) and Ronnie had contacted the record label asking for guest passes and a chance for young Michael to meet the band. Of course we said yes, only too eager to rub shoulders with the most infamous Englishman in Rio. We were staying on in the city for another day or two, so we were invited to Ronnie's home the following evening for one of his infamous barbecues.

301

But come the next day, after a trip out with *NME* photographer Derek Ridgers, to shoot some moody holiday snaps for their front cover, we were due to perform on what turned out to be the weirdest, most surreal TV show we've ever appeared on. *Milkshake* was Brazil's top pop show, kind of like *Top Of The Pops* but on acid or as Terry Staunton described it, 'like *Crackerjack* without the pencils'. We arrived to find out that we were supposed to be miming to the two singles from *Children*, 'Tower Of Strength' and 'Beyond The Pale', but no one had thought to provide the TV company with the edited single versions, so we were obliged to mime to the full-length album versions, both about eight minutes long each. The TV studio occupied a small theatre packed with an audience full of rowdy teenagers, most of whom had probably never even heard of The Mission. The stage was decorated with a giant milkshake and straw, an old-style red British telephone box, a Harley-Davidson motorbike, a bar, and a New York yellow taxi split down the middle. We were herded into the taxi to take our seats and told to wait for our cue. The studio audience was quietened down and then the stage was invaded by a cast of precocious youths dressed in silly costumes. There was a skateboarder zipping all over the place on his skateboard, a James Dean lookalike slouching against the bar, a West Side Story Jet and a Shark faking a fight, and a bevy of Day-Glo mini-skirted, go-going real-life Barbie dolls. A clapperboard was rattled down and the chief Barbie, the hostess of the show, Angélica – the one with the tallest beehive hairdo and the most lurid Day-Glo mini-dress – stepped forward to speak to the camera. She stamped her foot in mock impatience, studying her watch as she pretended to thumb a lift. It was acting of the highest calibre; give the girl an Oscar now. And this charade seemed to go on for yonks. In the meantime, the four of us were sat in the back of the split-down-the-middle NYC cab, tittering and sniggering at each other with no clue as to what was going on or even what song we were supposed to be miming to first. Then Craig exclaimed, 'Ah, bollocks.'

'What's up, mate?'

'I've just farted and followed through', he lamented.

Before we could even laugh in response, Angélica threw her arms in the air and announced: 'Ah, da Mission!' A big cheer, as much in relief as anything else I suspect, went up from the audience, which acted as the signal for the four of us to climb from the taxi, Craig a little more cautiously than the rest of us. He was wearing a white jacket, but fortunately for him he had on black trousers, otherwise it coulda got even more embarrassing for him than it already was – for all of us. At times like this we had a band motto, a philosophy applied to the strange situations we often found ourselves in: *Give it your best shot, laugh it off, and fuck it anyway.* We ambled across the stage, past neon signs burning the legends of 'Whoom!', 'Blam!', 'Kaboosh!' and 'Buumm', to a small podium that was set up with a drum kit and a microphone on a stand, and the stage manager instructed the audience to stand up and scream as if we were New Kids On The Block.

First up was 'Beyond The Pale', which has a long, slow guitar intro before the track kicks in, which largely dissipated any anticipation there may have been building for us. When it eventually does kick in, we go through our moves and our poses, although Craig is strangely a little more stationary than usual, while the onstage cast cavort and prance around us in a manner that probably, and should have, shamed them when they watched the clip back in later years once puberty had passed. The Skateboard Kid was still whizzing around, narrowly missing both Simon and me, with Simon ready to take his guitar off and swing it and knock the bugger off his board if he got any closer. Elsewhere, Mick's drum kit was slipping away from him and he's shouting at Craig to come and gently manoeuvre it with his foot back into position and then stand there holding it in place. He made very sure not to stretch too much, did Craig.

There's a *long* instrumental section in the middle of the album version of 'Beyond The Pale', which leaves me with nothing to do.

Feeling like a bacon sarnie in a vegan deli, I spied the telephone box and with great poise and assuredness I casually sauntered across, entered and pretended to make a telephone call which, funnily enough, lasted about as long as the guitar break. Back at the microphone for the first words of the last verse, my timing was impeccable. Sod the Oscar for Angélica, give it to me.

Next up was 'Tower Of Strength', which has about three minutes of drum machine before the 'proper' drums pile in, so Mick, entering into the spirit of it all and challenging me for the Oscar, vacated his drum stool and strode purposefully over to the Harley-Davidson, straddling the gleaming chrome beast. Unfortunately for him, though, he accidentally hit the stand with a stray boot and the bike crashed to the studio floor. No Oscar for Mick then. Undeterred, he gave the camera a raised fist salute and the audience loved him for it, roaring their approval, and Mick once again took the popular vote. Simon, in the meantime, had just had his foot run over by the Skateboard Kid. He was seething. The Kid knew now to keep away from Slink for the remainder of the song.

Another instrumental break and this time I wandered over to sit at the mock bar and pretended to order a drink from a disco dolly gyrating away on top of it. I was getting good at this acting lark. With still two minutes of instrumental outro to go I thought, sod this, I'm off, and left the stage and headed back to our dressing room to pour myself a real drink while t'other three had to endure to the bitter end. Once it was all over we left as soon as it didn't seem rude to, and in the relative sanity of our minibus we looked at each other and all asked 'What the fuck was that?'

The thing is, all bands, once they attain a certain level of success, find themselves in these kinds of bizarre scenarios. I guess some *artistes*, who may be concerned with their *credibility* (ho hum), when confronted with what we'd just been asked to do might balk and just say bugger this, and walk out. But one strength The Mission had was the ability to laugh at ourselves and each other and have fun doing so. Being in the band was, mostly, great merriment. You visit Brazil, or Italy or Portugal or wherever, and you have to surrender yourselves to the spirit of the place and its people, enjoy the fact that it's different from being back at home in staid ol' England. We enjoyed our lives and particularly during this period. Heady daze. What was there to not enjoy? We weren't the kind of people to sit around and moan about our lot, or the silly, embarrassing things we sometimes had to do as a band. Just get on with it, have fun, have a laugh. I never understood the young bands who'd blather on in interviews about 'the hardships of having to tour'. For me, and for t'other three as well, that was always the best thing about being in a band. My opinion is somewhat different now as I've reached the late autumn of my days. Touring can be gruelling, and without the 'aids' – the booze, white powders, and other stimulants and distractions – energy is premium and I do everything I can to preserve for the shows what little I have left, and at the end of every long tour I vow never again. Until the next one, of course. But back in 1988, as a band we were up for *it*. Of course there were days when we'd fall out and couldn't stand the sight of each other, but we never took that onto the stage with us. And more often than not it was onstage where our differences would be settled and forgotten via the euphoria of playing a blinder. In 1988 we were still as close a band as we'd ever been; we harboured a deep-rooted affection for each other and the band itself. We were one of the very best bands in the world at that time. All four of us believed it so and I personally will not countenance any argument against that assertion.

So, after *Milkshake*, it was a quick dash back to the hotel for Craig to shower and change his underpants and then off to Ronnie's for caipirinhas and samba. Our moanin' Minnie of the ol' 4-string fretboard tried to persuade us he didn't wanna go, but we weren't allowing him to spend an evening stuck on his own in his hotel room, racking up more huge telephone bills, the boring git.

We arrived at the Biggs residence in the hills overlooking Rio some three hours later than scheduled, partly due to having to mime to the looooonnnggg versions of two of our songs and partly because Craig pooed his pants, an excuse that Ronnie took with good grace and a huge cackle of a laugh. The evening was jolly and with a bit of cachaça inside us we were soon all up on our feet around the pool, trying our hand (shouldn't that be feet?) at samba with Selma, a neighbour of Ronnie's who was an award-winning samba dancer. Most of us were made to look pitiful but, surprise surprise, Craig, with a caipirinha in one hand and his other arm around Selma's waist, showed us all how it was done with panache and style. Craig had been into Northern Soul all-nighters when he was a young 'un so he knew his way around a dance floor. A friend of Ronnie's was playing along to the music on a traditional Brazilian percussion instrument called a cuica. The cuica is basically a hollow drum with a stick inside attached to the underside of the skin, which the player rubs frantically with a wet cloth while tapping away with his fingers on the topside of the skin. It emits an unholy racket of a squeak, not unlike a scared monkey. Craig, ever on the look-out for ways to annoy us, brokered a deal with the man. For some reason Craig had brought with him on this South American jaunt his Leicestershire bagpipes. When we'd been at Stanbridge Farm rehearsing prior to this trip we'd visited a folk instrument shop in nearby Crawley. We all bought a bunch of esoteric instruments. Both Simon and I bought a sitar, a mandolin and a bouzouki each (quite sensible, really), Mick a gaggle of ethnic percussion instruments, and Craig bought some bloody bagpipes. Why? Because he's bloody weird like that sometimes. While we all tried to master our new instruments we'd have to put up with him making a god-awful cacophonous drone at all hours. Quite why he decided to bring them on tour to South America I don't know. I can only assume he was looking for further opportunities to piss us all off again. Anyway, he bartered his bagpipes for the cuica. I don't know what was soddin' worse, the bagpipes or the cuica. Needless to say, neither made it onto a Mission record, praise the heavens.

A little later in the evening when things had quietened down a bit, a TV and a video player were wheeled out onto the patio to give us all an exclusive pre-release screening of *Prisoner Of Rio*[8], a feature film co-scripted by Ronnie depicting the attempts of Scotland Yard to extradite the titular character, our congenial host, back to Blighty, including a bungled attempt to illegally kidnap him. The film was being premiered in London's West End a few weeks after our return from South America and as Ronnie obviously could not attend he asked if I would be Raimunda's consort for the evening. Of course, with the promise of a party, I said yes. Young Michael was also flying over to attend. A limo was sent to pick me up from my hotel which then went onto pick up Raimunda from hers. We arrived at the cinema and I escorted her up the red carpet – yes, it was that kind of do – with Fleet Street snappers' flashbulbs popping all over the place. As famous as I thought I was at the time barely any of 'em knew me. 'Hey, Raimunda, where's Ronnie tonight? Who's that with you, love? Your toy boy? A bit young for you, innee?' was a popular, and cruel, taunt flung at us from the gathered photographers. The film itself is so-so at best but, in recompense for sitting through it, a party was held afterwards in a nearby club, where I was rubbing shoulders with the likes of celebrity madam Cynthia Payne[9] and various cast members from *Eastenders* and *Brookside* as well as the film itself. At one point I had to accompany Raimunda onto the stage where there was a telephone set up on a table and a call was put into Ronnie back in Rio. One by one those of us onstage, maybe five or six of us, had to have a quick word with Ronnie, which was amplified throughout the club. When it was my turn Ronnie warned me to keep my hands off Raimunda (as if!), or he'd have the boys sent around. I was as good as gold that night. That was one threat I took seriously.

307

Anyway, to recap, we did have fun at Ronnie's. He could tell a tale, although I suspect some of them were perhaps a little taller than they should have been (but we're all guilty of that, aren't we?), and I have to say that he and his family were good company and likeable. Thinking about it now though – and I don't know this for certain – I strongly suspect that dollars changed hands for the (dubious) privilege of spending time with Britain's most wanted man. Anyway, it made a good story for the *NME* and got us on their front cover.[10]

A day or so later we flew out of Rio to São Paulo. I have very little recollection of my first time in the city that has become home for me for the last 20 years as I was mostly incapacitated by a right ol' stinker of a cold and confined to my bed. As regular as England getting knocked out of a major championship by penalties, I always seem to catch a cold on a tour of any length. Bloody miserable they can be, too. I have to say, though, that I used to have fewer colds when I was shovelling white powders up my nose, drinking a lot more and sleeping less. I've become more susceptible to the buggers as the years have progressed and my temperance has accelerated. Not sure what conclusion to draw from that fact.

We had two shows to play at Projeto SP, a large 5,000-capacity indoor venue. Hopped up on a heavy dose of Vitamin C, various cold cures and a B12 happy shot, I managed to get through the first show without much to-do. Back to the hotel, back to bed. A day off and stay in bed. Next day, next show, same routine. We managed to play for about an hour and ten minutes before I completely lost my voice and the will to continue. I walked offstage and the band followed. A discussion ensued backstage and it was explained to me, and the band, that we had more than fulfilled our contractual obligation. I believe the clause was for a performance of a minimum length of one hour and we'd done that. However, the show was substantially shorter than the two hours we'd generally been playing and we felt we were short-changing our audience who'd paid good money to come and see us. It transpired that the venue was free for the next couple of nights and we weren't due in Paraguay until four days hence. Despite the protestations of management, promoter and tour manager but with, more importantly, the band's support, I walked back onstage with a translator and announced in a barely audible croak that we were curtailing that night's show but that everyone in attendance could come back in two days' time with their ticket stub for a re-scheduled show, by which time I hoped to have recovered my voice. And I did, and it was a stormer of a show, the São Paulo audience celebrating the fact that, in essence, they'd got two Mission shows for the price of one by giving us one of the best receptions we've ever received.

Next day we flew out to Asunción for the final show of our South American expedition. As I mentioned earlier, we were the first non-South American band to play in Paraguay. It was a big deal. The country at the time was under the regime of dictator Alfredo Stroessner and his Colorado Party, and had been since 1954. His rule had been marked by extensive human rights abuses; torture and execution were rote for political opponents. When we were met at the airport by the promoters we were shunted into long black limousines and on the drive into the city every radio station we tuned into was playing The Mission. We passed palatial luxury homes with banners strewn across the streets at We passed palatial luxury homes with banners strewn across the streets at regular intervals, welcoming us to Paraguay and promoting our show. welcoming us to Paraguay and promoting our show. There were pockets of people on the sidewalks waiting to wave to us as if we were visiting dignitaries as we sped by. As we travelled closer to the city centre the poverty became more evident, with entire families sleeping in the doorways of closed and boarded-up shops. We were informed that the limos actually belonged to Stroessner's family, and the radio stations were all owned by his son-in-law, who was also partly promoting our show. Without wanting to bore you with the politics of it all, Paraguay was a country on the verge of change. The advanced age of Stroessner, the nature of his regime, the economic problems the majority of the population faced and its international isolation were all catalysts for anti-regime demonstrations and seditious public statements by outspoken opposition, too many and too relentless for suppression.

Stroessner's popularity was at an all-time low when we arrived and it was explained to us that our visit was a relaxing of his government policy to prohibit foreign musicians from performing in order to curry favour with the younger generation, with whom he was particularly unpopular and who were particularly vocal in their calls for government reform. On our arrival at the city centre hotel there was a press conference planned for us and we were strongly advised not to say anything overtly political even if we were asked. Of course you couldn't ask those kind of things at the time and expect a 'no comment' from me. And so the question was asked of us, what did we think of Alfredo Stroessner? Being the dimber-damber of our gang I answered as diplomatically as I could... something along the lines of: 'We don't feel qualified to have an opinion as we know next to nothing of the history, politics and culture of Paraguay. However, and I'm sure I can say this on behalf of my fellow band mates too, we believe that every human being has the right to voice an opinion, and should have the freedom to live their lives without fear of oppression whatever their colour, creed, nationality, gender or sexual orientation, and to be governed by a fairly elected representation. I understand our being invited here may be politically motivated but I can assure you that politics has nothing to do with us saying yes to the invitation. We are here solely just to play our music to those of you that wanna hear it. And we're very happy to be here for that reason and that reason alone.' The entire assembly of attending journalists stood and applauded. I have to say, that was quite a moment for me. I've never been particularly politically motivated. My personal feeling is that politicians are all a bunch of self-serving lying twits, with a few exceptions. I'm sure a lot of people go into politics ideal-istically and with the best of intentions, only to get corrupted and compromised along the way. Maybe that's too broad an assumption but that is how I have generally perceived politicians during my life. You see a politician being interviewed and they so rarely actually answer the question they're being asked – they're evasive, slimy, slip-pery, disingenuous. I just don't, can't, believe them. But surely freely elected governments are always gonna serve a population better than autocracy, despotism, totalitarianism or monarchy, because we can choose to elect a different sleaze-bag to office every four years if we so wish. Very occasionally the electorate does get it right.

We saw a lot of poverty on our travels in South America, more so than anywhere else I'd been up to that point in my life, but Asunción was the worst. We were sat in the hotel restaurant eating dinner and I spotted a small, filthy child creep into the room and crawl between the chairs, stealing bread off the tables when the waiters weren't looking. I beckoned the child over to me. He looked terri-fied but he crawled over to our table. I gave him all the bread in our bread basket and all the food from my plate, wrapped in a serviette. He made a dash for the door and a waiter tried to stop him but I called out and demanded, 'No, no, let him go.' The waiter acceded to my request and the urchin turned and looked at me and gave me a huge smile before he disappeared out the door.

In the hotel bar late that first night I met a young Scotsman who claimed he was on the run from the long arm of British law. For what exactly he offered no explanation. He was buying the drinks and my company, and also paying the piano man to play our favourite old blue Sinatra songs as we sat, drank, smoked and chewed the cud on the balcony overlooking the town square. While watching the BBC News back at home just a few months later in early February 1989 they were reporting on the military coup in Paraguay that was ousting Stroessner from power and they were filming from exactly the same spot the Scotsman and I had been sat.

Our show in Asunción was at the Estadio de Tennis y Yacht Club – a small outdoor stadium situated right next to the Paraguay River. There was a heavy military police presence, I guess to make sure we didn't incite the audience to start a revolution. You could tell they weren't too familiar with how to put on a rock show of this magnitude, though, because they lined up *in front* of the front of stage barrier, not behind it as is usually the custom. As soon as we walked onstage there was a huge surge forward and the military police were crushed against the wooden barricade. They soon worked out that they needed to stand in the area *between* stage and barrier. We were advised before we went onstage to spray mosquito repellent on the areas of our skin that were exposed to the elements. I didn't heed the advice, believing that a few mozzy bites wouldn't be a problem. However, being right next to a big body of water and under bright stage lights attracted millions of the blighters and they stung the living daylights out of me throughout the performance. I woke up the next morning looking like the Elephant Man what with all the swelling on my face, hands and arms. It wasn't much fun heading back to the UK that day, the flight proving especially uncomfortable for me.

Endnotes

1   Favela slum areas occupy the outskirts of the larger Brazilian cities, particularly Rio and São Paulo. The great wave of migration from the Brazilian countryside to the cities between the 1940s and 1970s led to the proliferation

of these shanty towns. Poor and with no hope of meeting the exorbitant price of already-scarce land and housing, migrants had little choice but to squat on vacant land and construct dwellings from salvaged or found materials. From 1950 to 1980 the number of people living in favelas in Rio alone jumped from 170,000 to more than 600,000, and by the early 21st century it was estimated there were as many as 1,000 favelas in the city.

2   It was deemed necessary after the fracas of our first US tour to appoint a North American manager. Pamela Burton came highly recommended to us by Ian Copeland, our US agent. She'd worked at Ian's FBI NYC-based office but was leaving and looking for a new challenge. We were that challenge. She rented space in U2's Manhattan office, appointed Elise Margolis as her assistant and managed us until 1992. Both Pamela and Elise became much-valued – and adored – members of the extended Mission family.

3   Craig did that quite a lot in them days. A perfect example is the front cover of the *NME* issue reporting on this trip. Mick and I are casually leaning against railings, with Sugarloaf Mountain in the background. I'm in a baggy, dark suit (looked better than it sounds); Mick is in black jeans and a Mission 'Slob Crew' T-shirt; and Simon is lounging on a bench in front of us, wearing black jeans, a purple scarf over his head (again, it looks better than it sounds), a brightly coloured tie-dye T-shirt (it looks about how it sounds, but it was 1988, so it was cool at the time) and holding a ciggie in his right hand. We're all wearing shades and look like quite a good-looking band, if I may say so myself. Stood away from us at the back is Craig, looking decidedly like a confused tourist rather than a member of an internationally renowned rock band. There's always one, isn't there?

4   The real, pronounced 'hey-al' (plural: reais, pronounced 'hey-ice'), is the official currency of Brazil. The real replaced the cruzeiro real in 1994.

5   I always felt it was one of the few songs we didn't play particularly well live, so we dropped it from the set. We have, however, got better at playing it over the years and now we can muster up a damn fine version. We're not one of those bands that refuses to play our most popular songs, but I don't believe in giving an audience *everything* they want. Sometimes they're gonna get a little of what I want them to have, whether they like it or not.

6   I bumped into Phil Rodriguez again just a couple of years or so ago, backstage at a Radiohead stadium show in São Paulo. He'd seen my name

on the band/crew's guest list and had looked me up when I arrived at the Allianz Parque, home to Palmeiras football club. It transpires that Phil and his company, Move Concerts, have gone from strength to strength in the intervening years, Move now the biggest independent concert promoter in Latin America with offices in Argentina, Brazil, Colombia, Costa Rica, Dominican Republic, Peru and Puerto Rico, while his headquarters remain in Miami. We had a good catch-up and reminisce about our first joint venture back in 1988. He reminded me of a couple of incidents involving certain members of our party which are perhaps best not to mention here. Shush, your secret's safe with me... I'll email you my bank details...

7   Regularly included in 'best films of all time' lists, *Sunset Boulevard* (1950) is the classic film noir and stars Gloria Swanson as Norma Desmond, a former silent film star who pulls struggling screenwriter Joe Gillis, played by William Holden, into a deranged fantasy where she dreams of a return to former glory on the big screen. The sorry tale starts with a floating body in the swimming pool and ends with the immortal line from Norma as she descends the stairs, 'All right, Mr DeMille, I'm ready for my close-up now.'

8   Directed by Lech Majewski and starring Steven Berkoff, Paul Freeman and Peter Firth, the film was released in 1988 to tepid reviews.

9   Cynthia Payne, brothel keeper and party hostess, made headlines in the 1970s and 1980s when she was convicted of running a brothel in south London. She became infamous in 1978 when her home was raided during a sex party. Men paid to dress up in lingerie and be spanked by young women, also in lingerie. It was reported that 53 men were there, which included an MP, a peer of the realm, solicitors and several vicars. An apocryphal story did the rounds at the time: a vicar, found in bed with a scantily clad woman, when confronted by a police officer was purported to exclaim, 'I demand to see my solicitor, he's in the next bedroom!'

10 I used the *NME* feature mentioned here – published over two issues on 24/09/1988 and 01/10/1988 and written by Terry Staunton, who accompanied us on part of our South American tour – as a prompt for my own memories. Thanks, El Tel.

CHAPTER 15

For Relaxing Times, Make It Suntory Time

PLAYLIST:
1. Belief – The Mission (*Live At The BBC* – CD1)
2. The Grip Of Disease – The Mission (*Live At The BBC* – CD1)
3. Deliverance – The Mission (*Live At The BBC* – CD1)
4. Down To Earth – Curiosity Killed The Cat
5. Hymn For The Dudes – Mott The Hoople
6. *Ambient 1: Music For Airports* (album) – Brian Eno
7. Lexington Queen – Ryuichi Sakamoto
8. My Body Is A Cage – Peter Gabriel   9. Five To One – The Doors
10. Brass Neck – The Wedding Present
11. Banks Of The Nile – Fotheringay (feat. Sandy Denny)
12. Slaughter On 10th Avenue – Mick Ronson
13. Rain Song – Led Zeppelin   14. Mambo Sun – T.Rex
15. Maggie May – Rod Stewart

The first thing Mick and I did on our return from South America was go for an HIV test. Linda Greaves, who was Tony Perrin's assistant, booked us both in at a Harley Street specialist. It wasn't that either of us were exhibiting any symptoms but we just wanted a peace-of-mind check-up after visiting a part of the world where AIDS and other STDs were apparently rife. We saw the doctor, and his memorable advice to us was, 'I know having sex with your fans is your way of saying thank

you to them but sometimes just an autograph will suffice, you know.'
We then had to see a nurse for her to take blood and urine samples.
She was, it has to be said, quite attractive. As we were going through
the various procedures and being asked about recent sexual partners
– when, where, how many, and all that kind of gubbins – Mick tried
to chat her up, eventually asking her, as he was handing over his urine
sample, if she'd like to go for a drink with him. Flattered as I'm sure
she was, laughingly, but unsurprisingly, she declined the tempting invitation. Once we were done we were then told we'd have to wait for
a few days for the test results to come back and revisit the office to
receive them, since they refused to give out test results over the phone.
Neither Mick nor I were especially worried but there is always that
little niggle in the back of your mind, isn't there?

Well, a couple of days passed and our office received a call from the
doctor's office. It was explained that, 'Mr Hussey's samples have gotten
mixed up with someone else's so could he please return to give new
blood and urine samples?' My initial reaction, of course, was to panic,
not believing a word of it and fearing the worst, my thinking being
they were asking for new samples to confirm results that weren't good
news. Mick came with me, as his result had come back and he was
informed it was negative. Phew, I was happy for him but that didn't
really ease my troubled mind. A couple more days of escalating unease
and we got the call to say my results were in. Mick accompanied me
again, for moral support this time, because by now I had pretty much
convinced myself I was positive. We were asked by the attending nurse,
different from the one that had taken the tests, if we'd like to be together
when I received my results. Without thinking we said, sure, why not,
only realising that she thought Mick and I were a couple when she
said, 'It's important to remember that just because one of you has a
certain test result doesn't mean the other has the same. As partners you
need to support each other and be honest with each other and if you
engage in any sexual activity outside of your relationship then you must

get tested regularly.' That didn't sound too promising did it? I felt like she was preparing us for the worst. Then she looked down at the piece of paper in front of her and, after taking a time that bordered on sadistic to read the result, disclosed that I was negative too. Resisting the urge to jump up and dance around her office, the relief, nonetheless, was overwhelming and I silently vowed to mend my libidinous ways – yet another vow that didn't last very long. So as not to disappoint or embarrass the nurse, Mick and I bounced out of the office together holding hands.

A few days later we entered the hallowed portals of the BBC Maida Vale Studios to record a session for Liz Kershaw's show on Radio 1. Like most bands, we took advantage of recording sessions for radio to 'demo' new songs. The sessions at Radio 1 took four or five hours to record and mix, usually four songs. Basically, bash 'em down live with a couple of overdubs here and there, some backing vocals maybe, and then mix 'em. No messing about. Sometimes the results were arguably better than the recordings we released on 'official' albums, somehow capturing a spirit and an energy that often gets lost when a song is worked on for days, weeks, even months in the studio. And sometimes they just sound like demos. On this particular session, first broadcast on September 21, 1988, we recorded three of the new songs we'd been playing live on the South American tour – 'Belief', The Grip Of Disease' and 'Deliverance', along with an admittedly fairly ropey version of the piano-led 'Kingdom Come'. The three aforementioned songs are notable for their lyrics, which were all works in progress at the time, with 'Deliverance' particularly ending up really quite different to the *Carved In Sand* album version. We were actually quite fortunate to be invited back to the BBC studios, as on our previous appearance, sometime towards the end of 1986, we'd disgraced ourselves with quite some aplomb and been threatened with a ban.

Flashback to said session: We'd been taken out by the record company the evening before, along with Curiosity Killed The Cat who were flying high in the Top 10 at the time, to celebrate both bands' albums – *God's Own Medicine* in our case – having just been certified Gold in the UK. There was an enormous amount of alcohol involved along with other stimulants, which were shared with a Cat or two in the toilet cubicles. I don't believe any of us actually made it to bed that night and we had a fairly early morning alarm call for a BBC session, again at Maida Vale, being produced by Dale Griffin, former drummer with one of my favourite early Seventies bands, Mott The Hoople. Also, this same week, *Melody Maker* and *Sounds* had just announced their annual readers' polls and we, as both a band and individually, had featured highly. Anyway, we rolled into the studio bleary-eyed and considerably the worse for wear, and proceeded to attempt to play a handful of songs we'd been playing handsomely and routinely on tour for the best part of the past year. We just couldn't do it. We could barely stand and we had to break off in the middle of each recording for one or more of us to rush off to the loos to put our heads down the porcelain thrones. On one occasion we were all laughing at Simon's pitiful attempts to play the EBow part on 'Wasteland', with Mick quipping, 'Look at 'im. He's just been voted number three best musician in the country and he can't even hold his guitar, let alone play it.' With that, the man nicknamed Slink downed his instrument and made a dash for the bathroom with his hand over his mouth. He didn't quite make it.

Sitting in the lobby waiting to record another session were members of the world-renowned and highly esteemed BBC Symphony Orchestra. Crashing through the swing doors from Studio One came our Si, hand covering mouth and vomit spraying out from between his fingers all over the waiting musicians. Needless to say, they weren't best pleased with our behaviour and we were threatened with ejection from the building there and then. Our record company radio plugger, Mark Howell, was called. 'You better get down here quick, there's a bit of a situation,' he was informed. He arrived in minutes and walked into the control room, where we were all slumped in various postures of hungover slouch, and asked what was going on. 'It's the record company's fault for taking us out last night and getting us pissed when they knew we had a radio session today,' we remonstrated. 'We're too fucked up to play properly'. And he lost it and let us have it. We'd never been shouted at by anyone like that – before or since. 'You stupid, irresponsible brats. Who do you think you are? We've worked damn hard to help get you where you are. It's *your* problem if you can't handle your own drinking and drugging, don't you dare blame the record label. You knew you had a session this morning, you're grown men, it was your responsibility to be here on time and fit and able to record. Now, can you go back in there [pointing to the studio] and play those bloody songs properly? They've [Dale and the engineer] had enough of you and are just about ready to abort this session. They do that and you're finished here at the BBC, you'll never be invited back and they won't play your records ever again.' We sobered up pretty quickly at Mark's vicious but well-deserved scolding and agreed to give it our best shot. We traipsed back into the studio, tails firmly between our legs.

Much gentle persuasion and negotiation was needed on Mark's part to convince the Beeb to even allow us to stay in the building, let alone to try and finish the session. An uneasy concord was struck. We'd be allowed to stay as long as we managed to keep it together enough to record full band versions of 'Blood Brother' and 'And The Dance Goes On'. For the two additionally required tracks we were able to substitute *God's Own Medicine* pre-recorded instrumental backing tracks, for which I had to record new vocals – 'Wasteland' and 'Severina', I believe. It has to be said it wasn't our finest moment in a long line of not-our-finest-moments. If you're curious enough to wanna hear the results, and I don't particularly advise it, they are both available on the (should be... *Barely*) *Live At The BBC* release, CD1. We did get invited back to the Beeb, of course, but it was almost two years later (September 1988), and our singles always struggled to pick up Radio 1 airplay, possibly as a consequence of our earlier vomit-induced *faux pas*.

Early October and we were flying off for our first visit to Japan. On arrival at Tokyo's Haneda Airport we were greeted by a horde of black-clad teenagers, many of whom had brought presents for us. We were ferried to the hotel, again in minibuses, to find waiting fans, again with armfuls of presents for us. There were even presents in our hotel rooms, from both the record label and the promoters. Bottles of sake,[1] sake decanting sets, jewellery, stationery, cuddly toys, ornaments, and articles of clothing including kimonos. I was even given a small koto.[2] The Japanese are very generous. They are also very courteous, always bowing their heads when they greet you. It's a little disconcerting at first, and it feels slightly subservient on their part, until you accept it's just part of their culture and this is the way they traditionally greet people. I have to agree with the actor Bill Murray when he once said, 'They're very polite, but you feel like a joke is being played on you the entire time you're there.'

There was a small gathering of girls waiting for us in the hotel lobby at all hours, never really bothering us, just staring and giggling behind their hands when we looked their way. If we stopped to say hello then we'd be inundated with yet more gifts.

The record company rep assigned to look after us introduced himself as Cashbox. Not a very Japanese name, we thought, but we soon realised why: he paid for everything during our stay. Wherever we went − clubs, restaurants, bars − out would come his wallet and cash to pay the bills. We quickly realised Cashbox wasn't his real name and he was, indeed, playing a joke on us.

The first night we were in Tokyo we were taken out for dinner and then, because of the long flight and all of us feeling fairly fatigued, we decided on what for us was an early night. I showered and retired to my bed. Laid down, closed my eyes and I couldn't sleep a wink. With Japan being eight hours in front of the UK, jet lag had kicked in. I had never suffered jet lag before in all my travels. Weary as hell but not at all sleepy (I usually paid good money to feel that way), I tossed and turned all night. I tried listening to gentle music – Eno's *Ambient 1: Music For Airports* is always a good bet to curb insomnia – reading, drinking some of the sake I'd received earlier, flicking through the channels of late-night Japanese TV, watching the pay-per-view in-room porn channel and making sure I got my money's worth in the hope of tiring myself out, but nothing worked. My first night in the Land of the Rising Sun and I ended up lying there, staring at the ceiling, waiting for the sun to rise. When breakfast began to be served I ventured down to the restaurant, expecting it to be more or less empty, but sat there scoffing away were most of the members of our travelling entourage. Very rarely did any of us make it to breakfast, so this was a surreal moment. It transpired that all of them had suffered the same fate as me. We'd all sat alone in our rooms, climbing the walls because slumber wouldn't come, not realising our compadres in the very next rooms were going through the same ordeal. If only we'd known we could've gone for a wander or midnight splash in the hotel pool. Every time I travelled any lengthy distance after this occasion I suffered jet lag. Still do, but I don't travel now without sleeping pills. It helps.

By the time breakfast was finished and I'd made it back to my room I was ready to crash. I'd just laid my head on the pillow and closed my eyes when the telephone next to my bed rang. Bugger. 'Hello, Wayne, this is Cashbox. Did you sleep well? Are you ready to start your interviews? We're waiting for you downstairs in the lobby.' Double bugger. While the rest of the band and the crew all slunk back to bed I had to get up and talk about how excited I was to be in Japan to a roomful of strangers, none of whom spoke English.[3] Such is the plight of being the front man in a rock'n'roll band. And asking for drugs to help you get through the day was an absolute no-no in Japan. No one would even entertain the request. We had been forewarned but it didn't stop us from trying.

'Cashbox, can we get any drugs?'

'Why, do you have a headache? I can get you some aspirin.'

'Err, no, that's not quite what I mean.'

'Oh, you mean like cocaine or hashish? No, they're very illegal here.'

'Well, they're very illegal pretty much everywhere in the world but usually we can get something if we ask nicely enough.'

'No, you have drugs and the police find out then you go to prison. Remember Paul McCartney?'[4]

'Okay, so... that aspirin...'

It was at one of these early morning interviews I was handed a magazine by a chap who explained that he wrote for this particular journal. He was very eager to bring to my attention the fact that The Mission were at number two in their chart this month. At number one was Eric Crapton. This is neither a spelling mistake nor printing error.

After that first sleepless night in Tokyo we spent every other evening in the arms of the Lexington Queen; very generous with her hospitality and favours, she was. Situated in the Roppongi district of the city, the celebrated Lexington Queen was a nightclub run by an affable American chap named Bill Hersey who invited visiting bands and models into his establishment for free. And then didn't charge any of 'em for drinks. The Lex was always full of beautiful international models from afar – Australia, New Zealand, the UK, Europe and the US – who were just aching to meet visiting rock stars. Even we qualified as such back in 1988. Being sequestered in Tokyo on long-term modelling contracts, the models were often quite desperate for companionship other than Japanese men, so us visiting musos were the more-than-willing beneficiaries of their desire for fun and frivolity. How Bill managed to make it all work financially is beyond me. Admittedly the booze tasted suspiciously watered down, but we couldn't really complain as we were never charged a yen, and our sleepless nights were spent in the company of stunningly beautiful women willing to help us combat that jet lag.

The centre of Tokyo was ablaze with neon. The overwhelming incursion of the commercial West came as a slight disappointment, though; I was expecting and hoping for a little more Japanese tradition and culture. It was there but you had to seek it out and it paid to have someone with you that knew where to go, knew the secret passwords and could speak the lingo. The tone and mood of the wonderfully nuanced Sofia Coppola film *Lost In Translation*, starring Bill Murray as a fading actor who befriends recent college graduate Scarlett Johansson in Tokyo amid scenes of dislocation and disconnection, is a perfect crystallisation of how I remember my first stay in the city.

We played two nights at the Seinenkan Hall, memorable only for a couple of things. First, the punctuality of the Japanese. If the schedule said we were being picked up at 3.17 p.m. then we'd be picked up at that exact time – not a minute before or after. If the soundcheck was at 4.03 p.m. then we'd be making noise at 4.03 p.m. The whole thing was executed with military precision. Fortunately for them, and for us – and perhaps surprisingly – none of us was habitually late, and we readily observed lobby and bus call times. The ridiculously early stage time of 6 p.m. on the dot meant that the entire event was over by 8 p.m. and we could be showered and changed and visiting with the Lex Queen by 9.30 p.m.

While we're performing, they're stood up, dancing around and singing along, going as crazy as audiences do anywhere else in the world. When the song finishes, there's a brief smattering of applause and then complete and utter silence. No heckling, no screaming, no one shouting song requests, or 'get 'em off, Hussey' (or was I fooling myself and it was really 'get off, Hussey'?). You can hear a pin drop. It was later explained to us that it's because the audience want to hear every utterance from the stage, and believe it disrespectful to be making noise when we are being quiet. It is beautifully observed but, as with much of Japanese culture that was new to us, it's disquieting and takes some getting used to. We were more used to our audiences being noisy and rude.

The most memorable moment of those two shows, though, involved Craig Adams. We were stood in the wings, stage left, with our guitars slung around our necks and drinks in our hands, awaiting the predetermined moment in our intro music when we make our entrance for the most dramatic effect. Craig was first on; as anyone who has seen The Mission perform will know, he stands on the right-hand side of the stage.

Anticipation and excitement was at fever pitch, the crowd rapt, and as the intro music hits the crescendo Craig totters off onto the stage. He is wearing very pointy winkle-picker boots. About halfway across the stage, one of his winkle-pickers gets caught under a guitar cable that hasn't been taped down properly to the floor and he trips. The three of us trailing him onto the stage are in hysterics, all pomp and ceremony forgotten for a moment as we watch our band mate flying through the air. Somehow though he manages to land on his bum without damaging his bass guitar or spilling a single drop from the glass of wine he is holding. It is perhaps the single most impressive moment of all three of our shows in Japan.

Our third show in the country was in Osaka, which meant a trip on the famed Shinkansen, or the 'Bullet Train'. Today I guess its speed and comfort wouldn't be considered as spectacular as it was back in 1988; some of the Euro trains are now of a comparable standard (a train I caught from St Petersburg to Moscow just a couple of years ago was equally as impressive). However, compared to the delays of departures and arrivals, the over-full carriages, the interruptions of 'work on the rails', and the general comparative slower speed of good ol' British Rail, the Bullet Train was decidedly futuristic.[5] As with all things Japanese, the Bullet Train arrived and departed to the second of its scheduled time. On the journey to Osaka we got to see the magnificent snow-capped Mount Fuji off in the distance. Travel truly is one of life's greatest pleasures.

The day after the show, we stopped off in Kyoto on way back to the capital. I'd been craving Japanese tradition and culture since we arrived, and I finally found it and more in Kyoto. Recognised as the cultural capital of Japan, Kyoto is a heaven. With its numerous Buddhist temples and Shinto shrines, Fujin the God of Wind and Raijin the God of Thunder reside side by side in the Kaminarimon gate that guards the entrance to the Sanjusangendo temple. Fantastic palaces and enchanted gardens with lily-covered pools and ponds full of friendly koi and stepping stones, the love charms and the wind chimes, ceremonial teas, and the 1001 statues. Kyoto *is* magic and special. It is also a major tourist destination. It must've been that way in 1988 as well, but I don't remember it being crowded at all the day we visited. Oddly, though, we did have our gaggle of gigglers who had followed us from Tokyo to Osaka and now again a day later to Kyoto on the train, traipsing behind us as we walked around sightseeing. They kept their distance, never really bothering us, but whenever we turned around and caught sight of them they would all put their hands over their mouths and giggle. I'm sure they meant no harm but it was strangely unnerving and faintly sinister. Stalkers aside, Japan was very enjoyable. I loved it, and couldn't wait to go back.

One thought has just struck me.

The shows themselves observed what we came to recognise as the *normal* etiquette of Japanese audiences, which did initially take us by surprise and took some getting used to. However, our own performances were perhaps a lot more controlled than normal too, maybe something to do with the tempering of our pre-show consumption because of the early hour. And, perhaps, because these were the first shows we'd played, the first place we'd visited, where we couldn't procure any drugs.

In the early years of the band our shows had been largely fuelled by alcohol and speed and, in all honesty, could be erratic. There were some performances that were supernal and some that were absolute shambles, but very few *just* average. The very best gigs were the ones where I felt transported, where I lost my mind to the performance, to the onstage persona I had created and that had evolved over the first couple of years; the shows where it all felt just a bit out of control, when no one, least of all us, knew where the performance might go. They were raw, spontaneous, and we could be brilliant and the best band in the world, and other times the most shambolic. The art is in the balance between surrender and control. Too much control and the show becomes predictable, not enough and the whole shebang could career into utter chaos.

Most of our songs have a set structure but there are also a few that have sections we can stretch out and improvise, letting the song go where the mood takes it. So much of the success of a Mission show is the communion between us and our audience but there are occasions where the audience plays little or no part, and the music goes where it goes because we, as the musicians onstage, surrender to the moment. The audience doesn't always see it, feel it, sense it or recognise it, but at that moment it doesn't matter. It's not applause or validation from our audience that we are striving for, it is transcendence, a luminous, shamanistic altered state of consciousness. It didn't, still doesn't, happen very often but when it does it's because we're all in a receptive state induced or helped along by a surrendering of control. We have become far more consistent as a live band through the years, very rarely playing a poor show now, much more in control, but the price paid for that consistency is we very rarely hit those same numinous, ineffable heights we did more often in the early years. But we couldn't maintain that lifestyle. There was bound to be casualties at some point along the way if we had. We'd almost imploded on our first US tour when the *lifestyle* took over everything else. I am convinced that if we had *cracked* America, made it there in the late Eighties on a par with our stature in the UK and Europe, then I wouldn't be sat here today writing this. I think America would've been the death of me. Literally. And I don't think I would've been the only one. What is it that Jim Morrison sang? 'No one here gets out alive'… By 1988 we were adjusting to our position as one of Britain's biggest rock bands and had started to rein in our excesses somewhat, but there were still occasions where we binged, and we did still abide, although moderated, by our same pre-show rituals and routines – as we do today. I guess you could call it the survival instinct.

In November 1988, one of the biggest bands in the UK at the time – The Mission, just in case you're wondering – played a series of five free shows in tiny venues across Britain for our Mission World Information Service members. Among them were shows at my old fave hangout in Liverpool, Planet X, and two nights of pandemonium at the Borderline, just off Charing Cross Road, London. When you get used to playing the city halls and the Apollos, and then you play venues where the audience are literally in your face, can reach out and grab any part of your anatomy they want, where they're spilling over the monitors and onto the stage, propelled by the crush behind them, and are soaked and sticky with sweat and excitement just as we are, it's a timely reminder of what being in a band really should be all about. Particularly when your upcoming shows include Wembley Arena and Birmingham NEC.

But first we had a flying visit to the Iberian Peninsula to contend with. Porto and Lisboa were our first shows in Portugal (destined to become one of my favourite countries to both play and visit[6]), and a short run of shows in Spain, our first since even before 'Serpents Kiss' had been released.

Before the soundcheck at the Madrid venue there was a press conference held for us, the four of us and a translator sat at a long table facing this Spanish inquisition. The very first question lobbed like a hand-grenade at us was, 'Why are All About Eve better than The Mission?'

327

First, how can you answer such a question? Second, this kind of journalistic guff I expected from the UK hack-pack but not, up to now, from their mainland European counterparts. The constant vile bile spewed by the Brit press was obviously proving contagious and we were starting to receive similar hack-flak abroad. Now, my reaction wasn't because the journalist may have been correct in his assumption, or that I had any issue with the idea that someone might enjoy AAE more than they do The Mission. That's their prerogative and it all comes down to taste in the end anyway, but what did fire my ire was the blatant attempt to offend and get a rise out of me. Well, he succeeded. Piqued, I picked up the glass of water that was sat on the table in front of me and flung its contents in the direction of the agitator and stormed off in a stroppy tantrum, leaving the other three to quickly bring to an end the farcical event. And some people wonder why most bands despise the music press.

Less than a week later we kicked off our completely sold-out UK tour at the Cornwall Coliseum in St Austell. The dates would also include shows at the 8,000-capacity Birmingham NEC and 12,500-capacity Wembley Arena. Who needs the soddin' press when you reach this level?

The NEC show was the first in a venue of this size that was *ours* and not us supporting someone else. It was an amazing feeling to walk out on that stage in front of 8,000 people, knowing they had all come to see us, The Mission. In hindsight it was perhaps the zenith of The Mission's ascendency, the fruition of three years of solid work, the realisation of what we'd been aiming for. Somehow we managed to play the NEC, and Wembley, and conjure an intimate atmosphere that belied the vastness of the venues. To look out at the audience as we were playing 'Tower Of Strength', with our stage lights turned on them and away from us, and to see 8,000 people standing with their arms in the air, right to the very back of the auditorium, and hear everybody singing 'you are a tower of strength to me' was one of the most memorable, momentous moments of my life. I remember bouncing over to Craig on the stage as we were playing and, with both of us staring out at the audience, saying to him, 'Bloody hell, mate, look at that, that's for us. *We've* done this!'

Just a month previous we'd been playing at the Borderline in London to 250 fanatical faithful, and now a legion of 12,500 at Wembley. And as if further evidence was needed of our place in the *scheme of things* at the tail end of 1988, to further confirm my own belief that we were arguably the best band in the world at that time, *Sounds* and *Melody Maker* both published their readers' polls results for the year. Well, you know me, not one to bang my own drum... oh, go on then, here goes.

Melody Maker:

The Mission were voted best band (U2 were number two); best LP was *Children*; best single 'Tower Of Strength'; we were best live act; second best video was 'TOS'; I was second best male singer, beaten out by Morrissey, but I beat Moz to number one chap of the year (ha). I was also voted number six best instrumentalist, number five best dresser and number six best haircut, which was a strange one 'cos I never had my hair cut that year.

Sounds:

The Mission were voted best band (U2 number two again, Guns N' Roses number three); best album was *Children*; 'Tower Of Strength' shared the number one single spot with U2's 'Desire', with 'Beyond The Pale' at number five; we were best live act; I was voted number two musician after U2's The Edge and Prince at number three, Jimmy Page at four and Slink at number five; I was voted best male vocalist, beating Moz into second place this time; I was also voted number one best person, with Mikhail Gorbachev[7] not quite as popular as me (!!!???)

329

at number two; our *From Dusk To Dawn* video collection was number one retail video; and 'Tower Of Strength' made number two and 'Beyond The Pale' number three in the best promo video category.

Even the most cynical of readers must concede that was quite the haul…

Not such a surprise, however, was that once again we didn't merit one mention in the *NME* readers' polls. Maybe it really was because the *NME* readership didn't care one jot about us one way or the other, but I was disappointed not to have even appeared in the 'Creep Of The Year' category. But then I did have stiff competition in the eventual winner Margaret Thatcher and the Goss bros. of boyband Bros. I wouldn't want to cast any further aspersion as to the integrity of the *NME* any more than I have done previously, so I'll leave it up to you to draw your own conclusions from that observation.

Another Leeds-based band (and no, not The Sisters Of Mercy), The Wedding Present, were voted best band in the *NME* in 1988. I've got nothing against David Gedge and his cohorts – we probably nodded at each other in the Leeds Warehouse back in the day – but I'd have to say that they were more your typical *NME* fare – coming across as a bit dour, earnest, looking like they'd bought their clothes in a church jumble sale, ramshackle and politically correct – characteristics only one of which The Mission could be occasionally accused of. It begins with R, in case you really need to be told, although I did once buy a fantastic faux corduroy blue paisley shirt in a jumble sale. But credit where its due, they did plough their own furrow and ended up accruing 18 (yes, 18 – six more than us!) Top 40 hits in the UK, 12 of which all came in one year! They weren't my cuppa, as I'm sure we weren't their tipple, but it did feel good to be part of a group of bands from Leeds that was firmly putting the city on the musical map in the UK after years of Manchester, Liverpool and Scotland's dominance of the alternative scene.

For The Mission to feature so highly in the readers' polls was, for us, a validation of sorts after all the spiteful invective and vilification we had endured from the metaphorical quills of the music scribes. It was their *readers* that voted in the polls, not the journalists themselves, so it was a good ol' poke in the eye for 'em when we did so well. I'm not sure how many people actually made the effort to vote, probably not that many to be frank; it was a lot of effort to fill in the poll, place it in an envelope, address it and then trudge to the local post office in all weathers to buy a stamp, then deposit the envelope in the red letter pillbox situated outside on the pavement – who'd go to all that bother? Well, our audience, nothing if not zealous and committed, seemingly did. As did I too when I was a teenager. I would go to those very same lengths myself to vote for my favourites in the readers' polls and would be as pleased as punch when the music papers printed the results and I'd see the bands I'd voted for featured. To see Mick Ronson up against Jimmy Page in the best guitarist category, Queen and Roxy Music among the best new bands, T.Rex as best pop act, Bowie vying with Rod Stewart and Robert Plant for best male vocalist, Fairport Convention's Sandy Denny losing out to Stone The Crows' Maggie Bell as best female vocalist, *Electric Warrior* winning out over *Every Picture Tells A Story* as best album. I dreamt about being there among them myself one day and there I was in the second half of the Eighties atop the pile. I'm not sure how much it all really meant, or how much notice anyone really took of the polls in all honesty, and in reality there were a lot of artists that sold more records and were more well-known than us, but very few enjoyed audiences that were as partisan as ours. And even though their number has dwindled somewhat since the heady daze of the late Eighties, they still are.

After the highs of playing to a sold-out Wembley Arena and the clean sweep in the music rags' readers' polls, *NME* aside, we flew out to Athens, Greece, to play two nights at the relatively small Rodon

Club. Weirdly, the first night was completely sold out while the second night, our last show of 1988, a year where we'd scaled the heights, saw only a handful of people turn up. Back down to Earth with a resounding bump.

Looking back at it now, I'd say 1988 was The Mission's apex. We'd toured the world, playing over a hundred shows in 30 different countries, pretty much sold out everywhere (except Athens). *Children* had sold over half a million copies and we'd appeared on *TOTP* several times and on countless covers of music magazines. But the biggest achievement as far as I'm concerned was that the four of us in the band had survived it all intact and ended the year as close as we'd always been. It's impossible to share all those fantastic, bizarre, surreal, life-changing experiences together and not be bonded, to not care deeply for each other. And not just the band either, but the extended family of our core crew and management. We were looking forward to what 1989 would bring but, of course, when you've reached the summit where is there for you to go?

My girlfriend, Sheryl, who I hadn't seen for a few months, flew over from California towards the end of the year. She arrived with several full suitcases, seemingly ready to stay for a while. We spent a peaceful and happy Christmas and New Year together at my folks' place in Bristol.

Endnotes

1   Sake, pronounced *sah-kee*, is the Japanese national beverage, also referred to as Japanese rice wine. With a higher alcohol content than either beer or wine, it is often served warmed in a small earthenware or porcelain decanter and sipped from little porcelain cups called sakazukis.

2   The national instrument of Japan, a half-tube zither played by plucking.

3   When visiting some countries where speaking English perhaps wasn't very common we were, thankfully, given translators. But there were often occasions when we'd be asked a question and we'd answer with just one or two words but the translator would give a very long-winded reply. Made you wonder what indeed they were saying on our behalf. And the opposite happened too. When I gave a reply that was perhaps a bit longer than usual, the translator might answer on my behalf monosyllabically. So I'll state here and now that I can't be held accountable for everything that I am supposed to have said in interviews, okay?

4   McCartney was notoriously arrested on his arrival at Tokyo Narita Airport in January 1980 for possession of a sizeable amount of marijuana, found in his luggage. He spent nine days in a Japanese jail before his lawyers, and some say Yoko Ono, intervened on his behalf and negotiated his release and immediate deportation.

5   Sadly, my more recent experiences of privatised British trains are much the same as they were with British Rail, it has to be said: very expensive, and seemingly still trailing behind in technology, punctuality and efficiency. How can they justify charging you for a seat and then very often you find yourself having to stand for at least part of your journey because of overcrowded carriages?

6   Hello Bernardo, Sara, Tomas, Vicente, and Dinis, my favourite Portuguese family.

7   Former leader of the Soviet Union and widely regarded as one of the most significant world figures of the second half of the 20th century. He received the Nobel Peace Prize for his pivotal role in ending the Cold War and introducing new political freedoms in the Soviet Union, implementing glasnost, a policy that saw increased transparency in government institutions and activities in the USSR. Personally, as flattered as I was I think the electorate got that one wrong and I hereby now cede first place to Gorbachev. As long as I'm second and still above Morrissey!

CHAPTER 16

You'll Never Walk Alone

PLAYLIST:
1. You'll Never Walk Alone – Gerry & The Pacemakers
2. Get It On – T.Rex   3. Starman – David Bowie
4. Sweet Talkin' Guy – The Chiffons
5. Roll Away The Stone – Mott The Hoople   6. Time – Pink Floyd
7. Strange Days – The Doors   8. Fascinating Rhythm – Bassomatic
9. Come On In My Kitchen – Robert Johnson
10. Smokestack Lightnin' – Howlin' Wolf
11. Men With Broken Hearts – Hank Williams (aka 'Luke The Drifter')
12. Walk The Line – Johnny Cash   13. Hurricane – Bob Dylan
14. No Time To Die – Billie Eilish
15. The Girl In The Fur-Skin Rug – The Mission
16. Wuthering Heights – Kate Bush
17. The Man With The Child In His Eyes – Kate Bush
18. Butterfly On A Wheel – Wayne Hussey demo
19. There She Goes – The La's   20. Strawberry Fields Forever – The Beatles
21. You Can't Put Your Arms Around A Memory – Johnny Thunders
22. Come Back – The Mighty Wah!

Saturday, April 15, 1989 is a date indelibly incised on the psyche and collective memory of the city of Liverpool. Many, 97 to date, lost their lives while attending an FA Cup semi-final between Liverpool and Nottingham Forest at Hillsborough, Sheffield Wednesday's home ground. The Mission organised and played a benefit show at the Liverpool Royal Court Theatre two weeks later on Saturday, April 29, 1989.

What a glorious welcome we received when we walked onstage, and it's no overestimation to say the communion between us and the audience was highly charged with raw emotion. We blasted through a set of firm fan faves interspersed with a couple of new songs, 'Amelia' receiving its first live airing. At one point during our set, all the power in the building went down. We were plunged into darkness and silence. But not for long. While our crew were frantically scrambling around the stage using hand-held torches to find the fault, the entire audience spontaneously erupted into a rousing version of Liverpool FC's anthem, 'You'll Never Walk Alone', hundreds of cigarette lighters held aloft. It was a timely reminder of why we were all actually there.

I've enjoyed many great moments in my life but that right there, for me, was the single most emotional moment of my professional career. Tears were streaming down my face, as they were with the rest of the band, our crew, the house crew and security, and looking out at the audience I could see the vast majority were in tears too. It wasn't for the gig, it wasn't about the bands – it was about a show of support, a communal outpouring of grief for those that had lost their lives at Hillsborough just two weeks previously. I have never, and will never, forget it.

A fashionable opinion seems to be that the late Eighties was the nadir of a particularly poor decade for pop and rock music and that's why a band like The Mission were able to exist, and even flourish and excel. Whether that's true or not is subjective. And a load of bollocks. We were, and are, good enough to have existed at any time during the last 60 years. We're not to everyone's taste, I'm only too aware of that, but then who is? Admittedly there wasn't an awful lot of competition around at the time – only U2, The Smiths (although they split up in 1987, so Morrissey then), The Cure, Depeche Mode, Siouxsie & The Banshees, Echo & The Bunnymen, New Order, The Pogues, The Waterboys, The Cult, The Cocteau Twins, R.E.M.,

335

The Jesus & Mary Chain, The Sisters Of Mercy, Fields Of The Nephilim, and let's not forget the *NME* faves, the mighty Wedding Present. Also hot on our heels were The Wonder Stuff, Pop Will Eat Itself, My Bloody Valentine, The House Of Love, The Stone Roses, The Happy Mondays, and the whole Madchester and Shoegazing clans...

By its very nature music is subjective, music is really only any good if *you* like it. That is the only important criterion. You can, however, *acknowledge* the technical abilities of certain musicians without enjoying in the least what they create. It can't be denied that Mariah Carey, for example, can really sing, but would you have any of her music in your house? Nah, neither would I. Yngwie Malmsteen can undoubtedly play the guitar but, bugger me, what an unholy racket. Richard Clayderman can tickle those ivories, but it's the elevator music of the lift down to hell. As with any art, beauty is in the eye (ear) of the beholder. There are millions of technically proficient musicians but unless the music they are performing touches *you* in some personal way then all the technical ability in the world is, quite simply, not that impressive, is it?

Not forgetting the Chopins, Mozarts and Beethovens of the past, who never had the opportunity to hear their music recorded, there's been loads of brilliant music created in every decade since electrical recording was invented in the early 1900s. And conversely, there's been a lot of music I regard as rubbish. It all comes down to personal taste in the end and, of course, tastes are shaped by a whole heap of life experiences: the discs our parents were spinning at home as we were growing up; what was popular and fashionable when we first started seriously listening to music (T.Rex and Bowie for me); what we shared with friends and sweethearts; the first youth club disco ('Sweet Talking Guy' by The Chiffons brings that particular memory back for me every time); the first gig (Pink Floyd at the Bristol Hippodrome, November 1974, cost me £1); losing your virginity (mine was 'Roll Away The Stone' by Mott The Hoople, and we didn't even get to the first chorus before it was all over and done with...); first time dropping acid (The Doors' 'Strange Days') and ecstasy (Bassomatic's 'Set The Controls For The Heart Of The Bass') and smoking dope (err, I can't remember); number ones on the day our children were born – music is part of the fabric of our very being, the soundtrack to our lives. It's part of every culture across the world, fundamental and essential to human social and emotional interaction. Music can be entertainment. It can be ceremonial, spiritual, hymnal, tribal. It's work songs and shanties, dance songs and trance-inducing; it's played at weddings and funerals, major sporting events, in every shop in every shopping mall, in factories, bars, pubs, clubs and restaurants. We play it at parties and social gatherings, in the car while driving to work or over headphones on the bus or train. And we play it when we're alone when we want, or have, no other company other than the music itself. Music is a salve; it excites us, elevates us, calms us, comforts us, consoles us. Music is everywhere. There isn't a single person in the world that hasn't been exposed to at least *some* music. However, there is a relatively recently recognised neurological condition known as musical anhedonia, which is characterised by an inability to derive pleasure from music. The very small percentage of people with this condition can recognise and understand music but fail to enjoy it. A bit like listening to Level bloody 42 or Simple Minds, I would imagine. Maybe they just haven't heard the *right* music yet? But can you even begin to contemplate suffering with such a condition? How much poorer our lives would be, how much colour would be missing. But we're lucky, aren't we? I'm assuming you like music because you're sat there reading this book, written by someone who is known primarily as a musician. Or at least I like to think I am but I guess there might be some, maybe even you, that might argue that contention. The point is, you like music, just as I do. The odds are, though, that while we might like a couple of the same things, we probably have very different tastes in music. That's normal; there won't be any two human beings with exactly the same taste. And the world is a better place for it.

337

The worst period of music for me was probably the Noughties (and whoever came up with that daft term deserves a stint in the stocks and rotten fruit bunged at 'em), but even then there must've been a few records released during the decade that I liked. Try as I might, though, I just can't remember any. But if you were young during that period, just as I was in the Sixties and early Seventies, then no doubt you'll harbour a fondness for the music produced, our teenage years perhaps being when we're at our most impressionable, and when bonding over music is as good a way as any to gain acceptance from our peers. Personally, I spent most of the Noughties going backwards in time in my listening: immersing myself in the old Delta and Chicago blues, the complete works of Hank Williams and Luke The Drifter and Johnny Cash, and falling for Bob Dylan in a huge I'd-marry-him-in-an-instant-and-have-his-babies way, never really *getting it* before. Dylan is one of those artists that once you're converted, you become a fanatical zealot. You never hear someone say, 'Oh, Bob Dylan, yeah, he's alright.' It's either 'God, I hate his voice' or 'Bob is God'.

I had young parents (they were 19 when I was born), so I grew up with all the Fifties and Sixties pop music in the home, things like Elvis, Little Richard, Chuck Berry, The Everly Brothers, Buddy Holly, Gene Vincent, Jerry Lee Lewis, Eddie Cochran – all that really cool early rock'n'roll. And then a little later it was The Beatles, the Stones, The Kinks, The Walker Brothers, The Animals, Small Faces, to name just a very few. Nothing avant-garde or highbrow – aside from the Mormon Tabernacle Choir, it was just the pop music of their day.

For me the best decade, and not just for music, was the Sixties. I believe there were three pivotal events in the very early years of that decade which were the hair-triggers for the sociocultural changes wrought in the ensuing years.

First, in 1960, conscription was abolished in the UK. Healthy young men between the ages of 17 and 21 were no longer mandatorily obliged to complete their two years of National Service. The military – and I understand why – is built on conformity and erasing the individual: the uniforms; the short back and sides crew-cut; unquestioningly obeying orders from superior officers; discipline and endless drills; becoming just one of the rank and file. The abolition of conscription completely changed the mindset of young *men* in Britain.

Second, the contraceptive pill was introduced in 1961. The pervading morality through the Fifties and into the early Sixties was that courtship[1] involved an implied promise: if the woman became pregnant then the man would be obliged to marry her in a shotgun wedding,[2] a convention leading to many ultimately unhappy marriages in which the husband would be expected to go out to work while the wife would stay at home, keeping house and raising a brood of kids. With the pill (available initially in Britain *only* to married women who had, generally, already started families but had decided they didn't want any more children) women were now able to control when and if they got pregnant. Previously, the onus was on the man to provide protection, but the advent of the pill put that choice, that decision, into the hands of women for the first time. The impact was more far-reaching than anticipated and ushered in what was regarded as a more permissive age, where women could be sexually active without running the risk of unwanted pregnancies. The pill completely changed the mindset of young *women* in Britain.

Finally, at 3 p.m. on Saturday, August 18, 1962, under the stewardship of the legendary Bill Shankly, Liverpool FC resumed playing in the top division after an eight-season absence, kicking off a period of unrivalled national and European domination. That very same evening, The Beatles, themselves among the first of their generation to avoid mandatory National Service, became the four mop-tops the world would come to know and love. Ringo Starr, replacing the recently ousted drummer Pete Best, played his first show with John, Paul, and George at Hulme Hall in Birkenhead. The Swinging Sixties was off and running.

Each year, PolyGram would hold an annual conference, which was basically a huge booze-up. They'd invite all their employees, including the various sales teams from around the country, and they'd try to persuade as many of their signed acts as possible to attend, the idea being that the minions got to hang out with the pop stars they'd been promoting. They were actually quite good fun. The first one we were invited to, in 1987, was held in a hotel in Torquay, with PolyGram taking over the entire establishment for the night.[3] That's how I ended up with Steven Severin (of The Banshees) in my room at the end of the festivities. I remember being sat up till the early hours with him, debating – no, make that arguing – whether The Beatles or the Sex Pistols had made the biggest sociocultural impact. I was for The Beatles, obviously, while Steven was expounding the merits of the Pistols. We both had very valid arguments. Both bands had immeasurable influence on their times, that can't be denied – in music, fashion, culture, art, and the breaking down of conventional and traditional music business practices; a cleansing, a purging if you want, which is an absolute necessity every now and then. We're due another soon, aren't we? You could probably add Bowie to the argument, too, although his influence didn't have quite as much of an effect on the *business* of music. The biggest difference, for me at least, was that The Beatles helped *shape* the decade they existed in, while the Sex Pistols (the better band name I have to concede, okay, Steven?) were more a *reaction* to the times in which they emerged.

The Beatles' success, of course, was on a massive global scale and change was affected while they were still a band, making records and growing up (fast) together in public. Just look how much they changed over the course of the decade: from the mop-top Beatles of 1963, to the mods of 1965's *Rubber Soul*, the psychedelic classic of 1967, *Sgt Pepper's Lonely Hearts Club Band*, and then the bearded, long-haired hippies of 1969's *Abbey Road*. How quickly they grew and evolved as musicians and human beings and how different they looked with each passing year, and they weren't merely reflecting the ever-changing trends and fashions but forging them. The Beatles were at the vanguard of the Sixties' countercultural revolution. The Sex Pistols' success was more fleeting, with their influence taking longer to infiltrate and reshape the mainstream, but perhaps, as Severin argued, to ultimately no less a degree than that of The Beatles. There can be no argument that both bands inspired multitudes of their own generations to pick up instruments and make music of their own.

Before The Beatles, very few bands or singers wrote their own songs; it was the professional songwriters (some of whom went on to successful solo careers in their own right) – among them such greats as Gerry Goffin & Carole King, Barry Mann & Cynthia Weil, Jeff Barry & Ellie Greenwich, Leiber & Stoller, the Neil's Sedaka and Diamond – who staffed the Brill Building and Tin Pan Alleys of New York and London, and would churn out the hits for the vocal groups and teen idols of the late Fifties and early Sixties. Then The Beatles came along and they blew the whole kit and caboodle wide open. More and more bands followed in their footsteps, demanding to write their own material and, as they became more adept at doing so, gradually the Brill Building/Tin Pan Alley songwriting production line ground to a halt. Since then, most artists worth their salt, including the Sex Pistols, have written their own songs and that practice is, fortunately, still prevalent today. Of course, there has always been, and will remain, the huge production teams that write and produce for 'pop' acts: Chinn & Chapman, who wrote massive Top 10 hits for the likes of The Sweet, Mud and Suzi Quatro in the Seventies; Stock Aitken Waterman, who produced hits in the late Eighties and early Nineties for a huge cast of characters including Kylie Minogue, Bananarama and Rick Astley, and who scored their first UK number one with my old chums Dead Or Alive with the dance-floor smash 'You Spin Me Round (Like A Record)'; and today, an awful lot of pop hits are being written by professional songwriters once again, sometimes by committees of four or five, or more. What was I saying about the music business needing a cleansing, a purging again? Yeah, it's all become about *streams* and *views*, and *likes* and *online followers*, and in the race to a billion streams, pop music, to these gnarled ol' ears of mine at least, has become largely anodyne again. The generic and formularised chord sequences and melodies and excessive use of vocal Autotune software comes across to me as mostly contrived, calculated and characterless. Today, most major record companies aren't interested in signing new artists unless they have, I dunno, a million Instagram followers. And to attract those million followers you either have to follow the formula and make *easy* pop music, or show some skin or be exceptionally pretty. Or even in some cases all three. It's *always* been that way, of course, but it's all-encompassing now with the influence of social media. Of course there are exceptions to those rules, and thank the heavens for that. Billie Eilish, strikingly beautiful but with her beauty made up of many component parts and not just the way she looks, and her brother Finneas – exceptional, once-in-a-generation talents who both appear as genuinely *authentic* – write and produce their own records and it is, in my humble, pop music of the highest order, comparable to the best pop of bygone eras. Pop music has always needed the context of its own time, its own era, its own age to be understood and accepted.

But for me, the Sixties – the decade of cultural revolution, when youth around the world demanded to be heard – was the most colourful, vivid, changeable, progressive, shocking, permissive, extraordinary, hopeful, liberal, open-minded and exciting decade. It began in monochrome, with Britain shaking off the greyness of the Fifties and the shackles of repressive traditions, and ended in widescreen Technicolor that bloomed and flowered and promised so much (although we mustn't overlook the way that optimism came to a grinding halt, with the Manson murders, Altamont, the Kent State University shootings, the ongoing war in Vietnam, 'Tricky Dicky' Nixon in the White House and the undoubtedly dubious Edward

Heath soon to be behind the desk at 10 Downing Street). If nothing else though, the Sixties gave us an incredible cornucopia of amazing music – more than any other decade, I believe – a huge proportion of which I have loved and still do.

I felt inspired enough to write a song, using the infamous story of the Stones' drug bust at Keith Richards' Redlands country home in February 1967, as a metaphor for the best of the Sixties. 'The Girl In A Fur-Skin Rug', which references Mick's then-girlfriend Marianne Faithfull, who was clad in nothing but a fur-skin rug when the police burst in, was included on 2013's *The Brightest Light*. Lyrics reproduced by kind permission of me, again.

It's a time of martyrs and assassins
Demonstration reigns everywhere
Crowds of people are amassing
There's a revolution in the air
Anarchy and fighting on the city streets
A new voice is shouting loud in the searing heat
It's a time of prophets with protest songs
Tryin' to make it right their fathers' wrongs
Rail against the pricks of the grey-haired guard
Fight against the bullies of the old school yard
Fists raining hard, playground thugs
We all love the girl in a fur-skin rug.

It's a time of butterflies on the wheel
Take a magic trip and they throw 'em in jail,
And Sergeant Pilcher he's going down
For taking a bribe of half a crown,
What a clown, planting drugs
On the girl in a fur-skin rug.
I wasn't there, just too young for that,

But I've watched the film and read the book
And though I swear it's the same old hat
Nostalgia sells and we love the look
Of the girl in a fur-skin rug.

The dream is over long time gone
The old brigade just carries on
It was all a con
But I'd still love to hug
The girl in the fur-skin rug.

I was, and am, a huge fan of Kate Bush. I've loved her music from the very first time (in 1978) I heard 'Wuthering Heights' and the album that spawned it, *The Kick Inside*. Her 1985 album, *Hounds Of Love*, is so good that listening to it almost made me give up on the idea of being a singer before I'd even hollered my first note in anger.

Kate has always been totally unique, so quintessentially English in the very best of ways (a romantic notion, I know, but somehow like an English rose garden in full bloom during summer), a sonic pioneer, a master supreme at perfectly voicing the characters that inhabit her songs. Her influence has been vast, but she is completely inimitable and peerless. A then 19-year-old Kate was the first female artist to hit number one in the UK singles chart with a song she had written herself. The follow-up single, the hauntingly beautiful 'The Man With The Child In His Eyes', which also reached the Top 10, was written when she was just 13! A few years ago I made the drive from the South Rim of the Grand Canyon to LA – about eight hours long – and the only music I played the whole journey was Kate Bush. It struck me at the time that while her music could only be British, it worked perfectly with the desert landscapes of Arizona and Southern California. Just me, Kate's voice at blistering volume, the long, straight roads that lay before me, and the desert. The drive was transcendent.[4]

A polaroid photo of me in some random hotel room looking particularly dishevelled, circa autumn 1988. © Wayne's personal collection

Being followed by a group of girls in Kyoto, Japan. They never spoke to us unless we spoke with them first, choosing to just follow us around at a distance. Weird. October 1988. © Craig Adams

Me having just exited the pool at Stanbridge Music Farm rehearsal studios in Sussex, smoking a ciggy and reading the latest edition of *Viz*. We were, and remain, highly cultured. Summer 1989. © Craig Adams

Me having a whale of a time in the pool at Jacob's Studio, Surrey, while recording *Carved In Sand*, summer 1989. © Craig Adams

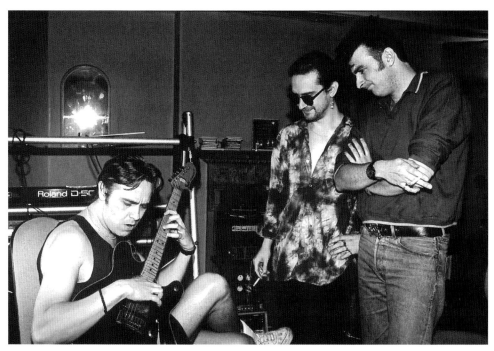

In the studio at Jacob's with Mick showing me and producer Tim Palmer how it's done. 'What chord is that, Mr Huss?' 'Fuck if I know.' Courtesy of Tim Palmer

Mick laying down some tracks – Scalextric that is – at the Music Farm rehearsal studios, Sussex, in the summer of 1989. © Nic Duncan

A very happy Slink having snagged the bottle of Bailey's from the rider. © Nic Duncan

Craig in hair net, summer 1989. © Nic Duncan

'Err, Jez, can you put me car back on the track, please, mate?' Summer 1989. © Nic Duncan

The legendary Metal Gurus at the Fulham Greyhound, December 1989. L to R: Rick Spangle, Mental Mick, Hipster Looney and Slink. © Wayne's personal collection

'Skin up, Wayne!' With our manager Tony Perrin, Black Mountains, 1989. © Wayne's personal collection

A promo photo shoot on the Brighton seafront in late 1989. Note the growth of a beard giving me the air of a more sophisticated, serious, wise man than previous incarnations. It was all a lie. I was still the 'frontman nincompoop' I'd always been. © Kate Garner

Yet another study in dishevelment, with me, having spectacularly fallen off the wagon, once again becoming a staunch practitioner. Oh, my weary head ... circa Spring 1990. © Wayne's personal collection

Me with Biffa, who was employed to primarily oversee overzealous house securities but ended up spending most of his time bailing me – and the rest of the band – out of trouble. Bands on tour could get away with all kinds of extreme behaviour that would put 'normal' people in prison. Spring, 1990. © Marc Binder

This could well be the last photo shoot we did with the original lineup of the band. Caught by the lens of Iggi Demello backstage at a warm-up show at Leeds Poly, March 1990. © Iggi Demello

Me casually posing on a flight case backstage at Leeds Poly, as you do. March 1990. © Iggi Demello

Anyway, in early 1989, when considering who to ask to sing on 'Butterfly On A Wheel', which would appear on The Mission's new album, I thought of Kate, not believing for a second she'd even entertain the idea. But what did I have to lose? The answer is always gonna be no unless you ask, right? On The Mission's previous two albums, Julianne Regan had come into the studio to sprinkle her special brand of vocal magic dust over a few of our songs. By the time we were starting to think about recording what was to become *Carved In Sand*, however, All About Eve were, quite rightly, distancing themselves from us, and so asking Julianne to be involved again wasn't an option.

So, Charlie Eyre at Phonogram made contact with Kate's assistant, Hilary Walker, who I then spoke with on the phone. Hilary suggested I send Kate a cassette of the demo and write a short accompanying note to go with it. Which I did. A week or so went past and then I received a note back from Kate herself, saying that she loved the song and would love to be involved. She suggested that after we'd recorded it with the band, we should send her a tape of a rough mix so she could listen and work out what to contribute before she came to the studio.

I was ecstatic. We then set to work on our album over the ensuing months and eventually, a good six or so months later, we got the song to a point that I believed was good enough to send to Kate. We ran off a rough mix to cassette and biked it over to Hilary. A few days later I received a phone call from Hilary, explaining that Kate had listened to the rough mix and loved it, thought it was fantastic and already so good that she couldn't hear anything she could add to make it better. And to compound matters, Kate herself was now incredibly busy putting the finishing touches to *The Sensual World* album and gearing up for its imminent release, so she no longer had the time to be involved. Of course I was hugely disappointed but took her comments as a compliment of sorts. Maybe Kate was telling the truth. I like to believe so. Cynicism hadn't yet become the reflex it later became with advancing years. And sadly, I lost the note Kate sent me too, along with my Christmas cards from Iggy, and a whole load of other memorabilia that has gone missing in my many moves around the globe. I probably used it as a bookmark or something and it'll turn up inside an old book someday. Or maybe Craig's got it all squirrelled away in his parents' attic.

It was being suggested to us by the record company that maybe we should tailor our sound a little more to the US market on the next record, go a little harder and heavier, much like The Cult had done with their 1987 album, *Electric*. Again, they felt we were falling between the cracks of radio formatting in the US – neither heavy enough for the rock stations, alternative enough for modern rock or college radio, and certainly not light enough for the pop stations. We entertained the idea to the extent that Canuck engineer/producer Mike Fraser, whose many credits include Aerosmith, AC/DC and Metallica, and who has been the preferred engineer for renowned big rock producers Bruce Fairbairn and Bob Rock,[5] was flown over from Canada to spend a few days with us in London's Marcus Studio to record a version of 'Belief'. Once finished, I flew out to Vancouver with Mike so that we could mix the track in the legendary Little Mountain Sound Studios, Mike's (and Fairbairn's and Rock's) favoured studio.

Mike is a genial, softly spoken, gentle, laid-back chap, easy to get along with and easy to work with. Perhaps too easy. The end result was, unfortunately, deemed as being a bit 'blah', as much the band's fault as it was Mike's.[6] I don't think we were cut out to go the out-and-out American 'big rock' route. It certainly didn't sit well with me anyway. We resisted Mike's entreaties to play big guitar power chords or chug (you already know my thoughts on chugging), both staple components in big rock music. We weren't our Phonogram label mates, Def Leppard, who were enjoying huge success at the time in the good ol' US of A.[7] You know damn well I had no problem with grandiloquent, melodramatic rock gestures, but they were always more of the northern European persuasion than the North American type. We'd kinda flirted with the

British big-rock-trousers classic rock to a degree with *Children*, but that was as 'rocky' as I could personally go. After much deliberation we felt we needed someone we could be comfortable with in the studio, with more energy – someone who *got us* but would have no qualms about pushing us, not if but when we needed it. And they had to be British.

Since we'd recorded *God's Own Medicine* with Tim Palmer, he'd gone up in the world, recording albums with both Robert Plant and David Bowie's Tin Machine. It just had to be Tim again. We knew him well and liked him, he worked fast and got things done, which is also how we liked to work in the studio. And Tim has always known how The Mission should *sound*. The fact that how he hears us and how I hear us has on occasion not tallied is more down to the fact that I've always had a tendency to wanna stray from *the formula*. While Tim has always recognised our strengths and our unique qualities and tried to get us to play to them, I have very often creatively fought against such straightjacketing. It's no coincidence that the albums we've released that *sound* most like how The Mission are perceived had some measure of Tim's involvement. Please understand that this is not an implied criticism of Tim and his working methods at all; he has always done good by us, and is exceptional at his job, as proven by his track record with a whole host of other diverse, and often enormously successful, bands and artists over the years. And when we've needed to make a record that *sounds* like The Mission, there's no one better to get the job done. Such was the case when it came to recording our third studio album, the one destined to be christened *Carved In Sand*.

Shortly after 7 p.m. on Wednesday, December 21, 1988, Pan Am Flight 103 from Frankfurt to Detroit (with stopovers scheduled at Heathrow and another in New York City) shockingly blew up in mid-air. The plane was destroyed by a bomb that had been planted on board, killing all 243 passengers and 16 crew. Large sections of the aircraft crashed in a residential street in Lockerbie in Scotland,

347

killing a further 11 residents. With a total of 270 fatalities, the Lockerbie bombing is the deadliest terrorist attack in UK history.

In early 1989, The Mission were asked if we'd play a benefit show for the Lockerbie Disaster Fund, in nearby Carlisle, just south of the border with England. It would be our first show of the year and was scheduled for March 18 at The Sands Centre. We readily agreed. Except it transpired I was in hospital on that weekend, so the show had to be moved to a later date.

The previous weekend I'd been admitted to hospital in south London for emergency surgery. I'll spare you the graphic details but let's just say that the episode involved a female employee at Phonogram, abundant amounts of sniff-sniff, and sexual deviancy using an assortment of restraints. The following morning came, a Saturday, and I was doubled up in agony on my couch, not able to move. It felt like the pain emanated from my stomach. I called Craig, who was also living in London at the time, he in Chiswick, and he came to my flat in Streatham Common. We managed to persuade a local doctor to visit me who, upon examination, immediately diagnosed me with testicular torsion[8] and insisted I rush straight to the nearest hospital for emergency surgery. Somehow, during the throes of white-line-fever lechery, one of my knackers had become twisted which cut off the blood supply to it. Craig and I jumped (well, Craig jumped while I kind of rolled) into a taxi, which took us straight to the hospital where I underwent surgery that same afternoon.

Upon waking from the general anaesthetic apparently the first thing I said to Craig, who was sitting patiently by my bedside, was 'How did Chelsea get on?' Where that came from I shall never know and I'm ashamed to admit it even now. Craig made sure I was alright and then made his way home, leaving me to enjoy the semi-consciousness of painkillers on drip. The attending doctor came to visit me the next morning, Sunday, and as I was still bleeding fairly heavily asked the nurse to re-dress my wound. 'Ah, the bleeding should stem throughout the day and be stopped by tomorrow,' he promised. Monday morning and I pull back my sheets and it's like the scene from *The Godfather* when the movie director wakes to find his bed is soaked with the blood of his prize horse's head. No horse's head between my legs, though; just a pair of very bloody testicles. The doctor was called and after conferring with other docs it was decided I should go back into surgery immediately, as it was definitely not as it should be.

So, I was prepped for surgery and wheeled off to the operating theatre again. When I came back to consciousness this time I was informed that during the previous procedure one of the veins in my testicle had been inadvertently nicked and not noticed when stitching me up. Hence, the profuse bleeding. The second surgery fixed me up and I then spent a few more days in hospital to make sure all was well. There was an 'official' news story released that week to the press that our Carlisle Sands Centre show was postponed because I had been admitted to hospital with 'abdominal pain'. We couldn't very well declare the truth now, could we? Whatever would my mum have thought?

I was released from hospital later that week and St Michael of Headingley, Leeds, volunteered to travel down from Yorkshire to stay and look after me while I recuperated. Having Mick Brown nurse me was the absolute best rehabilitation. Wearing baggy trousers around my crotch and moving very gingerly, within days we were going out to gigs, The Waterboys in Brighton being one of them, after which we ended up going back to their hotel bar for a late night drinkie-poo and singalong. We shared the same tour manager, the unflappable and ever-wise Harry Isles, and he had very kindly booked me and Mick a room.

Mike Scott and The Waterboys were one of those annoying bands that took their instruments into the bar after a show and played and sang all night long. That was their idea of after-show fun. And it was actually. And I bet they did the same on their tour buses, too, after shows – and at breakfast, and on travel days. 'Ah, we have an eight-hour drive today, what shall we do? I know, let's get the acoustic guitars, mandolins, fiddles and bodhrans out and jam.' It was just

349

something I could never imagine The Mission doing. Once *our* shows were over, the guitars went into their cases and it was straight into the booze and the party favours. Our travel days were spent getting stoned, drunk or tripping, and watching favourite films or listening to Craig's Roy Chubby Brown tapes. No bodhrans on our bus, although we did have to put up with Craig's bloody bagpipes for a while until he swapped 'em for the cuica drum, which is a far more irritating racket than a bodhran. We ended up making sure his cuica was hidden away in the equipment truck and not left on our bus.

A few evenings later, and still during my recuperation, Mick and I went to another gig, this time in London, and I bumped into the girl that had, um, put me in the hospital. She shimmied up to me and, beaming with what I perceived as pride, whispered in my ear, 'Ah, I know the real reason you were in hospital. Wanna show me your scar?' And with that, she took me by the hand and led me to the toilets, where we found an empty cubicle so she could inspect my stitches and test if everything was still in working order. It was a relief to find out that it was. Licking her lips she said, 'I love a man with scars.'

With the swelling between my legs gradually subsiding we found ourselves in a newly opened residential rehearsal studio, again just off the A23 somewhere between Crawley and Brighton. It was imaginatively named The Music Farm and was found a half mile or so down a dirt track. There were no neighbours anywhere near us, just open fields and meadows. It was an idyllic setting. The building itself was a long, prefabricated, single-storey construction that at one end housed six or seven bedrooms with a couple of bathrooms. The big rehearsal room was in the middle, with windows that looked out across the fields, and there was a large kitchen-cum-living room area at the entrance to the building. We were self-catering, so there were frequent trips to the local supermarket to stock up on essentials, and with Craig and Simon both fancying themselves as celebrity chef Keith Floyd, they took it in turns to don the *toque blanche* to serve up delicious dinners at the end of a long day's rehearsing. We were there for what felt like weeks, routining and honing the new songs for the new album. We had about 20 that we were knocking into shape, and a regular visitor was Tim Palmer, who was helping us with the process.

But there's only so much time you can spend in the rehearsal room. And so much television you can watch in the evenings (remember, there were still only four channels at this time (although Sky had just introduced their news and film channels)). Boredom began to set in, so one day we all went into nearby Crawley and each bought the biggest Scalextric[9] sets we could find. We joined the four sets together and made a huge racetrack that ran the length of the corridor and in and out of a couple of empty rooms. Mick, having owned a Scalextric set as a kid, knew how to soup up his car to go faster than the rest of ours. Cheating git. There were a couple of particularly treacherous bends, so we positioned Jez at one and Nipper at another to sit there and place our cars back on the track when they flew off. Well, they had to earn their wages somehow.

We were in the rehearsal room on the afternoon of Saturday, April 15, working on the intricacies of some song or other when, at just after 3 p.m., Jez popped his head around the door and said, 'Just watching *Grandstand* and there's a bit of a pitch invasion going on at Hillsborough. There's some Liverpool fans on the pitch, one of the first over the fence was wearing a Metallica T-shirt.' With Metallica being mates of ours we all had a giggle at that, not immediately realising the magnitude of what was unfolding in Sheffield. Jez left the room and we turned our attention back to what we were working on before the interruption. Jez, with strict instruction from yours truly to keep me updated on how the FA Cup semi-final between Liverpool and Nottingham Forest was proceeding, just a couple of minutes later came back into the room looking ashen, so my immediate thought was that Liverpool had conceded an early goal. 'Mate, you better come and see this, there's something awful happening at the match, there's fans being laid out on the pitch, it looks like the game's gonna be abandoned,' he explained.

We quickly downed our instruments and ran into the living room to watch the horrific scenes that were being transmitted live on television from Hillsborough. With each passing minute the unbelievable horror was escalating and it was quickly and clearly evident that there were people dying, being crushed to death in the pens behind the goal at the Leppings Lane end of the stadium. All I could do was just sit there and watch as this tragedy played out, tears streaming down my face as the reported death toll rose and kept on rising. I'd been a Liverpool supporter since the FA Cup final in 1965. I'd lived in the city from the beginning of 1978 through to the end of 1983, almost six years. I loved the city, its people and their warmth and wit, its history and culture, its uniqueness. I felt as Liverpudlian as much as I did Bristolian, my city of birth. Still do. I knew how much the city would be in shock, their suffering, mourning and grieving at this moment. I'd been living in Liverpool in December 1980 when John Lennon was murdered in NYC and knew how much his shocking death had affected the city, but this Hillsborough disaster was gonna be felt by the people of Liverpool in unimaginable ways and for decades to come. I phoned a couple of friends I was still in contact with in Liverpool to make sure they were okay, the disbelief at what had happened completely overwhelming. Everyone I knew in Liverpool knew somebody who had gone to the game. Everyone I knew also knew of somebody who had not come home.

Maybe it was that same evening, maybe it was the morning after, but I remember thinking that I had to do something to help if at all possible. After talking it through with the band I called Tony Perrin and told him we wanted to arrange a benefit show for the families of the bereaved. Tony, to his credit and my eternal thanks, got straight on to it and arranged a show at the Liverpool Royal Court for exactly two weeks later, Saturday, April 29. We also took the opportunity to reschedule the postponed Lockerbie Disaster gig in Carlisle for the day after, Sunday, April 30.

The enigmatic Liverpool band, The La's, offered their support, as did my old mate Pete Wylie of Wah! fame. Nasher, Ped and Mark O'Toole from Frankie Goes To Hollywood offered to come and play a set and also to back Wylie for his. In a matter of a couple of days it was all organised and ready to go. The show was announced and sold out instantly.

Being in the area rehearsing yet again, we played a hastily arranged warm-up show at Champagnes in Horsham, the fourth occasion, by my reckoning, we'd played at that sweat-pit dive. As always it was crammed and much fun was had by all. I remember there were plenty of Liverpool FC scarves being held aloft in the audience that night, one of which was given to me by a generous benefactor, which I still have among my vast collection of LFC/football memorabilia today. (How the hell have I ended up keeping all of that but lost most of my music-related memorabilia over the years?)

We travelled up to Liverpool the night before the show and checked into the city centre Holiday Inn, all rooms very kindly donated by the hotel. Let me just say at this juncture that everybody involved with the show gave of their time and services for free – us and the La's, Wylie, the stage crews, the venue crews and security, the PA (Tour Tech) and lights (Entec), the tour buses and transport, and with all profits from our merch sales donated, too. It really was an amazing show of solidarity from everyone involved.

On arrival, Pete Wylie brought us the unfortunate news that the Frankie boys had pulled out. He offered to play solo and we offered to back him on a couple of his tunes. Arrangements were made to have an extra-long soundcheck so we could run through a couple of Wah! hits with him.

Come showtime and the Royal Court was packed, the atmosphere electric. Just before The La's took to the stage I popped into their dressing room to say hello and thank them for being there. The air thick with smoke and pungent with an aroma of something I couldn't quite identify, they were polite if not effusive. Minutes later they were onstage playing a lovely set of their jingly–jangly bright-as-a-buttercup songs, the highlight of course being the seminal 'There She Goes'. Next up, it was our turn.

Today, remembering that show elicits a strange emotion in me. Even though our performance and the audience were both spectacular, it's still not something I can look back on and derive any amount of real satisfaction from because of the very reason we were there in the first place. I guess we did it hoping that it would help, maybe provide a salve, in some small way. We did raise a tidy sum but in very real terms it was just a drop in the ocean of what was really needed, and, anyway, no amount of financial recompense is any consolation at all to the bereaved.

I have, however, been heartened over the years by the number of people who have said they were there that night and that the event did help them. That's all I could truly hope for under the circumstances.

Anyway... after the audience had serenaded us with 'You'll Never Walk Alone', someone found the electric meter and put a few quid in and on we went with the show. The plan we had devised in cahoots with Wylie was that he would join us onstage towards the end of our set for a blast through Iggy's '1969'. After introducing Wylie I started the song by playing the riff and singing the first verse before the band joined in and the whole place erupted. At which point I looked behind me and saw Simon being Super Slink, Craig head down and rocking, Wylie strutting his stuff, and some other bloke thrashing away at a guitar. It took me a couple of seconds to realise it was Mick Jones from The Clash/Big Audio Dynamite. I had no idea he was gonna join us onstage – it was as much a surprise to me as it was to the audience. Mick and Wylie had been long-time friends and, as I found out later, Mick had offered to join Pete for his performance once he'd heard the Frankie boys had bailed. When '1969' was over, The Mission left the stage to Pete and Mick to play a couple of acoustic covers, the first being The Beatles' 'Strawberry Fields Forever', which Pete very kindly dedicated to me, as he knew it was one of my all-time fave songs. They followed it with the wonderfully poignant Johnny Thunders song 'You Can't Put Your Arms Around A Memory'. Once they'd finished, The Mission rejoined them both onstage for a rampage through Wah's 'Come Back', the Sex Pistol's 'Pretty Vacant' (that was quite a moment, playing the Pistol's classic with the guitarist from The Clash) and our own 'Shelter From The Storm'. And that was that. What an emotional rollercoaster that night was. Unforgettable.

After the show I was having a drink with Wylie and I asked if he'd like to come with us the next day to Carlisle to do it all again for the rescheduled Lockerbie Disaster benefit.

'Ah, I can't, Wayne, I promised I'd go over to Manchester to see my mates play,' he replied.

'Okay, who's that then?', I asked, my curiosity piqued as to whose company Pete was preferring to ours.

'Ah, they're called Happy Mondays.'

'Mmm, never 'eard of 'em, soz mate.'

'Hey, you soon will.'

Yeah, right, I thought.

The times they are a changin'...

Of course, after the emotional toll of the night in Liverpool the Carlisle Sands Centre show the next day could only be an anticlimax. Except it wasn't. Not as emotionally charged as the previous night, it was, nevertheless, another rollicking performance, remembered fondly by the hordes following us at the time.[10] In his review for *Melody Maker*, Paul Lester said of us, 'The Mission are still the most involving and multi-faceted adventure rock has to offer.' For once I wouldn't disagree. Again, just as in Liverpool, everybody gave freely of their time and services and another sizeable amount was raised for the Lockerbie Disaster Fund.

I must confess, I've not always been entirely comfortable aligning myself with various charities and performing benefit shows. I think one really has to examine one's reasons and motives for getting involved. But, looking back now, I'm glad that in April 1989, when perhaps we were at our most popular, we decided to perform these two shows and in our own small way tried to help. I like to feel we did.

Endnotes

1   Courtship, an archaic formal term rarely used these days, was a period during which a couple would develop a romantic relationship, especially with matrimony as its end-view. Dating is more widely used today, which is still very formal to my mind. In my world the question would more likely be, 'so, are you two shagging?'

2   A wedding arranged in order to avoid embarrassment due to premarital sex, usually as it has resulted in an unintended pregnancy. The phrase is based on the idea that the father of the bride-to-be threatens the reluctant groom with a shotgun in order to ensure that he follows through with the wedding. (Thanks, Wiki.)

3   The Mission didn't get to attend in 1988 (we were on tour in South America), but we did send a video message from Ronnie Biggs's house, which I'm sure was loudly jeered when shown. In 1989, the conference was held in the ballroom at The Dorchester, on London's Park Lane. And again we were hanging out with Siouxsie and her Banshees. They usually had a band or two or a newly signed artist performing. That night it was Level bloody 42. I don't know if I've mentioned previously (smirk) but I was never a fan of Mark 'Slap' King and his merry men. I can't rationalise my loathing, words fail me when I try to explain why I have such a dislike for them. They're probably decent blokes, although between you and me, I did hear a few grumbles from record company personnel as to how 'difficult' Slap Happy Mark could be. Don't tell

anyone I told you that though. Although to be fair to the chap, and not wanting to cast stones at the innocent, it's all just hearsay. I have since been assured by a reliable source that 'he seriously was very nice and polite. I daresay age has mellowed him like it does a lot of people, just like a certain other person I know.' I wonder who he could be referring to? That all being said, just because he's a decent bloke it doesn't make his music any more palatable to me. As it also works the other way, too – there are certain individuals who we all know are invidious, curmudgeonly strops, but we love them and their music, nonetheless. Anyway, Steve Severin and I took it upon ourselves as our duty to mankind to wend our way through, it has to be said, the scant crowd to stand in front of Mark King as he performed, and to heckle and hurl abuse his way, particularly between songs. After 10 minutes or so of this rollicking great fun the visibly disgruntled front man had a word with someone at the side of the stage and a mere couple of minutes later we had our shoulders tapped and we were 'escorted' away from the stage by four burly house security troglodytes and ejected from the ballroom to the bar. On entry into the bar we received a loud round of applause from the gathered throng. It seems we weren't alone in our antipathy of Level bloody 42.

4   While working on the final revisions for this book Kate Bush hit the number one spot in the UK singles chart with 'Running Up That Hill', some 38 years after its initial release, and has seen a mass resurgence in popularity, particularly among a brand-new generation of younger fans. Brilliant. There's hope for us yet.

5   Bruce Fairbairn (who sadly passed in 1999 at the age of only 49) and Bob Rock are esteemed Canadian record producers who preferred to work out of Vancouver's Little Mountain Sound Studios. Between them, they've produced most of rock music's royalty, including Bon Jovi, Van Halen, AC/DC, Aerosmith, Metallica, Mötley Crüe, Poison, Chicago, Kiss, Yes, The Tragically Hip, The Cult, Bryan Adams, David Lee Roth and The Offspring.

6   The version of 'Belief' recorded with Mike Fraser eventually saw the light of day on the 2006 release, *Anthology: The Phonogram Years*.

7   Being label mates, we bumped into Def Leppard a few times over the years while on promotional duties. Hailing from Sheffield, just as Slink does, the band were always good company; fun-loving Yorkshire blokes who liked a good natter about footie and classic British early Seventies bands such as

Mott The Hoople and The Faces. I remember once being in a hotel bar in Munich with them (both bands were appearing on the same TV show), and by the end of the night it was just myself, Mick Brown, and the Lepp's guitarist, the tragic Steve Clark, in the bar. Both Mick and I were about sixteen sheets to the wind between us and could barely stand. But we were both in far better shape than Steve. Even in our acute inebriation we were cognisant enough to realise that he was completely gone, and we had to get him to his room and into bed. Somehow between us we managed it. Less than a year later we heard the very sad news that Steve, an alcoholic who was on a six-month leave of absence from Def Leppard in an attempt to get well, had been found dead at his home in London, at the age of 30.

8   When the testicle rotates (testicular torsion), it twists the cord supplying blood to the loose bag of skin (scrotum) beneath the penis. This may occur after vigorous activity, a minor injury to the testicles, or even just sleep. Sudden, severe pain and swelling in the testicle are symptoms. Surgery is required. Treated promptly, the testicle can often be saved. A longer wait may affect fertility.

9   Scalextric slot-car racing sets first came around in the late 1950s and were manufactured by the English firm Minimodels. They became hugely popular, but they weren't cheap. I never had a set. My parents were never able to afford one for us.

10   The Carlisle show was particularly memorable for Graham Chisnall, a young chap who would become a very dear friend of mine in later years. I asked if there was someone in the audience who knew the words to 'Pretty Vacant', as I didn't. Chis put his hands up to volunteer and clambered up onstage, where I handed him the microphone. He didn't know the words at all, even less than I did, but to be fair to him he wasn't in the least intimidated and gave it his all, as if he'd been getting up onstage in front of thousands for years.

CHAPTER 17

Castles Carved In Sand

PLAYLIST:
1. Hi Ho Silver Lining − Jeff Beck   2. Sunshine Superman − Donovan
3. Lullaby − The Cure   4. Birthday − The Sugarcubes
5. Dreamtime − The Heart Throbs
6. It's Yer Money I'm After, Baby − The Wonder Stuff
7. Mr Pleasant − The Mission   8. Heaven Sends You − The Mission
9. Girl In A Jigsaw Puzzle − Katydids   10. Bird Of Passage − The Mission
11. Sea Of Love − The Mission   12. Lovely − The Mission

VIDEO PLAYLIST:
Waves Upon The Sand (documentary) − The Mission

Miles Hunt was gobbing off about me and The Mission in the music press. One of many, he wasn't the first and certainly not the last. As I've said before, I was an easy target, and *pop stars* back then always picked easy targets, particularly when the objects of their invective were in bands ahead of 'em in the popularity stakes. I did it myself when I first came along, mouthing off about all and sundry. However, 99 per cent of the people pillorying me had never met me. I guess you could say my reputation preceded me. One journalist was, apparently, so nervous about meeting 'the wild man of rock' (who me?), that he'd asked around ahead of the meeting and couldn't find anyone with a bad word to say about me. While that was nice to read I could definitely name a few that wouldn't necessarily concur with that sentiment.

Miles's band, The Wonder Stuff, were riding the crest of their first wave of acclaim and, as is usually the way with johnny-come-latelies, they were taking verbal potshots at the bands they had in their sights and saw as competition. The business of music is as cut-throat and competitive as any other – don't you believe otherwise – and one way of potentially damaging your competitors is by slagging 'em off in the music press. Be careful, though, because one day you just might bump into the object of your vilification and that could make for an uncomfortable moment...

In the first week of May 1989, we started recording our new album at the fabled RAK Studios in St John's Wood, London, a stone's throw from Regent's Park. RAK, one of the few studios we worked in during the Eighties that is still open and thriving today, was founded in an old Victorian school and church hall in 1976 by legendary record producer Mickie Most, famed for his hits with a whole litany of bands and artists, including The Animals, the Jeff Beck Group, Herman's Hermits, Donovan and Lulu to name a few. Mickie would turn up at the studio most days on his motorbike, which he parked directly outside the building, just to hang out. He'd be sat in the TV room, regaling whoever wanted to listen (I did!) with all these fantastic stories about the hitmakers he'd worked with in the Sixties and Seventies. He definitely liked a good yarn. It was Mickie that told me, knowing how big a Zeppelin fan I was, that both Jimmy Page and John Paul Jones had played on Donovan's monster hit 'Sunshine Superman'. His favourite thing to ask you was, 'Are you winning in there?'

With Tim Palmer loving how the drums sounded in Studio One, we were booked into RAK for two or three weeks to record the drum tracks for the album. Chris Sheldon, Tim's best friend since school days and today a top producer in his own right, was brought in to engineer. Mick set up his kit and a couple of days were spent getting a workable drum sound. We decided for this record to mostly dispense with playing with a click.[1] We wanted the songs to have their own natural ebb and flow rather than be played to a strict, rigid tempo. The natural tendency for us as musicians is to slightly slow down for verses and then, as we get excited, rush into and slightly speed up for choruses, and we wanted to imbue the songs with that natural dynamic. So, we plugged our guitars directly into the mixing desk in the control room so we could play along with Mick, otherwise he'd have nothing to play to and that ain't much fun for drummers now, is it? Some songs were recorded in just a few takes, others took longer and, long before Pro Tools was making everything easier, we even did some 24-track tape editing to get those drum tracks together, which was made all the more difficult by the absence of a click track. But it was worth it. For me, Mick's playing on *Carved In Sand* was a tour de force and the best he ever sounded.

One of Tim's stipulations for this new record was that he wouldn't work on weekends. He was newly married and wanted to stay that way. With a bit of success and having climbed a few more rungs up the ladder, he was throwing his weight around and making *his* demands of *us*. Cheeky bugger. But we didn't mind, as we had three consecutive weekends away in Europe anyway, playing with The Cure. They had recently released *Disintegration*, an album that would rightly go on to be regarded as a classic.

I was, and remain, a Cure fan, my fave album of theirs being 1982's *Pornography*, with all its austere beauty. I had first seen them play in 1979 at Eric's in Liverpool, a gig that was, as I later learned from the man himself, bassist Simon Gallup's first with the band.

On the first weekend (6 May) of our run of shows with The Cure, we played at Heerenveen in the Netherlands, a big indoor ice arena. At the end of the evening I knocked on their dressing room door to say hello. I was immediately invited in and very warmly received. I'd met keyboardist Roger O'Donnell before on tour in the US, when we'd played with The Psychedelic Furs, and Simon and I had spent an afternoon in a pub next door to the offices of *Melody Maker*. I'd not met the others before though. They were all lovely but, singers being singers, Robert Smith was initially a little shy and maybe suspicious of me at first (perhaps another example of my reputation preceding me?). But we soon hit it off, and Robert invited me to accompany them to a restaurant for an after-show meal. With me being the easy-to-persuade, capricious type, I ditched my fellow band mates and off we went. On The Cure's tour bus, Robert insisted I sit next to him, as he did at the restaurant, and we sat holding hands under the table for the rest of the evening. It was love, I was a smitten kitten.

The next morning, complete with thundering hangovers, we made our way back to the UK and back to RAK for another week of drum recording. We were already looking forward to the following weekend, Saturday, May 13, when we'd be flying out to Germany to appear as second on the bill to The Cure at the Loreley Bizarre Festival. We'd previously played the same festival in 1987 with The Banshees and Iggy, the amphitheatre gloriously situated atop a mountain overlooking the River Rhine. This year, The Sugarcubes and The Pixies were appearing on the bill too. I watched a bit of both bands from the side of the stage and marvelled at the extraordinary vocal acrobatics of The Sugarcubes' female singer, Björk. I wished she'd sang more of their songs rather than that Einar bloke, who just seemed to shout.

Backstage I caught up with my new chums The Cure, and we sat outside our Portakabin dressing rooms, taking in the afternoon sun while supping wine and beers and following the football results from back home. Simon Gallup was an Arsenal supporter[2], who at that point were neck and neck with Liverpool in vying for the league title, a race that would come right down to the final game of the season. We'll come back to that in a while… if we must.

After the show I was again invited to go with The Cure but back to their hotel this time, where we sat in the bar being serenaded on piano by Roberto, bass player with The Cure's tour support band, Shelleyan Orphan. As the drinks flowed so the quiet serenade soon degenerated into a riotous sing-song around the piano when Roberto started playing Abba classics. At the end of the night, much the worse for wear, I realised I had no idea where the Mission hotel was, so Simon very kindly offered me the couch in his room. In the morning The Cure's tour manager ascertained the name and address of our hotel, poured me into a taxi and bid me fond adieu until the following weekend.

Back in London, on Monday 15 May, I had an evening off. There was a band called The Heart Throbs who were causing a little stir in the music press that I quite liked the sound of and, perchance, they were playing at Dingwalls in Camden Lock. I was at a loose end so I thought I'd go and check them out. I was with a friend, can't remember exactly who now but it would've been somebody who could afford me a little security, as I was no longer in the habit of going out alone. The Mission might've been very popular in 1989 but being popular also meant there were as many if not more people out there who detested me and, with a few beers in 'em, they'd love to have a pop at me if they got the chance. That's why I stopped going out in Leeds when I still lived there. It wasn't so bad in London, as most places were used to seeing semi-famous people among their clientele. There, I was just one of the many 'pop stars' that were always around town. My point was proven when I walked through the door at Dingwalls. There, sitting at the bar, was Miles Hunt, the would-be usurper who'd been slagging me off in the music press. As I walked in he saw me and then turned his back on me. Whatever.

363

Dingwalls wasn't particularly busy that night and most everyone was down in front of the stage, watching the band. I walked over and sat down next to Miles. He ignored me. I tapped him on the shoulder. He turned and, with no small degree of asperity, said, 'What?'

'Let me buy you a drink?' I offered.

'Nah, you're alright.'

'Come on, you seem to have a lot to say for yourself. I'm here, you can say it to my face now, over a drink,' I insisted.

Miles grudgingly acceded to my request. We sat there and talked and gradually I could feel him warm to me. Alcohol will do that. And I think it came as a surprise to him that I understood some of his criticisms of me and The Mission. His biggest beef was the number of different formats we released with each single: a 7-inch vinyl, a 12-inch vinyl with extra tracks and remixes, maybe a cassette, a CD or two, and some format with special packaging aimed at the collectors. Yeah, it was too much, but we did try to make each release something special and unique in itself and, anyway, every other bugger was at it in the Eighties. The Wonder Stuff themselves would soon be doing just the same. Our first singles, released independently, were basically just a 7-inch and a 12-inch vinyl version – CD singles weren't really a thing yet – and that was yer lot. Once we signed to Phonogram, though, it became common practice to release each single in various formats, in hopes that the die-hard fans would buy all of them, thereby helping it into the charts.

It had started with the 'Stay With Me' single, our first on Phonogram, where we released a numbered limited edition – 5,000 gatefold-sleeve 7-inch singles, which were all signed – in addition to the normal 7-inch and 12-inch versions. And with each subsequent release the formatting became more expansive. It wasn't a practice I particularly endorsed or objected to – ambivalence would be how I'd best describe my attitude, with the occasional pang of guilty conscience. We couldn't force anyone to buy more than one format, that was up to the individual, but with every band there is a faction of the fan base that is so devout they want *everything* you release. I do wonder, though, how our singles would've fared without all the formatting and major label promotion. Not as well, my guess would be. But that's part of the reason we wanted to sign with a major label in the first place, making that particular pact with Beelzebub so we could compete with the big guns.

Anyway, I argued my case, pointing out that even Morrissey – one of Miles's biggest musical heroes at that point and once regarded as the saviour of independent music – had signed to the big, bad, evil corporate EMI and was now *playing the game*. Miles and I argued, debated and even occasionally agreed on a myriad of topics over the course of that evening, as we made our way from one drinking establishment to another, eventually ending up back at the Royal Court Hotel on Sloane Square where Miles was staying and where, more importantly, we could order drinks right through the night from the night porter. We sat, drank some more, and chatted like two old dears over the (metaphorical) garden fence, putting the world to rights. Miles remembers me playing him a rough mix on cassette of our newly recorded version of 'Mr Pleasant', he not realising that it was a cover of a Kinks song and thinking I'd written it. His reaction was, 'My God, that doesn't sound like The Mission, it sounds like The Wonder Stuff! You're gonna get battered in the music press for sounding like us.' As flattered as I was that he thought me capable of writing such a fine song, I explained it was a cover and confessed that at that point I hadn't really heard, apart from possibly a couple of singles, any of The Wonder Stuff's music. So Milo, as he shall henceforth be known, proceeded to play me the album they were currently recording, which would eventually be released later that summer as *Hup*. While I could hear a vaguely similar *joie de vivre*, I didn't really consider 'Mr Pleasant' to sound like the Stuffies; to me it was more arch and satirical, much like The Kinks' version in fact. I replied pointedly, 'Well,

I get a battering in the music press from all-comers, including your good self, so yet another slagging ain't gonna bother me. And anyway, you can't go wrong with a Kinks song.' With the sun already up we decided that we should get some sleep so we both crawled into Miles's bed and, after planting a goodnight smackeroo on his lips, we both managed to get some well-needed kip. It's fair to say that by the end of that first night we were the best of friends and have remained so ever since. Oh, by the way, The Heart Throbs were grand.

The following weekend was our final show that summer with The Cure, this time at the Rock am See Festival in Konstanz, Deutschland, again. The German band Die Toten Hosen (translates as Dead Trousers – apparently one of the brilliant Jürgen Klopp's3 favourite bands) were second on the bill, just above us. They were awful: a bit like Sham 69 but in German. Even Robert Smith was moved to comment from the stage that they were the worst band he'd ever heard. But what do we know? They're huge in Australia, Japan and South America and have come to be absolutely revered as national treasures in their Fatherland. And, well, you know, if Jürgen likes 'em then they can't be all bad, can they? I spied Robert watching us from the side of the stage during our performance and I remember him saying to me afterwards, 'I like that new 'butterfly' song, it's really beautiful – that should be a single.' Who was I to argue?

On our return to England we moved into Jacobs Studio[4], a short drive from Guildford in the Surrey countryside, for six weeks. Having finished all the drum recordings at RAK, we were there to record bass guitar, guitars, piano, keyboards, vocals and other nonsense. Like The Manor before it, Jacobs was fully residential and came replete with requisite heated swimming pool and tennis court. I've always preferred residential studios, where band and studio crew live in and can work to any schedule we please, avoiding hanging around the control room if we're not needed. While those who have never spent time in a studio might think it thrilling to watch musicians at work – and it can be – I can assure you that after a while it does get tedious unless you're actively involved in some way. Who wants to sit around and watch Craig spend hours finessing the same bass guitar part? Or Simon trying to get a guitar sound he can work with? Or watching me sing the same song 10 times over? Or worse, sit there while Mick spends two days programming a drum track, as he did with John Paul Jones on our previous album? Yes, a lot of time in the studio is spent just sitting around waiting for others to do their jobs. Of course, a major part of the engineer's and producer's job is to sit through it all and work with each musician in turn. No wonder they got paid the big bucks.

We developed a routine at Jacobs, which was essentially this: all up and about by 10 a.m., dressed and ready for our daily game of Tennis Football, come rain or shine. Fortunately we were at Jacobs through the June and July of 1989, and the weather was as decent as it gets in England. So we played three-a-side on the full-size hard tennis court. The rules and scoring were very much based on 'proper' tennis. The server could serve either by a drop-ball or the ball being placed on the ground behind the baseline. The equivalent of the underarm tennis serve, the drop-ball serve was the easier to execute of the two service methods, but the downside was that it was also easier to receive and control, as the ball didn't come over the net at quite the same pace as the placed-ball serve. The placed-ball serve was more difficult to execute, like the overarm in tennis, and only a couple of us ever bothered with it. This was how I'd serve, but very often my first serve would be a foul, either ploughing straight into the net or out of bounds on the other side of the court, so then I'd resort to the drop-ball for my second serve. I'm sure you wanted to know that.

As in tennis, the ball had to bounce in the service box, diagonally across the other side of the net. On receipt of the ball after a *good* serve, we were allowed as many touches as we could muster by any combination of the players on our side, as long as the ball only

bounced (touched the ground) three times while you were in possession of it. For example, I could receive the ball and skilfully control
it, let it bounce once or twice, keep it in the air with my knees
before knocking it up towards the net where Tim, being well over
six-feet tall, might be stood and he could head it back over the net
to the other side. Or, as Tim liked to do when he received a serve,
perform 'The Surge' – a move which entailed him controlling the
ball on his chest and then 'surging' forward with it before walloping
it over the net into the opposing side's half of the court. 'The Surge'
was a potent weapon.

Every day we'd have different captains who'd take it in turns to choose
their players from a pool of eight of us: the four band members, Tim
and Chris, and Jez and Nipper. Three-a-side with one substitute. The
good players were me (of course) and Tim and Jez, while Adams wasn't
bad, and Slink was okay but sometimes tried to be too clever. Mick
was as enthusiastic as a puppy chasing the ball and about as adroit at
kicking it; Nipper was similar, although good with his head; with poor
ol' Chris Sheldon being the runt of the litter and the last to be picked
every day. I used to hate it when Chris ended up on my team because
he was definitely a handicap. Chris or no Chris, though, I loved this
start to the day, but woe betide everyone else if I ended up on the
losing side. My competitive nature coming to the fore, I'd be in a foul
mood for hours afterwards if we hadn't won. Being the great producer
he is, Tim noticed this petulant behaviour of mine and, preferring a
more amenable working atmosphere, engineered it so I was indeed on
the winning side every day. Everybody else was in on it, so even if my
side were losing the opposing side would start making 'mistakes' just
so I could win. Of course, I was none the wiser and just thought I
was brilliant and the best player there… until we'd left Jacobs and the
truth was revealed to me. Bunch o' bastards…

After Football Tennis, we'd have a bit of breakfast and would be in
the studio working by midday, with me in a good mood. We'd work

through until teatime, when we'd all sit down in the dining room for a delicious meal cooked for us by Tiggi, Olly and Sara, the studio chefs. Afterwards we'd reconvene to the studio, usually wrapping up for the evening sometime just before midnight. Again, we didn't work on weekends as Tim insisted on going back home to London for a couple of days off with his wife and newly born daughter.

Everyone else stayed on at the studio, enjoying the amenities and accommodation, treating the time as a holiday, with the occasional trip into nearby Guildford. There was a pub nearby, which we visited once or twice and where I met a couple of ladies who came back to the studio with me. I showed them around and introduced them to everyone, and even ended up recording a vocal – 'Divided We Fall' – with them sat in the control room. Of course, bibulousness was abounding all through this and there may have been a bit of showing off from *moi*.

Anyway, the fact that I couldn't drive came up in conversation. Being a summer evening with the sun not yet setting, and because one of the girls owned a car, they insisted on taking me for a driving lesson down the country lanes that surrounded the studio. All three of us were mightily sozzled, so it was always a disaster waiting to happen. With me behind the wheel and still in first gear, hopelessly trying to co-ordinate how to use a clutch at the same time as changing gears, all while steering, I ended up rolling the car into a roadside ditch. Fortunately there was no damage – to us or the car, or even the ditch. I wasn't going bloody fast enough. But there was no way we could reverse it out; we just had to leave it there and go get someone to tow it. Fortuitously we hadn't actually travelled very far from the studio, only a couple of hundred yards, so we just walked the short distance back, both of the girls laughing uproariously at my ineptitude. As did the rest of the band on our very swift return. On the upside, it was too late in the evening to call out a tow truck, which meant that the girls ended up having to sleep the night with me in my bed. I paid for the truck in the morning, which was the least I could do. The girls did offer to return to give me more lessons, but I decided the world was a safer place without me driving. Plus, Sheryl, my girlfriend, was about to arrive from the US.

Sheryl had been back and forth a few times that year and it was always lovely to see her, but the truth is it wasn't what anyone could call a *serious* relationship, and certainly not exclusive. In fact, looking back, I think both of us liked being with each other and had fun when we were together, but we could only stand it for short periods of time. She came to the studio and stayed for a few days but then, getting bored, decided she would head to my flat in Streatham Common to visit friends of hers in London. I knew she was sharing her affections with others, but I was hardly a paragon of virtue myself and, if truth be known, it really didn't bother me. How could it, considering the way I behaved myself? What was good for the goose was good for the gander. It was just sex. What was important to us was how we treated each other when we were together.

It was during this period when we began to notice that Simon was withdrawing from the recording process. I know Simon was irked that I hadn't been able to use any of the tunes he'd submitted for consideration, while he wasn't entirely happy with the direction the new album was taking – which was a return to the more quintessential Mission sound rather than following the more 'classic rock vibe' of *Children*. Most of the new songs I'd written already had well-established guitar parts that I'd come up with and would play on the record, leaving less for Simon to do this time round. I still left the guitar solos to Si – he could solo better than I could; listen to 'Deliverance' and 'Belief' as evidence, yer honour – but all the basic guitars, with very few exceptions, were played by me. I'd written the riffs and arpeggios, so rather than waste time teaching them to Simon I'd gone ahead and recorded them myself. Personally, I don't think it matters who plays what in the studio; if whoever comes up with the idea can play it, they should record it. An exception would be Mick, for example, who couldn't play guitar but would come up with guitar ideas and sing them to me and I'd try to play 'em. Conversely, I couldn't play drums but I always had a good idea of what I wanted the drums to do, and Mick was always open to suggestions. I don't think I have an ego when I'm recording. If I don't have to play on a record at all I'm quite happy not to. The end result is what matters, not who played what. Without realising it, though, I was essentially marginalising Simon. And Simon, being the insecure type, contrary to his very different public image, was taking it to heart. As a form of creative release I guess, he would lock himself away in his bedroom and, using our TEAC 4-track recorder, spend almost all his time working on what he referred to as a solo instrumental album. I couldn't be bothered to deal with it; I was still writing lyrics and had an enormous amount to take care of on the record without worrying about whether our guitarist was happy or not. I just assumed, and hoped, it was a passing phase.

Friday 26 May, my 31st birthday. We'd had a good day in the studio and I was looking forward to the match that night (Liverpool v. Arsenal) being broadcast live on TV from Anfield. It was the last game of what had been a tumultuous season for us, what with the Hillsborough disaster, but it looked like ending with success. We'd just beaten Everton 3–2 in the FA Cup Final and were on for our second League and Cup double in four years. We were top of the table, three points above Arsenal with a slightly better goal difference. We could even lose the match 1–0 and still be crowned champions. 0–0 at half-time and all looked rosy. The band, Nipper, Jez, Tim and Chris brought in a birthday cake and sang 'Happy Birthday' to me. Very touching, it was. The second half started and I was still feeling pretty confident. Eight minutes in and Arsenal score through a header

371

from Alan Smith. 1–0 to the Arse. I still felt fairly certain we'd take the title. 90 minutes were up on the clock and all we had to do was see out the added-on extra couple of minutes. With seconds remaining, Michael Thomas raced on to a header from Smith, evaded a challenge from Stevie Nicol and slotted the ball home past the advancing Bruce Grobbelaar to score Arsenal's second. And the title-winning goal. Two fucking nil. I couldn't believe it. There were only 18 seconds left to play when Liverpool kicked off again. Tim, being an Arsenal supporter, was going bonkers, while the rest of the lads were all taking the piss out of me 'cos we'd lost.

Now, if you're a football fan you know how much a defeat can hurt, and certainly one of this consequence. But the worst thing is when other people gloat and rub yer nose in it. I hate football gloaters. I try not to do it with my friends as I know how painful it can be to be on the receiving end. And karma often has a nasty habit of coming back to sting you in the arse (see what I did there?) anyway. As I refuse to have any Manchester United supporters as friends, I will gloat every time we put one over on them. But otherwise, I ain't a gloater.

'Fuck off,' was my reaction to my band mates as I flounced out of the TV room. With Tim having left after the match to go home for the weekend, I grabbed Chris, who was still in residence. 'Come on, we're going to the studio. I'm gonna write a new song.' Locking the rest of the band out, I kept Chris working till the sun came up, writing the lyrics and recording from scratch (with a drum machine and playing all the instruments myself) a brand new song, which became 'Heaven Sends You'. A song that has nothing to do with football at all and everything to do with cunnilingus.

While working at Jacobs, we invited a few guests to come visit and contribute to our new platter. First, there was Chris's girlfriend of the time, Susie Hug, singer in the *NME*-championed (cursed, more like) up-and-coming band The Katydids. No Julianne, no Kate, no matter. Susie did a wonderful job singing the backing vocals on 'Bird Of Passage'.

I'd written 'Sea Of Love' as a kind of 'Dear Prudence' pastiche, based around a westernised Indian raga scale. Both Simon and I had each bought sitars a year or two previously but neither of us could really elicit anything more than a caterwaul from our instruments. My sitar was more of an ornament in my living room if I'm honest. It looked great. I'd occasionally have a go, but it took me about a week just to tune the bugger and then whatever I played was a horrendous din and no doubt disturbing to my neighbours. The upshot was that I wanted *real sitar* on the track, so Tim found Bahiji, a blind Indian sitar session player. Mick was entrusted with the task of picking up Bahiji from the local train station. 'How will I recognise him?' our drummer asked.

'Don't think you'll miss him, Mick. Look for an Indian guy with a white cane in one hand and a sitar case in the other. I don't think there'll be many people like that alighting at Guildford,' our producer replied, laughing.

On arrival, Bahiji warmed up with a few ragas while Chris set up the mics, and then he listened through to the track once and nailed it in one take. Amazing musicianship.

Elsewhere, we asked an old acquaintance of mine from my Liverpool days, Guy Chambers (who would go on to be Robbie Williams' right-hand man through the early years of his massive success) to score a piece I'd written on piano named 'Sweet Smile Of A Mystery' for an 80-piece orchestra. While he was visiting the studio to show us the score, we got him to play some piano dribbles on 'Grapes Of Wrath'. We'll come back to the recording of 'Sweet Smile Of Mystery' in a while.

Finally, we asked Simon's brother, David, who had previously played with Artery and Pulp, Slink's earlier bands, to come and play trombone on 'Mr Pleasant'. Among my parents' collection of Sixties 7-inch singles was The Kinks' 'Autumn Almanac', a typical Ray Davies jaunty little tune. But flip it over and there you'd find, in my humble, the superior B-side, 'Mr Pleasant'. I remember we spent a day in Nomis rehearsal studios, rather than rehearsing what we should've been rehearsing, just jamming through a whole bunch of Kinks songs, with 'Mr Pleasant' being the one we enjoyed playing the most. Probably because it wasn't one of The Kinks better-known songs and musically it being the complete antithesis of what our audience would ordinarily expect from us, we started playing it live, even at our headline Reading Festival appearance later that summer, raising eyebrows and gales of laughter both.

Sometime early in the process of recording the album we thought it'd be a great idea to film the proceedings and make a studio documentary, which would also follow us on our upcoming tour of the Scottish Highlands, culminating with our headline appearance down at Reading Festival. We met with a couple of video directors and the American Leo Sanchez won our vote, swung by the fact that he turned up to the studio in a Sixties red one-seater bubble car. The film, *Waves Upon The Sand*, opens with us nearing the end of our tenure at Jacobs, having a garden party. We'd run a competition through MWIS and a lucky four or five fan club members (and plus ones) were invited to the studio one weekend. We played our guests some of the close-to-being finished tracks we'd been working on, and showed them around the house, the studio and the grounds. A few had bought swimming costumes so, being a lovely English summer's day, they enjoyed a splish-splash in the swimming pool with some of us. A few games of Football Tennis were followed by a barbecue, with severely under-cooked chicken, sausages and steaks (obviously, none of us were veggie at this point). A cask full of beer on tap along with a few cases of wine, and the party was swinging. One thing I failed to mention is that a bunch of us had dropped acid – me, Mick, Simon, Nipper, Leo, and Tim and Chris being LSD virgins taking their very first trips. Jez and Craig were staunchly against hallucinogens at this time and stayed on the booze, preferring instead to be evil little shits trying to do in the heads of those of us that were tripping. I knew what they were up to, they couldn't fool me.

About an hour or so after dropping the tabs I bumped into Tim in the house. 'How's your trip going, man?' I asked.

'Ah, I'm not feeling anything, it's done nothing for me. But, hey, come and look at this tree outside in the garden, it's brilliant.'

'Okay, so you're not tripping then, eh?' I said, laughing.

A little later I stood and watched Leo, our video director, who was supposed to be filming all the shenanigans for our documentary, filming his own reflection in a mirror for about 20 minutes. A little narcissism at work there, me thinks.

A little later we all found ourselves sat on the grass in the garden, *Hounds Of Love* blaring out of the stereo. Somehow we had all ended up in a circle with Chris sat in the middle. This was his first trip, remember. Jez, the little bugger, knew damn well what he was doing as he'd done his own fair share of tripping previously, and he had a long stick that he kept poking Chris with. While everyone was laughing Chris would turn around and Jez would be looking away, all innocent. A few moments later Jez would move to another part of the circle and poke Chris again and Chris would swing around while we all laughed at him, having no idea what trick was being played on him or by whom. This went on for some minutes, although saying that, it's hard to know just how much time elapses when you're tripping – it coulda been seconds, it coulda been hours. Even though Chris had a fixed inane grin on his face, every time Jez poked him I could see the fear and paranoia encroaching in his eyes and, even in my addled state, I knew what Jez was doing was naughty. So I got up and took his stick off him and threw it away, and went and got Chris and dragged him from the middle of the circle to sit next to Tim, his best mate. Jez, though, still kept trying to torment whoever he could throughout the rest of the afternoon, the devilish imp. Chris today claims he had a really good time with no bad vibes at all, and can't remember the poking incident. All I'll say is he never dropped acid again. And neither did Tim for that matter.

One of the very last things we did before we left Jacobs around the middle of July was to record what became the final track on *Carved In Sand*, 'Lovely'. I wrote it as a kind of response to Lennon's 'God', which I love, and in which he sings a litany of things he doesn't believe in, except 'I just believe in me, Yoko and me'. I wanted to write a track which turned that concept around, something positive to conclude the album, and so I listed a bunch of things I *did* believe in (or at least I did at the time), culminating with 'but most of all I believe in you'. I daresay my list may well be quite different today. Here's an exercise for you: try to list the things you believe in and the things you don't believe in. Which is easier for you and which makes you feel better? Your answer will tell you a lot about yourself.

Anyway, 'Lovely' was recorded live in the garden on another beautiful sunny day. I'm sat cross-legged on the grass with a microphone set up in front of me, strumming my Gibson Hummingbird acoustic guitar and singing. Tim's baby daughter, Lauren, just a few months old, is sat in her baby-bouncer in front of me and I sing to her. Slink is walking around playing electric guitar through a tiny toy amp attached to his belt. Others are wandering around playing various percussion instruments, Tim whistling, Jez with some bells stuffed down his shorts jumping up and down in time to the music, all accompanied by the natural sounds of the garden: the summer, birds singing, cows mooing, sheep baa'ing, the gentle breeze. Hippies? Who, us?

Endnotes

1   A click is the name given to a metronome that is played to drummers in their headphones so that they can keep a rock-solid tempo. It makes life easier for any later editing and 12-inch dance-floor remixes that may need to be done, and also means you can run MIDI sequencers in synchronisation.

2   Simon gave up supporting Arsenal a few years later, when the Premier League was formed and money started taking over the game. He's been an avid Reading supporter ever since.

3   Liverpool Football Club's now legendary and sainted German football manager.

4   Owned and run by the lovely husband and wife team of Andy and Fran Fernbach, Jacobs was yet another storied residential studio that sadly went the way of the dodo, finally closing in 2006. Set in 20 acres of Surrey countryside, it was another idyllic spot to record. There's footage of us horsing around at Jacobs in the *Waves Upon The Sand* documentary. It was a great place to work, and a favourite of top musicians, as evidenced by the list of just some of its many impressive clients: Stevie Wonder, U2, Radiohead, R.E.M., Robert Plant, The Cult, The Smiths, Status Quo, David Bowie, Def Leppard, Police, Marc Almond, Primal Scream, Pavarotti, Echo & The Bunnymen, Goldie, Bryan Adams, Pulp, Robbie Williams, Ian Brown, Paul Weller, Placebo, Bloc Party, Babybird, Kevin Rowland, Gang Of Four, Psychic TV, The Verve, Charlatans, and our new mates, The Cure.

CHAPTER 18

Gasoline Rainbows

PLAYLIST:
1. God – John Lennon   2. My Old Man – Joni Mitchell
3. I Can't Read – Tin Machine   4. Into The Blue – The Mission
5. Divided We Fall – The Mission   6. Hungry As The Hunter – The Mission
7. A Forest – The Cure   8. Down In The Park – Gary Numan
9. Baby, You're A Rich Man – The Beatles
10. Sweet Smile Of A Mystery – The Mission   11. Amelia – The Mission
12. Luka – Suzanne Vega   13. Janie's Got A Gun – Aerosmith
14. Deliverance – The Mission

On arrival Margarita called me into her office. 'Wayne, I'm so sorry to have to tell you that the studio was broken into last night. The burglars came in through the skylight and I'm afraid some of your guitars have been stolen.'

Stunned, as this was only our second day at Swanyard Studios, situated at the end of a small alley behind the Highbury & Islington tube station, all I could reply was, 'Sod the guitars, what about the tapes, are they alright?' My immediate concern was that three months or so of studio work hadn't been stolen or damaged. Guitars, as much as there are some I love, are, after all, really just tools of the trade and mostly replaceable. Three months of work on tape could only be replaced by a further three months of work repeating what we'd already done. I don't think any of us could've faced that. Fortunately the tapes were safe and sound. When asked by *Melody Maker* for a comment about the robbery I made a quip along the lines of, 'Ah, the thieves probably had a quick listen to the tapes and thought, "Nah, this is rubbish, we won't get much for these, leave 'em, let's just take the *good* guitars."'

Which also means they left most of *my* guitars – my Fender Starcasters (I had three), my Vox 12-string Teardrops (I had three of them as well), my Aria Pro 12-string, the Coral Sitar – basically all guitars that were a little more esoteric, shall we say. I did however lose my Gibson Hummingbird six-string acoustic, which was beautiful and played and sounded like a dream, and my 12-string sunburst Ovation. I did replace both with similar models but neither were as good as the ones I had nicked. If anyone out there still has 'em, I wouldn't mind 'em back. As I'm sure Simon wouldn't mind his original Zemaitis, a veritable Rolls-Royce of a guitar, handmade and engraved by renowned luthier Tony Zemaitis, which was also stolen. There weren't many of them about; Ronnie Wood had one as did Jimi Hendrix and James Honeyman-Scott. However, Simon did manage to get Zemaitis to make a new one by way of replacement, made to the same specs. It's valued at over £25,000 now. Needless to say, he doesn't take *that* baby out on tour anymore. In fact, Zemaitis very kindly made a cheaper copy (worth about £4,000 in comparison) for him to use onstage.

A couple of Si's Yamaha SG-2000s also disappeared. Tim Palmer was perhaps the biggest victim, though, as he only had two guitars and they were both stolen: his lovely orange Gretsch Nashville and, weirdly, leaving my three Starcasters behind (one, a dark green that looks black; the second, a sunburst; and the third, a brown), they took Tim's blonde one. We did speculate whether it was an inside job, as the robbing bastards seemed to know what they were doing. They knew where the guitar cases were stashed and took the exact matches for the stolen guitars. Fortunately the studio was insured for such eventualities and we were immediately recompensed by Margarita.

We were back in London at Swanyard at the end of June, through July and into early August, to put the finishing touches to the album and to mix it. I resumed my budding bromance with my new best mate Milo, as The Wonder Stuff were recording just a mere mile away at The Greenhouse Studio. He would ride over on his motorbike – a Kawasaki 550 Custom that Rob 'The Bass Thing' Jones[1] had given him – after they had finished work for the day.

They started and finished earlier than we did. The first time he came over, for some reason it was only him and me left in the control room, the rest of the band having left for the evening. I thought I'd be hospitable so I bought a gram of coke from the studio's resident supplier (ey up, Toffee). I poured the contents of the wrap onto a table top and ceremoniously chopped out the whole gram into a big half circle, rolled up a note and proffered it to Milo. 'Nah, you're alright, mate, don't do it,' was his response. I didn't know that, so ostentatiously I bent over the desk, shoved the note up my nose and in one long snort the whole line disappeared. If I was to attempt that today I'm sure it would put me in a coffin. And Milo wasn't impressed, as I talked bollocks for the next 30 minutes without letting him get a word in edgeways. And if you know Milo, he doesn't like not being able to get a word in edgeways.

I didn't know this until I spoke with Milo while researching this book but while he had seen people doing cocaine, he hadn't really been around it before he'd met up with us. On subsequent evenings, when Milo would come over to the studio and the rest of the band were around, there would always be a bit of Charlie getting railed out on CD covers and being passed around. And every time Milo would be offered it and every time he would decline. He remembers that in the end I just shouted, 'Leave him the fuck alone, he doesn't want it.' He also remembers that we were doing lines every 10–15 minutes and he thought, 'What a shit drug if you gotta keep doing more of it every few minutes.' And that is a *very* good point. I always preferred speed – a lot cheaper and lasted a lot longer. Mind you, the first couple of toots of coke were usually alright, loosened me up, made me more sociable, and sex was hornier with orgasms more, err, orgasmic, but then, like drinking for some people, one line too many and I'd be off to the dark places in my mind, my psyche. I didn't like where cocaine took me when I did too much of it. I became cold, remote, dissociated and disconnected, cruel even and definitely perverse. It still occasionally turns up backstage when we're on tour but it gets ever easier to *do a Milo* and say no. The last couple of times I was tempted I instantly regretted it as soon as the gak hit the back of my throat. The problem is one line is never enough. It is one drug I really don't miss.

One night after we'd finished at the studio Milo came back with me to the flat that was being rented for me nearby. I'll let Milo tell you in his own words what happened:

'I think by then I had decided I didn't really ever wanna hear The Beatles again, which you couldn't believe. And you said "I bet you've never heard John Lennon's first solo album" and I'm like "You bet right, I haven't, no," and so you said "I'm putting it on and you can't say a fucking word, we're not speaking to each other until we get to the end of the album," and you lit the room really nicely, some candles and scarves draped over the lamps, and we were drinking some horrible wine and smoking ciggies but it was a really great experience, and yes, at the end of the night you sent me away with the CD. I've done that to people since with favourite records of mine 'cos I thought that was a brilliant way to be introduced to it.'

Aw, how romantic. Yes, I did indeed give Milo my CD of Lennon's *Plastic Ono Band*, an album I believe no home should be without –

and, in return, a few days later he gave me a copy of Joni Mitchell's *Blue*. A decent swap, I'd say, with Milo perhaps getting the slightly better end of the deal.

During our first week or so at Swanyard, Tin Machine, fronted by David Bowie, were in town playing a couple of shows. Tim, having co-produced Tin Machine's hugely underrated first album[2], was obviously on the guest list for the sold-out Town & Country Club show in Kentish Town. Unfortunately he couldn't blag it for me, as tickets – and particularly spots on the guest list – were like gold dust. Tin Machine then had a day off, so Tim invited their guitarist, Reeves Gabrels, to Swanyard to add guitar on a few tracks of ours. Reeves came in with this tiny guitar shaped a bit like a cricket bat, with no headstock as such, the guitar ending at the nut. It was tuned at the bridge and he had little buttons behind the bridge that would, when pushed in, make the notes jump up a predetermined interval in pitch. I'd never before seen or heard anything like it. There are now foot pedals that can do the same kind of thing, but not back in 1989. He plugged in to the Mesa Boogie amp we owned at the time and produced this amazing sound. The original idea was for him to only play lead guitar on 'Into The Blue' but as we watched and listened, it was suggested he play on more songs of ours, so eventually he played additional guitar on 'Divided We Fall' and 'Hungry As The Hunter'. To get the sounds Reeves got out of that strange-looking instrument was wizardry. It required amazing dexterity to use the push buttons at the same time as plucking the strings and moving fingers around the fretboard. It was fabulous, and an honour, to watch Reeves play up close. I remember Craig and Mick were as stunned as me. For some reason Simon wasn't present – he came in later that day after Reeves had left.

'Do you wanna hear it, Slink?' Tim asked.

'Ah, if you want, not really that fussed,' was his sullen reply.

'Ah, play 'em anyway, TP, I wanna hear 'em again,' was my input.

382

Simon sat there listening through the three different tracks that Reeves had played on. At the end of the playback one of us asked, 'So what do you think, Slink?'

'It's alright. I could've played that though.'

Mmmm. So why didn't you then? It was yet another in an ever-lengthening number of incidents where Simon's discontent and disaffection were being expressed, and mostly ignored. He wasn't happy about us bringing in a guest guitarist to play on the album, but that's exactly what Reeves was: a guest, adding his own unique colour to our own already very rich palette of sound. He was absolutely no threat to Simon, but I don't think Simon quite saw it like that. To him it was perhaps another example of him being sidelined.

As close as we were as a band – and we were like a gang of desperados riding into the mainstream together, plundering bounty and escaping to our hideaway to plot our next raid on the staid and established music business – we never really *talked* to each other. With a couple of notable exceptions, everyone I've played with in bands I've considered friends and I'm absolutely certain the affection between us has been genuine. But even with my closest male friends there has always been a distance between us. One to one we very often have little to say to each other, but we find some propinquity, our version of intimacy, by focusing on a third element rather than on ourselves. It used to be music, football, jokes, girls, booze and drugs, but these days it's more likely to be our ailments – aching backs, painful hands, weakening bladders, haemorrhoids, all the various mischiefs our bodies are visited with through the curse of ageing. We share remedies, pills and ointments, and attempt to outdo each other in the recital of our physical afflictions. That's how we get our kicks these days. None of us, though, would ever dream of talking about our *feelings*. That's just not the done thing between males, is it? Of course, we're always there for each other if there's some louring storm wreaking havoc in our lives, but more as a stout and sturdy pillar to lean on than as a confidante.

We balk at confidences, perceive them as weights we'd rather not be burdened with. Feelings and emotions shared among men can be very dangerous weapons. Maybe it's a generational thing. My generation is certainly more open than my parents' generation was, so maybe later generations are more willing to share their feelings than blokes my age. Maybe that's why I write songs: to give shape and body and voice to my feelings – with words that are still very often ciphered – that I can't fully express any other way.

Never once did anyone in the band ask me what a lyric was about or even make any comments, either positive or negative.[3] And I never volunteered the information or sought their approval. That was just never a conversation in any of the bands I have played with. When I was the guitarist in, say, The Sisters Of Mercy or Dead Or Alive, I didn't really pay much attention to the words that Andrew Eldritch or Pete Burns were singing. Maybe the occasional line would pop out as memorable, but generally I was more concerned about my own contributions as a musician than the words the singer was writing. Just like the members of Joy Division famously didn't take much notice of the lyrics Ian Curtis sang on the *Closer* album, where all the clues were hidden that foretold his tragic suicide. It's easy to hear with hindsight, but who was paying attention at the time? His band mates certainly weren't. And I think that's normal; pretty much every band of males work in the same way I would say. We just don't ordinarily have those kinds of conversations. Maybe if we had then we might've been able to forestall Slink's departure from the band less than 12 months later. In one interview at the time, Simon was quoted as saying, 'Mick knows me inside out, Craig knows me pretty well, Wayne's never really made an effort.' Mmmm. Well, I'd counter that with Mick knew us all inside out, there have been times when it's been a little fraught, shall we say, between Craig and Simon and I've had to play the peacemaker, and I think Simon made the same amount of effort as I did in us getting to know each other. I didn't really think we had a problem until we were recording *Carved In Sand*, and even then I didn't believe his problem was solely with me. I always felt we had got on fine, even if we weren't perhaps as close as the others. There was a dynamic within the band, well-defined roles that seemed to me to be working. I understood Simon's creative frustrations but I believe he just made matters worse for himself by withdrawing from the daily recording process. And I had neither the time nor the patience to deal with it. If only we could've *talked*.

While he was there with us at Swanyard I did ask Reeves if he could put me on the guest list along with Tim for Tin Machine's show the following night, at the National Ballroom in Kilburn. Which he very kindly did. I loved the show; it seemed to me that Bowie had got his mojo back after a few years in the creative wilderness, as evidenced by the run of dodgy albums he'd made in the Eighties, commencing with, in my opinion, the disappointingly orthodox but huge hit that was *Let's Dance*. Personally I think Tin Machine was the beginning of an artistic renaissance for Bowie, where he would start making albums again that would take his audience by surprise. All through the Seventies there was anticipation tempered with curiosity whenever Bowie released a new album, as you were never quite sure what kind of record to expect from him, and every one of 'em, from 1970's *The Man Who Sold The World* through to 1980's *Scary Monsters*, was brilliant. It's difficult to pick a fave, mine probably being a choice between *Diamond Dogs* (1974), *Station To Station* (1976) and *Low* (1977). I bet your faves are different from mine and I wouldn't be able to disagree with you, as I do love 'em all.

I bumped into Reeves a couple of times in later years, once in LA when both he and I got up onstage to play guitar with The Cure. I'd played with The Cure a couple of times previously, the first time being a drunken jam in in late '95 at St Catherine's Court, a rural

15th-century Tudor mansion near Bath owned by actress Jane Seymour. The Grade I listed former monastery was being rented by The Cure to record their *Wild Mood Swings* album. A year later, Radiohead would also rent the place to record their magnum opus, *OK Computer*. I seem to remember framed photographs of Ms Seymour in various glamour poses adorning the walls of the ground floor of the house, with more provocatively attired photos of her in the bathrooms. I thought that a little strange. You wouldn't catch me doing that in my house. What guest of mine would wanna sit there on the throne looking up at photos of me in my skimpy undies? Apologies for putting that thought in your head. I have to say, though, that it was a sumptuous location to record an album, despite all the tales of ghostly ghouls and hauntings, tales well believable considering its age, history and ambience. It wasn't a house I'd want to be left alone in. Apparently Henry VIII housed his illegitimate daughter at the location when it was a monastery.

The next time I played with The Cure was at their LA Great Western Forum show in August 1996. It was the second night of a two-night stint and The Cure then had the best part of a week off before their next show. I was over there on holiday myself at the time, visiting family. I'd gone to the show the first night and learned that Robert was flying home to England directly after the second show to see his wife, Mary, for a few days. He needed to make a quick getaway before the audience even clocked he'd left. So, he asked if I'd join 'em onstage and play the planned second encore with them. Yeah, of course I would, I'd love to. The idea was that we'd play 'A Forest', in which Robert would start the song and then when it got to the long instrumental outro section, I would take over, playing the improvised lead guitar parts while he left the stage to jump into a waiting big black car which would speed him to LAX and back to Blighty. To make sure that Robert had enough time to escape it was suggested we play one more song, an instrumental, a song I hadn't heard and didn't know called 'Forever'. To help me out, Simon Gallup wrote the chords on the inside of my left arm so I could follow what was going on. That was fun, playing a Cure song I'd never heard before in front of 20,000 rabid Cure fans. It worked, though; Robert got clean away and made his late-night flight home. He still owes me for that.

The next time I played with The Cure was at a KROQ radio special show at the American Legion Hall in LA in October the following year, 1997, by which time I was actually a resident of Southern California. I joined 'em onstage and played 'In Between Days' (which we'd played with The Mission a few times) and 'A Forest' again. Earlier in the set Reeves had also got up to play a couple of songs. I do believe that was the very first time Reeves had played with The Cure, and here we are today with him now a permanent member of the band for the last 10 years or so. Even though Perry Bamonte, lovely man, was still in The Cure at the time, I do wonder if that was some kind of guitar play-off between Reeves and me, some kind of audition that Robert had instigated for future reference. Well, I was never gonna win that one, was I? Reeves is a fabulously incendiary guitar player; it's like playing with a grown-up when you play with him. Mind you, there was the time when Perry left The Cure and I was sat by the phone waiting for the call that never came. The Cure were the only band I'd have considered leaving The Mission for, but I don't know how long I would've lasted in all honesty. I do enjoy being 'Our Glorious Leader' and I'm pretty sure Robert wouldn't have allowed that to happen if I'd joined The Cure. And anyway, they got Reeves in, which I have to concede was the better move for them. Actually, I've just realised I'm fibbing. I almost left The Mission in the summer of 1990 to join All About Eve as their guitar player, an episode I'll come back to another time.

While we're about it, getting up and joining mates onstage while I lived in Southern California became a fairly common occurrence.

A few months later, in May 1998, my good friend Gary Numan came through town and was playing at the Hollywood Palace, the scene of Craig's freak-out on our first US tour in 1987. Gary had emailed me and asked if I'd play guitar on a couple of songs, again songs I didn't know, but I went out and bought the CDs and dutifully learnt the guitar parts. Now, if you've ever seen Gary perform live you'll know that a lot of care is taken with how the entire show looks, from the lighting and staging, to how Gary and the band are dressed and made up. Watching in the dressing room as they all prepared for the stage I must confess I did begin to feel a little dowdy. I had turned up to soundcheck wearing a pair of black Caterpillar work boots, a black front-zipped short jacket and Quiksilver baggie green corduroy trousers (still have 'em and they still fit), which were all the rage among the hip kids at the time (I know; seems implausible now, doesn't it, but surely corduroy is due a comeback soon?) and Gemma, Gary's brilliant wife who doesn't ever hold her tongue (or her belches and farts, if truth be known), asked me when I was gonna change for the show.

'Err, I thought I'd wear this,' was my sheepish reply. 'I ain't brought anything else with me.'

'What, you're going onstage in green cords?' she exclaimed.

'Yeah.'

'You pillock.'

God, I love Gemma.

Right, let's wind this tape back to July 1989 and Swanyard Studios, shall we?

I'd written one of the tunes for *Carved In Sand* on the piano and thought, as we had a decent recording budget, that I'd like an orchestra to play it. I was suggested Guy Chambers as someone who could score the piece for me. I'd known Guy as a young kid; he used to come into the studio after school and play with Hambi & The Dance, the band I was playing with at the time in Liverpool. He was precociously musically talented.

I visited him in his London flat one afternoon and played him the tune on his piano, which he recorded to cassette. I left it with him and he later came down to Jacobs to show us his ideas and to play a mock-up he'd put together using a string synthesiser. Satisfied with the result, we booked the nearby Angel Studio in Islington for an afternoon and an 80 (yes, 80!) piece orchestra was installed for the session. The Angel was one of the very few recording studios in London that could accommodate an orchestra of that size, Abbey Road Studios being one of the others. In retrospect I really wish I'd pushed to use Abbey Road instead. Being such a Beatles fanatic it seems almost bizarre that through the years when we had recording budgets to do so, I never recorded at Abbey Road. Still time to cross that one off the bucket list, I guess. I have, however, walked across *the* zebra crossing, but then everyone's done that.

As it happens, the Angel Studio session was helmed by renowned engineer John Timperley, who had started in the music business in the late Fifties and could count Bing Crosby, Tony Bennett, Shirley Bassey, Count Basie, Stephane Grappelli, and Cream's debut album among his many impressive credits. More interestingly to me, though, he'd engineered the orchestral sessions for The Beatles' *Magical Mystery Tour*, 'I Am The Walrus' being the orchestral stand-out from what is perhaps my favourite Beatle album.

Widely regarded by even The Beatles themselves as 'not a proper album', rather it was a collection of EPs, singles and music written and recorded for the ill-conceived hodgepodge film of the same name, and initially put together and repackaged as an album by the band's US record label, Capitol. Nonetheless, it captures the dazzling musical potpourri the band were producing at the time, from the surrealist 'I Am The Walrus', to the music-hall singalong 'Your Mother Should Know'; to arguably the best single ever, the double

A-side of Lennon's 'Strawberry Fields Forever' and McCartney's 'Penny Lane'. George Harrison was on top form, too, contributing the Laurel Canyon-inspired floating psychedelia of 'Blue Jay Way' and the money-isn't-everything jibe (isn't it always folk with loads of the green stuff that say that?) of 'Baby, You're A Rich Man'. It all culminated with the idealised world peace anthem 'All You Need Is Love'. Perfect psychedelic pop music for late 1967/early 1968. Significantly, though, it was perhaps the first time the mainstream media were seen to turn against the once lovable mop-tops. The accompanying film, screened on BBC One on Boxing Day, drew derision, and the 'Strawberry Fields Forever'/'Penny Lane' single was the band's first since 1963's 'From Me To You' to miss the top spot in the UK singles chart. Perhaps the most damning critic, though, was HRH, The Queen, who only two years previously had honoured the band with MBEs but was now quoted as saying, 'The Beatles are turning awfully funny, aren't they?'

So, yes, John Timperley of *Magical Mystery Tour* fame was now engineering 'Sweet Smile Of A Mystery', my well-intentioned but ultimately grandiloquent paean to womanhood.

By the time I turned up at the Angel Studio all the musicians were in place and playing through the piece. Each part was written out by hand on a separate manuscript – that's some job in itself – and Guy was stood on a podium in front of the orchestra, swinging his baton, conducting the musicians. I walked into the studio and the sound was overwhelmingly powerful, as loud as any rock band I've ever heard with the possible exceptions of Motörhead[4] and Sigur Ros. Can you imagine how it feels to hear an 80-piece orchestra playing a piece of music you've written? It was one of *those* moments in my life.

When they'd finished their run-through, Guy introduced me as the 'composer' of the music and all 80 members of the orchestra stood up and applauded. That felt weird. I'd hazard a guess that this is orchestra protocol, but nonetheless it took me by surprise and made me blush somewhat. I retired to the control room, where I was hoping that John Timperley might regale me with some Beatles tales I'd never heard before, but no such luck. He was too busy with the job in hand and unsurprisingly reticent when quizzed.[5] How many times in his life must he have been asked? A bit like me and the question I get asked too bloody frequently, 'What's Eldritch *really* like?'[6]

Tim and Chris (Sheldon, our album engineer) were also in attendance, keeping an eye on proceedings and learning a few tricks from the uber-master. Chris remembers that one of the tuba players, who only had a couple of 'blurts' to play in the whole piece, spent most of his time reading the *Daily Mail*. Glancing every now and then at his partitura, when the time came for him to play one of his two notes, he'd drop his newspaper to the floor, play his note, and then pick up the paper again and resume reading.

After the session at the Angel had ended we bade farewell to John, Guy and the orchestra, and walked the 500 yards or so back to Swanyard. On arrival, Chris set up the Shure SM57 we'd been using as my vocal microphone[7] for the album and a pair of headphones for me in the studio, and threaded up the new multi-track on the 24-track machine and excitedly hit playback. I started singing along and it quickly became apparent that the whole track was in the wrong key for my voice. It was pitched too low. Uh-oh. I'd written the song in C sharp minor, D minor (the saddest of all keys), being the key I often preferred to sing in. I hadn't really thought to check the key before I'd played the song to Guy, as at that point I hadn't yet written lyrics or even a vocal melody. Try as I might I had no one else to blame but myself. Unfortunately. We tried setting the microphone up in the control room and playing the track over the speakers to see if that would help with my pitching. Still too bloody low. In the end, Tim suggested slightly speeding the track up in small increments so that the pitch would be raised too until we found the one where I could actually sing the bloody thing. When we'd recorded a vocal we were reasonably happy with we slowed the machine back down to its normal speed and it sounded very strange. So strange in fact that in the end the track only ended up as a single B-side and didn't even make it onto the album. It was one of the most expensive B-sides ever… by anyone. The whole shebang cost in the region of £15,000! For one track! With inflation that would be over £33,000 today! For a fucking B-side! If I tell you that the last Mission album, *Another Fall From Grace*, released in 2016, in its entirety cost less than £20,000 to produce then you'll have some idea at how excessive 'Sweet Smile Of A Mystery' was. It was the Eighties, after all, and excess in the music business was rife.

When we'd more or less completed all the tracks we thought it a good idea to rifle through the names and addresses of our MWIS subscribers to find members that lived fairly local to Swanyard and invite them to the studio for a playback. Maybe 10–12 people turned up on the given day, mostly girls. Strange that. We sat them all in the control room and armed them with a pen and paper and asked them to give their marks and make comments about the songs as they listened. Of course, during the afternoon I found myself in a cupboard with one of our guests. God, I was incorrigible and insatiable. Fornication aside it was an interesting, and fun, exercise and we did take note of what our guests had to say, even more than we did of management and key record company personnel when we held a similar playback for them. No shagging in a cupboard that evening – well, not for me anyway, although I did hear tale that Slink had slunk off with one of our management team for a quickie. But I do remember Charlie Eyre, our A&R manager at Phonogram, sat there listening intently to 'Butterfly On A Wheel' and as the song finished he turned around and said those same immortal and prophetic words George Martin had once said to

The Beatles: 'Congratulations, lads, you've just made your first number one single!' How right George Martin was. Charlie was too, but not quite to the same magnitude – 'Butterfly...' did make it to number one in South Africa, at a time when apartheid was still in full effect, and all our royalties earned in the country were donated to the ANC.[8.] It didn't make it to number one anywhere else.

I hate regrets. I really do try to avoid them if I can. One of the very few I do have professionally is allowing the choosing by committee of the track listing and the title itself for what became *Carved In Sand*, the committee being the band, management and certain record company folk. We came up with a few prospective title options, mainly derived from the lyrics within; everyone had a vote and *Gasoline Rainbows* was neck and neck with *CIS* right up to the last minute, although *Lovely* was my own personal favourite until I found out that The Primitives' debut album released the previous year boasted the same title. Up to *CIS* I had pretty much the last word on album titles, and what songs were going on them and in what order – I would spend weeks working out the running order, which was vitally important in the days of vinyl and even CDs, before random play function and programmable CD players were introduced, another case of progress not always being for the better. I relinquished this degree of control for *CIS* and I regret it. I've not done it since. My instincts may not always be correct but they are my own, and if mistakes have been made then they've been mine and I much prefer it being that way than having to blame someone else. That being said, of course I confer with the other people involved and will always listen to and take on board their opinions, but the final creative decisions have always rested with me. Now I can't imagine the *Carved In Sand* title being anything other than what it became. The same can't be said for the final track listing of the album.

I'll refer to the vinyl version here, as that is how I still think of it, side one and side two. Side one is pretty much a damn perfect Mission side, if I may say so myself, starting off with the screaming rush of 'Amelia', a song I penned in response to an anonymous letter I received through the MWIS from a young girl that was being sexually abused by her father. There was no name and no return address, so having no way to reply directly I felt compelled to write the song. I chose the name 'Amelia' because it's the name of one of my sisters, and I have always seen the relationship that she enjoyed with my dad as being very tactile; she would, as a youngster, always cuddle up on Dad's lap to watch TV together. All very innocent and born out of love, with absolutely nothing sinister there at all, I hasten to add. And observing them after I'd received the letter made me realise how lucky I was to have the family I did, and even with the ups and downs that are natural in every family, how close and healthy mine and my siblings' relationships with our mum and dad were – and remain.

In the late Eighties, I really felt the mainstream media largely ignored the issue of sexual abuse within families and that it was often swept under the carpet when questions did arise. And it wasn't just within the family either. Habitual, institutionalised sexual abuse was occurring, and had been forever, as history has since proven – in churches, children's homes and schools, committed by very public, high-ranking figures in positions of immense power. It was a taboo subject that was never raised in polite conversation and a problem that was a lot more prevalent than anyone cared to admit. I remain convinced that it touched all our lives far more than we were ever really aware of.

And I wasn't the first to broach the subject, and I haven't been the last. Notably, Suzanne Vega's 'Luka' and Aerosmith's 'Janie's Got A Gun' came before, but certainly 'Amelia' was as direct as I could possibly make it. I didn't see the point of writing a subtle song about an issue that desperately needed to be raised in the public's consciousness. I had a point to make with the song and so made it very clearly. Perhaps my approach was polemical. It certainly caused an amount of controversy in the music press, with some for it and others staunchly against. The *NME*, with boring predictability, criticised the song 'for attacking the delicate subject of child abuse with a mallet' and they even went as far as phoning the NSPCC to try and elicit an official censorious reaction, only to be told by an NSPCC spokesperson, 'A lot of our work is about public awareness and this can only help. Obviously the more people know about sexual abuse the more we can do to stop it, so it's best to bring it out as an issue.'[9]

Some have said it was a brave move putting 'Amelia' as track one, side one. For me, however, there was only ever one place on the album the track could go and that was as the opener. Why hide it away as track three, side two, for example, if the motivation for the song was to highlight an issue that needed highlighting?

Over the years since its release I have received all kinds of comments from friends, and foes, regarding the song. I remember one incident during the week of its release, I was in Soho Square, London, trying to wave a taxi down. As I was waiting one pulled up. A passenger was alighting so I quickly grabbed the door before it was closed to claim the soon-to-be vacant Hackney. I looked up and the passenger was Bob Geldof. I'd met Bob a couple of times previously, as we were on the same record label.

He said, 'Hey Wayne, well done on that child abuse song.'

'Ah, thanks,' I said, then dumbly enquired, 'do you like it?'

Geldof replied, 'That's not what I'm saying, I haven't heard it. I'm saying well done on raising the issue.'

Even now there are people who come to our shows that will mention to me they find it hard to hear 'Amelia' because of its lyrical bluntness and because of their own experiences of abuse. I understand that it can make people feel uncomfortable. It shouldn't be a comfortable issue, although my hope was the song would help the victims of sexual abuse. There are others that thank me for the song and for helping them through their own traumatic experiences. It's as current and topical a song today as any from the Mission oeuvre and still just as polemic. I can perform 'Amelia' and feel every word passionately all over again, with the performance putting me in an angry mood that often takes me a few songs to recover from. There is an emotional investment demanded by this song that I am not always capable of meeting, hence I don't play it too often.

Following 'Amelia' as second track was 'Into The Blue'. Far more oblique than 'Amelia', this is a drug song. Charlie Eyre, our A&R manager, was aghast at the lyrics of this one, particularly the 'mumbo-jumbo hocus-pocus' couplets, but then again I'd put money on the fact that he'd never ingested hallucinogens. As I sing in 'Belief', 'if I have to explain then you'll never understand'.

Next up was 'Butterfly On A Wheel'. In terms of online streaming, this is our globally most played song across all platforms. It was destined to be the first single from the album. However, I do know there is a certain *very* small faction of our otherwise very loyal UK-based present-day core audience (hello Graham and Coups) that despise the song. When we play it live there's usually a heckle or two and then they use the opportunity to either skip to the loo, pop out for a smoke or get another round in at the bar. They should thank me for giving them the opportunity to avail themselves of these facilities. If we played a set where there wasn't a single song they were prepared to miss they'd be gagging for a ciggie and, at our age, pissing their pants. And we wouldn't want that now, would we?

Again, lyrically this song has its detractors. For me, the lyric is very pointed at the two protagonists in the song – Julianne and Simon – and every line pertains specifically to them. It's not for the rest of the world. Unlike 'Tower Of Strength', it wasn't written for our audience. Can't please them buggers all the time anyway and not *everything* I do is done with their approval in mind. Far from it. I get it, though: it has been our most popular song internationally and is perhaps the favourite of the more casual, shall we say, of our audience – you know, the type that go to one show a year, or buy our greatest hits album because 'aw, I love that song, it's so pretty'. It's our 'Friday I'm In Love' or 'Just Can't Get Enough'.

Following on from our most despised/popular song is the heavily-influenced-by-The-Beatles 'Sea Of Love', complete with sitars and a lyric that includes 'if wishes are stallions then kisses are galleons'... get it? If not, what can I tell you?

Side one of the record closes with 'Deliverance', a quintessential Mission anthem with an instant communal singalong chorus. Hugely influenced at the time as I was by *The Mists Of Avalon*, Marion Zimmer Bradley's retelling of the King Arthur legend, perhaps the song may have enjoyed a wider reach if I hadn't been so obsessed with fable, lore and the oneiric. But that was who I was in 1989. If you like The Mission at all then odds are you'll love side one of *Carved In Sand*.

Perhaps the same can't be said for side two, though, which commenced with the low-key chilled synth muzak of 'Grapes Of Wrath', my 'Springsteen song'. I've said this many times before and I'll say it again in case you've not read it previously: I read the John Steinbeck book of the same title and was deeply affected by it to the extent that I sat down and wrote this song. I say 'wrote' but I've always felt this song came *through* me rather than *from* me. I originally wrote the song on acoustic guitar, with Simon playing mighty fine piano on the demo we recorded together. When we came to record it for the album, though, it was felt that the piano and acoustic guitar instrumentation was too conventional, so we took it off into a totally different direction, one that, again in retrospect, perhaps misses the spot.

'Belief', by far the best track on side two, is next up and has become another venerable live fave of both ours and our audience.

397

Then came two tracks that, left up to me at the time, wouldn't have made the album at all – 'Paradise (Will Shine Like The Moon Tonight)', featuring what I consider to be perhaps my worst throw-away lyric (and I know there's a few contenders) that meant absolutely nothing to me at the time of writing it or since, followed by the rocker 'Hungry As The Hunter'.

'Lovely' rounds off the album with a suitable two minutes of verdant, bucolic, looney, hippie idealism; a perfect closer.

This is where we can argue what should've, could've been included instead to make *Carved In Sand* the defining Mission album that side one promised it to be. My personal choices would've included 'The Grip Of Disease', 'Heaven Sends You' and 'Bird Of Passage' instead of 'Grapes', 'Paradise' and 'Hunter'. You'd might well argue some other combination of tracks, which also included 'Divided We Fall', 'Mr Pleasant', 'Sweet Smile Of A Mystery' and an early version of 'Hands Across The Ocean'. Take yer pick.

My take on *Carved In Sand* these days is that it was the work of a band that had manoeuvred themselves into a comfortable position and were quite content to maintain that equilibrium, ultimately ending up being a mostly safe and formulaic record released at a time when, if we had been a bit braver and more willing to take bigger 'creative' risks 'we', as I paraphrase Terry Malloy[10], 'coulda been contenders'. Instead, we allowed outside influences to impact our own internal decision making and that's a regret I've had to learn to live with. And learn from. The fact that *Carved In Sand* went on to be our biggest-selling album globally is no real consolation.

Endnotes

1   The Wonder Stuff's bass guitarist, who left the band in December 1989 and moved to NYC, where he would sadly pass away in July 1993 at the tender age of 29. The first time I encountered Rob I was walking through the bar at the Columbia Hotel in London and I heard someone shout out 'Wanker!' and, knowing it was aimed at me, I turned around and saw him staring at me, to which he hollered, 'Yeah, I mean you,' in front of a bar full of people. Nice. With his mohawk and pierced nose he was a fearsome-looking individual. Until you got to know him, that is, and then he was still pretty fearsome but I could see through the act and we actually ended up getting on pretty well. I was sad when he left The Wonder Stuff, for Milo more than anything 'cos I know he was hurt by Bob's defection, but it has to be said The Bass Thing was the least personable of the band. But you knew exactly where you stood with him and you gotta respect that. And he did look great onstage with the Stuffies.

2   Tim also co-produced *Tin Machine II*, which again was another criminally underrated album upon release, with one review stating that it 'didn't quite match up to their wonderfully overwrought but sadly under bought debut'. Ouch. It's almost reassuring to read that even Bowie suffered bad reviews in his lifetime. Today, both Tin Machine albums have been afforded a favourable critical re-evaluation and are now recognised as being the very good albums they are, and sparking Bowie's creative renaissance. Death'll do that.

3   After his departure from the band Simon didn't hold back: his very public criticisms of me, my songwriting, particularly my lyrics, the musical direction of the band, and making very evident his belief that I wielded too much control and that he should have been entitled to make a bigger musical contribution to the band all appearing in print. He wanted us to sound like Aerosmith and Metallica. 'Nuff said.

399

4   That old Lemmy chestnut: when once soundchecking he was reputed to have stopped the band in mid-song and asked, 'What's that fucking 'orrible noise? Turn it up!'

5   A gentleman of the 'old school', John sadly passed in 2006 with leukaemia, at the age of 65.

6   Answer: How would I bloody know? I haven't seen him for over 20 years. I'd like to believe he's changed for the better, as I like to think that I have, in the interim. If you wanna know what I thought of him when I worked with him then please see *Salad Daze*.

7   The Shure SM57 is a classic dynamic microphone – revered primarily for mic'ing up guitar amps and other instruments. Fairly cheap, still less than £100 even today. When we started recording vocals for *Carved In Sand* Tim and Chris set up a bunch of microphones for me to try, some of them vintage and very expensive. The SM57 came out on top. Tim tells me that he also recorded both David Bowie and Bono using the SM57 so I am in good company. Personally, I've been using a Neumann U87 microphone to record my vocals since I bought a pair when recording the *Masque* album in 1991.

8   The African National Congress (ANC) is a social-democratic political party in South Africa that was outlawed between the years of 1960 and 1990. In February 1990, after much international pressure, President F. W. de Klerk repealed the ban on the ANC and released Nelson Mandela from prison after 27 years of incarceration. Mandela would go on to lead the ANC at the 1994 general election – the first time that black South Africans were allowed to vote – and be elected as president, thereby ending almost 50 years of apartheid in South Africa.

9   As quoted word for word in the *NME* the week *CIS* was released.

10 Terry Malloy, the character played by Marlon Brando in the 1954 classic *On The Waterfront*.

CHAPTER 19

As Sure As God Made Wine You Can't Wrap Your Arms Around A Memory

PLAYLIST:

1. Candleland – Ian McCulloch   2. Heaven Or Las Vegas – Cocteau Twins
3. Pump Up The Volume – Star Turn On 45 (Pints)
4. This Is The Sea – The Waterboys   5. Trail Of Scarlet – The Mission
6. Sowing The Seeds Of Love – Tears For Fears
7. John Wayne Is Big Leggy – Haysi Fantayzee
8. The Sensual World – Kate Bush
9. Deliverance (The Sorcerer's Mix) – The Mission
10. Metal Guru – T.Rex
11. The Ballroom Blitz – The Sweet   12. Virginia Plain – Roxy Music

VIDEO PLAYLIST:

1. Butterfly On A Wheel – The Mission   2. Deliverance – The Mission

Sometime in late July 1989 I found myself with funny man Bunnyman Ian McCulloch and the Cocteau Twins' Robin Guthrie in a toilet cubicle on a boat on the River Thames. There wasn't enough room for the Cocteau Twin's vocalist, the heavily pregnant Liz Fraser, so she was waiting outside for us. Let's just say Robin had a big bag of party favours he was sharing around and we were playing lucky dip, shall we? Mac was about to release his first solo album, *Candleland*, which Liz had blessed with some of her exquisite warbling and the Cocteaus, label mates of ours at the time, were working on what would become their masterpiece, *Heaven Or Las Vegas*. We were all there together at the invitation of The Cure who had just completed their European tour with three nights at Wembley Arena and were celebrating by throwing their end-of-tour party on a boat. The entertainment for the evening was Star Turn On 45 (Pints), a novelty act who'd scored a hit the previous year with their northern-cabaret-club-circuit pastiche of 'Pump Up The Volume'. Star Turn were playing their versions of Cure hits, a joke that wore thin pretty quickly, it has to be said.

I look back at incidents like this now and realise how easily I was taking it all for granted; the rubbing shoulders and more with bands and artists whose music I loved. It must be remembered that like most everyone else who gets into making music, I did so because I love music. And the musicians who make the music I love were, and are, my heroes. I've been fortunate enough to meet and even in some cases work with a fair number of them over the years. I realise that most were once perceived as my peers, particularly during this period, but their music has stayed in my affections and has grown in importance to me over time. A few I am still good friends with, some I keep in occasional contact with, but most are now as remote to me as they are to you. My memories of meeting musicians I looked up to are as cherished as I know some people cherish their memory of meeting me. As weird as that realisation is I trust it doesn't come across as being egotistical and vain on my part (although of course I am prone to bouts of both) to suggest that there have been times I've spent the merest of moments with people who treasure the encounter and carry the memory fondly for the rest of their lives. I've lost count the number of times I've been asked, 'Do you remember me?', followed by the reminder, 'We met backstage at your gig in [*insert town of your choice*] in [*insert year of*

402

your choice],' or some such other random location and occasion. And, of course, there are others who have forgotten me as soon as I've left the room.

Come August and as the finishing touches were being made to *Carved In Sand* we were also busy preparing for an eight-show traverse through the Highlands and islands of Scotland. Bypassing the usual tour stops of Glasgow and Edinburgh, we kicked off this little jaunt at Fat Sam's in Dundee, with all venue capacities for the tour being between two and three hundred. Remember, among our last UK shows had been sell-outs at Wembley Arena and Birmingham NEC.

Just for the hell of it we were going back to the band's very early days, travelling in a minibus driven by Mick, staying in cheap B&Bs and playing tiny venues. The pressure valve of having spent the last few months in the studio, with the slowly mounting tensions aggravated by Slink's bruised ego, needed to be released. We needed to be, to feel, like a band again. Being in the studio with nothing to do for days, weeks on end gives one far too much time to *think* about things. It's always better to be *doing*. And the situation was exacerbated by the fact that by this time, we were all doing different drugs.

In the early days of the band our communal drug of choice was amphetamine. One drug, one mind. Now, though, Simon was smoking a lot of spliff again and, in my experience, heavy smoking very often induces paranoia. I'm convinced this was a factor in his increasing disengagement from the band. Craig had sworn off the hallucinogens but he'd like a spliff in the evening with a line or two. The yin and yang, the up and down. Craig had also recently settled down with Leona and together they'd bought a house in Chiswick. He was as settled as I would ever know him, aside from today. Mick still did it all and was, amazingly, always the most cognisant of all of us, while I just stuck with white powders and acid – up and out of this world. There'd be moments when we were all in the same mental and emotional space but they became more fleeting and occasional. Alcohol was the only constant binder. Piling into a minibus and being stuck in the same small, enclosed space for endless hours as we travelled across Scotland forced us to re-evaluate our personal relationships. The Scottish Highland tour was a healing time for us as a band as much as anything else. Or a papering over the cracks.

We'd sold a season ticket for the tour to members of MWIS, a reduced one-price-for-all eight shows. We restricted the number to 101, the Dalmatians they were called, so that at least *some* locals were able to get tickets for the shows. As well as venues on the Mainland in off-the-beaten-track towns such as Elgin, Aviemore and Dingwall, we also had to catch the ferry across to Stornoway on the Isle of Lewis to play in the function room at the Seaforth Hotel, the same hotel we were staying in. All very cosy. We arrived the day before the show, so we enjoyed a night off in Stornoway, which we spent crawling the pubs and bars of the small town along with the Dalmatians. One bar I found myself in was offering live music entertainment; some local chap sat on a stool with an acoustic guitar singing his Scottish folk songs, and very good he was too. But as the audience was mostly made up of the travelling Dalmatians, I was being pestered to get up on the stage and sing a song or two. The local chap very graciously offered me the use of his acoustic guitar and stool and I drunkenly stumbled my way through a couple of Mission songs just to stop the Dalmatians yapping. After I'd finished I was sat at the bar sipping on a whiskey and chatting to one of the elder local residents, a fisherman by trade. 'That was alright, that were,' he complimented. 'We had that dobber Mike Scott of The Waterboys in here recently and he's Scottish, he is, but the bampot thinks he's Irish, he does. He should remember where he's from. The patronising git was singing "I wish I was a fisherman". Well, I wish I were a bloody pop star, I do.' Let me just clarify that I was and remain a big fan of The Waterboys and the Big Music triptych of *A Pagan Place*, *This Is The Sea* and *Fisherman Blues*, all three being stonkingly fine albums.

From the Isle of Lewis we had to catch the ferry to Portree on the Isle of Skye. There was only one ferry crossing per day and so we, the band and crew, boarded with the 101 Dalmatians to the astonishment of the locals, who had never seen anything like it. Even though it was August, it was windy and raining and the crossing was rough. Much imbibing by all at the onboard bar during the crossing and there were soon a fair few hangdogs leaning over the sides of the creaking old vessel gipping up their guts into the roiling brine.

Upon arrival, the Isle of Skye reminded me a little of *The Wicker Man*'s Summerisle[1], a feeling compounded by the fact that we were playing at The Gathering Hall. We checked into a small family-run guest house, our accommodation for the duration of our stay. After the show, which was suitably riotous, your well lubricated numbskull author on return to the hostelry decided to set off a fire extinguisher, leaving the breakfast room covered in a dry white powder before crawling off to bed. At six the following morning there was a loud pounding on my door, to match the loud pounding in my head. I staggered out of bed in just a pair of paisley briefs to answer, and there stood Big Pete Turner with the lady of the house, the owner of the hotel. 'Right, you,' she started, 'you may think you're a bloody pop star and can go letting off fire extinguishers in hotels willy-nilly and then just get someone else to clear up your mess. Not here you can't. You make a mess here, you have to clean it up yourself. Get your bloody clothes on *now* and get yourself down to the breakfast room and clear up that bloody mess. I have to serve breakfast in there from seven so you have exactly one hour to do it.'

I looked at Pete for some moral support and he just grinned and said, 'You best do what the lady says. Me and Stevie did offer to clean it up but she insisted that we wake you to do it.'

'Five minutes, downstairs,' demanded the battle-axe. 'Understand?'

I had no choice. I nodded assent and closed the door. I immediately went to the bathroom, stuck my fingers down my throat and puked up the contents of my stomach from the previous night's sottish inebriation until I was just retching bile. I took a couple of paracetamol washed down with two or three full glasses of tap water and felt marginally human. I dressed in black leggings, a T-shirt and a pair of black suede moccasins and found my way downstairs. On entry into the breakfast room I almost retched again seeing the mess I'd made the night before. Stupid sod. The Sgathaich[2] was stood there in the doorway with Pete and Stevie Sex-Pistol and all three just watched as I proceeded with brooms and brushes to clean the room in time for breakfast. As 7 a.m. was approaching and it was clearly evident I wasn't gonna finish the job on time on my own, the termagant relented and allowed Stevie and Pete to assist me. I've never set off another fire extinguisher for fun ever again.

We finished our summer 'get-away' in Scotland in Dunfermline, before heading south to headline Reading Festival for the second time in three years, this time the Sunday, closing night. 1989 marked a deliberate policy change away from the heavy metal and punk emphasis that had dominated previous years' festival line-ups, and alongside New Order and The Pogues, who headlined the Friday and Saturday nights, respectively, The Mission represented the changing of the guard.[3] The organisers had even persuaded the venerated champion of alternative music, John Peel, to compere the event, although true to form, he refused to announce us just as he had refused to play 'Serpents Kiss' when it had appeared in his Festive 50 in 1986.

Our mates The Wonder Stuff were on directly before us and proved themselves well adept at handling audiences of this size. It was easy to see that they were a band on the rise, and they would go on to headline the same festival themselves a year or two later.

By this time, we were getting used to playing shows of this magnitude. In the early days, playing festivals was an opportunity to reach a wider audience than would ordinarily come to see our shows. By the time we were headlining festivals across Europe the simple truth is, aside from the status that it conferred, we were doing it for the money. Festivals can and do pay huge fees compared to what we could earn by playing our own shows in 'normal' venues. We didn't particularly like playing them, though, as there were so many things beyond our control that could and did go wrong. But with time we'd learned to be less precious, more relaxed and easy-going, and if things did go awry, usually technical mishaps, then we were able to just get on with it and laugh it off. One thing to remember as a headliner at a festival is that by the time you hit the stage most of the audience are completely zonked out of their skulls anyway, and as long as you play a few tunes they recognise and can sing along with then they'll be happy.

We played a stormer in 1989. Adhering to the John Paul Jones truism – make the first three songs of your set songs the audience know and love, then you can play what the hell you like – we started with 'Beyond The Pale', 'Wasteland' and 'Like A Hurricane' and from then on in it was a huge communal celebration. We were at the height of our popularity, cocky and assured, confident enough to drop five new tunes into our 20-song set. We were joined onstage by an overcome Clint Mansell from Pop Will Eat Itself, who ran from the wings uninvited to sing 'Pretty Vacant' with us – a good job too, as I didn't know the words.[4]

We even enjoyed some decent reviews in the weeklies for a change, perhaps the best coming from the pen of *Melody Maker*'s Everett True: 'The appeal of The Mission is very straightforward: it's a fix, a charge, a yearning for succour and the bright lights of home… The Mission fulfil a deep need inside all of us, the need for comfort, for warmth, for reassurance. They do this well, astonishingly well in fact, their music sweeping down from the stage, and enabling those who wish to lose themselves, to do so effortlessly, in nowhere. Everything is geared to finding that moment, that crescendo when the world stops right there, tears run down your face and you vow that this is the life… The Mission are perfect for this occasion.'

407

After the success of our performance at Reading we flew out to Europe to play a few more festivals, in Italy, Austria and Switzerland, before our annual MWIS 'Shindig', an all-dayer this year, at Sheffield Polytechnic towards the end of September. For the bargain price of £1 MWIS members could get to see us play two sets: one of completely new material from our soon-to-be-released new album, and a second set of favourite songs as voted for by the attendees. Also for their money they got to enjoy sets from The Wonder Stuff, Claytown Troupe, Rosetta Stone and, fronted by the Leeds legend that is Stevie Vayne, The Vaynes (previously known as Dead Vaynes – Craig had enjoyed a brief stint with them between the time we'd left TSOM and formed The Mission). Stevie had recently pierced his dick with a small silver snake and was intent on showing off his handiwork to one and all. 'Look,' he enthused manically, seizing the opportunity for a joke he'd obviously been preparing for days, 'Serpents Piss!'[5]

There were competitions and raffles being run throughout the day with such dubious prizes as a pair of football boots as worn by me, an old hat or two, my floor-length purple crush velvet coat as worn on *TOTP* one time, and other sundry items as donated by the rest of the band. The master of ceremonies for the day was our very own Jez Webb, replete with dinner jacket and dickie bow. 'Number 667,' he announces one of the winning raffle tickets, 'the neighbour of the beast.'

This Shindig has gone down in Mission folklore as being the last time the majority of the original Eskimos were in attendance together, many choosing this as their jumping off point before we went back out on tour the following year playing city halls and arenas in support of *Carved In Sand*. Most had been with us since the summer of 1986 and been instrumental in helping us get to where we were; without them, it may not have happened for us in quite the same way as it did. But they didn't enjoy us playing the bigger venues and saw our expanding audience as a threat to the access to the band they'd enjoyed up to now. It's natural and understandable, even if it was sad for us to see their numbers dwindle as our general audience grew. The Eskimos weren't what you would call goths, their attire far too slovenly to be considered as such. Goths took a lot of care over the way they dressed and looked – The Eskimos not so much, if at all. And by 1989, most of them were getting to the age of having to face up to joining the workforce, some even getting wed and settling down and starting families. I remember bumping into Stoko[6] – along with Ramone, co-author of the highly irreverent *Eskimo* fanzine – in London sometime later, having not seen him in a while, and he was wearing a suit and carrying a portfolio on his way to a job interview as an architect. I couldn't believe my eyes or stop myself from laughing, but I felt a strange pride and sense of awe that Stoko had gotten it together and was no longer the slob that used to nightly blag his way onto our guest list and snaffle our rider, giving me lip about being a *pop star*, and generally taking the piss whenever he could. You would never think he and Ramone actually liked the band, the amount of stick they gave us. Mind you, I think it's all gone downhill for both of them these last few years, as Stoko's now one of the 17 bass guitarists in the Ramone-managed band Evil Blizzard. Both Ramone and Stoko and other original Eskimos do make it along to a show every now and then and it's always a treat to see 'em, even though we do have to hide our rider and put aside our sensitive egos.

Back at the hotel after the Shindig I was sat in the bar with Milo having a quiet drink away from the madding crowd. He asked me if I knew where Sheryl was. I said something like, 'No, I ain't seen her since before we went onstage,' and half-jokingly followed it with, 'she's probably off shagging Malc somewhere.'

This is Malcolm Treece, guitarist with The Wonder Stuff, to be clear.

'So you know then?' he asked.

'Know what, that she's shagging Malc? I didn't know for sure but suspected. You've just confirmed it.'

'You don't mind?' Milo asked incredulously.

'How can I with what I get up to? See Alexa from Yugoslavia[7] sat over there?' I nod my head discreetly in the direction of a raven-haired beauty sat among a group of Eskimos on the other side of the bar, 'we've just shagged in our spare room upstairs.'

The Mission had booked an extra room at the hotel for any such eventualities and in case someone turned up unexpectedly.

'How long's it been going on, Sheryl and Malc?' I enquired.

'It started when we played Reading Festival together.'

'Mmm, about a month then. Who knows?'

'Well, all our lot do. She's been to the studio with Malc a couple of times, and I believe some of your chaps do, too,' he replied.

'And none of 'em dared tell me? That figures. You reap what you sow, eh, mate? Wanna 'nother drink?'

Milo and I talked and drank some more until it felt like time to go to bed. I got to the room I was sharing with Sheryl and she was already under the covers although still awake.

'Alright, love, have a good evening, did you?' I asked.

'Yeh, it was good. And you?'

'Yeh, great, been down in the bar chatting with Milo.'

'About what?'

'About you and Malc actually.'

Sheryl didn't answer.

I went on, 'Yeh, he told me. You been with him tonight, right? Have fun? You know, I don't mind, I just wish I'd known before everyone else did. Is it serious or just a bit of fun?'

'I don't know,' she replied.

'Well, I guess you need to make up your mind. I don't care if you shag around, that's only fair as I do it all the time, you must know that?'

'Yeah, of course.'

'But if you're emotionally involved though, that's something else entirely. You best have a think about that,' I suggested.

We didn't argue, no voices were raised, and very little else was said that night. But something felt broken.

The truth is, I was hurt that Sheryl had been having an affair with Malcolm, not that she was having the affair but that it was with someone reasonably close to me, and while everyone around me seemed to know but no one thought to tell me. That's just stupid male pride talking there, though, isn't it? I didn't care about the one-night stands and brief flings she'd had with people even closer to me than Malc because it had just been sex with no real emotional investment, but this thing with Malc, an emotionally charged intimacy so close to home, did feel like a betrayal. The human heart is a curious and complex organ. Was it possessiveness? Was it jealousy? Was it pride? It was certainly hypocritical.

I never blamed Malc, why would I? I'd have done the same thing and worse in his situation with absolutely no regard for the feelings of anyone else involved. He and I always got on fine even after the affair ended, and The Wonder Stuff toured as our support in Europe and the US. Malc even stood in for Slink for a few of the US shows. There was never ever any animosity between us, maybe a little embarrassment and uneasiness but certainly no rancour.

After we'd been home for a few days Sheryl told me that she'd decided she wanted to stay with me and would end her relationship with Malcolm. She asked if she could go visit him and spend one last night with him. I agreed. It would've been ungracious not to, eh?

This whole episode was exorcised in the song 'Trail Of Scarlet', which I wrote for the later *Masque* album with a fair amount of poetic license exercised.[8]

Phonogram had decided to make us an international priority with the release of *Carved In Sand*. Basically, what that meant was our promotion budgets would be increased in every territory around the globe, and each local label would have to report back to the main office (in the Netherlands at the time) each week on sales, radio and video plays etc. The stakes had just gotten higher. We'd released two albums that had sold very decently internationally, if not quite the numbers the label was hoping for (each half a million plus), so by making us a priority they were essentially betting on us to take our sales and global popularity to the next level with the release of *Carved In Sand*.

The album was finished and ready to go but its release date had been put back to the new year because the label was releasing the new Tears For Fears album, *Seeds Of Love*, in September 1989 and didn't want ours to get lost in its slipstream. Record company politics. TFF were huge internationally, particularly in the US, and the label had already spent well over £1 million on just recording the bugger. They were banking on another huge international seller and they were well on their way, with the release of the first single from the album, the nouveau psychedelic 'Sowing The Seeds Of Love'. It was okay for us, we didn't mind; it gave us time to properly prepare for *our* release.

A stylist was brought in to smarten us up and we were given a budget of £10,000 (over £22,000 in today's money) to spend on new clobber. Craig, Simon and Mick all got £2,000 each and with me being the front man I had £4,000 spent on me. The stylist took me around to London's posh designer shops – Katherine Hamnett, Michiko Koshino, Gucci etc. – where I bought a bunch of designer shirts, jackets, trousers and shoes, the butterfly shirt I wore on *TOTP* and the long-sleeved red tunic shirt with the gold Nehru collar that I wore a lot onstage and in photos being just two of them. Both Craig and I had Nehru jackets tailor-made at a cost of £500 each, as modelled by the pair of us in the video for 'Butterfly On A Wheel'. In fact, all four of us are togged out in our new apparel for the 'Butterfly...' video shoot. Simon, when quizzed recently, remembers only getting a new scarf and shirt. I'd suggest that is his selective memory at work, as I remember him purchasing some snug-fitting leather pants as well as a waistcoat or two and a snazzy red jacket, the malady of his growing discontent obviously colouring his memory. There are several photo sessions from around this period where we do look quite well presented in our new natty threads rather than the scruffbags we ordinarily were. I wouldn't have dared walk into one of those posh shops on my own before, or since, and none of us would've ever considered spending that much money on clothes if we hadn't been 'gifted'[9] the money by the record company.

We were also persuaded to move on from the artwork of Sandy Ball for this new release. Sandy's illustrations had been the basis of our artwork from the beginning, and was as identifiably *The Mission* as much as our logo and our hats and shades. By now, Sandy and Mick had split up, but Sandy had still been involved with the artwork for *Children* and its attendant singles, although Mick had taken a more active role during this period. So, for *Carved In Sand* we decided to work with an established artist – Keith Breeden – with plenty of previous experience designing album covers[10], award-winning in some cases. He came up with a new font for us, dispensed with the Celtic knot logo (what blasphemy!) and, after asking for our star signs, devised a design based on the four elements – Craig being Aries and fire, Mick Taurus and earth, Simon Scorpio and water, while I'm 'born of the sign of air and The Twins'. The cover was definitely a move away from the uniqueness of our previous artwork – perhaps, dare I say it, more corporate. In general I liked it. The new font used on the cover would look great on T-shirts and stencilled on the back of leather jackets, although it was largely illegible when used to list the credits on the inner sleeve. Keith would also go on to design the covers for the singles from the album – 'Butterfly...', 'Deliverance and 'Into The Blue', which, arguably, were better than the album cover.

413

The band photos included in the artwork were all taken by Kate Garner who, earlier in the Eighties, alongside DJ Jeremy Healy, had scored a huge hit as Haysi Fantayzee with 'John Wayne Is Big Leggy'. Kate had given up the music malarkey and was now branching out into photography, having already photographed a whole host of subjects, including iconic shots of Sinead O'Connor. We travelled down to Brighton for the day and took with us various outfit changes, the idea being that by changing our clothes it would look like more than one photo shoot and we could use some of the resulting shots for promo and the album artwork. In the morning, we were photographed walking/ messing around on the sea front, and with it being late in the year and an icy breeze whipping in from the sea, we were dressed accordingly in long coats and leather jackets. I'd also been growing a beard for the last few weeks so when we took a break for lunch I nipped off to the nearest Sweeney Todd for a shave. I'd never had one like that before; the ceremony of lying back in the barber's chair with hot towels on my face, and then being lathered up with the barber stood over me wielding his cut-throat blade (now I know from where the phrase 'close shave' derives). Somehow we'd wangled exclusive use of the interior of the Royal Pavilion for the afternoon and, revelling in its opulence, we changed into recently acquired outfits becoming of such ostentation. It was a far cry from our first photo shoot in early 1986 at the Headingley Bear Pit[11], near the Co-op on Leeds' Cardigan Road.

Next up for us was shooting the videos for both 'Butterfly...' and 'Deliverance'. It had already been decided that those two tracks were gonna be the first two singles from the album. Much of the footage for the 'Deliverance' video had been shot during our performance at Reading Festival, but Leo, our bubble-car-driving video director, wanted some more close-up shots. So we had to set up the complete stage set, exactly as it was at Reading, in a large, cold warehouse, and wear exactly the same togs we'd worn for the show so that he could get the extra shots he needed. Puh. Was it really necessary, all

414

that expense and extra time? Did it make much difference? I think not. The 'Butterfly...' shoot was another day in a large, cold warehouse, which I spent largely rolling around in dead leaves scattered on the concrete floor in my nice, new, expensive clothes. Oh, the memories...

Neither of the videos are, in my opinion, great works of art, although of the two my preference would be 'Deliverance', purely because it visually documents our appearance at Reading Festival that year and reminds me of how popular we were at the time.

Some bands establish a look, a feel, an aesthetic through their videos, forming an integral part of their image, their *brand* if you want. Depeche Mode, The Cure, Radiohead and Massive Attack, among a host of others have all managed it. The Mission, though, I feel floundered in this regard, and we were never entirely comfortable with the medium or managed to establish a style of our own. I still contend the best video we ever made was 'Serpents Kiss' – unscripted jollity, the four of us having a lark in a park. Not sure we could've kept that concept up over the course of the intervening years, though, and the many videos we have since made. No one could've had *that* much fun, not even us.

Tim Palmer and I were booked into the mix room at Olympic Studios to produce an extended remix of 'Deliverance' for the 12-inch single release. A night or two before, I had a very vivid dream. I dreamt how the remix should be structured, and wrote it down immediately on waking so as to not forget. I'd recently watched the film *Excalibur*, starring Helen Mirren as the enchantress Morgana, and dialogue from the film featured heavily in the remix, sampled from the VHS I owned of the film. Sampling was still relatively new and a free for all at that point, and you could pretty much sample anything from any source without having to obtain permission. Nowadays, and quite rightly so, you have to jump

415

through many hoops to use anything – even a single line from a film or TV show or another record.

Still smarting from Kate Bush's backing out of singing on 'Butterfly...', we also sampled her 'mmm, yes' from her recently released single 'The Sensual World'. So... I did get to sing my duet with Kate after all, albeit unwittingly on her part. Couldn't get away with it these days. The funniest part of that remix, though, is the spoken monologue over the outro. That's Tim. After quickly scribbling down what he was gonna say, he set up a mic and recorded himself, but instead of saying 'from the bosom of the lake' he mistakenly pluralised bosom. We ended up keeping it in because the rest of the take was perfect and we figured that if his *faux pas* made us laugh so much then others would get it too. No one's ever mentioned it, though, preferring, I believe, to take it seriously.

The Metal Gurus world tour of 1989 was, in fact, just two dates: the Fulham Greyhound on December 20 and, the following day, we supported The Wonder Stuff at Aston Villa Leisure Centre. The Gurus, featuring Rick Spangle on bass guitar, Mental Mick on drums, Slink on guitar and Hipster Looney on vocals and guitar, were a new band causing a bit of a stir as unashamed glamsters. As their press release at the time stated, Hipster and Rick had met when they were young rockers and Hipster had posed the question: Cliff Richard or Elvis Presley? Rick had answered, 'Cliff, of course,' and a life-long friendship ensued. They started a band and enlisted the services of guitarist Slink, a semi-pro pigeon fancier they'd met in their local pub, The Tripe Throwers Arms. The drummer's stool was filled by Lucky, a hod carrier by trade but who fancied his chances of 'pulling more birds' if he learnt to play the drums. They called themselves The Mental Gnus, but the printers of their first, and only, tour poster made a spelling mistake and it came out as The Metal Gurus. It stuck.

The Gurus were a near-mythical band. Marc Bolan of T.Rex even wrote a song about them. What was most striking about them was not their music, but their clothes – unashamedly glam rock, as though punk had never happened. Slink's hero was evidently Noddy Holder of Slade, to the extent that he wore a mirrored top hat along with a feather boa over his furry chest-revealing crushed velvet top. Lucky plumped for tight lurex hot pants, while Hipster sported the prerequisite feather boa over a fetching silver sequinned top and revealing see-through lace loons. The pick of the bunch, though, was Rick Spangle. Never have you seen such a sight. Like a sausage wrapped up tightly in Bacofoil, he was crammed into a silver all-in-one jumpsuit, teetering on stripy platform boots, topped off with silver shoulder-length hair, not unlike Overend Watts of Mott The Hoople, another major influence on the Gurus. The music they played, like their clothes, was also unashamedly glam rock, covering all the great chart hits from 1972 to 1973: The Sweet, Roxy Music, Bowie, T.Rex, the original Mr Bacofoil himself Gary Glitter, Status Quo, Mott, Cockney Rebel and more.

Of course, The Metal Gurus was just us having some fun, letting off some steam. We'd all got into music as kids through listening to glam rock and we'd quite often, when we should've been rehearsing for something else, spend our time messing about with glam-rock songs.

When The Wonder Stuff had played our MWIS Shindig in Sheffield they'd done so for free. All we had to do was stump up for their hotel for the night. In return, we agreed that we'd support them at one of their three Christmas shows at the Aston Villa Leisure Centre. However, we wanted to do something a bit different. Hence, The Metal Gurus. We played a warm-up gig at the Fulham Greyhound with Ned's Atomic Dustbin supporting. Obviously word got out that The Metal Gurus were, in fact, The Mission under another guise, so the place was full to bursting. Most of the audience, too young to really know much glam rock, just stood gaping nonplussed as we tottered around the stage in our platform boots, performing such classics as 'Ballroom Blitz' and 'Virginia Plain', the Roxy Music hit for which Mick took over vocal duties. Singing drummers, eh?

The following night in Birmingham was much the same. Let Milo explain:

'Whatever the reasoning behind this absurd creation it certainly typified the "offstage" Mission that I had become acquainted with, perhaps a little too well. Without doubt they performed the songs as deftly as anyone would expect, but the real hilarity of The Metal Gurus lay in how they looked. Oddly, it never occurred to us that the assembled masses would not get the joke; I had imagined three and a half thousand people rolling about laughing as the Gurus went through their ludicrous routine, but barely a soul realised who in reality the band actually were and so The Metal Gurus found themselves playing to a somewhat bemused gathering. A gathering that was almost certainly left wondering why it was that The Wonder Stuff had asked a, most likely, local glam-rock tribute band to play that night instead of the much-advertised 'Very Special Guests'. Not that it seemed to matter much to The Mission. They had successfully entertained and amused themselves and at the outcome, I guess that is all it was really about.' And so say all of us.

A day or so later, after the demise of The Metal Gurus, I flew out to the US to spend Christmas with Sheryl and her mum and dad, who I'd be meeting for the first time. I left a bitterly cold and blustery England to arrive in the dry desert warmth of Las Vegas. This was the first Christmas I was to spend away from England. With clear blue skies and blazing sunshine, it did feel alien being in that climate at Christmas time, fake snow in the windows of their tract home in the gated community on the outskirts of the city, a fake Santa standing in their garden and the fake Christmas tree adorned with lights and baubles standing in the corner of their living room. Everything felt fake. Even the relationship between Sheryl and me. I think we both realised it was coming to an end and this was perhaps our last hurrah, a feeling compounded when I opened, on Christmas morning, the present she'd bought me: a pair of white-and-silver snakeskin cowboy boots. They were ghastly. We'd been together for almost two years, admittedly not actually spending that much time together during that period, but didn't Sheryl know me well enough by now to know I wouldn't dream of wearing such horrendous footwear? Okay, I know what you're thinking; you've seen the photos of me in the Eighties and there's no way I can plead my case when it comes to sartorial taste, but there were some items of apparel that were beyond the pale (sorry) even for me. And snakeskin cowboy boots were one of them.

'Oh, wow,' was my dazzled reaction as I opened the shoe box.

'Do you like them?', she asked all excitedly.

'They're certainly eye-catching,' was my response.

'Try them on,' suggested Sheree, Sheryl's mum.

Oh, bloody hell.

'Them are some boots there, young Wayne,' her dad, Merle, helpfully chipped in. I could tell, even with a name like Merle, he wouldn't wanna be seen dead in those cowboy boots either.

So, there I was, feigning delight, parading around the living room in Las Vegas on Christmas morning in a pair of cowboy boots even Garth Brooks[12] would've considered tacky. With Sheryl being an only child there was just the four of us sat around the dinner table that day, tucking into a ham and mashed spuds. Of course I wore the boots.

Later in the day, when Sheryl and I were alone, she said, 'You know, if you don't like the boots we can go back to where I bought them from and exchange them.'

Thank fuck for that. 'Yes, please,' was my immediate response.

We ended up going the next day and I traded my snakeskin cowboy boots for a pair of suede moccasins. Come on, that's all they had –

cowboy boots or moccasins. What would you have done? Anyway, I liked a good pair of moccasins.

With Christmas over, we then took a driving trip – well, Sheryl drove and I looked out the window at the stunning views – to LA and then up the Pacific Coast Highway to Monterey and on into San Francisco, perhaps one of the world's most spectacular drives, so we stopped off at random various spots en route. While in the Bay Area, we went to see the Grateful Dead at the Oakland Coliseum. They played for hours, almost as long as The Cure play for, but one thing that really interested me was that they had an area cordoned off behind the mixing desk where Deadheads, the Dead's equivalent of our Eskimos, could set up personal equipment to record the shows. Some would come with quite elaborate set-ups – reel-to-reel recorders and not just portable handheld devices. The idea was that by allowing people to record the shows it would cut down on the amount of illegal bootlegs.

Bootlegs were, and are still, a lucrative business, and bands and artists with a hardcore audience (think Bob Dylan and the *Basement Tapes*, perhaps the most famous bootleg of all time until the recordings were officially released many years later) would find that vast sums were changing hands in exchange for illegal, and quite often very poor audio quality, recordings. The Grateful Dead's idea was that fans of the band could exchange recordings of their shows, and a whole community existed doing just that. I thought it was a brilliant idea, and on my return to the UK, after conferring with the rest of the band and our manager Perrin, we drew up a press release to the effect that on our upcoming *Carved In Sand* world tour anyone wanting to record the show could do so on handheld devices. Personally, I can't listen to live bootlegs, particularly Mission ones, but I resented the fact that there were a fair few poor-quality releases of our shows out there and that we had no control over it, and that the more zealous of our audience would pay extortionate amounts to possess such recordings. I recognise that for some fans, having a recording of a show they attended and enjoyed is perhaps the most significant memento to them, and I believed it would mean even more to them if it was a recording they'd made themselves. Our hope was that we could set up a tape exchange facility via MWIS and bypass the bootleggers all together, to the extent the market for Mission bootlegs would die off.

However, PolyGram threw a real hissy fit when the news was announced in the music press. Their argument was that by encouraging our audience to record the shows we'd be harming sales of our 'official' record releases. What poppycock. Any fan wanting to listen to live tapes of us would surely already own the 'official' releases. But the label demanded we publicly retract our statement and, forced to do so, we did, although we have since had it written into every contract for a live show to this day – both for The Mission and my solo shows – that anyone recording the show with a handheld device is completely free to do so. And it is generally well-known among our audience that they can. I have absolutely no problem with people exchanging live tapes as long as no money changes hands.

After driving back down the coast to LA, New Year's Eve 1989 arrived, with Sheryl and me getting blind drunk in a fleapit of a motel in Hollywood, our last night together. Perhaps the cowboy boots episode being the final nail in the coffin, we both realised that, as a romantic relationship, we were done. There were no tears, no recriminations, no regrets. We both recognised it had run its course. The next day, January 1, 1990, the very same day that 'Butterfly On A Wheel' was released as a single, I flew back to Heathrow.[13]

421

Endnotes

1   The cult-classic early Seventies British folk horror film starring Christopher Lee and Edward Woodward. The inhabitants of Summerisle, an isolated island off the coast of Scotland that has forgone Christianity in favour of a form of Celtic paganism, require a human sacrifice for their May Day ceremony to save that summer's crop of fruit trees. I love the film but it's not to everyone's taste. Apologies for the overt objectification here, but *The Wicker Man* also features the delectable Ingrid Pitt. As a red-blooded young teenage boy with a raging, out-of-control libido, the vampiric Pitt and her ravishing décolletage in the Hammer Horror films fuelled a thousand erotic fantasies of mine. Just the thought of Ingrid sinking her fangs into my neck as she pulled my head into her heaving bosom and I would gladly have surrendered my human life to her.

2   A legendary Scottish warrior woman associated with the Isle of Skye, where she resided in her 'Fortress of Shadows' (Dún Scáith). She is also known as 'the Shadow' and 'Warrior Maid'.

3   Reading, later adding its sister festival in Leeds over the same weekend, hasn't looked back since, becoming one of Europe's most prestigious and best attended music festivals.

4   Clint would go on to become a celebrated, award-winning, Golden Globe and Grammy-nominated Hollywood film composer. Jammy bugger.

5   As 'borrowed' from Neil Perry's *Sounds* report of the day, issue dated October 14, 1989.

6   Our appearance at Reading Festival a month earlier had been Stoko's 100th Mission show. I'd given him a shout-out from the stage, 'Ton up, Stoko.'

7   After the Yugoslav wars of the Nineties, Yugoslavia dissolved into what we know today as the sovereign countries of Bosnia and Herzegovina, Croatia, Montenegro, North Macedonia, Serbia and Slovenia. Kosovo is a partially recognised independent state, declaring independence from Serbia on 17 February 2008.

8   The lyrics for 'Trail Of Scarlet', reproduced by kind permission of me:

> It was the word from Milo a word to the wise
> That set me straight about your cheating and your lies
> Set down between us like the bottle that we shared
> He had to tell me 'cause no one else dared
> I'm so disappointed I'm so very, very let down
> You can have the bed and the stains on the sheets
> I'll sleep on the floor I can't bear your deceit
> You gave yourself away for the sake of a thrill
> And for the price of my conceit you were a steal
> I'm so devastated I'm so very, very let down
> And isn't it just like you to shake the faith in me
> I gave you all I had to give but I couldn't give you all you need
> And something that had died was all we had to lose
> And the worst thing I ever did to you was ask you to choose
> I'm so very lonely I'm so very, very let down
> And didn't we once have it all held it in our hands
> It's too easy to deceive a trust that makes no demands
> You leave a trail of scarlet like footsteps in the snow
> You leave a trail of scarlet everywhere you go
>
> And I'm the last to know

9   We were never gifted anything by the record company, it was all recoupable. Every penny spent on us and on our behalf was entered into the deficit column of our account. Every drink, meal, taxi, hotel, flight, video and photo shoot, studio cost, producer, engineer, remixer, touring subsidy, everything. We've ended up selling over 4 million albums for Universal (Universal bought out PolyGram years ago) and yet we're still over a million quid un-recouped. Our recording contract, signed with Phonogram in 1986, was for 'In Perpetuity', meaning they own the master recordings forever, a standard business practice at the time. I am waiting, however, for the day that Universal follows Sony's recent lead and wipes out the un-recouped debts of all artists signed before 2000. We'd actually be able to make some money on our back catalogue at last if they do. It's not as if they haven't made the money back that they spent on us; they have and more.

10   Some of the album covers Keith designed were Pink Floyd's *Division Bell*, The Cult's *Electric*, Roxy Music's *Street Life*, and a bunch for Fine Young Cannibals and Scritti Politti.

11 The Headingley Bear Pit, still there today, was originally part of the long-expired Leeds Zoo and Botanical Gardens.

12 The world-famous American country & western singer of dubious taste, who has enjoyed huge mainstream success, particularly in the US during the Nineties and ever since. Based on albums alone, he is the second-biggest bestselling artist of all time in the Land of the Free (only The Beatles have topped him).

13 I was to see Sheryl only once or twice again when we played in the US. She came to the shows to say hello, as much to the rest of the band and the crew, with whom she was friendly, as me. She did get in touch a few years later to ask if I was still in contact with John Paul Jones, and could I ask him to play at a birthday party she was organising for her husband, who was a huge Zeppelin fan. I couldn't help her, having lost touch with JPJ. I later heard the unbearably sad news that her husband had committed suicide, and Sheryl took her own life shortly thereafter as she couldn't face a life without him.

CHAPTER 20

The Fates And The Furies

PLAYLIST:
1. To Cut A Long Story Short – Spandau Ballet
2. Enjoy The Silence – Depeche Mode
3. Missing In Action – The Comsat Angels   4. Winning – The Sound
5. Dreaming Of Me – Depeche Mode
6. Never Let Me Down Again – Depeche Mode
7. Kashmir – Led Zeppelin   8. I Feel You – Depeche Mode
9. Gone – Martin L. Gore
10. Knockin' On Heaven's Door – Bob Dylan
11. Amelia – The Mission   12. I Want Your Love – Transvision Vamp

VIDEO PLAYLIST:
1. Butterfly On A Wheel – The Mission (at San Remo Festival)
2. The Mission at Kilburn National Ballroom (*Rock Steady*)
3. Wayne Hussey (on *The James Whale Radio Show*)

I woke up in my hotel room in Montreal on Monday 23 April, 1990, with a slightly fuzzy head. The curtains were drawn shut but the outside light of the late morning was sneaking in around the edges. I lit up my first fag of the day, always needing a couple before I could even get out of bed. Filthy habit. It was great back then, though; you could smoke anywhere and everywhere – hotel rooms, aeroplanes, restaurants, recording studios, tour buses, on TV, in radio stations, trains and buses, taxis and limos, bars and pubs, bordellos and clubs. I lay there inhaling deep heady drags and played back the events of the evening before in my mind. The show at the Metropolis had been the first of our scheduled six-week *Carved In Sand* North American tour. There'd been a bit of a ruckus in our dressing room afterwards. Seemingly intent on sabotaging our performance by purposely playing like a twat and trashing his gear, Slink had pushed over his amps and kicked his stage monitors into the pit between the stage and the audience, forcing us to curtail our planned set. I gotta say at this juncture that this behaviour was really out of character for Simon. Slink was, and is, slow to anger; but this had been building for months, possibly even years. We got back to the dressing room and he started slinging things around: chairs, plates, glasses, cans, bottles and accusations. Mick was trying to calm Slink down but he was having none of it. I was sat on a chair on the opposite side of the room, just letting him vent. Craig was sat between us. Simon threw a chair that smashed against a wall and then came at me. I have never seen, before or since, such hatred and fury on his face. Before he could get to me, Craig was up and at him like the rabid terrier he could be and stood between us snarling at Slink, 'Don't you fucking touch my mate or I'll break every fucking bone in your hands and you'll never play guitar again. Got it? Now calm the fuck down, you wanker.' Or words to that effect. Simon then stormed out of the dressing room and apparently made his own way back to the hotel. The rest of us travelled back on our tour bus. 'Ah, he'll be alright when he's calmed down,' ventured Mick. 'Good job we've got a travel day tomorrow to Toronto – we can have a clear-the-air chat en route,' suggested Stevie Sex-Pistol.

We all went straight to our rooms on arrival back at the Holiday Inn, foregoing the usual congregation in the bar or someone's room for a nightcap. None of us felt like it, or could be bothered to search out Simon and try to fix what was evidently a bit of a problem. Let's all just sleep on it, was the consensus; the cold light of day would bring clarity and clear thinking. It was while I was puffing away on my second nicotine fix the next morning that I looked at the telephone sat on the bedside table with the red message light flashing. I picked up the receiver and put it to my ear and pressed the button to listen to the voice message...

Roll back the clock to the beginning of the year and my arrival back in England after my adventures on the US West Coast over Christmas and the New Year. 'Butterfly On A Wheel' had just been released and was selling very well, the midweek chart putting us at number four! In the past we had generally shoehorned most of our promotional duties into our tours, afternoons on show days very often spent conducting interview after interview, or being ferried from one radio station to a TV station and on to another radio station, and all before soundcheck. Sometimes we'd even have interviews between soundcheck and showtime, and sometimes – the most dangerous time of all – after the show.

The worst, though, was having to rise at some ungodly hour to appear for 30 seconds or so on some schlocky breakfast show. I remember one time in Oslo on one of the early tours, after a late stage time the night before, having to get up and be on camera by 8 a.m., outside in the kind of cold that freezes your breath as you breathe out, on a ski slope with snow on the ground and a pair of skis on my feet and ski poles in hand, pretending I'd just glided down the slopes. As if. Of course, I was dressed in the perfect skiing attire of my black bolero hat, sunglasses and a long black crushed-velvet coat. What nonsense. More fool me for agreeing to do it.

On-tour promo was time-consuming and exhausting, and distracted from the real purpose, the priority of the day which should always be the *show*. Despite the adrenaline, wine and speed, and the energy you feed off from an audience, I would very often find that by the end of the night I was running on fumes alone. How to counteract that? Drink more wine and take more speed. Vicious circle.

For the release of *Carved In Sand*, we realised promo duties would intensify, so to accommodate the increased demand – on my time in particular – we'd set aside six weeks before the tour dedicated solely to promo. Basically, the next month and a half of my life: two weeks in the UK speaking to every magazine, fanzine, TV and radio show that would have me; two weeks jetting around the capitals of Europe doing the same; and two weeks in the US, a week each in LA and NYC. Aside from the occasional TV playback when the whole band would be needed and would fly out to wherever I was, I could handle most of it myself. Mick spent a few days here and there alongside me, in fellowship and for moral support as much as anything else. And Craig travelled to the US to keep me company and help with those mind-numbing, unremitting phoners that would take up most of the day.

By this time, Simon, however, was refusing to do anything that didn't involve the whole band. Although it did feel at the time like he was shirking his responsibilities – yet another example of our increasing schisms and ever-widening differences – I can't say I particularly blame him, as promo is tedious at best. Can you imagine spending all day, every day talking about yourself and your work, answering the same questions over and over? As John Lennon once said, 'I spend half my life making music, and the other half justifying it.'

Usually I enjoyed the first couple of interviews when we released a new album, as it was very often the first time I was forced to sit down and contemplate the music we'd created, and I'd come to revealing hitherto unrealised observations and conclusions. I never analysed the music during the writing and recording, relying instead on instinct and impulse, making creative decisions based on nothing more than whim. But day after day of repeating myself in interviews led me to feel like I was starting to lie and I couldn't remember from one to another what 'down-pat' answers I'd already used. As explained earlier, to counteract this tedium I started entertaining myself by spinning yarns and tall-tales,

428

fabricating stories and explanations. It was the only way to hold on to sanity and have a bit of fun doing so.

While we were in NYC, Craig and I were interviewed for MTV's *120 Minutes*, a show that exclusively featured alternative music. While there, we were asked if we'd like to be one of the first bands to appear on a new show they'd just recently premiered, called *Unplugged*. We declined the offer on the grounds of believing that we wouldn't be shown in our best light and, more importantly, the premise was ill-judged and *Unplugged* wasn't gonna take off. Bugger. The only thing ill-judged was our decision, and this was another prime example of a blundering misstep for us in America, yet again incurring the wrath of the record label, but worse, alienating MTV.

With its high midweek chart position, it was a crushing disappointment when the official chart was announced the Sunday after release and, even though it was that week's highest new entry, 'Butterfly On A Wheel' had only made it to number 17. Still, it was enough to get us another appearance on *TOTP*, after which we hit Top 5 again the following midweek. But once again, we missed the Top 10 in the official chart, the single only climbing to 12, and then the following week slumping all the way down to 29 on its way out of the chart and to landfill. I must confess I thought, as did some at Phonogram, that this single could be the one to blow things wide open for us, but our judgement was proven errant, not at all helped by the fact we'd breached the rules on formatting and were penalised with lower chart positions than sales were indicating. Excuses, excuses.

A few days later we found ourselves in Rome to appear on another TV show. The rest of the band had flown in to join me and we were staying at a posh hotel out near the airport. Early evening on arrival we'd convened to the bar and found ourselves in the company of Spandau Ballet. Both bands eyed each other suspiciously until a few drinks had been sunk and Gary Kemp approached me. He sidled up and said, 'Congrats on that 'Butterfly...' single, it's a really good, well-written song.' That broke the ice and we spent the rest of the evening fraternising with the Spands.

The following day we performed on a typically bonkers Italian talk/pop TV show, with us starting out sat among the audience until we were called to the stage to mime to the single. Come evening and we were invited to see the Spands in concert at some enorma-dome in Rome, a huge indoor arena packed with mostly screaming teenage girls. Afterwards, we made our way back to their dressing room. I got talking to *Martin* Kemp this time and he asked what I thought of the show.

'Mmm, yeh. The kick drum sounded huge, the band played tight. It sounded good,' was my non-committal reply.

'You didn't like it much, did you?' he said, laughing, seeing right through my disingenuousness.

'Nah, soz, it's not really my thing, but, you know...,' I trailed off.

'Ah, it's alright, mate, I don't like your band much either,' he said with a grin. I admired his honesty and frankness and lack of airs and graces.

Another knees-up with the Spands ensued back at the hotel, once they'd escaped the hordes of waiting girls outside the stage door. They were alright, Spandau Ballet, all decent cockneys up for a laugh, quite the contrary to my preconceived notion of them. But then, I'm gonna surmise that I was probably not quite what they expected either.

I'd first seen Depeche Mode playing one of their very first shows in September 1980, supporting The Comsat Angels at the Canning Town Bridge House pub. I was, and am, a big fan of Sheffield's finest, the Comsats,[1] having seen them on many occasions around this time, including supporting Captain Beefheart, Siouxsie & The Banshees and U2. They were my favourite band for a while, hence travelling down from Liverpool to London to see them. Their debut album, *Waiting For A Miracle*, is a classic of the post-punk genre and is, in my opinion, one of two albums from this period that was criminally overlooked at the time and still is, the other being The Sound's *From The Lion's Mouth*. We all know the debut albums of Joy Division, The Cure and Echo & The Bunnymen, but The Comsat Angels and The Sound debuts deserve to be just as venerated alongside 'em.

Anyway, this particular night at the Bridge House, the Comsats had this funny little synth band supporting – four geeky New Romantic kids, three of them playing synths to a drum machine while the fourth was a whirling dervish who sang. Being a devoted guitar aficionado myself, Depeche Mode really wasn't my thing but their songs were as catchy as gonorrhoea, each one boasting a hook that could snare even the wiliest muskellunge, and it was obvious that we were going to be seeing them in the pop charts very soon. But who'd have put money on them back then becoming the behemoth *Depeche Mode* we know today, the international *brand*, the much respected doyens of the dark synth scene who've inspired a level of devotion bordering on religious?

After seeing them support The Comsat Angels, I didn't take much notice of them again until we were recording *Children*, during which they released 'Never Let Me Down Again' as the single from the album *Music For The Masses*, which I bought and played incessantly while we were at The Manor. In fact, the beat, the drive, the feel, the grandiloquence of that track is not dissimilar to our own 'Tower Of Strength'. A lot of people have speculated that 'Tower Of Strength' was inspired by my love of Led Zeppelin, and 'Kashmir' in particular, and maybe it was in part. But just as equally, I can hear Depeche Mode in 'Tower Of Strength' too.

The best thing that ever happened to Depeche Mode, undoubtedly, was Vince Clarke leaving them after the release of their first album to form, first, Yazoo and then Erasure. The boy ain't done bad for himself since, with his penchant for writing those snazzy pop hooks, but his departure meant that Martin Gore took over as chief song-writer, which arguably was the making of the Modes. It took him a

431

while to grow into the role but Martin brought a darkness to both lyrical themes and melodies and developed into one of the finest songwriters of our generation. His songs are *very* smart and nuanced, but sound deceptively simple, almost, subject matter aside, nursery rhyme-ish at times. And still indecently catchy. It is high art.

Depeche Mode are one of the rare breed of bands who get better with age. For the record, my favourite album of theirs is *Songs Of Faith And Devotion*, and that was their eighth! Aligned with Martin's burgeoning songwriting chops, Alan Wilder's classically trained consummate musicianship, and Dave Gahan developing into a great singer and one of the best front men I've ever seen – up there with Mercury, Jagger, Plant, Bono and the like – exercising complete control over the massive audiences they play to, Depeche Mode rose from being four nerdy Essex boys playing frothy, lightweight synth-pop to become one of the world's biggest, and most respected (particularly by their peers) bands. I don't know anybody that doesn't like Depeche Mode and I can't think of another artist I can say the same about, not even The Beatles.

And what does Depeche Mode have to do with us? Well, in 1990 we were invited to appear as a guest at the San Remo Music Festival, a long-standing institutional annual Italian song contest and awards ceremony broadcast live on national television since the early Fifties. Among the many Italian acts competing for the best song award (which is a bit like the Eurovision Song Contest), several international artistes of repute (ill perhaps, in our case) are invited to perform at the prestigious event to bring a bit of glitz, glamour and panache to proceedings amid the many Italiano canzones. It was indeed a much-coveted TV appearance so why they asked us I really have no clue. Fellow guests that year included Liza Minnelli, Tina Turner and Rod Stewart. At least we had allies in Depeche Mode, who were miming to 'Enjoy The Silence'.

After rehearsals, there was nothing for us to do but wait around in our dressing rooms until it was time to perform. We weren't invited into Liza's, Tina's or Rod's dressing rooms but Mick, Craig, Jez and me did end up in Depeche's, where we all sang along to the glam-rock songs Martin was banging out on guitar. For some reason Simon declined to join us and chose to stay in our dressing room, drinking on his own. When it was time, both bands did our thing in front of the seated theatre audience, with Depeche in particular receiving a rapturous reception. Our performance was notable for my total lack of effort to mime; instead I preferred to expose the pretence of it all by using the microphone and stand as mere props to swing around while 'singing'. Pretentious in pointing out the pretension, eh? It's on YouTube if you fancy a gander.

That evening, when the work was done, there was a party thrown in a local club. Of course, The Mission and Depeche staggered along. Also in attendance were a bunch of other bands and singers: Sinéad O'Connor, Belinda Carlisle, Jimmy Somerville, Curiosity Killed The Cat, and The Alarm, to name just a few I can remember (neither Liza, Tina or Rod made an appearance, or at least I didn't see 'em). Much frivolity ensued and everybody was having a grand ol' time until various members of The Alarm, Vitamin Z and Curiosity decided to get up on the stage, which had a drum kit and several guitars, amps and mics set up, to regale us with 'the blues'. Now... I love *old blues*, but I detest modern pissed-up, pub-rock, white-boy electric blues, and once 'Alarm Killed The Vitamin' started jamming, it brought down the mood of the entire place. The only people enjoying it were the people onstage playing it, and I'm not entirely convinced that even they were, apart from Mike Peters[2] that is.

Encouraged by the Depeche lads and the bravado that alcohol brings, me and Daryl Bamonte, who was there looking after the Modes and who I had spent a riotous night with celebrating his 21st birthday[3] a few years earlier in Bochum, Germany, took it upon ourselves to bring 'the blues' to a halt. So, we sneaked up onstage behind the amps and unplugged the guitars. They then plugged themselves back in and carried on, boring everyone to death. So we unplugged them again, to loud

433

cheers from the gathered throng. This went on for a while until both me and Daryl realised we needed to pee. But rather than scuttling off to the loo and letting them get away with murdering an entire genre, we decided to whip 'em out and urinate on the stage. That stopped them well good and proper – partly through fear of electrocution but mostly they didn't want to get their footwear sullied by our rapidly spreading puddle of piddle. They downed their instruments and exited the stage with much haste much to the audience's, and our, relief.

A few minutes later The Mission were cajoled by Daryl to get up and do a bit of our Metal Gurus act, with Depeche's Martin Gore joining us on guitar and backing vocals. I had no qualms about standing in my own piss if it was in the name of art. We shambled through a few glam classics before realising that we were so totally blottoed we couldn't actually play and were making an unholy racket, possibly worse than 'Curiosity Alarmed The Z'. There we were, voted the world's best live band in both *Sounds* and *Melody Maker* just a couple of short months previously, disgracing ourselves in front of a group of our peers who just stood laughing, if not with us then at us.

The night ended with Mick and me adjourning to Dave Gahan's hotel room and sitting up to the early hours with him and a couple of others and, fuelled by a small mound of sniff-sniff, talking utter gibberish. Jez and Craig, coincidentally, grabbed a carrier-bagful of miniatures from their hotel mini-bars and headed to the beach, bumping into Jimmy Somerville en route and inviting him to join 'em. He, perhaps wisely, declined the invitation, leaving our undaunted *gli amici* to watch the sunrise on their own. Where to and with whom Slink disappeared I have no memory but, as was becoming more and more frequent, he wasn't with any of us.

The situation with Simon had been slowly simmering throughout the recording of *Carved In Sand* but now that the album was done and dusted, we had tours of the UK, Europe, North America, Mexico,

Australasia and Japan to look forward to over the ensuing months. Whatever tensions were brewing would hopefully be dissipated by being onstage night after night, playing to the adoring legions. That was where we all preferred to be, and any and all stresses and problems melted away for those couple of hours or so we played *rock gods*. Or so I thought.

In my experience, though, guitarists are a funny breed. And I am qualified to make that assertion as I was 'just' the guitarist in most of the bands I'd played with previous to The Mission. They are usually the most egotistical and insecure in the band, certainly the fucking loudest. The hearing in my left ear is pretty much destroyed due to the ear-drum crushing volume of the various guitarists that have stood to my left onstage. Not quite captain of the ship, usually second in command, and bristling with resentment that the singer gets the most attention, guitarists in retaliation like to make the biggest noise.

During my time spent as 'chief mate', I very often craved a little more recognition. Maybe ultimately that was a driving motivation for me wanting to become a singer, although I don't think I'd quite rationalise it that way. As stated earlier, I feel I kind of inherited the job with The Mission by default. All that aside, though, I do know that Simon became uncomfortable with the more 'pop' direction I leaned towards, and he came to absolutely detest the attendant shenanigans being demanded of us in order to promote ourselves and our records. I can't say I blame him for feeling that way because I have come to loathe it too, but back in the second half of the Eighties I was more than up for the good fight and recognised that I – we – had a responsibility to the records to promote them any way we could. To be fair, Slink today is more than willing to take some of the weight of interviews and promotion off my shoulders, but by the beginning of 1990, when the amount of promo was immense, he was dead set against it.

During that six-week period of promo for *Carved In Sand* we were all sat in the back of a big black car somewhere in Europe and, having

435

been out on my own doing promo for a week or so, I was feeling particularly emotionally highly strung. Slink said something glib that I took offence to. I turned around in my seat and punched him in the face. As soon as I hit him I burst into tears; one, because of how mentally ragged I was, and two, because I instantly regretted it. Violence never solves any problems, only makes more. Simon didn't punch me back so he won that fight by claiming the moral high ground. The truth is, physically he is a lot bigger than me and could probably lay me out without much effort, but he chose not to. Well, not that night anyway.

Simon is a dichotomy. Onstage he has always had a swagger – hence the appellation of Slink – which came across often as arrogance. Offstage he could also play that part to the hilt if he was allowed or encouraged to do so. Just as I could easily play the 'pop tart' both on and offstage. I think that is how we largely saw each other back in *them days*. But today, having known Simon some 36 years or so, I've come to see him as a tender, often unsure and insecure, kind and thoughtful sweetheart. Mind you, he still plays too bleedin' loud and can be a pompous ass when he's had a cider too many. Of course, I'm perfect and I'm sure Simon would concur.

By the way I never hit Craig or Mick or any other member of the band or crew – and there's been a few maybe deserving of a slap – but, as hard as you may find this to believe, I've definitely had a shout at some of 'em. I did once throw a pint of water over Mark Gemini Thwaite[4], though, while arguing over whether there was a C chord in 'Knocking On Heaven's Door'. It turns out Mark was right: there is a C chord, in both Bob Dylan's and Guns N' Roses' versions, but we preferred the darker A minor in The Sisters Of Mercy, and the Sisters' version is all the better for it. I did apologise to Mark many years later when I realised my mistake, an apology that he took full opportunity to rub in my face by saying, 'I told you so.' Don't you just hate it when people do that?

Carved In Sand was released during the third week of February 1990, and entered the UK album chart at number seven, a slight disappointment after *Children* had debuted at number two. If our crown wasn't yet quite slipping it was certainly askew by this point. Again, the album was certified Gold within two or three days of release and would end up being our biggest-selling album globally, but it all felt a little anticlimactic, like treading water.

Nonetheless, touring was our métier and our travels that year kicked off with a secret warm-up show at the newly relocated Marquee on London's Charing Cross Road.

The following day we were at the Kilburn National Ballroom to record a performance for Channel 4's TV show *Rock Steady*. With 3,000 lucky members of MWIS in attendance, full of adrenaline and who knows what else, we entered the stage and I immediately launched into the ferocious acoustic guitar strumming of 'Amelia', spitting out the lyrics chronicling familial sexual abuse with real intent and intensity. Just before the rest of the band were due to crash in and join me, I felt a tap on my shoulder. I turned around and it was one of the TV crew technicians. Sheepishly he said, 'Um, sorry, we weren't ready for you, can you please start again?' Obviously the moment was completely ruined for me, my intensity being burst like a balloon sat on by a sumo wrestler. All I could think to say to the audience was, 'Well, fuck me, eh?' Once we got the go-ahead that the cameras were at last rolling we started again, but it was difficult to imbue the song with any degree of feeling other than irritation. I was annoyed and, with my concentration shot to bits, things went from bad to worse as we were plagued with various technical difficulties. About 20 minutes in, just as we started 'Butterfly...', I called proceedings to a halt, ripped up the agreed set-list and started taking requests from the audience. The TV people didn't know what to do, as we'd all spent tedious hours during the day going through the set so the technicians could practise their planned camera moves and angles.

Backstage, Tony Perrin was taking the flak from the *Rock Steady* producer, who was screaming, 'I'll make sure they never record another TV show ever again!' We'd heard that one before. Back onstage I was losing it big time, and all in front of the TV cameras. I was inciting the audience to chant '*Rock Steady* is shit!', offering to give everybody back the £3 it had cost them for a ticket, and throwing myself from the stage into the seething throng in the mosh pit in a desperate bid to escape the travesty that was being played out onstage. It was anarchic, bedlam, and I was so angry that this shambolic mess of a show, all initiated because the soddin' camera crew weren't filming when we first hit the stage, was to be broadcast on Channel 4.

This all reads as if I was having a giant strop and throwing a tantrum and I suppose I was. I've never been one to hide how I'm feeling when onstage. Anyone that has seen us play live more than a few times will know that I am occasionally prone to letting anger get the better of me when things aren't going quite as I'd want. Sometimes I get annoyed with our equipment or the crew, sometimes the band or the audience, but most of all myself. Many fans love The Mission on these nights, much like the *Rock Steady* audience in the National Ballroom did on that particular night – they become favourite shows among the diehards. No one quite knows what's gonna happen next and that's what enthrals the audience.

As the last chord of the last song rang out in the Ballroom, I declared, 'You let us get away with murder.' Still, *Rock Steady* broadcast the show in all its gory glory and, weirdly, the producer faxed Perrin a few days later to say it ended up being the best and most watched show of the series.

Elsewhere on the *Carved In Sand* tour, we found ourselves again back in arenas, city halls and Apollos, and after our previous experience in venues of that size it was felt that it would help the show visually if I could put my guitar down more often, so as not to be rooted to the spot and thereby freeing me up to be the prancing, preening 'rock god front man'. So, we had to draft in a replacement guitarist. Someone, probably either Craig or Mick or even both, suggested Dave 'Wolfie' Wolfenden, who'd previously played guitar in Red Lorry Yellow Lorry with Mick, and the Expelaires with Craig. We all knew and, more importantly, liked Wolfie from the time the Lorries had supported us on a previous tour. The only member of the band that seemed a little reticent towards the idea was Slink. Knowing now how insecure Simon was and his state of mind at the time, I'd proffer that bringing Wolfie in, albeit even temporarily, posed a threat to Simon in his mind. It was never intended for Wolfie to be a musically contributing member of the band; rather he was simply there to join us onstage for half a dozen songs a night towards the end of the set, to take over my guitar parts. So we went ahead with the plan, despite the misgivings we assumed Simon was feeling.

Wolfie, who looked a little like Eric Morecambe from the classic comedy duo Morecambe & Wise, was a constant source of amusement and prone to mishap. One day off, somewhere in Europe, he'd gone for a walk around the city. Not looking where he was walking, he'd fallen into a deep hole left by workmen who had nipped off for lunch. He had to be helped out by passers-by. Fortunately, no damage was done, apart from a loss of dignity.

Another time we were playing 'Beyond The Pale' at an outdoor venue and there was a tree overhanging the stage. After the long, quiet intro, the band all crashes in together, at which point Wolfie, getting carried away by the moment, leapt into the air, attempting a Pete Townshend scissor-kick, and nearly knocked himself out hitting his head on an overhanging branch.

A little later in the year, just a couple of days before we were due to head off to Finland to play a festival with The Cramps and The Stone Roses, we were playing football on a piece of grassland near our rehearsal room. With no one anywhere near him, Wolfie comically stood on the ball and fell over. We were all in hysterics as he was rolling around on the grass, screaming in his high-pitched whinny-whiney broad Yorkshire accent, 'I've broken my wrist, you twats, I've broken my wrist!' He was taken to hospital where he was diagnosed with a severely bruised wrist but thankfully no broken bones.

Another occasion, he'd gone for a night walk around some European city and got taken short. Being in a quiet part of town there was nowhere open he could nip into, and he was a fair distance from the hotel. The street was dark, with minimal street lighting and very little traffic and, as far as he could ascertain, no one else around. He found a hedge, and squatted, pulling his trews and undies down around his knees and proceeded to relieve himself. Just about then a bus came around the corner and stopped right in front of him, triggering motion sensor lights that illuminated a bus stop that Wolfie hadn't noticed right next to the hedge. He was lit up like the Copacabana on New Year's Eve as the passengers alighting from the bus passed him, looking on with surprise and distaste while the rest sat on the bus staring out of the windows, their mouths agape. It could only happen to Wolfie.

After a couple of days of production rehearsals, the tour 'proper' kicked off at Liverpool's Royal Court on Sunday 4 March and passed me by in a blur. Having not really toured in 1989 and being newly single again, I immersed myself into on-tour hedonism with renewed vim and vigour.

We employed our own security guard for this tour, Nigel 'Biffa' Thomas, who had represented Wales as a boxer in his youth. He was also a staunch Welsh nationalist as a young 'un and a member of a Welsh liberation organisation. He boasted once that he was part of a crew that blew up a reservoir on the border of Wales and England in the Seventies, the idea being that the destroyed dam would flood a village on the English side of the border. Except they got their calculations wrong and the water flowed to the Welsh side, flooding

440

a Welsh village instead. I can't vouch for the veracity of Biffa's story, my online sleuthing only unearthing the tale of Tryweryn dam being blown up by Welsh freedom fighters in protest at the flooding of the Welsh village of Capel Celyn in 1963, which would've made Biffa about two years old at the time. Not sure if even the Welsh would recruit insurgents at that tender age. Now, before I get outlawed forever from entering Wales, let me just clarify that I am indeed half Welsh, my mum being born in Cardiff.

Anyway, Biffa was employed by us for two reasons. First, to oversee the security at all the venues. Because we'd had many a run-in with house security crews being too aggressive and physical with our audiences, we decided we needed our own *man* to be in charge. I never saw Biffa having to be physical with anyone, ever. His presence alone was intimidating enough to keep the peace. And second, to look after the band and keep us out of trouble. That was probably the harder of the two tasks he was entrusted with.

I loved having Biffa around; we got on really well and I always felt incredibly safe, even if I did give him the runaround at times. One night, when I was being too lairy, he marched me to my hotel room and locked me in. After about 10 minutes I quietly opened my door to see if the coast was clear and he was stood there on guard. 'Get back in yer room, Hussey. I'm staying here until I can hear you snoring.' Fifteen minutes later I tried again. He was still there. This went on for about an hour before I finally gave up and went to bed. Besides me, Biffa also looked after Wendy James from Transvision Vamp on tour. The biggest problem he had with her was, apparently, having to carry her vanity case which was, by all accounts, quite large and heavy. Mine was just a couple of lipsticks and a bit of blusher, and I carried those myself.

During the first week of the tour we released 'Deliverance' as the second single from *Carved In Sand*. It entered the UK chart at number 30 and climbed to 27 the following week. We were invited to appear on *TOTP* again, and fortuitously for us we had a day off so we were able to accept.

On the same broadcast, a band that had already been around for a few years had recently reinvented themselves and were making their *TOTP* debut with 'Loaded'. Of course, it was Primal Scream — destined to become one of the best, and one of my favourite, bands of the Nineties. After both our performances on the show, the Primal's single climbed into the Top 20 while ours stalled at number 27, perhaps not best helped by my notorious appearance a day later on a popular-with-the-piss-heads-just-home-from-the-pub late-night Friday talk show, *The James Whale Radio Show*. It was broadcast on Radio Aire in Leeds and simulcast on national telly via Yorkshire Television.[5]

I had never previously watched James Whale, but the rest of the band had, and they all warned me that Whale could be very often patronising, even condescending, towards his guests and would go out of his way to try and make them look like idiots. Well, he didn't need to bother with me as I did that all by myself.

We had just played a sold-out show at Sheffield City Hall and I'd been whisked away from the after-show celebrations and driven to the TV studios in Leeds, coincidentally not too far from where I used to live. I did mention earlier that the most dangerous time to conduct an interview, particularly for me, was *after* a show. And so it proved this particular night. I was already well oiled, what with the normal pre-stage routine and then drinking through the performance and, high on the euphoria of playing a raucous show to an ecstatic audience, carrying on when we came offstage and during the half-hour journey to Leeds. Biffa came with me to make sure I didn't get into trouble. This was one night when he failed miserably. *James Whale* was broadcast live and, determined to get my insults and barbs in first, the very first words out of my mouth were 'Who gives a fuck!' and from there it quickly degenerated into an attempt to see how many times I could say 'fuck' live on air before I'd get kicked off the show. At one point I called Whale a 'pillock' (and in my head I heard a nation cheer) and I also took off my moccasins and threw them at the camera. After an aborted attempt to read my astrological chart via computer, Whale had had enough and tried to escort me off the set and out a side door to the outside of the building. Biffa, bless him, blocked Whale's way and wouldn't let me be ejected, with Whale having to resort to 'roll VT, roll VT' and my last words being 'Fuck off' before they cut to a video. Watching it now while researching for this book it does make me laugh because it's like watching somebody I used to know. But I also cringe because I know it is me. It's 'car-crash TV', the clip being aired regularly on pretty much every 'TV's worst moments' show on British TV since, alongside famous footage of Oliver Reed and George Best and others behaving disgracefully on camera. When I phone my mum, which I do regularly, she occasionally says, 'You were on telly again last night.'

'Doing what?'

'Being drunk and swearing and throwing your shoes at the camera.'

'Aw, God, not that again.'

She must be so proud of me.

In the eyes of the Great British public, this one incident is perhaps what I am best known for. I can't count how many people I've met who remember that over any of the records we released. *I'm* so proud of me. Do I regret it? No, not really. That's who I was in 1990 and that clichéd, drunken, licentious, degenerate, libidinous rock star bears very little resemblance to the person I am today. Unfortunately. I still swear, mind.

Once they managed to remove me from the studio, Biffa and I found ourselves in an outer office at Yorkshire Television. The telephones were ringing. I picked up a receiver. 'Oh, hello. I'm ringing to complain about the disgraceful behaviour and language on your show this evening,' griped the irate caller.

'What, you mean like 'fuck off', do you?' was my reply, followed by me slamming the phone down.

I answered a few more calls in a similar vein before we were ordered to finally leave the building. The episode even made Page Three of the following Sunday's *News Of The World*, and knowing how much they loved a scandal, my only disappointment was that the story didn't make the front page. You'd think that I'd be banned from Yorkshire Television forever after that little escapade but no, I was welcomed back on the *James Whale Radio Show* later that same year, with Noddy Holder and The Metal Gurus (Noddy and Jim Lea from Slade produced the Metal Gurus single and Noddy performed 'Merry Xmas Everybody' with us). I was a little less inebriated on my second visit and, despite Whale's best attempts to goad me, I held my tongue, much to his frustration. The pillock.[6]

Maybe it was karma, but too many late and excessive nights on the tour led to me falling sick with a particularly virulent strain of the now regular-as-clockwork tour cold, and we had to cancel a show at Newport Centre. The doctors came and gave me shots and whatnot, but all to no avail. That was the first of only two shows *I've* ever had to cancel because of illness, the second being a solo show in Milan many, many years later – the fact that I was holed up in Paris had nothing to do with my cancelling Milan, honest guv.

We've had to cancel shows because of illness of other members of the band and for other reasons beyond our control but, as far as I can recollect, no matter how bad I've felt, I've always managed to drag myself out of bed and onto the stage, aided by pharmaceuticals both legal and illegal, and *medicinal* wine, finding some reserve of energy from somewhere. On occasion we've even played with me pretty much having lost my voice, so we've resorted to getting members of the audience up onstage to sing the songs for us. It's made for a unique audience experience and is better than the alternative of cancelling, right? Right.

I was prescribed antibiotics in Newport with the strict instruction not to mix them with alcohol. The next show, two days later, at the Bristol Hippodrome (where I saw my first-ever gig in 1974, Pink Floyd on their *Dark Side Of The Moon* tour) was terrifying because of my enforced sobriety, not ever having played a Mission show sober up to that point.

The Irish and UK leg of our tour culminated with sell-out shows at Wembley Arena and Birmingham NEC again. What was I saying about the feeling of treading water? And then it was into Europe.

To kick it off we, the band, flew to Paris for an in-store acoustic show at the Virgin Megastore on the Champs-Élysées. The place was absolutely jam-packed with people spilling out onto the pavement and those that could get in hanging over the balconies, attempting to get a peek at us. We played an eight-song set to promote *Carved In Sand*, including Craig's spirited *a capella* version of 'Champagne Charlie'. He had decided that from now on during this tour he was only going to drink champagne. That resolution lasted about the length of an afternoon; he was soon drinking whatever he could get his hands on, his resolve being about as strong as mine. Once we'd finished entertaining the masses we then stood there for a couple of hours and signed *millions* of autographs as the queuing crowds traipsed past, proffering record and CD sleeves, various other bits of memorabilia, and the occasional body part.

My best friend, Miles Hunt, had been in the doldrums. Rob 'The Bass Thing' Jones had recently left The Wonder Stuff and moved to NYC to marry Michelle Robinson, who was the last girlfriend of the ill-fated Sid Vicious.[7] We'd have our regular late-night telephone conversations with Milo bemoaning his lot. Not being sure what was happening with the band and his enthusiasm for it at an all-time low, he wasn't even certain he wanted to carry on. I'd heard enough. 'Come on holiday with us,' I suggested.

445

'What do you mean?'

'Find yourself a new bass player – any bugger will do, it's only four strings, it ain't hard – and come out on tour with us to Europe and the States,' I said. And that's what happened. The Stuffies found a young, malleable bass player, a lot less scary than 'The Bass Thing', and came out on tour to Europe as our support.

Our first night together, in Utrecht, Milo and I stayed up all night in the hotel emptying his minibar and putting the world to rights, and both of us had to be poured onto our respective tour buses in the morning. It was fortunate for us that the following day was a long drive up to Stockholm, without having to play that night. We'd started as we meant to carry on.

It was great motivation for us having a band as good as The Wonder Stuff supporting us. We'd got to the stage where we were playing venues across most of Europe comparable to the size of those we played in the UK and with a hugely partisan audience it sometimes felt like we didn't have anything to prove. Having a *happening*, new, young band onstage before us who could raise the temperature and who had an audience of their own made us raise our own game night after night. We may have had our own festering internal personal problems, but once we hit the boards all of that was forgotten and we played some of the best shows we'd ever played. With unanimously favourable reviews for us throughout this tour, even the press were impressed for a change, particularly at our skill of making arena shows feel like sweaty, intimate, inclusive club gigs.

The tour swept through Europe without a hitch, until we reached Italy. We played in Milan and when Dave, the Wonder Stuff manager, went to collect their fee after the show the promoter refused to pay, bringing a gun out and placing it on the table in front of him. Dave, probably wisely, decided not to push the issue and left the room, and venue, unpaid. He then instructed the band that they wouldn't be going to Rome with us the following day; they were getting the heck out of Italy and would meet up with us in Lyon, France, in a couple of days. We went on to Rome to play at the Tenda Strisce, a big circus tent in the city centre, a show that was interrupted with a police raid and them pulling the power on us, claiming we were playing too loud. Much shouting and bickering in Italian was going on backstage between the promoters and the police so, with the audience getting restless and booing, the power was restored and I grabbed my Ovation 12-string acoustic and went back onstage to play acoustic versions of 'Butterfly...' and 'Love Me To Death'. With the police appeased by the drop in volume, they departed the venue, and as soon as we were sure they had left the vicinity, the rest of the band rejoined me onstage and we were back to full volume, blasting through the rest of the set to a clearly excitable and ecstatic audience. Post show, the promoters took us out to a nightclub to celebrate. On arrival they herded us into an empty back office. We were starting to worry what was going to happen next, having heard the story about Dave and the gun from the previous night, when a guy walked in with a big silver platter with THE MISSION chopped out in six-inch long lines of cocaine. I bagsied the M.[8]

Over the last few days Slink had been starting to complain about not feeling very well. Initially we put it down to overindulgence and the normal stresses and strains of touring. After he'd hoovered up at least one of the S's in Rome, he went downhill fast the following day on the bus journey to Lyon, coming out in a bright red rash that covered most of his body. When we arrived at the hotel a doctor was called out to see him and immediately diagnosed him with the highly contagious scarlet fever. We immediately cancelled our two remaining shows – in Lyon and Paris – and arrangements were made for Simon to fly home to Sheffield the very next day. The rest of us travelled back to England on the tour bus. Simon then had to stay at home, quarantining and recovering for a couple of weeks.

To allow time for Slink to recover, we cancelled the first week of scheduled shows of our North American tour, which was due to start on April 16 in Port Chester, New York. The new start date was the 22nd, in Montreal. Craig, Mick and I, along with Stevie Sex-Pistol, flew as originally planned to New York and spent the time doing extra promo, visiting friends, sightseeing and partying. Simon, Wolfie and our tour manager Harry Isles flew into NYC on April 21 and were picked up at the airport by the tour bus, en route to picking us up at the hotel. The crew had gone on ahead on their bus and with the equipment. We climbed onto the bus, having stowed our luggage in the hold, and saw Wolfie and Harry sat at one of the tables in the front lounge.

'Hello chaps,' chirruped Wolfie.

We all sat down and exchanged pleasantries. The bus moved off on its way out of Manhattan to Montreal.

Mick: 'How was your flight?'

Harry: 'Fine, ta.'

'Where's Slink?' I asked.

Wolfie: 'Ah, he's in the back lounge.'

Just then we heard voices and laughter emanating from the back of the bus.

Craig: 'Who's that with him?'

Harry: 'Oh, that's Suzanne and Steve.'

'What, Steve, his mate from Sheffield?' I asked.

'Yep,' confirmed Wolfie.

'Bloody 'ell, how long's he staying around for?' Craig asked rhetorically.

Curious, we walked down the bus aisle and there, sprawled out in the back lounge, was Simon with his friend, Steve, and his girlfriend, Suzanne.

'Alright, Si, how're you feeling now?' one of us asked.

'Great, rarin' to go,' he replied.

'Hello Steve, hello Suzanne,' someone else said.

'Alright,' they chorused.

'Si, can we have a quick word in the front lounge, please?' someone asked, more than likely me.

Simon got up and followed us to the front lounge, where we all sat down.

'So, what's happening, Si?'

'What do you mean?'

'How long are you planning to have Suzanne and Steve on the bus for?'

'Ah, Suzanne's gonna get off in Toronto and go home to see her family [she's Canadian]. Steve is gonna stay for the whole tour.'

'Okay, but you haven't asked us and this is the first time any of us has heard anything about this. You know what the band bus rules are,' I said.

The rule was, and still is, that partners and friends were allowed on the bus but only for a couple of days at most and, as a courtesy, everybody had to be asked first. To turn up on the first day of a six-week tour with two friends in tow without even asking was just not on. We didn't have a problem with Suzanne; she'd only be on the bus for two or three days. And we liked Suzanne. She'd been our tour manager when we'd toured with The Psychedelic Furs and, having toured extensively with other bands too, she knew how tour bus etiquette worked. The problem was Steve. None of us liked him. At all. And he'd never been on a tour bus before.

'Well, we're gonna have to talk about this later,' I said.

The bus is our sanctum. It's our inviolable private space when we're on tour. It was just us four band members, and Wolfie, Stevie Sex-Pistol and Harry. And the bus driver, of course. Anyone else would only ever be a temporary passenger. Even Tony Perrin, our manager, would come out for just a few days and then leave us to it.

Simon returned to the back lounge for the remainder of the journey while the rest of us sat at the front, bitching and moaning about how disrespectful his behaviour was. It was decided among us that we'd have to tell Simon that Steve couldn't stay for the whole tour – a few days and then he'd have to leave.

We arrived in Montreal and checked in to the hotel. Just before we retired to our rooms we asked for another quiet word with Slink, just the four of us. We told him what we'd decided. He didn't say much, just 'Okay, I'll tell him then,' but it was clear that he was *very* unhappy.

The following day at the Metropolis soundcheck the subject came up again and heated words were exchanged between the band and Simon. The ever-reasonable Mick was trying to smooth things over and explain to Simon our collective position. Craig and I were less diplomatic: 'The fucker's gotta go, man.' After soundcheck we stayed at the venue while Simon disappeared. He returned just before stage time, with Suzanne and Steve making themselves scarce while we prepared for the show. The dressing room was graveyard quiet, the atmosphere as cold as death, nary a word uttered by any of us. Stevie Sex-Pistol came in to tell us that the intro music was playing and we made our way to the side of the stage. Jez handed us our guitars and we walked on… for the last time as the original line-up of The Mission.

The following morning I listened to the voice message… it was Stevie Sex-Pistol.

'Huss, we gotta bit of a problem. There was a note pushed under my door this morning from Slink. He said he's checked out and left the hotel and left the band. He's gone.'

'Fucking hell,' was all I could say as I lit up my third cigarette before even getting out of bed.

END OF PART TWO

Endnotes

1   In 1991 or '92, when The Mission were looking for a new guitarist to replace Simon, fellow Sheffielder and the Comsats' singer/guitarist, Stephen Fellows, came to my home in Herefordshire to audition for the vacant role. We played together for a bit and got on well. He showed me a few Comsat guitar riffs, which was the highlight of his visit for me. But it was apparent from the off that Stephen still had so much to offer himself rather than be playing second fiddle to the likes of me, which, if he had joined, he would've had to do. Sadly, Stephen and the Comsats never enjoyed the commercial success they were deserving of, but that being said, they have devout followers and are still highly regarded by those in the know. I've had conversations with Martin Gore (Depeche Mode's primary songwriter) about our mutual love for the Comsats, Martin even going as far as covering the Comsat's 'Gone' for his *Counterfeit e.p.*, released in 1989.

2   The Alarm's lead singer.

3   Please see *Salad Daze* for the full account of how Daryl lost his watch, jacket and mind on his 21st birthday, and ended up sleeping in a gutter.

4   Mission guitarist from 1992 through to when I knocked it on the head for the first time in 1996, and from 1999 to 2001 when we reformed, and then again from 2005 to when I broke up the band for a second time in 2007. Mark's guitar playing features on the *Neverland*, *Blue*, *Aura* and *God Is A Bullet* albums, as well as various compilations, live albums and music videos.

5   Now known as ITV Yorkshire.

6   I was invited to do a phone radio interview with James Whale just a few years ago when promoting a recent Mission album. Much of the interview was, of course, taken up with my memorable first appearance on his TV show and, again, he was trying to get a rise out of me. By now, of course, I'd become an adult and was wise to his ruse. I wish the man no ill; he's

enjoyed a long career in talk radio so he must have been doing something right. And if he was a pillock then so was I. It was all just a game we played.

7   Michelle found Sid Vicious in her bed, dead from a heroin overdose, on 2 February 1979. The fatal dose was reputedly procured and administered by Sid's mum, Ann Beverly. Michelle changed her name to Jessica Ronson in the late Eighties, before she met and married Rob 'The Bass Thing' Jones who, himself, sadly died of a suspected drug overdose in 1993.

8   I gotta say that I do love Italy but it has always been absolute chaos working there, whether with TSOM, The Mission or solo. The only way to ensure a show will go anywhere close to plan is if you take a full crew and production with you. And even then if you have to rely on locals for anything then nothing is guaranteed. Don't get me wrong, the people are lovely, and I have some very good Italian friends and always love visiting, but you have to go into working in Italy with a completely relaxed mindset and be prepared for anything and everything to go tits up.

Acknowledgements

My eternal love and thanks to Cinthya, my wife, my soulmate, my partner, my inspiration, and our menagerie of pets present and past – Tinkerbell, Scarlett, Meggy, Babi, Charlotte, Brutus, Monroe, Blanche, Pacino, Mel, Crystal, Fluffy-Head, Baby-Boy, Tigger, Jolie, Freckles, Sawyer and Hissy.

Special thanks, love and respect to Craig Adams, Simon Hinkler, and Mick Brown for accompanying me on this surreal and amazing journey. Only the four of us will ever really know what we went through and experienced together.

Thanks and acknowledgements to:

Lucy Beevor, my editor, who foraged her way through my oft times hyperbolic verbalism with sensitivity and empathy and a particularly beady eye on potentially libellous content, and pruned my words to a manageable and, hopefully, altogether legal read.

David Barraclough for his unswerving support, encouragement, and guidance. Still 'Up the Mariners!'

Claire Browne for her prompt email replies and enthusiasm, diligence, negotiation and organisational skills, and longanimity with my finickiness.

Debra Geddes for getting the word out, and for sharing my love for the greatest football club in the world.

David Stock for persuading people to buy my book.

Greg Morton for doing some of my leg work.

Imogen Gordon Clark for getting the ball rolling before she moved to pastures anew.

And everyone else at Omnibus Press.

James Mountford for his help in sourcing photographs and their provenance and for pointing us in the right direction with the cover. And for the colourisation of a few of the 'older' photos. All invaluable practice for putting his own forthcoming book together, entitled "*On A Wing And A Prayer: A Photographic History of The Mission*" scheduled for publication November 2024.

Paul Skellet for his inimitable cover art (based on a photo from 1986 by Martyn Strickland).

Alex Jaworzyn for proofreading.

And, in no particular order, for their contribution to the story: Jez Webb, Pete Turner, Phil Wiffen, Miles Hunt, Tim Palmer, Alex Daniele, Mats Lernaby, Tim Parsons, Mark Lee, Graham Christensen, Daryl Bamonte, Nipper Bayes, Eds Barlow, Harry Isles, Sian Thomas, Tony Perrin, Martin Horne, Charlie Eyre, Chris Sheldon, Julianne Regan, Adam Stevenson, Linda Greaves, Neil 'Spud' Perry, Mat Smith, Steve Sutherland, John Paul Jones, Mark 'Spike' Stent, Dave 'Wolfie' Wolfenden, Paul 'Grape' Gregory, Pamela Burton, Elise Margolis, The Eskimos, Sandy (Ball) Holden, Nic Duncan, everyone that contributed photos unwittingly or not, and Liverpool FC.

Last word:

The landscape is ever changing and since I finished writing this book Queen Elizabeth II died as did Fletch from Depeche Mode. Perry Bamonte rejoined The Cure, Bob Dylan announced yet more shows, and Kate Bush hit number one in the UK hit parade with 'Running Up That Hill' some 37 years after its initial release, and has enjoyed a huge, and welcome, career renaissance. Mike Kelly left The Mission after serving admirably for ten years to be replaced by the younger and eager-as-a-puppy, Alex Baum. Memories contrary to mine have been voiced by some of the players in this book but rather than amend to accommodate their version of events I have left the stories as I've remembered them. It is my book after all. That doesn't make the stories any more or less precise. Memory is never precise.

Anyway, as the cliché goes, why let truth get in the way of a good story, eh?